Computer Graphics for Java Programmers

Computer Graphics for Java Programmers

SECOND EDITION

Leen Ammeraal

Hogeschool Utrecht

Kang Zhang

University of Texas at Dallas

BICENTENNIAL
1807
WILEY
2007
BICENTENNIAL

John Wiley & Sons, Ltd

Copyright © 2007   John Wiley & Sons Ltd, The Atrium, Southern Gate, Chichester,
West Sussex PO19 8SQ, England

Telephone (+44) 1243 779777

First published 1998 (0-471-98142-7), reprinted September 1998, May 2000, March 2001, February 2002

Email (for orders and customer service enquiries): cs-books@wiley.co.uk
Visit our Home Page on www.wiley.com

Other Wiley Editorial Offices

John Wiley & Sons Inc., 111 River Street, Hoboken, NJ 07030, USA

Jossey-Bass, 989 Market Street, San Francisco, CA 94103-1741, USA

Wiley-VCH Verlag GmbH, Boschstr. 12, D-69469 Weinheim, Germany

John Wiley & Sons Australia Ltd, 42 McDougall Street, Milton, Queensland 4064, Australia

John Wiley & Sons (Asia) Pte Ltd, 2 Clementi Loop #02-01, Jin Xing Distripark, Singapore 129809

John Wiley & Sons Canada Ltd, 6045 Freemont Blvd, Mississauga, ONT, L5R 4J3, Canada

Wiley also publishes its books in a variety of electronic formats. Some content that appears
in print may not be available in electronic books.

Library of Congress Cataloging-in-Publication Data

Ammeraal, L. (Leendert)
    Computer graphics for Java programmers / Leen Ammeraal. – 2nd ed.
        p. cm.
    Includes bibliographical references.
    ISBN-13 978-0-470-03160-5 (alk. paper)
    ISBN-10 0-470-03160-3 (alk. paper)
  1. Computer graphics. 2. Java (Computer program language) I. Title.
    T385.A488 2007
    006.6′63 – dc22

                             2006029327

British Library Cataloguing in Publication Data

A catalogue record for this book is available from the British Library

ISBN-13: 978-0-470-03160-5 (PB)
ISBN-10: 0-470-03160-3 (PB)

Typeset in 10/12 Sabon by Laserwords Private Limited, Chennai, India
Printed and bound in Great Britain by Bell & Bain, Glasgow
This book is printed on acid-free paper responsibly manufactured from sustainable forestry
in which at least two trees are planted for each one used for paper production.

Contents

CONTENTS

C H A P T E R 4 – Some Classic Algorithms   **91**
4.1   Bresenham's Algorithm for Line Drawing   92
4.2   Doubling the Line-Drawing Speed   97
4.3   Circles   102
4.4   Cohen–Sutherland Line Clipping   107
4.5   Sutherland–Hodgman Polygon Clipping   113
4.6   Bézier Curves   120
4.7   B-Spline Curve Fitting   130
Exercises   135

C H A P T E R 5 – Perspective   **139**
5.1   Introduction   140
5.2   The Viewing Transformation   141
5.3   The Perspective Transformation   146
5.4   A Cube in Perspective   148
5.5   Some Useful Classes   152
5.6   A General Program for Wire-Frame Models   168
Exercises   174

C H A P T E R 6 – Hidden–Line Elimination   **177**
6.1   Line Segments and Triangles   178
6.2   Tests for Visibility   179
6.3   Specification and Representation of 3D Objects   190
6.4   Holes and Invisible Line Segments   192
6.5   Individual Faces and Line Segments   194
6.6   Automatic Generation of Object Specification   198
6.7   Hidden-Line Elimination with HP-GL Output   207
6.8   Implementation   209
Exercises   213

C H A P T E R 7 – Hidden–Face Elimination   **219**
7.1   Back-Face Culling   220
7.2   Coloring Individual Faces   225
7.3   Painter's Algorithm   226
7.4   Z-Buffer Algorithm   234
Exercises   246

C H A P T E R 8 – Fractals   **249**
8.1   Introduction   249
8.2   Koch Curves   250
8.3   String Grammars   253
8.4   Mandelbrot and Julia Sets   264
Exercises   276

Preface

During the eight years since the publication of the first edition of *Computer Graphics for Java Programmers*, the programming language Java has increasingly become the language of choice in many industrial and business domains. Hence the skills for developing computer graphics applications using Java have been highly in demand but are surprisingly lacking in the computer science curricula. Meanwhile, for the past five years the second author has been teaching Computer Graphics at his current university using the first edition of this textbook, and felt that there was a need to update the book. We therefore decided to jointly write this second edition.

This edition continues the main theme of the first edition, that is, graphics programming in Java, with plenty of source code available to the reader. The new edition has, however, been updated as follows:

1) The contents of some chapters have been updated, as a result of the authors' years of classroom experience and recent feedback from our students.
2) An instructor's manual has been created to include lecture slides and answers to exercise questions.
3) Chapter 8 has been replaced by a new chapter covering the topic of fractals.
4) A beta version of a companion software package has been added, which demonstrates the working of different algorithms and concepts introduced in the book.
5) More illustrative examples have been included in several chapters and various minor errors in the first edition have been corrected.

Over the past few years, Java has evolved into more powerful programming environments. The most notable development related to computer graphics is its support for 3D graphics. Many application examples illustrated in this book could be readily implemented using Java 3D without any understanding of the internal working of the implementation, which we consider undesirable for computer science students. We therefore believe that this textbook continues to serve as an indispensable introduction to the foundation of computer graphics, on which many application program interfaces (APIs) and graphics libraries could be developed, and more importantly, *how* they are developed.

x   PREFACE

As in the first edition, the example programs can again be downloaded from the Internet at:

`http://home.planet.nl/~ammeraal`

or at:

`http://www.utdallas.edu/~kzhang/BookCG/`

In writing this second edition, several people need to be acknowledged for their direct or indirect contributions. We would first like to thank the UT-Dallas graduate students Bill Fahle, Andy Restrepo, Janis Schubert, and Subramanya Suresh, who contributed to different parts of the demonstration software. In particular, we appreciate the great effort of Janis Schubert in developing and integrating different parts of the software while striving to maintain the same look and feel of the user interfaces. Finally, we thank Jonathan Shipley of John Wiley and Sons for his enthusiastic support and assistance in publishing this edition.

Leen Ammeraal, The Netherlands
`l.ammeraal@hccnet.nl`

Kang Zhang, USA
`kzhang@utdallas.edu`

Chapter 1

Elementary Concepts

This book is primarily about graphics programming and mathematics. Rather than discussing general graphics subjects for end users or how to use graphics software, we will deal with more fundamental subjects, required for graphics programming. In this chapter, we will first understand and appreciate the nature of discreteness of displayed graphics on computer screens. We will then see that x- and y-coordinates need not necessarily be pixel numbers, also known as device coordinates. In many applications logical coordinates are more convenient, provided we can convert them to device coordinates. Especially with input from a mouse, we also need the inverse conversion, as we will see at the end of this chapter.

1.1 LINES, COORDINATES AND PIXELS

The most convenient way of specifying a line segment on a computer screen is by providing the coordinates of its two endpoints. In mathematics, coordinates are real numbers, but primitive line-drawing routines may require these to be integers. This is the case, for example, in the Java language, which we will use in this book. The Java Abstract Windows Toolkit (AWT) provides the class *Graphics* containing the method *drawLine*, which we use as follows to draw the line segment connecting A and B:

```
g.drawLine(xA, yA, xB, yB);
```

The graphics context *g* in front of the method is normally supplied as a parameter of the *paint* method we are using, and the four arguments of *drawLine* are integers, ranging from zero to some maximum value. The above call to *drawLine* produces exactly the same line as this one:

```
g.drawLine(xB, yB, xA, yA);
```

We will now use statements such as the above one in a complete Java program. Fortunately, you need not type these programs yourself, since they are available from the Internet, as specified in the Preface. It will also be necessary to install the Java Development Kit (JDK), which you can also download, using the following Web page:

```
http://java.sun.com/
```

If you are not yet familiar with Java, you should consult other books, such as some mentioned in the Bibliography, besides this one.

The following program draws the largest possible rectangle in a canvas. The color red is used to distinguish this rectangle from the frame border:

```
// RedRect.java: The largest possible rectangle in red.
import java.awt.*;
import java.awt.event.*;

public class RedRect extends Frame
{  public static void main(String[] args){new RedRect();}

   RedRect()
   {  super("RedRect");
      addWindowListener(new WindowAdapter()
```

```
        {public void windowClosing(WindowEvent e){System.exit(0);}});
      setSize (200, 100);
      add("Center", new CvRedRect());
      show();
   }
}

class CvRedRect extends Canvas
{  public void paint(Graphics g)
   {  Dimension d = getSize();
      int maxX = d.width - 1, maxY = d.height - 1;
      g.drawString("d.width  = " + d.width,  10, 30);
      g.drawString("d.height = " + d.height, 10, 60);
      g.setColor(Color.red);
      g.drawRect(0, 0, maxX, maxY);
   }
}
```

The call to *drawRect* almost at the end of this program has the same effect as
these four lines:

```
g.drawLine(0, 0, maxX, 0);       // Top edge
g.drawLine(maxX, 0, maxX, maxY); // Right edge
g.drawLine(maxX, maxY, 0, maxY); // Bottom edge
g.drawLine(0, maxY, 0, 0);       // Left edge
```

The program contains two classes:

RedRect: The class for the frame, also used to close the application.
CvRedRect: The class for the canvas, in which we display graphics output.

However, after compiling the program by entering the command

```
javac RedRect.java
```

we notice that three class files have been generated: *RedRect.class*, *CvRe-
dRect.class* and *RedRect$1. class*. The third one is referred to as an *anonymous
class* since it has no name in the program. It is produced by the two program
lines

```
addWindowListener(new WindowAdapter()
   {public void windowClosing(WindowEvent e){System.exit(0);}});
```

which enable the user of the program to terminate it in the normal way. We could have written the same program code as

```
addWindowListener
(  new WindowAdapter()
    {  public void windowClosing(WindowEvent e)
      {  System.exit(0);
      }
    }
);
```

to show more clearly the structure of this fragment. The argument of the method *addWindowListener* must be an object of a class that implements the interface *WindowListener*. This implies that this class must define seven methods, one of which is *windowClosing*. The base class *WindowAdapter* defines these seven methods as do-nothing functions. In the above fragment, the argument of *addWindowListener* denotes an object of an anonymous subclass of *WindowAdapter*. In this subclass we override the method *windowClosing*. A further discussion of this compact program code for event handling can be found in Appendix B.

The *RedRect* constructor shows that the frame size is set to 200×100. If we do not modify this size (by dragging a corner or an edge of the window), the canvas size is somewhat less. After compilation, we run the program by typing the command

```
java RedRect
```

which produces the output shown in Figure 1.1.

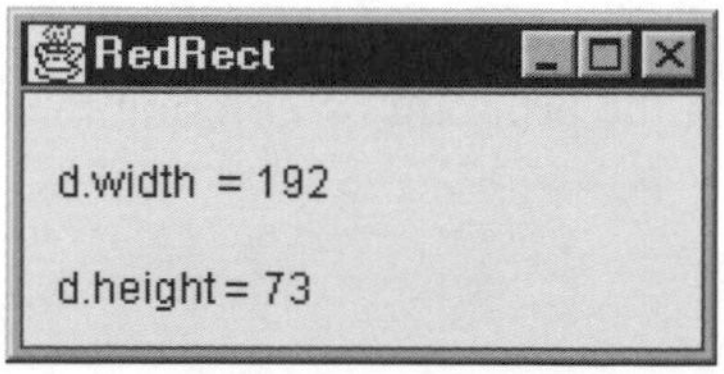

○ **Figure 1.1: Largest possible rectangle and canvas dimensions**

The blank area in a frame, which we use for graphics output, is referred to as a *client rectangle* in Microsoft Windows programming. We will consistently use a *canvas* for it, which is a subclass, such as *CvRedRect* in program *RedRect.java*, of the AWT class *Canvas*. If, instead, we displayed the output directly in the frame, we would have a problem with the coordinate system: its origin would be in the top-left corner of the *frame*; in other words, the *x*-coordinates increase from left to right and *y*-coordinates from top to bottom. Although there is a method *getInsets* to obtain the widths of all four borders of a frame so that we could compute the dimensions of the client rectangle ourselves, we prefer to use a canvas.

The tiny screen elements that we can assign a color are called *pixels* (short for *picture elements*), and the integer *x*- and *y*-values used for them are referred to as *device coordinates*. Although there are 200 pixels on a horizontal line in the entire frame, only 192 of these lie on the canvas, the remaining 8 being used for the left and right borders. On a vertical line, there are 100 pixels for the whole frame, but only 73 for the canvas. Apparently, the remaining 27 pixels are used for the title bar and for the top and bottom borders. Since these numbers may differ in different Java implementations and the user can change the window size, it is desirable that our program can determine the canvas dimensions. We do this by using the *getSize* method of the class *Component*, which is a superclass of *Canvas*. The following program lines in the paint method show how we obtain the canvas dimensions and how we interpret them:

```
Dimension d = getSize();
int maxX = d.width - 1, maxY = d.height - 1;
```

The *getSize* method of *Component* (a superclass of *Canvas*) supplies us with the numbers of pixels on horizontal and vertical lines of the canvas. Since we begin counting at zero, the highest pixel numbers, *maxX* and *maxY*, on these lines are one less than these numbers of pixels. Remember that this is similar with arrays in Java and C. For example, if we write

```
int[] a = new int[8];
```

the highest possible index value is 7, not 8. Figure 1.2 illustrates this for a very small canvas, which is only 8 pixels wide and 4 high, showing a much-enlarged

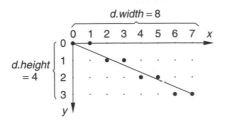

○ **Figure 1.2: Pixels as coordinates in an** 8 × 4 **canvas (with** *maxX* = 7 **and** *maxY* = 3**)**

screen grid structure. It also shows that the line connecting the points (0, 0) and (7, 3) is approximated by a set of eight pixels.

The big dots approximating the line denote pixels that are set to the foreground color. By default, this foreground color is black, while the background color is white. These eight pixels are made black as a result of this call:

```
g.drawLine (0, 0, 7, 3);
```

In the program *RedRect.java*, we used the following call to the *drawRect* method (instead of four calls to *drawLine*):

```
g.drawRect(0, 0, maxX, maxY);
```

In general, the call

```
g.drawRect(x, y, w, h);
```

draws a rectangle with (x, y) as its top-left and $(x + w, y + h)$ as its bottom-right corners. In other words, the third and fourth arguments of the *drawRect* method specify the width and height, rather than the bottom-right corner, of the rectangle to be drawn. Note that this rectangle is $w + 1$ pixels wide and $h + 1$ pixels high. The smallest possible square, consisting of 2×2 pixels, is drawn by this call

```
g.drawRect(x, y, 1, 1);
```

To put only one pixel on the screen, we cannot use *drawRect*, because nothing at all appears if we try to set the third and fourth arguments of this method to zero. Curiously enough, Java does not provide a special method for this purpose, so we have to use this call:

```
g.drawLine(x, y, x, y);
```

Note that the call

```
g.drawLine(xA, y, xB, y);
```

draws a horizontal line consisting of $| xB - xA | + 1$ pixels.

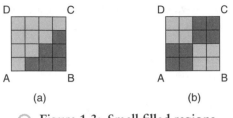

Figure 1.3: Small filled regions

1.2 THE BOUNDARIES OF FILLED REGIONS

In mathematics, lines are continuous and have no thickness, but they are discrete and at least one pixel thick in our graphics output. This difference in the interpretation of the notion of lines may not cause any problems if the pixels are very small in comparison with what we are drawing. However, we should be aware that there may be such problems in special cases, as Figure 1.3(a) illustrates. Suppose that we have to draw a filled square ABCD of, say, 4×4 pixels, consisting of the bottom-right triangle ABC and the upper-left triangle ACD, which we want to paint in dark gray and light gray, respectively, without drawing any lines. Strangely enough, it is not clear how this can be done: if we make the diagonal AC light gray, triangle ABC contains fewer pixels than triangle ACD; if we make it dark gray, it is the other way round.

A much easier but still non-trivial problem, illustrated by Figure 1.3(b), is filling the squares of a checker-board with, say, dark and light gray squares instead of black and white ones. Unlike squares in mathematics, those on the computer screen deserve special attention with regard to the edges belonging or not belonging to the filled regions. We have seen that the call

```
g.drawRect(x, y, w, h);
```

draws a rectangle with corners (x, y) and $(x + w, y + h)$. The method *fillRect*, on the other hand, fills a slightly smaller rectangle. The call

```
g.fillRect(x, y, w, h);
```

assigns the current foreground color to a rectangle consisting of $w \times h$ pixels. This rectangle has (x, y) as its top-left and $(x + w - 1, y + h - 1)$ as its bottom-right corner. To obtain a generalization of Figure 1.3(b), the following method, *checker*, draws an $n \times n$ checker board, with (x, y) as its top-left corner and with dark gray and light gray squares, each consisting of $w \times w$ pixels. The bottom-left square will always be dark gray because for this square we have $i = 0$ and $j = n - 1$, so that $i + n - j = 1$:

```
void checker(Graphics g, int x, int y, int n, int w)
{   for (int i=0; i<n; i++)
        for (int j=0; j<n; j++)
        {   g.setColor((i + n - j) % 2 == 0 ?
                Color.lightGray : Color.darkGray);
            g.fillRect(x + i * w, y + j * w, w, w);
        }
}
```

If we wanted to draw only the edges of each square, also in dark gray and light gray, we would have to replace the above call to *fillRect* with

```
g.drawRect(x + i * w, y + j * w, w - 1, w - 1);
```

in which the last two arguments are $w - 1$ instead of w.

1.3 LOGICAL COORDINATES

1.3.1 The Direction of the Y-axis

As Figure 1.2 shows, the origin of the device-coordinate systems lies at the top-left corner of the canvas, so that the positive y-axis points downward. This is reasonable for text output, where we start at the top and increase y as we go to the next line of text. However, this direction of the y-axis is different from normal mathematical practice and therefore often inconvenient in graphics applications. For example, in a discussion about a line with a positive slope, we expect to go upward when we move along this line from left to right. Fortunately, we can arrange for the positive y direction to be reversed by performing this simple transformation:

$$y' = maxY - y$$

1.3.2 Continuous vs. Discrete Coordinates

Instead of the discrete (integer) coordinates we are using at the lower, device-oriented level, we want to use continuous (floating-point) coordinates at the higher, problem-oriented level. Other usual terms are *device* and *logical* coordinates, respectively. Writing conversion routines to compute device coordinates from the corresponding logical ones and vice versa is a bit tricky. We must be aware that there are two solutions to this problem, even in the simple case in which increasing a logical coordinate by one results in increasing the device coordinate also by one. We want to write the following methods:

$iX(x)$, $iY(y)$:   the device coordinates of the point with logical coordinates x and y;

$fx(x)$, $fy(y)$:   the logical coordinates of the point with device coordinates x and y.

With regard to x-coordinates, the first solution is based on *rounding*:

```
int iX(float x){return Math.round(x);}
float fx(int x){return (float)x;}
```

For example, with this solution we have

$$iX(2.8) = 3 \text{ and } fx(3) = 3.0$$

The second solution is based on *truncating*:

```
int iX(float x){return (int)x;}           // Not used in
float fx(int x){return (float)x + 0.5F;}  // this book.
```

With these conversion functions, we would have

$$iX(2.8) = 2 \text{ and } fx(2) = 2.5$$

With both solutions, the difference between any value x and $fx(iX(x))$ is not greater than 0.5. We will use the first solution throughout this book, since it is the better one if logical coordinates frequently happen to be integer values. In these cases the practice of truncating floating-point numbers will often lead to worse results than we would have with rounding.

Besides the above methods iX and fx (based on the first solution) for x-coordinates, we need similar methods for y-coordinates, taking into account the opposite directions of the two y-axes. At the bottom of the canvas the device y-coordinate is $maxY$ while the logical y-coordinate is 0, which may explain the two expressions of the form $maxY - \ldots$ in the following methods:

```
int iX(float x){return Math.round(x);}
int iY(float y){return maxY - Math.round(y);}
float fx(int x){return (float)x;}
float fy(int y){return (float)(maxY - y);}
```

Figure 1.4 shows a fragment of a canvas, based on $maxY = 16$.

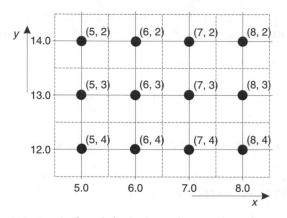

⬭ **Figure 1.4: Logical and device coordinates, based on *ymax* = 16**

The pixels are denoted as black dots, each placed in the center of a square of dashed lines. In this discussion and elsewhere in this book, let us write x and y for logical and X and Y for device coordinates. (Since it is customary in Java to use lower-case letters at the beginning of variable names, we will not write X and Y in program text.) In Figure 1.4, the device-coordinates (X, Y) are placed between parentheses near each dot. For example, the pixel with device coordinates $(8, 2)$, at the upper-right corner of this canvas fragment, has logical coordinates $(8.0, 14.0)$. We have

```
iX (8.0)  = Math.round (8.0) = 8
iY (14.0) = 16 - Math.round (14.0) = 2
fx (8)    = (float)8 = 8.0
fy (2)    = (float) (16 - 2) = 14.0
```

The dashed square around this dot denotes all points (x, y) satisfying

$$7.5 \leq x < 8.5$$
$$13.5 \leq y < 14.5$$

All these points are converted to the pixel $(8, 2)$ by our methods iX and iY.

Let us demonstrate this way of converting floating-point logical coordinates to integer device coordinates in a program that begins by drawing an equilateral triangle ABC, with the side AB at the bottom and the point C at the top. Then, using

$$q = 0.05 \; p = 1 - q = 0.95$$

we compute the new points A′, B′ and C′ near A, B and C and lying on the sides AB, BC and CA, respectively, writing

```
xA1 = p * xA + q * xB;
yA1 = p * yA + q * yB;
xB1 = p * xB + q * xC;
yB1 = p * yB + q * yC;
xC1 = p * xC + q * xA;
yC1 = p * yC + q * yA;
```

We then draw the triangle A′B′C′, which is slightly smaller than ABC and turned a little counter-clockwise. Applying the same principle to triangle A′B′C′ to obtain a third triangle, A″B″C″, and so on, until 50 triangles have been drawn, the result will be as shown in Figure 1.5.

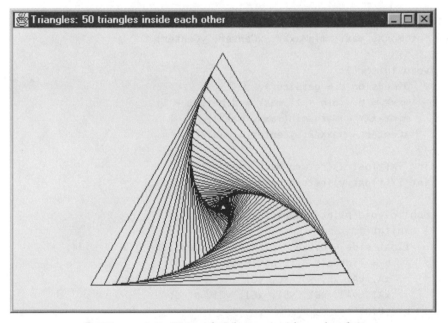

○ **Figure 1.5: Triangles drawn inside each other**

If we change the dimensions of the window, new equilateral triangles appear, again in the center of the canvas and with dimensions proportional to the size of this canvas. Without floating-point logical coordinates and with a *y*-axis pointing downward, this program would have been less easy to write:

```
// Triangles.java: This program draws 50 triangles inside each other.
import java.awt.*;
import java.awt.event.*;
```

```java
public class Triangles extends Frame
{  public static void main(String[] args){new Triangles();}

   Triangles()
   {  super("Triangles: 50 triangles inside each other");
      addWindowListener(new WindowAdapter()
         {public void windowClosing(WindowEvent e){System.exit(0);}});
      setSize (600, 400);
      add("Center", new CvTriangles());
      show();
   }
}

class CvTriangles extends Canvas
{  int maxX, maxY, minMaxXY, xCenter, yCenter;

   void initgr()
   {  Dimension d = getSize();
      maxX = d.width - 1; maxY = d.height - 1;
      minMaxXY = Math.min(maxX, maxY);
      xCenter = maxX/2; yCenter = maxY/2;
   }
   int iX(float x){return Math.round(x);}
   int iY(float y){return maxY - Math.round(y);}

   public void paint(Graphics g)
   {  initgr();
      float side = 0.95F * minMaxXY, sideHalf = 0.5F * side,
         h = sideHalf * (float)Math.sqrt (3),
         xA, yA, xB, yB, xC, yC,
         xA1, yA1, xB1, yB1, xC1, yC1, p, q;
      q = 0.05F;
      p = 1 - q;
      xA = xCenter - sideHalf;
      yA = yCenter - 0.5F * h;
      xB = xCenter + sideHalf;
      yB = yA;
      xC = xCenter;
      yC = yCenter + 0.5F * h;
      for (int i=0; i<50; i++)
      {  g.drawLine(iX(xA), iY(yA), iX(xB), iY(yB));
         g.drawLine(iX(xB), iY(yB), iX(xC), iY(yC));
```

```
        g.drawLine(iX(xC), iY(yC), iX(xA), iY(yA));
        xA1 = p * xA + q * xB;
        yA1 = p * yA + q * yB;
        xB1 = p * xB + q * xC;
        yB1 = p * yB + q * yC;
        xC1 = p * xC + q * xA;
        yC1 = p * yC + q * yA;
        xA = xA1; xB = xB1; xC = xC1;
        yA = yA1; yB = yB1; yC = yC1;
      }
   }
}
```

In the canvas class *CvTriangles* there is a method *initgr*. Together with the other program lines that precede the *paint* method in this class, *initgr* may also be useful in other programs.

It is important to notice that, on each triangle edge, the computed floating-point coordinates, not the integer device coordinates derived from them, are used for further computations. This principle, which applies to many graphics applications, can be depicted as follows:

$$\begin{array}{cccccccc} float & \rightarrow & float & \rightarrow & float & \rightarrow & float \\ \downarrow & & \downarrow & & \downarrow & & \downarrow \\ int & & int & & int & & int \end{array}$$

which is in contrast to the following scheme, which we should avoid. Here *int* device coordinates containing rounding-off errors are used not only for graphics output but also for further computations, so that such errors will accumulate:

$$\begin{array}{cccccccc} float & & float & & float & & float \\ \downarrow & \nearrow & \downarrow & \nearrow & \downarrow & \nearrow & \downarrow \\ int & & int & & int & & int \end{array}$$

In summary, we compare and contrast the logical and device coordinate systems in the following table, in terms of (1) the convention used in the text, but not in Java programs, of this book; (2) the data types of the programming language; (3) the coordinate value domain; and (4) the direction of the positive *y*-axis:

Coordinate system	Convention	Data type	Value domain	Positive *y*-axis
logical	lower-case letters	float	continuous	upward
device	upper-case letters	integer	discrete	downward

1.4 ANISOTROPIC AND ISOTROPIC MAPPING MODES

1.4.1 Mapping a Continuous Interval to a Sequence of Integers

Suppose we want to map an interval of real logical coordinates, such as

$$0 \le x \le 10.0$$

to the set of integer device coordinates $\{0, 1, 2, \ldots, 9\}$. Unfortunately, the method

```
int iX(float x){return Math.round(x);}
```

used in the previous section is not suitable for this purpose because for any x greater than 9.5 (and not greater than 10) it returns 10, which does not belong to the allowed sequence $0, 1, \ldots, 9$. In particular, it gives

```
ix (10.0) = 10
```

while we want

```
ix (10.0) = 9
```

This suggests that in an improved method iX we should use a multiplication factor of 0.9. We can also come to this conclusion by realizing that there are only nine small intervals between ten pixels labeled $0, 1, \ldots, 9$, as Figure 1.6 illustrates. If we define the pixel width ($= pixelWidth$) as the distance between two successive pixels on a horizontal line, the above interval $0 \le x \le 10$ of logical coordinates (being real numbers) corresponds to $9 \times pixelWidth$. So in this example we have:

$$9 \times pixelWidth = 10.0 \text{(the length of the interval of logical coordinates)}$$
$$pixelWidth = 10/9 = 1.111\ldots$$

In general, if a horizontal line of our window consists of n pixels, numbered $0, 1, \ldots, maxX$ (where $maxX = n - 1$), and the corresponding (continuous)

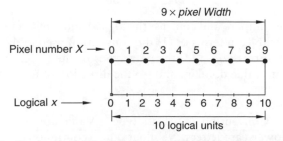

○ Figure 1.6: Pixels lying 10/9 logical units apart

interval of logical coordinates is $0 \le x \le rWidth$, we can use the following method:

```
int iX(float x){return Math.round(x/pixelWidth);}
```

where *pixelWidth* is computed beforehand as follows:

```
maxX = n - 1;
pixelWidth = rWidth/maxX;
```

In the above example the integer n is equal to the interval length $rWidth$, but it is often desirable to use logical coordinates x and y satisfying

$$0 \le x \le rWidth$$

$$0 \le y \le rHeight$$

where *rWidth* and *rHeight* are real numbers, such as 10.0 and 7.5, respectively, which are quite different from the numbers of pixels that lie on horizontal and vertical lines. It will then be important to distinguish between *isotropic* and *anisotropic mapping modes*, as we will discuss in a moment.

As for the simpler method

```
int iX(float x){return Math.round(x);}
```

of the previous section, this can be regarded as a special case of the improved method we have just seen, provided we use *pixelWidth* $= 1$, that is $rWidth = maxX$, or $rWidth = n - 1$. For example, if the drawing rectangle is 100 pixels wide, so that $n = 100$ and we can use the pixels $0, 1, 2, \ldots, 99 = maxX$ on a horizontal line, this simpler method iX works correctly if it is applied to logical x-coordinates satisfying

$$0 \le x \le rWidth = 99.0$$

The point to be noticed is that, due to the value *pixelWidth* $= 1$, the logical width is 99.0 here although the number of available pixels is 100.

1.4.2 Anisotropic Mapping Mode

The term *anisotropic mapping mode* implies that the scale factors for x and y are not necessarily equal, as the following code fragment shows:

```
Dimension d = getSize();
maxX = d.width - 1; maxY = d.height - 1;
pixelWidth  = rWidth/maxX;
pixelHeight = rHeight/maxY;
```

```
...
int iX(float x){return Math.round(x/pixelWidth);}
int iY(float y){return maxY - Math.round(y/pixelHeight);}
float fx(int x){return x * pixelWidth;}
float fy(int y){return (maxY - y) * pixelHeight;}
```

We will use this in a demonstration program. Regardless of the window dimensions, the largest possible rectangle in this window has the logical dimensions 10.0×7.5. After clicking on a point of the canvas, the logical coordinates are shown, as Figure 1.7 illustrates.

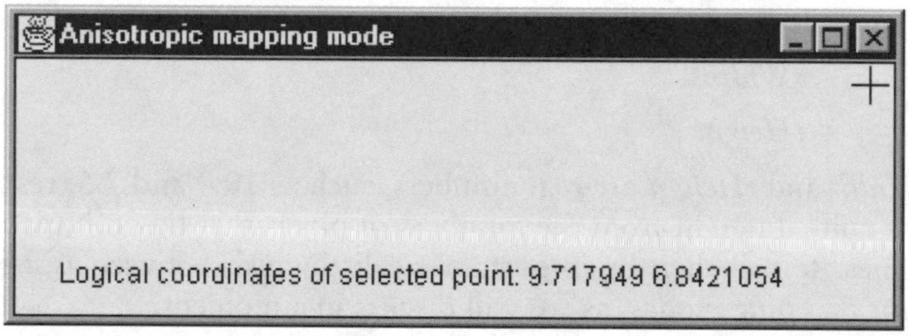

○ **Figure 1.7: Logical coordinates with anisotropic mapping mode**

Since there are no gaps between this largest possible rectangle and the window edges, we can only see this rectangle with some difficulty in Figure 1.7. In contrast, the screen will show this rectangle very clearly because we will make it red instead of black. Although the window dimensions in Figure 1.7 have been altered by the user, the logical canvas dimensions are still 10.0×7.5. The text displayed in the window shows the coordinates of the point near the upper-right corner of the rectangle, as the cross-hair cursor indicates. If the user clicks exactly on that corner, the coordinate values 10.0 and 7.5 are displayed. This demonstration program is listed below.

```
// Anisotr.java: The anisotropic mapping mode.

import java.awt.*;
import java.awt.event.*;

public class Anisotr extends Frame
{  public static void main(String[] args){new Anisotr();}

   Anisotr()
   { super("Anisotropic mapping mode");
     addWindowListener(new WindowAdapter()
```

```
          {public void windowClosing(WindowEvent e){System.exit(0);}}});
       setSize (400, 300);
       add("Center", new CvAnisotr());
       setCursor(Cursor.getPredefinedCursor(Cursor.CROSSHAIR_CURSOR));
       show();
   }
}

class CvAnisotr extends Canvas
{ int maxX, maxY;
  float pixelWidth, pixelHeight,
      rWidth = 10.0F,
      rHeight = 7.5F,
      xP = -1, yP;

   CvAnisotr()
   { addMouseListener(new MouseAdapter()
     {  public void mousePressed(MouseEvent evt)
        {  xP = fx(evt.getX()); yP = fy(evt.getY());
           repaint();
        }
     });
   }
   void initgr()
   {  Dimension d = getSize();
      maxX = d.width - 1; maxY = d.height - 1;
      pixelWidth  = rWidth/maxX; pixelHeight = rHeight/maxY;
   }

   int iX(float x){return Math.round(x/pixelWidth);}
   int iY(float y){return maxY - Math.round(y/pixelHeight);}
   float fx(int x){return x * pixelWidth;}
   float fy(int y){return (maxY - y) * pixelHeight;}

   public void paint(Graphics g)
   {  initgr();
      int left = iX (0), right = iX(rWidth),
          bottom = iY (0), top = iY(rHeight);
      if (xP >= 0) g.drawString(
         "Logical coordinates of selected point: "
         + xP + " " + yP, 20, 100);
      g.setColor(Color.red);
      g.drawLine(left, bottom, right, bottom);
```

```
        g.drawLine(right, bottom, right, top);
        g.drawLine(right, top, left, top);
        g.drawLine(left, top, left, bottom);
    }
}
```

With the anisotropic mapping mode, the actual length of a vertical unit can be different from that of a horizontal unit. This is the case in Figure 1.7: although the rectangle is 10 units wide and 7.5 units high, its real height is less than 0.75 of its width. In particular, the anisotropic mapping mode is not suitable for drawing squares, circles and other shapes that require equal units in the horizontal and vertical directions.

1.4.3 Isotropic Mapping Mode

We can arrange for horizontal and vertical units to be equal in terms of their real size by using the same scale factor for x and y. Let us use the term *drawing rectangle* for the rectangle with dimensions *rWidth* and *rHeight,* in which we normally draw graphical output. Since these logical dimensions are constant, so is their ratio, which is not the case with that of the canvas dimensions. It follows that, with the isotropic mapping mode, the drawing rectangle will in general not be identical with the canvas. Depending on the current window size, either the top and bottom or the left and right edges of the drawing rectangle lie on those of the canvas.

Since it is normally desirable for a drawing to appear in the center of the canvas, it is often convenient with the isotropic mapping mode to place the origin of the logical coordinate system at that center. This implies that we will use the following logical-coordinate intervals:

$$-1/2 \; rWidth \leq x \leq +1/2 \; rWidth$$

$$-1/2 \; rHeight \leq y \leq +1/2 \; rHeight$$

Our methods *iX* and *iY* will map each logical coordinate pair (x, y) to a pair (X, Y) of device coordinates, where

$$X \in \{0, 1, 2, \ldots, maxX\}$$

$$Y \in \{0, 1, 2, \ldots, maxY\}$$

To obtain the same scale factor for x and y, we compute *rWidth/maxX* and *rHeight/maxY* and take the larger of these two values; this maximum value, *pixelSize*, is then used in the methods *iX* and *iY*, as this fragment shows:

```
Dimension d = getSize();
int maxX = d.width - 1, maxY = d.height - 1;
pixelSize = Math.max(rWidth/maxX, rHeight/maxY);
```

```
centerX = maxX/2; centerY = maxY/2;
...
int iX(float x){return Math.round(centerX + x/pixelSize);}
int iY(float y){return Math.round(centerY - y/pixelSize);}
float fx(int x){return (x - centerX) * pixelSize;}
float fy(int y){return (centerY - y) * pixelSize;}
```

We will use this code in a program that draws a square, two corners of which touch either the midpoints of the horizontal canvas edges or those of the vertical ones. It also displays the coordinates of a point on which the user clicks, as the left window of Figure 1.8 shows.

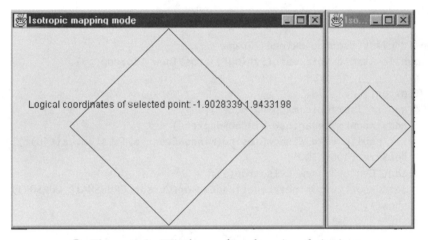

○ **Figure 1.8: Windows after changing their sizes**

In this illustration, we pay special attention to the corners of the drawn square that touch the boundaries of the drawing rectangle. These corners do not lie on the window frame, but they lie just inside it. For the square on the left we have:

Figure 1.8, left	logical coordinate y	device coordinate $iY(y)$
top corner	$+rHeight/2$	0
bottom corner	$-rHeight/2$	$maxY$

By contrast, for the square that has been drawn in the narrow window on the right, it is the corners on the left and the right that lie just within the frame:

Figure 1.8, right	logical coordinate x	device coordinate $iX(x)$
left corner	$-rWidth/2$	0
right corner	$+rWidth/2$	$maxX$

The following program uses a drawing rectangle with logical dimensions $rWidth = rHeight = 10.0$. If we replaced this value 10.0 with any other positive constant, the output would be the same.

```java
// Isotrop.java: The isotropic mapping mode.
//    Origin of logical coordinate system in canvas
//    center; positive y-axis upward.
//    Square (turned 45 degrees) just fits into canvas.
//    Mouse click displays logical coordinates of
//    selected point.
import java.awt.*;
import java.awt.event.*;

public class Isotrop extends Frame
{  public static void main(String[] args){new Isotrop();}

   Isotrop()
   { super("Isotropic mapping mode");
     addWindowListener(new WindowAdapter()
        {public void windowClosing(WindowEvent e){System.exit(0);}});
     setSize (400, 300);
     add("Center", new CvIsotrop());
     setCursor(Cursor.getPredefinedCursor(Cursor.CROSSHAIR_CURSOR));
     show();
   }
}


class CvIsotrop extends Canvas
{  int centerX, centerY;
   float pixelSize, rWidth = 10.0F, rHeight = 10.0F, xP = 1000000, yP;

   CvIsotrop()
   { addMouseListener(new MouseAdapter()
     {  public void mousePressed(MouseEvent evt)
        {  xP = fx(evt.getX()); yP = fy(evt.getY());
           repaint();
        }
     });
   }

   void initgr()
   {  Dimension d = getSize();
      int maxX = d.width - 1, maxY = d.height - 1;
```

```
        pixelSize = Math.max(rWidth/maxX, rHeight/maxY);
        centerX = maxX/2; centerY = maxY/2;
    }

    int iX(float x){return Math.round(centerX + x/pixelSize);}
    int iY(float y){return Math.round(centerY - y/pixelSize);}
    float fx(int x){return (x - centerX) * pixelSize;}
    float fy(int y){return (centerY - y) * pixelSize;}

    public void paint(Graphics g)
    {  initgr();
        int left = iX(-rWidth/2), right = iX(rWidth/2),
            bottom = iY(-rHeight/2), top = iY(rHeight/2),
            xMiddle = iX (0), yMiddle = iY (0);
        g.drawLine(xMiddle, bottom, right, yMiddle);
        g.drawLine(right,yMiddle, xMiddle, top);
        g.drawLine(xMiddle, top, left, yMiddle);
        g.drawLine(left, yMiddle, xMiddle, bottom);
        if (xP != 1000000)
            g.drawString(
            "Logical coordinates of selected point: "
            + xP + " " + yP, 20, 100);
    }
}
```

1.5 DEFINING A POLYGON BY USING THE MOUSE

We will use the conversion methods of the previous program in a more interesting application, which enables the user to define a polygon by clicking on points to indicate the positions of the vertices. Figure 1.9 shows such a polygon, just after the user has defined successive vertices, ending at the first one on the left, which is marked with a tiny rectangle.

The large rectangle surrounding the polygon is the drawing rectangle: only vertices inside this rectangle are guaranteed to appear again if the user changes the dimensions of the window. The very wide window of Figure 1.9 was obtained by dragging one of its corners. After the polygon was drawn, the dimensions of the window were again changed, to obtain Figure 1.10. It is also possible to change these dimensions during the process of drawing the polygon. We now summarize the requirements for this application program:

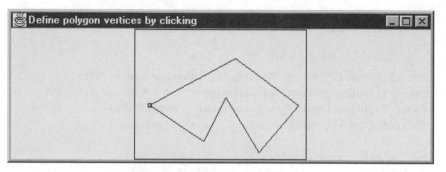

○ **Figure 1.9: Polygon defined by a user**

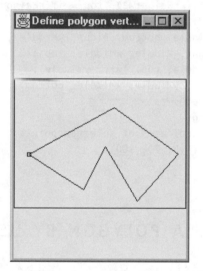

○ **Figure 1.10: Polygon still in the center of the window after resizing the window**

- The first vertex is drawn as a tiny rectangle.

- If a later vertex is inside the tiny rectangle, the drawing of one polygon is complete.

- Only vertices in the drawing rectangle are drawn.

- The drawing rectangle (see Figures 1.9 and 1.10) is either as high or as wide as the window, yet maintaining its height/width ratio regardless of the window shape.

- When the user changes the shape of the window, the size of the drawn polygon changes in the same way as that of the drawing rectangle, as does the surrounding white space of the polygon.

We will use the isotropic mapping mode to implement this program, and use a data structure called *vertex vector* to store the vertices of the polygon to be drawn. We then design the program with the following algorithmic steps:

1. Activate the mouse;
2. When the left mouse button is pressed
   2.1 Get *x*- and *y*-coordinates at where the mouse is clicked;
   2.2 If it is the first vertex
       Then empty vertex vector;
       Else If the vertex is inside the tiny rectangle (i.e. last vertex)
           Then finish the current polygon;
           Else store this vertex in vertex vector (i.e. not last vertex);
3. Draw all vertices in vertex vector.

The last step to draw all the polygon vertices can be detailed as follows:

1. Obtain the dimensions of the drawing rectangle based on logical coordinates;
2. Draw the drawing rectangle;
3. Get the first vertex from vertex vector;
4. Draw a tiny rectangle at the vertex location;
5. Draw a line between every two consecutive vertices stored in vertex vector.

In both Figures 1.9 and 1.10 the drawing rectangle has a width of 10 and a height of 7.5 logical units, as the following program shows:

```java
// DefPoly.java: Drawing a polygon.
// Uses: CvDefPoly (discussed below).
import java.awt.*;
import java.awt.event.*;

public class DefPoly extends Frame
{  public static void main(String[] args){new DefPoly();}

   DefPoly()
   {  super("Define polygon vertices by clicking");
      addWindowListener(new WindowAdapter()
         {public void windowClosing(WindowEvent e){System.exit(0);}});
      setSize (500, 300);
      add("Center", new CvDefPoly());
      setCursor(Cursor.getPredefinedCursor(Cursor.CROSSHAIR_CURSOR));
      show();
   }
}
```

The class *CvDefPoly*, used in this program, is listed below. We define this class in a separate file, *CvDefPoly.java*, so that it is easier to use elsewhere, as we will see in Section 2.13:

```java
// CvDefPoly.java: To be used in other program files.
//    A class that enables the user to define
//    a polygon by clicking the mouse.
// Uses: Point2D (discussed below).

import java.awt.*;
import java.awt.event.*;
import java.util.*;

class CvDefPoly extends Canvas
{  Vector v = new Vector();
   float x0, y0, rWidth = 10.0F, rHeight = 7.5F, pixelSize;
   boolean ready = true;
   int centerX, centerY;

   CvDefPoly()
   {  addMouseListener(new MouseAdapter()
      {  public void mousePressed(MouseEvent evt)
         {  float xA = fx(evt.getX()), yA = fy(evt.getY());
            if (ready)
            {  v.removeAllElements();
               x0 = xA; y0 = yA;
               ready = false;
            }
            float dx = xA - x0, dy = yA - y0;
            if (v.size() > 0 &&
               dx * dx + dy * dy < 4 * pixelSize * pixelSize)
               ready = true;
            else
               v.addElement(new Point2D(xA, yA));
            repaint();
         }
      });
   }

   void initgr()
   {  Dimension d = getSize();
      int maxX = d.width - 1, maxY = d.height - 1;
      pixelSize = Math.max(rWidth/maxX, rHeight/maxY);
```

```
        centerX = maxX/2; centerY = maxY/2;
    }

    int iX(float x){return Math.round(centerX + x/pixelSize);}
    int iY(float y){return Math.round(centerY - y/pixelSize);}
    float fx(int x){return (x - centerX) * pixelSize;}
    float fy(int y){return (centerY - y) * pixelSize;}

    public void paint(Graphics g)
    {  initgr();
       int left = iX(-rWidth/2), right = iX(rWidth/2),
           bottom = iY(-rHeight/2), top = iY(rHeight/2);
       g.drawRect(left, top, right - left, bottom - top);
       int n = v.size();
       if (n == 0) return;
       Point2D a = (Point2D)(v.elementAt (0) );
       // Show tiny rectangle around first vertex:
       g.drawRect(iX(a.x)-2, iY(a.y)-2, 4, 4);
       for (int i=1; i<=n; i++)
       {  if (i == n && !ready) break;
          Point2D b = (Point2D)(v.elementAt(i % n));
          g.drawLine(iX(a.x), iY(a.y), iX(b.x), iY(b.y));
          a = b;
       }
    }
}
```

The class *Point2D*, used in the above file, will also be useful in other programs,
so that we define this in another separate file, *Point2D.java*:

```
// Point2D.java: Class for points in logical coordinates.
class Point2D
{ float x, y;
  Point2D(float x, float y){this.x = x; this.y = y;}
}
```

After a complete polygon has been shown (which is the case when the user has
revisited the first vertex), the user can once again click a point. The polygon
then disappears and that point will then be the first vertex of a new polygon.

Note that the comment line

```
// Uses: CvDefPoly (discussed below).
```

occurring in the file *DefPoly.java*, indicates that the file *CvDefPoly.java* should be available in the current directory. Since the comment line

```
// Uses: Point2D (discussed below).
```

occurs in the file *CvDefPoly.java*, the program *DefPoly.java* also requires the class *Point2D*. Comments such as those above are very helpful if different directories are used, for example, one for each chapter. However, since class names are unique throughout this book, it is possible to place all program files in the same directory. In this way, each required class will be available.

EXERCISES

1.1 How many pixels are put on the screen by each of the following calls?

```
g.drawLine (10, 20, 100, 50);
g.drawRect (10, 10, 8, 5);
g.fillRect (10, 10, 8, 5);
```

1.2 Replace the triangles of program *Triangles.java* with squares and draw a great many of them, arranged in a chessboard, as shown in Figure 1.11.
As usual, this chessboard consists of $n \times n$ normal squares (with horizontal and vertical edges), where $n = 8$. Each of these actually consists of k squares of different sizes, with $k = 10$. Finally, the value $q = 0.2$ (and $p = 1 - q = 0.8$) was used to divide each edge into two parts with ratio $p : q$ (see also program *Triangles.java* in Section 1.3), but the interesting pattern of Figure 1.11 was obtained by reversing the roles of p and q in half of the $n \times n$ 'normal' squares, which is similar to the black and white squares of a normal chessboard. Your program should accept the values n, k and q as program arguments.

1.3 Draw a set of concentric pairs of squares, each consisting of a square with horizontal and vertical edges and one rotated through 45°. Except for the outermost square, the vertices of each square are the midpoints of the edges of its immediately surrounding square, as Figure 1.12 shows. It is required that all lines are exactly straight, and that vertices of smaller squares lie exactly on the edges of larger ones.

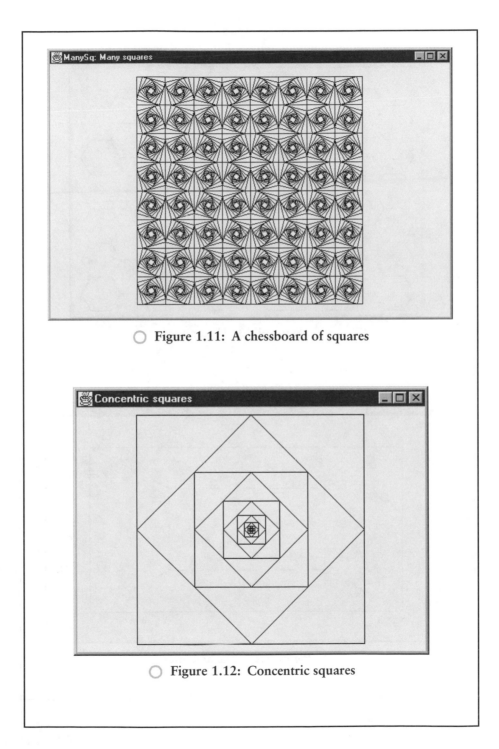

Figure 1.11: A chessboard of squares

Figure 1.12: Concentric squares

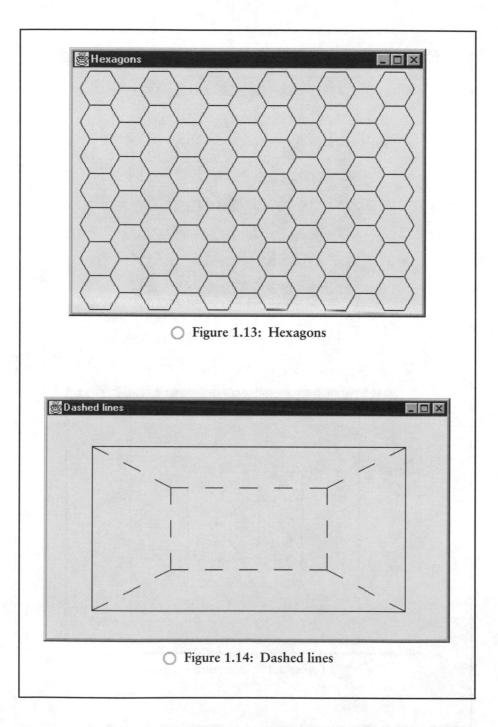

Figure 1.13: Hexagons

Figure 1.14: Dashed lines

1.4   Write a program that draws a pattern of hexagons, as shown in Figure 1.13. The vertices of a (regular) hexagon lie on its so-called circumscribed circle. The user must be able to specify the radius of this circle by clicking a point near the upper-left corner of the drawing rectangle. Then the distance between that point and that corner is to be used as the radius of the circle just mentioned. There must be as many hexagons of the specified size as possible and the margins on the left and the right must be equal. The same applies to the upper and lower margins, as Figure 1.13 shows.

1.5   Write a class *Lines* containing a static method *dashedLine* to draw dashed lines, in such a way that we can write

```
Lines.dashedLine(g, xA, yA, xB, yB, dashLength);
```

where *g* is a variable of type *Graphics*, *xA*, *yA*, *xB*, *yB* are the device coordinates of the endpoints A and B, and *dashLength* is the desired length (in device coordinates) of a single dash. There should be a dash, not a gap, at each endpoint of a dashed line. Figure 1.14 shows eight dashed lines drawn in this way, with *dashLength* = 20.

Chapter 2

Applied Geometry

Before we proceed with specific computer-graphics subjects, we will discuss some mathematics, which we will often use in this book. You can skip the first four sections of this chapter if you are very familiar with vectors and determinants. After this general part, we will deal with some useful algorithms needed for the exercises at the end of this chapter and for the topics in the remaining chapters. For example, in Chapters 6 and 7 we will deal with polygons that are faces of 3D solid objects. Since polygons in general are difficult to handle, we will divide them into triangles, as we will discuss in the last section of this chapter.

2.1 VECTORS

We begin with the mathematical notion of a vector, which should not be confused with the standard class *Vector*, available in Java to store an arbitrary number of objects. Recall that we have used this *Vector* class in Section 1.5 to store polygon vertices.

A *vector* is a directed line segment, characterized by its length and its direction only. Figure 2.1 shows two representations of the same vector $\mathbf{a} = \mathbf{PQ} = \mathbf{b} = \mathbf{RS}$. Thus a vector is not altered by a translation.

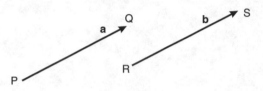

Figure 2.1. Two equal vectors

The sum $\mathbf{c}$ of the vectors $\mathbf{a}$ and $\mathbf{b}$, written

$$\mathbf{c} = \mathbf{a} + \mathbf{b}$$

can be obtained as the diagonal of a parallelogram, with $\mathbf{a}$, $\mathbf{b}$ and $\mathbf{c}$ starting at the same point, as shown in Figure 2.2.

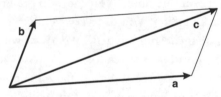

Figure 2.2: Vector addition

The length of a vector $\mathbf{a}$ is denoted by $|\mathbf{a}|$. A vector with zero length is the zero vector, written as $\mathbf{0}$. The notation $-\mathbf{a}$ is used for the vector that has length $|\mathbf{a}|$ and whose direction is opposite to that of $\mathbf{a}$. For any vector $\mathbf{a}$ and real number c, the vector $c\mathbf{a}$ has length $|c||\mathbf{a}|$. If $\mathbf{a} = \mathbf{0}$ or $c = 0$, then $c\mathbf{a} = \mathbf{0}$; otherwise $c\mathbf{a}$ has the direction of $\mathbf{a}$ if $c > 0$ and the opposite direction if $c < 0$. For any vectors $\mathbf{u}$, $\mathbf{v}$, $\mathbf{w}$ and real numbers c, k, we have

$$\mathbf{u} + \mathbf{v} = \mathbf{v} + \mathbf{u}$$
$$(\mathbf{u} + \mathbf{v}) + \mathbf{w} = \mathbf{u} + (\mathbf{v} + \mathbf{w})$$
$$\mathbf{u} + \mathbf{0} = \mathbf{u}$$

$$\mathbf{u} + (-\mathbf{u}) = \mathbf{0}$$
$$c(\mathbf{u} + \mathbf{v}) = c\mathbf{u} + c\mathbf{v}$$
$$(c + k)\mathbf{u} = c\mathbf{u} + k\mathbf{u}$$
$$c(k\mathbf{u}) = (ck)\mathbf{u}$$
$$1\mathbf{u} = \mathbf{u}$$
$$0\mathbf{u} = \mathbf{0}$$

Figure 2.3 shows three unit vectors $\mathbf{i}$, $\mathbf{j}$ and $\mathbf{k}$ in a three-dimensional space. They are mutually perpendicular and have length 1. Their directions are the positive directions of the coordinate axes. We say that $\mathbf{i}$, $\mathbf{j}$ and $\mathbf{k}$ form a triple of orthogonal *unit vectors*. The coordinate system is right-handed, which means that if a rotation of $\mathbf{i}$ in the direction of $\mathbf{j}$ through $90°$ corresponds to turning a right-handed screw, then $\mathbf{k}$ has the direction in which the screw advances.

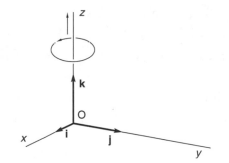

Figure 2.3: **Right-handed coordinate system**

We often choose the origin O of the coordinate system as the initial point of all vectors. Any vector $\mathbf{v}$ can be written as a *linear combination* of the unit vectors $\mathbf{i}$, $\mathbf{j}$, and $\mathbf{k}$:

$$\mathbf{v} = x\mathbf{i} + y\mathbf{j} + z\mathbf{k}$$

The real numbers x, y and z are the coordinates of the endpoint P of vector $\mathbf{v} = \mathbf{OP}$. We often write this vector $\mathbf{v}$ as

$$\mathbf{v} = [\ x \quad y \quad z\ ] \qquad \text{or} \qquad \mathbf{v} = (x, y, z)$$

The numbers x, y, z are sometimes called the *elements* or *components* of vector $\mathbf{v}$.

The possibility of writing a vector as a sequence of coordinates, such as (x, y, z) for three-dimensional space, has led to the use of this term for sequences in general. This explains the name *Vector* for a standard Java class. The only aspect this *Vector* class has in common with the mathematical notion of vector is that both are related to sequences.

2.2 INNER PRODUCT

The *inner product* or *dot product* of two vectors **a** and **b** is a real number, written as $\mathbf{a} \cdot \mathbf{b}$ and defined as

$$\mathbf{a} \cdot \mathbf{b} = |\mathbf{a}||\mathbf{b}| \cos \gamma \qquad \qquad \text{if } \mathbf{a} \neq 0 \text{ and } \mathbf{b} \neq 0 \qquad (2.1)$$

$$\mathbf{a} \cdot \mathbf{b} = 0 \qquad \qquad \text{if } \mathbf{a} = 0 \text{ or } \mathbf{b} = 0$$

where γ is the angle between **a** and **b**. It follows from the first equation that $\mathbf{a} \cdot \mathbf{b}$ is also zero if $\gamma = 90°$. Applying this definition to the unit vectors **i**, **j** and **k**, we find

$$\mathbf{i} \cdot \mathbf{i} = \mathbf{j} \cdot \mathbf{j} = \mathbf{k} \cdot \mathbf{k} = 1$$

$$\mathbf{i} \cdot \mathbf{j} = \mathbf{j} \cdot \mathbf{i} = \mathbf{j} \cdot \mathbf{k} = \mathbf{k} \cdot \mathbf{j} = \mathbf{k} \cdot \mathbf{i} = \mathbf{i} \cdot \mathbf{k} = 0 \qquad (2.2)$$

Setting $\mathbf{b} = \mathbf{a}$ in Equation (2.1), we have $\mathbf{a} \cdot \mathbf{a} = |\mathbf{a}|^2$, so

$$|\mathbf{a}| = \sqrt{|\mathbf{a} \cdot \mathbf{a}|}$$

Some important properties of inner products are

$$c(k\mathbf{u} \cdot \mathbf{v}) = ck(\mathbf{u} \cdot \mathbf{v})$$

$$(c\mathbf{u} + k\mathbf{v}) \cdot \mathbf{w} = c\mathbf{u} \cdot \mathbf{w} + k\mathbf{v} \cdot \mathbf{w}$$

$$\mathbf{u} \cdot \mathbf{v} = \mathbf{v} \cdot \mathbf{u}$$

$$\mathbf{u} \cdot \mathbf{u} = 0 \text{ only if } \mathbf{u} = 0$$

The inner product of two vectors $\mathbf{u} = [u_1 \quad u_2 \quad u_3]$ and $\mathbf{v} = [v_1 \quad v_2 \quad v_3]$ can be computed as

$$\mathbf{u} \cdot \mathbf{v} = u_1v_1 + u_2v_2 + u_3v_3$$

We can prove this by developing the right-hand side of the following equality as the sum of nine inner products and then applying Equation (2.2):

$$\mathbf{u} \cdot \mathbf{v} = (u_1\mathbf{i} + u_2\mathbf{j} + u_3\mathbf{k}) \cdot (v_1\mathbf{i} + v_2\mathbf{j} + v_3\mathbf{k})$$

2.3 DETERMINANTS

Before proceeding with vector products, we will pay some attention to determinants. Suppose we want to solve the following system of two linear equations for x and y:

$$\begin{cases} a_1x + b_1y = c_1 \\ a_2x + b_2y = c_2 \end{cases} \qquad (2.3)$$

We can then multiply the first equation by b_2, the second by $-b_1$, and add them, finding

$$(a_1b_2 - a_2b_1)x = b_2c_1 - b_1c_2$$

Then we can multiply the first equation by $-a_2$, the second by a_1, and add again, obtaining

$$(a_1b_2 - a_2b_1)y = a_1c_2 - a_2c_1$$

If $a_1b_2 - a_2b_1$ is not zero, we can divide and find

$$x = \frac{b_2c_1 - b_1c_2}{a_1b_2 - a_2b_1} \qquad y = \frac{a_1c_2 - a_2c_1}{a_1b_2 - a_2b_1} \tag{2.4}$$

The denominator in these expressions is often written in the form

$$\begin{vmatrix} a_1 & b_1 \\ a_2 & b_2 \end{vmatrix}$$

and then called a *determinant*. Thus

$$\begin{vmatrix} a_1 & b_1 \\ a_2 & b_2 \end{vmatrix} = a_1b_2 - a_2b_1$$

Using determinants, we can write the solution of Equation (2.3) as

$$x = \frac{D_1}{D} \qquad y = \frac{D_2}{D} \qquad (D \neq 0)$$

where

$$D = \begin{vmatrix} a_1 & b_1 \\ a_2 & b_2 \end{vmatrix} \quad D_1 = \begin{vmatrix} c_1 & b_1 \\ c_2 & b_2 \end{vmatrix} \quad D_2 = \begin{vmatrix} a_1 & c_1 \\ a_2 & c_2 \end{vmatrix}$$

Note that D_i is obtained by replacing the ith column of D with the right-hand side of Equation (2.3) ($i = 1$ or 2). This method of solving a system of linear equations is called *Cramer's rule*. It is not restricted to systems of two equations (although it would be very expensive in terms of computer time to apply the method to large systems). Determinants with n rows and n columns are said to be of the nth order. We define determinants of third order by using the equation

$$D = \begin{vmatrix} a_{11} & a_{12} & a_{13} \\ a_{21} & a_{22} & a_{23} \\ a_{31} & a_{32} & a_{33} \end{vmatrix} = a_{11}M_{11} - a_{12}M_{12} + a_{13}M_{13}$$

where each so-called *minor determinant* M_{ij} is the 2×2 determinant that we obtain by deleting the ith row and the jth column of D. Determinants of higher order are defined similarly.

Determinants are very useful in linear algebra and analytical geometry. They have many interesting properties, some of which are listed below:

(1) The value of a determinant remains the same if its rows are written as columns in the same order. For example:

$$\begin{vmatrix} a_1 & b_1 \\ a_2 & b_2 \end{vmatrix} = \begin{vmatrix} a_1 & a_2 \\ b_1 & b_2 \end{vmatrix}$$

(2) If any two rows (or columns) are interchanged, the value of the determinant is multiplied by -1. For example:

$$\begin{vmatrix} a_1 & b_1 & c_1 \\ a_2 & b_2 & c_2 \\ a_3 & b_3 & c_3 \end{vmatrix} = - \begin{vmatrix} a_1 & b_1 & c_1 \\ a_3 & b_3 & c_3 \\ a_2 & b_2 & c_2 \end{vmatrix}$$

(3) If any row or column is multiplied by a factor, the value of the determinant is multiplied by this factor. For example:

$$\begin{vmatrix} ca_1 & b_1 \\ ca_2 & b_2 \end{vmatrix} = c \begin{vmatrix} a_1 & a_2 \\ b_1 & b_2 \end{vmatrix}$$

(4) If a row is altered by adding any constant multiple of any other row to it, the value of the determinant remains unaltered. This operation may also be applied to columns. For example:

$$\begin{vmatrix} a_1 & b_1 & c_1 \\ a_2 & b_2 & c_2 \\ a_3 + ka_1 & b_3 + kb_1 & c_3 + kc_1 \end{vmatrix} = \begin{vmatrix} a_1 & b_1 & c_1 \\ a_2 & b_2 & c_2 \\ a_3 & b_3 & c_3 \end{vmatrix}$$

(5) If a row (or a column) is a linear combination of some other rows (or columns), the value of the determinant is zero. For example:

$$\begin{vmatrix} a_1 & b_1 & c_1 \\ a_2 & b_2 & c_2 \\ 3a_1 - 2a_2 & 3b_1 - 2b_2 & 3c_1 - 2c_2 \end{vmatrix} = 0$$

In many cases, determinant equations expressing geometrical properties are elegant and easy to remember. For example, the equation of the line in R_2 through the two points $P_1(x_1, y_1)$ and $P_2(x_2, y_2)$ can be written

$$\begin{vmatrix} x & y & 1 \\ x_1 & y_1 & 1 \\ x_2 & y_2 & 1 \end{vmatrix} = 0 \tag{2.5}$$

This can be understood by observing, first, that Equation (2.5) is a special notation for a linear equation in x and y, and consequently represents a straight line in R_2, and second, that the coordinates of both P_1 and P_2 satisfy this equation, for if we write them in the first row, we have two identical rows. Similarly, the plane in R_3 through three points $P_1(x_1, y_1, z_1)$, $P_2(x_2, y_2, z_2)$, $P_3(x_3, y_3, z_3)$ has the equation

$$\begin{vmatrix} x & y & z & 1 \\ x_1 & y_1 & z_1 & 1 \\ x_2 & y_2 & z_2 & 1 \\ x_3 & y_3 & z_3 & 1 \end{vmatrix} = 0 \tag{2.6}$$

which is much easier to remember than one written in the conventional way.

2.4 VECTOR PRODUCT

The *vector product* or *cross product* of two vectors **a** and **b** is written

$$\mathbf{a} \times \mathbf{b}$$

and is a vector **v** with the following properties. If $\mathbf{a} = c\mathbf{b}$ for some scalar c, then $\mathbf{v} = 0$. Otherwise the length of **v** is equal to

$$|\mathbf{v}| = |\mathbf{a}||\mathbf{b}| \sin \gamma$$

where γ is the angle between **a** and **b**, and the direction of **v** is perpendicular to both **a** and **b** and is such that **a**, **b** and **v**, in that order, form a right-handed triple. This means that if **a** is rotated through an angle $\gamma < 180°$ in the direction of **b**, then **v** has the direction of the advancement of a right-handed screw if turned in the same way. Note that the length $|\mathbf{v}|$ is equal to the area of a parallelogram of which the vectors **a** and **b** can act as edges, as Figure 2.4 shows.

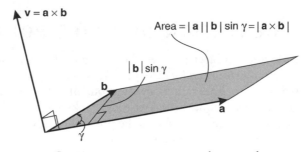

○ **Figure 2.4: Vector product a × b**

The following properties of vector products follow from this definition:

$$(k\mathbf{a}) \times \mathbf{b} = k(\mathbf{a} \times \mathbf{b}) \qquad \text{for any real number } k$$

$$\mathbf{a} \times (\mathbf{b} + \mathbf{c}) = \mathbf{a} \times \mathbf{b} + \mathbf{a} \times \mathbf{c}$$

$$\mathbf{a} \times \mathbf{b} = -\mathbf{b} \times \mathbf{a}$$

In general, $\mathbf{a} \times (\mathbf{b} \times \mathbf{c}) \neq (\mathbf{a} \times \mathbf{b}) \times \mathbf{c}$. If we apply our definition of vector product to the unit vectors **i**, **j**, **k** (see Figure 2.3), we have

$$
\begin{array}{lll}
\mathbf{i} \times \mathbf{i} = 0 & \mathbf{j} \times \mathbf{j} = 0 & \mathbf{k} \times \mathbf{k} = 0 \\
\mathbf{i} \times \mathbf{j} = \mathbf{k} & \mathbf{j} \times \mathbf{k} = \mathbf{i} & \mathbf{k} \times \mathbf{i} = \mathbf{j} \\
\mathbf{j} \times \mathbf{i} = -\mathbf{k} & \mathbf{k} \times \mathbf{j} = -\mathbf{i} & \mathbf{i} \times \mathbf{k} = -\mathbf{j}
\end{array}
$$

Using these vector products in the expansion of

$$\mathbf{a} \times \mathbf{b} = (a_1\mathbf{i} + a_2\mathbf{j} + a_3\mathbf{k}) \times (b_1\mathbf{i} + b_2\mathbf{j} + b_3\mathbf{k})$$

we obtain

$$\mathbf{a} \times \mathbf{b} = (a_2b_3 - a_3b_2)\mathbf{i} + (a_3b_1 - a_1b_3)\mathbf{j} + (a_1b_2 - a_2b_1)\mathbf{k}$$

which can be written as

$$\mathbf{a} \times \mathbf{b} = \begin{vmatrix} a_2 & a_3 \\ b_2 & b_3 \end{vmatrix} \mathbf{i} + \begin{vmatrix} a_3 & a_1 \\ b_3 & b_1 \end{vmatrix} \mathbf{j} + \begin{vmatrix} a_1 & a_2 \\ b_1 & b_2 \end{vmatrix} \mathbf{k}$$

We rewrite this in a form that is very easy to remember:

$$\mathbf{a} \times \mathbf{b} = \begin{vmatrix} \mathbf{i} & \mathbf{j} & \mathbf{k} \\ a_1 & a_2 & a_3 \\ b_1 & b_2 & b_3 \end{vmatrix}$$

This is a mnemonic aid rather than a true determinant, since the elements of the first row are vectors instead of numbers.

If $\mathbf{a}$ and $\mathbf{b}$ are neighboring sides of a parallelogram, as shown in Figure 2.4, the area of this parallelogram is the length of vector $\mathbf{a} \times \mathbf{b}$. This follows from our definition of vector product, according to which $|\mathbf{a} \times \mathbf{b}| = |\mathbf{a}||\mathbf{b}| \sin \gamma$ is the length of vector $\mathbf{a} \times \mathbf{b}$.

2.5 THE ORIENTATION OF THREE POINTS

We will now deal with a subject that will be very useful in Chapters 6 and 7. Suppose that we are given an ordered triple (A, B, C) of three points in the xy-plane and we want to know their orientation; in other words, we want to know whether we turn counter-clockwise or clockwise when visiting these points in the given order. Figure 2.5 shows the possibilities, which we also refer to as *positive* and *negative* orientation, respectively.

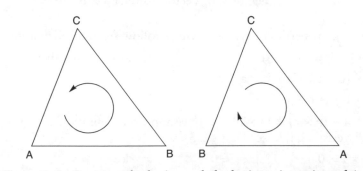

◯ Figure 2.5: Counter-clockwise and clockwise orientation of A, B, C

There is a third possibility, namely that the points A, B and C lie on a straight line. We will consider the orientation to be zero in this case. If we plot the points on paper, we see immediately which of these three cases applies, but we now want a means to find the orientation by computation, using only the coordinates $x_A, y_A, x_B, y_B, x_C, y_C$.

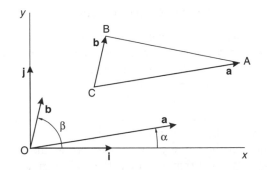

○ **Figure 2.6: Using vectors a and b instead of triangle edges CA and CB**

Let us define the two vectors $\mathbf{a} = \mathbf{CA}$ and $\mathbf{b} = \mathbf{CB}$, as shown in Figure 2.6. Clearly, the orientation of the original points A, B and C is positive if we can turn the vector $\mathbf{a}$ counter-clockwise through a positive angle less than $180°$ to obtain the direction of the vector $\mathbf{b}$. Since vectors are only determined by their directions and lengths, we may let them start at the origin O instead of at point C, as Figure 2.6 shows. Although this orientation problem is essentially two-dimensional, and can be solved using only 2D concepts, as we will see in a moment, it is convenient to use 3D space. As usual, the unit vectors $\mathbf{i}$, $\mathbf{j}$ and $\mathbf{k}$ have the directions of the positive x-, y- and z-axes. In Figure 2.6, we imagine the vector $\mathbf{k}$, like $\mathbf{i}$ and $\mathbf{j}$ starting at O, and pointing towards us. Denoting the endpoints of the translated vectors $\mathbf{a}$ and $\mathbf{b}$, starting at O, by $(a_1, a_2, 0)$ and $(b_1, b_2, 0)$, we have

$$\mathbf{a} = a_1\mathbf{i} + a_2\mathbf{j} + 0\mathbf{k}$$
$$\mathbf{b} = b_1\mathbf{i} + b_2\mathbf{j} + 0\mathbf{k}$$

and

$$\mathbf{a} \times \mathbf{b} = \begin{vmatrix} \mathbf{i} & \mathbf{j} & \mathbf{k} \\ a_1 & a_2 & 0 \\ b_1 & b_2 & 0 \end{vmatrix} = \begin{vmatrix} a_1 & a_2 \\ b_1 & b_2 \end{vmatrix} \mathbf{k} = (a_1 b_2 - a_2 b_1)\mathbf{k}$$

This expresses the fact that $\mathbf{a} \times \mathbf{b}$ is a vector perpendicular to the xy-plane and either in the same direction as

$$\mathbf{k} = \mathbf{i} \times \mathbf{j}$$

or in the opposite direction, depending on the sign of $a_1 b_2 - a_2 b_1$. If this expression is positive, the relationship between $\mathbf{a}$ and $\mathbf{b}$ is similar to that of $\mathbf{i}$ and $\mathbf{j}$: we can turn $\mathbf{a}$ counter-clockwise through an angle less than $180°$ to obtain the direction of $\mathbf{b}$, in the same way as we can do this with $\mathbf{i}$ to obtain $\mathbf{j}$. In general, we have

$$a_1 b_2 - a_2 b_1 \begin{cases} > 0 : \text{orientation of A, B and C positive (counter-clockwise)} \\ = 0 : \text{A, B and C on the same line} \\ < 0 : \text{orientation of A, B and C negative (clockwise)} \end{cases}$$

2.5.1 An Alternative, Two-dimensional Solution

It would be unsatisfactory if we were unable to solve the above orientation problem by using only two-dimensional concepts. To provide such an alternative solution, we use the angles α between vector $\mathbf{a}$ and the positive x-axis and β between $\mathbf{b}$ and this axis (see Figure 2.6). Then the orientation we are interested in depends upon the angle $\beta - \alpha$. If this angle lies between 0 and π, the orientation is clearly positive, but it is negative if this angle lies between π and 2π (or between $-\pi$ and 0). We can express this by saying that the orientation in question depends on the value of $\sin(\beta - \alpha)$ rather than on the angle $\beta - \alpha$ itself. More specifically, the orientation has the same sign as

$$\sin(\beta - \alpha) = \sin\beta\cos\alpha - \cos\beta\sin\alpha = \frac{b_2}{|\mathbf{b}|}\frac{a_1}{|\mathbf{a}|} - \frac{b_1}{|\mathbf{b}|}\frac{a_2}{|\mathbf{a}|} = \frac{a_1 b_2 - a_2 b_1}{|\mathbf{a}||\mathbf{b}|}$$

Since the denominator in this expression is the product of two vector lengths, it is positive, so that we have again found that the orientation of A, B and C and $a_1 b_2 - a_2 b_1$ have the same sign. Due to unfamiliarity with the above trigonometric formula, some readers may find the former, more visual 3D approach easier to remember.

2.5.2 A Useful Java Method

The method *area2* in the following fragment is based on the results we have found. This method takes three arguments of class *Point2D*, discussed at the end of Chapter 1. We will use the class *Tools2D* for several static methods, to be used as two-dimensional tools (see also Section 2.13). Note that, in accordance with Java convention, we use lower-case variable names a, b, c for the points A, B and C:

```
class Tools2D
{   static float area2(Point2D a, Point2D b, Point2D c)
    {  return (a.x - c.x) * (b.y - c.y) - (a.y - c.y) * (b.x - c.x);
    }
    ... // See Section 2.13
}
```

As we will see in Section 2.7, this method computes the area of the triangle ABC multiplied by 2, or, if A, B and C are clockwise, by -2. If we are interested only in the orientation of the points A, B and C, each of type *Point2D*, we can write:

```
if (Tools2D.area2(a, b, c) > 0)
{  ... // A, B and C counter-clockwise
}
else
{  ...
```

```
    // A, B and C clockwise (unless the area2 method return 0;
    // in that case A, B and C lie on the same line).
}
```

2.6 POLYGONS

A *polygon* is a sequence P_0, P_1, ..., P_{n-1} of vertices, where $n \geq 3$, with associated edges P_0P_1, P_1P_2, ..., $P_{n-2}P_{n-1}$, $P_{n-1}P_0$. In this book we will restrict ourselves to simple polygons, of which non-adjacent edges do not intersect. Figure 2.7 shows two simple and two non-simple polygons, for all of which $n = 5$.

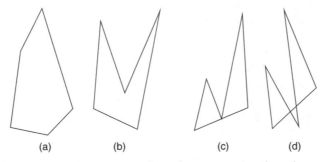

(a)   (b)   (c)   (d)

Figure 2.7: Two simple and two non-simple polygons

Besides non-simple polygons, such as those in Figure 2.7(c) and (d), we usually also ignore polygons in which three successive vertices lie on the same line. A vertex of a polygon is said to be *convex* if the interior angle between the two edges meeting at that vertex is less than 180°. If all vertices of a polygon are convex, the polygon itself is said to be convex, as is the case with Figure 2.7(a). Non-convex vertices are referred to as *reflex*. If a polygon has at least one reflex vertex, the polygon is said to be *concave*. Figure 2.7(b) shows a concave polygon because the vertex in the middle is reflex. All triangles are convex, and each polygon has at least three convex vertices.

If we are given the vertices P_0, P_1, ..., P_{n-1} of a polygon, it may be desirable to determine whether this vertex sequence is counter-clockwise. If we know that the second vertex, P_1, is convex, we can simply write

```
if (Tools2D.area2(p[0], p[1], p[2]) > 0)
    ... // Counter-clockwise
else
    ... // Clockwise
```

The problem is more interesting if no information about any convex vertex is available. We then have to detect such a vertex. This is an easy task, since any vertex whose x- or y-coordinate is extreme is convex. For example, we can use a vertex whose x-coordinate is not greater than that of any other vertex. If we do not want to exclude the case of three successive vertices lying on the same line, we must pay special attention to the case of three such vertices having the minimum x-coordinate. Therefore, among all vertices with an x-coordinate equal to this minimum value, we choose the lowest one, that is, the one with the least y-coordinate. The following method is based on this idea:

```
static boolean ccw(Point2D[] p)
{  int n = p.length, k = 0;
   for (int i=1; i<n; i++)
      if (p[i].x <= p[k].x && (p[i].x < p[k].x || p[i].y < p[k].y))
         k = i;
   // p[k] is a convex vertex.
   int prev = k - 1, next = k + 1;
   if (prev == -1) prev = n   1;
   if (next == n) next = 0;
   return Tools2D.area2(p[prev], p[k], p[next]) > 0;
}
```

We should be aware that one very strange situation is still possible: all n vertices may lie on the same line. In that case, the method *ccw* will return the value *false*.

We will use this method in Section 2.13, in which program *PolyTria.java* will divide a user-entered polygon into triangles.

2.7 THE AREA OF A POLYGON

As we have seen in Figure 2.4, the cross product $\mathbf{a} \times \mathbf{b}$ is a vector whose length is equal to the area of a parallelogram of which $\mathbf{a}$ and $\mathbf{b}$ are two edges. Since this parallelogram is the sum of two triangles of equal area, it follows that for Figure 2.6 we have

$$2\,\text{Area}(\triangle ABC) = |a \times b| = \begin{vmatrix} a_1 & a_2 \\ b_1 & b_2 \end{vmatrix} = a_1 b_2 - a_2 b_1$$

Note that this is valid only if A, B and C are labeled counter-clockwise; if this is not necessarily the case, we have to use the absolute value of $a_1 b_2 - a_2 b_1$.

Since $a_1 = x_A - x_C, a_2 = y_A - y_C, b_1 = x_B - x_C, b_2 = y_B - y_C$, we can also write

$$2\,\text{Area}(\triangle ABC) = (x_A - x_C)(y_B - y_C) - (y_A - y_C)(x_B - x_C)$$

After working this out, we find that we can replace this with

$$2 \text{ Area}(\triangle ABC) = (x_A y_B - y_A x_B) + (x_B y_C - y_B x_C) + (x_C y_A - y_C x_A)$$

Although the latter expression seems hardly an improvement, it is useful to prepare for a more general one, which we can use to compute the area of any polygon, convex or concave, which has the vertices $P_0 P_1, P_1 P_2, \ldots, P_{n-2} P_{n-1}, P_{n-1}$, labeled counter-clockwise:

$$2 \text{ Area}(P_0 \ldots P_{n-1}) = \sum_{i=0}^{n-1} (x_i y_{i+1} - y_i x_{i+1})$$

where (x_i, y_i) are the coordinates of P_i and P_n is the same vertex as P_0. As you can see, our last formula for the area of a triangle is a special case of this general one, in which the area of a polygon is expressed directly in terms of the coordinates of its vertices. A complete proof of this formula is beyond the scope of this book.

2.7.1 Java Code

As we have seen in Section 2.6, we use the method *area2* to determine the orientation of three points A, B and C. Recall that the digit 2 in the name *area2* indicates that we have to divide the return value by 2 to obtain the area of triangle ABC, that is, if A, B and C are counter-clockwise; otherwise, we have to take the absolute value $|area2(A, B, C)/2|$.

The same applies to the following method *area2*, whose return value divided by 2 gives the area, possibly preceded by a minus sign, of a polygon.

```
static float area2(Point2D[] pol)
{   int n = pol.length,
        j = n - 1;
    float a = 0;

    for (int i=0; i<n; i++)
    {   // i and j denote neighbor vertices
        // with i one step ahead of j
        a += pol[j].x * pol[i].y - pol[j].y * pol[i].x;
        j = i;
    }
    return a;
}
```

Note that this second *area2* method provides another means of deciding the orientation of a polygon vertex sequence: this orientation is counter-clockwise if *area2* returns a positive value and clockwise if it returns a negative one. However, the method *ccw* discussed in Section 2.6 is faster, especially if *n* is large, because for most vertices it will only perform the comparison

```
p[i].x <= p[k].x
```

while *area2* performs some more time-consuming arithmetic operations for each vertex.

We could add this second method *area2* to the class *Tools2D*, but you will not find it in our final version of this class in Section 2.13 because we will never use it in this book; since we will use *Tools2D* several times, we prefer to omit superfluous methods for economic reasons.

2.8 POINT-IN-TRIANGLE TEST

Determining the orientation of three points as we have just been discussing is useful in a test to see if a given point P lies within a triangle ABC. As Figure 2.8 shows, this is the case if the orientation of the triangles ABP, BCP and CAP is the same as that of triangle ABC.

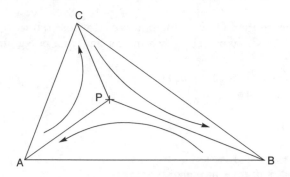

○ **Figure 2.8: Orientation used to test if P lies within triangle ABC**

Let us assume that we know that the orientation of ABC is counter-clockwise. We can then call the following method to test if P lies within triangle ABC (or on an edge of it):

```
static boolean insideTriangle(Point2D a, Point2D b, Point2D c,
    Point2D p) // ABC is assumed to be counter-clockwise
{  return
```

```
        Tools2D.area2(a, b, p) >= 0 &&
        Tools2D.area2(b, c, p) >= 0 &&
        Tools2D.area2(c, a, p) >= 0;
}
```

In this form, the method *insideTriangle* also returns the value *true* if P lies on an edge of the triangle ABC. If this is not desired, we should replace $>= 0$ with > 0. The above form is the one we will need in Chapters 6 and 7, in which we will use this method to triangulate complicated polygonal faces of 3D objects.

Incidentally, with a floating-point value x, we might consider replacing a test of the form $x >= 0$ with $x >= -epsilon$ and $x > 0$ with $x > epsilon$, where *epsilon* is some small positive value, such as 10^{-6}. In this way a very small rounding-off error (less than *epsilon*) in the value of x will not affect the result of the test. This is not done here because the above method *insideTriangle* works well for our applications.

2.8.1 An Alternative Method *insideTriangle*

The above method *insideTriangle* is reasonably efficient, especially if point P does not lie within the triangle ABC. In such cases the chances are that not all three calls to *area2* are executed because the first or the second of the three tests fails. However, it should be mentioned that there is an entirely different way of solving the problem in question, as we will see in Exercise 3.5. The corresponding alternative method *insideTriangle* (listed in Appendix F), is slightly faster than the one above if a single triangle ABC is to be used for several points P. It is also more general in that it does not rely on ABC being counter-clockwise. We will not discuss this alternative method here because it is easier to understand after the discussion of matrix multiplication and inverse matrices in Chapter 3. To avoid confusion we will normally use the *insideTriangle* version discussed in this section and occurring in the file *Tools2D.java*, even in cases where the one in Exercise 3.5 might be slightly faster.

2.9 POINT-IN-POLYGON TEST

The notion of orientation is also useful when we need to determine whether a given point P lies within a polygon. It will then be convenient if a method is available which accepts both the polygon in question and point P as arguments, and returns *true* if P lies inside and *false* if it lies outside the polygon. If P lies on a polygon edge, we do not care: in that case the method may return *true* or *false*. The method we will discuss is based on the idea of drawing a horizontal half-line, which starts at P and extends only to the right. The number of intersections of this horizontal half-line with polygon edges is odd if P lies within the polygon and even if P lies outside it. Imagine that we move to the right, starting at point P. Then our state changes from *inside* to *outside* and vice versa each time we cross a polygon edge. The total number of changes is therefore odd if P lies within the polygon and even if it lies outside the polygon. It is not necessary to visit all intersections strictly from left to right; the only thing we want to know is whether there are an odd or an even number of intersections on a horizontal line through P and to the right of P. However, we must be careful with some special cases, as shown in Figure 2.9.

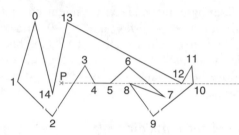

Figure 2.9: Polygon and half-line starting at P

We simply ignore horizontal polygon edges, even if they have the same y-coordinate as P, as is the case with edge 4–5 in this example. If a vertex occurring as a 'local maximum or minimum' happens to have the same y-coordinate as P, as is the cases with vertices 8 and 12 in this example, it is essential that this is either ignored or counted twice. We can realize this by using the edge from vertex i to vertex $i + 1$ only if

$$y_i \leq y_P < y_{i+1} \text{ or } y_{i+1} \leq y_P < y_i$$

This implies that the lower endpoint of a non-horizontal edge is regarded as part of the segment, but the upper endpoint is not. For example, in Figure 2.9, vertex 8 (with $y_8 = y_P$) is not counted at all because it is the upper endpoint of both edge 7–8 and edge 8–9. By contrast, vertex 12 (with $y_{12} = y_P$) is the lower endpoint of the edges 11–12 and 12–13 and thus counted twice. Therefore, in this example, we count the intersections of the half-line through P with the seven edges 2–3, 3–4, 5–6, 6–7, 10–11, 11–12, 12–13 and with no others.

Since we are considering only a half-line, we must impose another restriction on the set of edges satisfying the above test, selecting only those whose point of intersection with the half-line lies to the right of P. One way of doing this is by using the method *area2* to determine the orientation of a sequence of three points. For example, this orientation is counter-clockwise for the triangle 2-3-P in Figure 2.9, which implies that P lies to the left of edge 2–3. It is also counter-clockwise for the triangle 7-6-P. In both cases, the lower endpoint of an edge, its upper endpoint and point P, in that order, are counter-clockwise. The following method is based on these principles:

```
static boolean insidePolygon(Point2D p, Point2D[] pol)
{  int n = pol.length, j = n - 1;
   boolean b = false;
   float x = p.x, y = p.y;
   for (int i=0; i<n; i++)
   {  if (pol[j].y <= y && y < pol[i].y &&
          Tools2D.area2(pol[j], pol[i], p) > 0 ||
          pol[i].y <= y && y < pol[j].y &&
          Tools2D.area2(pol[i], pol[j], p) > 0) b = !b;
      j = i;
   }
   return b;
}
```

This static method, like some others in this chapter, might be added to the class *Tools2D* (see Section 2.13).

2.9.1 The *contains* Method of the Java Class *Polygon*

There is a standard class *Polygon*, which has a member named *contains* to perform about the same task as the above method *insidePolygon*. However, it is based on integer coordinates.

For example, to test if a point $P(xP, yP)$ lies within the triangle with vertices A(20, 15), B(100, 30) and C(80, 150), we can use the following fragment:

```
int[] x = {20, 100, 80}, y = {15, 30, 150}; // A, B, C
Polygon p = new Polygon(x, y, 3);
if (p.contains(xP, yP)) ... // P lies within triangle ABC.
```

If P lies exactly on a polygon edge, the value returned by this method *contains* of the class *Polygon* can be *true* or *false*.

2.10 POINT-ON-LINE TEST

Testing whether a point P lies on a given line is very simple if this line is given as an equation, say,

$$ax + by = h \tag{2.7}$$

Then all we need to do is to test whether the coordinates of P satisfy this equation. Due to inexact computations, such a test may fail when it should succeed. It may therefore be wise to be slightly more tolerant, so that we might write

```
if (Math.abs(a * p.x + b * p.y - h) < eps) // P on the line
```

where *eps* is some small positive value, such as 10^{-5}.

If the line is not given by an equation but by two points A and B on it, we can use the above test after deriving an equation for the line, as discussed in Section 2.3, writing

$$\begin{vmatrix} x & y & 1 \\ x_A & y_A & 1 \\ x_B & y_B & 1 \end{vmatrix} = 0$$

which gives the following coefficients for Equation (2.7):

$$a = y_A - y_B$$
$$b = x_B - x_A$$
$$h = x_B y_A - x_A y_B$$

Instead, we can benefit from the *area2* method, which we are now familiar with. After all, if and only if P lies on the line through A and B, the triangle ABP is degenerated and has a zero area. We can therefore write

```
if (Math.abs(Tools2D.area2(a, b, p)) < eps) // P on line AB
```

Again, if we simply test whether the computed area is equal to zero, such a test might fail when it should succeed, due to rounding-off errors.

2.10.1 Testing Whether a Point Lies on a Line Segment

If three points A, B and P are given, we may want to determine whether P lies on the closed line segment AB. The adjective *closed* here means that we include the endpoints A and B, so that the question is to be answered affirmatively if P lies between A and B or coincides with one of these points. We assume that A and B are different points, which implies that $x_A \neq x_B$ or $y_A \neq y_B$. If $x_A \neq x_B$ we test whether x_P lies between x_A and x_B; if not, we test whether y_P lies between y_A and y_B, where in both cases the word *between* includes the points A and B themselves. This test is sufficient if it is given that P lies on the infinite line AB. If that is not given, we also have to perform the above test, which is done in the following method:

```
static boolean onSegment(Point2D a, Point2D b, Point2D p)
{  double dx = b.x - a.x, dy = b.y - a.y,
```

```
        eps = 0.001 * (dx * dx + dy * dy);
    return
        (a.x != b.x &&
        (a.x <= p.x && p.x <= b.x || b.x <= p.x && p.x <= a.x)
        || a.x == b.x &&
        (a.y <= p.y && p.y <= b.y || b.y <= p.y && p.y <= a.y))
        && Math.abs(Tools2D.area2(a, b, p)) < eps;
}
```

The expression following *return* relies on the operator && having higher precedence than ||. Since both operators && and || evaluate the second operand only if this is necessary, this test is more efficient than it looks. For example, if $x_A \neq x_B$ the test on the line of the form ($a.y \mathrel{<=} \ldots$) is not evaluated at all. The positive constant *eps* in the above code has been chosen in such a way that the area of triangle ABP is compared with a fraction of another area, for which the square of side AB is used. In this way, the compared areas depend in the same way on both the length of AB and the unit of length that is used.

Instead of testing if P lies on the segment AB, we may want to apply a similar test to the projection P′ of P on AB, as Figure 2.10 shows.

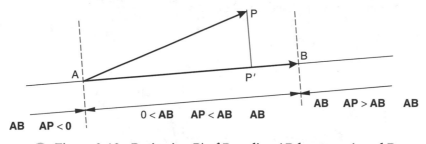
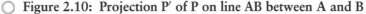

○ **Figure 2.10: Projection P′ of P on line AB between A and B**

We can solve this problem by computing the dot product of the vectors **AB** and **AP**. This dot product **AB** · **AP** is equal to 0 if P′ ≡ A (P′ coincides with A) and it is equal to **AB** · **AB** = AB² if P′ ≡ B. For any value of this dot product between these two values, P lies between A and B. We can write this as follows in a program, where *len2* corresponds to **AB** · **AB**, *inprod* corresponds to **AB** · **AP**, and *eps* is some small positive value, as discussed for the above method *onSegment*:

```
// Does P' (P projected on AB) lie on the closed segment AB?
static boolean projOnSegment(Point2D a, Point2D b, Point2D p)
{   double dx = b.x - a.x, dy = b.y - a.y,
```

```
    eps = 0.001 * (dx * dx + dy * dy),
    len2 = dx * dx + dy * dy,
    inprod = dx * (p.x - a.x) + dy * (p.y - a.y);
  return inprod > -eps && inprod < len2 + eps;
}
```

To determine whether P′ lies on the *open* segment AB (not including A and B), we replace the return statement with

```
return inprod > eps && inprod < len2 - eps;
```

2.11 DISTANCE BETWEEN A POINT AND A LINE

We can find the distance between a point P and a line *l* in different ways, depending on the way the line is specified. If two points A and B of the line are given, we can find the distance between a point P and the (infinite) line *l* through A and B by using the first of the two methods *area2* defined in Section 2.7:

$$\text{distance between P and line AB} = d = \frac{|area2(\text{A,B,P})|}{|\textbf{AB}|}$$

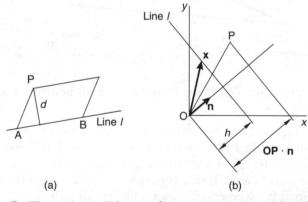

(a)   (b)

○ **Figure 2.11: Distance between point P and line *l***

This follows from the fact that the absolute value of *area2*(A, B, P) denotes the area of the parallelogram of which A, B and P are three vertices, as shown in Figure 2.11(a). This area is also equal to the product of the parallelogram's base AB and its height *d*. We can therefore compute *d* in the above way.

If the line l is given as an equation, we assume this to be in the form

$$ax + by = h$$

where

$$\sqrt{a^2 + b^2} = 1$$

If the latter condition is not satisfied, we only have to divide a, b and h by the above square root. We can then write the above equation of line l as the dot product

$$\mathbf{x} \cdot \mathbf{n} = h$$

where

$$\mathbf{n} = \begin{pmatrix} a \\ b \end{pmatrix} \text{ and } \mathbf{x} = \begin{pmatrix} x \\ y \end{pmatrix}$$

The normal vector $\mathbf{n}$ is perpendicular to line l and has length 1. For any vector $\mathbf{x}$, starting at O, the dot product $\mathbf{x} \cdot \mathbf{n}$ is the projection of vector $\mathbf{x}$ on $\mathbf{n}$. This also applies if the endpoint of $\mathbf{x}$ lies on line l, as shown in Figure 2.11(b); in this case we have $\mathbf{x} \cdot \mathbf{n} = h$. We find the desired distance between point P and line l by projecting $\mathbf{OP}$ also on $\mathbf{n}$ and computing the difference of the two projections:

$$\text{Distance between P and line } l = |\mathbf{OP} \cdot \mathbf{n} - h| = |ax_P + by_P - h|$$

Although Figure 2.11(b) applies to the case $h > 0$, this equation is also valid if h is negative or zero, or if O lies between line l and the line through P parallel to l. Both $\mathbf{OP} \cdot \mathbf{n}$ and h are scale factors for the same vector $\mathbf{n}$. The absolute value of the algebraic difference of these two scale factors is the desired distance between P and l. We will refer to this algebraic difference $\mathbf{OP} \cdot \mathbf{n} - h = ax_P + by_P - h$ as a *signed distance* in the next section.

2.12 PROJECTION OF A POINT ON A LINE

Suppose that again a line l and a point P (not on l) are given and that we want to compute the projection P′ of P on l (see Figure 2.10). This point P′ has three interesting properties:

1. P′ is the point on l that is closest to P.
2. The length of PP′ is the distance between P and l (computed in the previous section).
3. PP′ and l are perpendicular.

As in the previous section, we discuss two solutions: one for a line l given by two points A and B, and the other for l given as the equation $\mathbf{x} \cdot \mathbf{n} = h$.

With given points A and B on line l, the situation is as shown in Figure 2.10. Recall that in Section 2.10 we discussed the method *projOnSegment* to test if the projection P′ of P on the line through A and B lies between A and B. In that method, we did not actually compute the position of P′. We will now do this (see Figure 2.10), first by introducing the vector **u** of length 1 and direction **AB**:

$$\mathbf{u} = \frac{1}{|\mathbf{AB}|}\mathbf{AB}$$

Then the length of the projection AP′ of AP is equal to

$$\lambda = \mathbf{AP} \cdot \mathbf{u}$$

which we use to compute

$$\mathbf{AP}' = \lambda\mathbf{u}$$

Doing this straightforwardly would require a square-root operation in the computation of the distance between A and B, used in the computation of **u**. Fortunately, we can avoid this by rewriting the last equation, using the two preceding ones:

$$\mathbf{AP}' = (\mathbf{AP} \cdot \mathbf{u})\mathbf{u} = \left(\mathbf{AP} \cdot \frac{1}{|\mathbf{AB}|}\mathbf{AB}\right)\frac{1}{|\mathbf{AB}|}\mathbf{AB} = \frac{1}{|\mathbf{AB}|^2}(\mathbf{AP} \cdot \mathbf{AB})\mathbf{AB}$$

The advantage of the last form is that the square of the segment length AB is easier to compute than that length itself. The following method, which returns the projection P′ of P on AB, demonstrates this:

```
// Compute P' (P projected on AB):
static Point2D projection(Point2D a, Point2D b, Point2D p)
{  float vx = b.x - a.x, vy = b.y - a.y, len2 = vx * vx + vy * vy,
      inprod = vx * (p.x - a.x) + vy * (p.y - a.y);
   return new Point2D(a.x + inprod * vx/len2,
                   a.y + inprod * vy/len2);
}
```

So much for a line given by two points A and B.

Let us now turn to a line l given by its equation, which we again write as

$$\mathbf{x} \cdot \mathbf{n} = h$$

where

$$\mathbf{n} = \begin{pmatrix} a \\ b \end{pmatrix} \text{ and } \mathbf{x} = \begin{pmatrix} x \\ y \end{pmatrix}$$

and

$$\sqrt{a^2 + b^2} = 1$$

Using the 'signed distance'

$$d = \mathbf{OP} \cdot \mathbf{n} - h$$

as introduced at the end of the previous section and illustrated by Figure 2.11, we can write the following vector equation to compute the desired projection P′ of P on *l*:

$$\mathbf{OP'} = \mathbf{OP} - d\mathbf{n} = \begin{pmatrix} x_{\mathrm{P}} \\ y_{\mathrm{P}} \end{pmatrix} - d \begin{pmatrix} a \\ b \end{pmatrix}$$

This should make the following method clear:

```
// Compute P', the projection of P on line l given as
// ax + by = h, where a * a + b * b = 1
static Point2D projection(float a, float b, float h,
   Point2D p)
{  float d = p.x * a + p.y * b - h;
   return new Point2D(p.x - d * a, p.y - d * b);
}
```

2.13 TRIANGULATION OF POLYGONS

In many graphics applications, such as those to be discussed in Chapters 6 and 7, it is desirable to divide a polygon into triangles. This triangulation problem can be solved in many ways. We will discuss a comparatively simple algorithm. It accepts a polygon in the form of an array of *Point2D* elements (see Section 1.5), containing the polygon vertices in counter-clockwise order. The *triangulate* method that we will discuss takes such an array as an argument. To store the resulting triangles, it also takes a second argument, an array with elements of type *Triangle*, which is defined as follows:

```
// Triangle.java: Class to store a triangle;
//    vertices in logical coordinates.
// Uses: Point2D (Section 1.5).

class Triangle
{  Point2D a, b, c;
   Triangle(Point2D a, Point2D b, Point2D c)
   {  this.a = a; this.b = b; this.c = c;
   }
}
```

If the given polygon has *n* vertices, this triangle array should have length
n − 2. The algorithm works as follows. Traversing the vertices of the polygon
in counter-clockwise order, for every three successive vertices P, Q and R of
which Q is a convex vertex (with an angle less than 180°), we cut the triangle
PQR off the polygon if this triangle does not contain any of the other polygon
vertices. For example, starting with polygon ABCDE in Figure 2.12, we cannot
cut triangle ABC, because this contains vertex D. Nor is triangle CDE a good
candidate, because D is not a convex vertex. There are no such problems with
triangle BCD, so that we will cut this off the polygon, reducing the polygon
ABCDE to the simpler one ABDE.

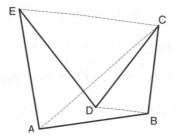

○ **Figure 2.12: Cutting off a triangle**

For this purpose we use the static method *triangulate*, which, along with some
others already discussed, is listed in the class *Tools2D* below:

```
// Tools2D.java: Class to be used in other program files.
// Uses: Point2D (Section 1.5) and Triangle (discussed above).

class Tools2D
{  static float area2(Point2D a, Point2D b, Point2D c)
   {  return (a.x - c.x) * (b.y - c.y) - (a.y - c.y) * (b.x - c.x);
   }

   static boolean insideTriangle(Point2D a, Point2D b, Point2D c,
      Point2D p) // ABC is assumed to be counter-clockwise
   {  return
        Tools2D.area2(a, b, p) >= 0 &&
        Tools2D.area2(b, c, p) >= 0 &&
        Tools2D.area2(c, a, p) >= 0;
   }

   static void triangulate(Point2D[] p, Triangle[] tr)
   {  // p contains all n polygon vertices in CCW order.
```

```
      // The resulting triangles will be stored in array tr.
      // This array tr must have length n - 2.
      int n = p.length, j = n - 1, iA=0, iB, iC;
      int[] next = new int[n];
      for (int i=0; i<n; i++)
      {  next[j] = i;
         j = i;
      }
      for (int k=0; k<n-2; k++)
      {  // Find a suitable triangle, consisting of two edges
         // and an internal diagonal:
         Point2D a, b, c;
         boolean triaFound = false;
         int count = 0;
         while (!triaFound && ++count < n)
         {  iB = next[iA]; iC = next[iB];
            a = p[iA]; b = p[iB]; c = p[iC];
            if (Tools2D.area2(a, b, c) >= 0)
            {  // Edges AB and BC; diagonal AC.
               // Test to see if no other polygon vertex
               // lies within triangle ABC:
               j = next[iC];
               while (j != iA && !insideTriangle(a, b, c, p[j]))
                  j = next[j];
               if (j == iA)
               {  // Triangle ABC contains no other vertex:
                  tr[k] = new Triangle(a, b, c);
                  next[iA] = iC;
                  triaFound = true;
               }
            }
            iA = next[iA];
         }
         if (count == n)
         {  System.out.println("Not a simple polygon" +
              " or vertex sequence not counter-clockwise.");
            System.exit(1);
         }
      }
   }

   static float distance2(Point2D p, Point2D q)
   {  float dx = p.x - q.x,
```

```
                    dy = p.y - q.y;
            return dx * dx + dy * dy;
       }
   }
```

In Appendix D we will use the method *distance2*, shown at the end of this class; it simply computes the square of the distance of two points P and Q. If we only want to compare two distances, we may as well compare their squares to save the rather costly operation of computing the square roots.

The program below enables the user to define a polygon, in the same way as we did with program *DefPoly.java* in Section 1.5, but this time the polygon will be divided into triangles, which appear in different colors. This program, *PolyTria.java*, uses the above classes *Triangle* and *Tools2D*, as well as the class *CvDefPoly*, which occurs in program *DefPoly.java* of Section 1.5. In our subclass, *CvPolyTria*, we apply the method *ccw*, discussed in Section 2.6, to the given polygon to examine the orientation of its vertex sequence. If this happens to be clockwise, we put the vertices in reverse order in the array *P*, so that the vertex sequence will be counter-clockwise in this array, which we can then safely pass on to the *triangulate* method:

```
// PolyTria.java: Drawing a polygon and dividing it into triangles.
// Uses: CvDefPoly, Point2D (Section 1.5),
//       Triangle, Tools2D (discussed above).

import java.awt.*;
import java.awt.event.*;
import java.util.*;
public class PolyTria extends Frame
{  public static void main(String[] args){new PolyTria();}

   PolyTria()
   {  super("Define polygon vertices by clicking");
      addWindowListener(new WindowAdapter()
         {public void windowClosing(WindowEvent e){System.exit(0);}});
      setSize (500, 300);
      add("Center", new CvPolyTria());

   setCursor(Cursor.getPredefinedCursor(Cursor.CROSSHAIR_CURSOR));
        show();
   }
}
```

```
class CvPolyTria extends CvDefPoly // see Section 1.5
{  public void paint(Graphics g)
   {  int n = v.size();
      if (n > 3 && ready)
      {  Point2D[] p = new Point2D[n];
         for (int i=0; i<n; i++) p[i] = (Point2D)v.elementAt(i);
         // If not counter-clockwise, reverse the order:
         if (!ccw(p))
            for (int i=0; i<n; i++)
               p[i] = (Point2D)v.elementAt(n - i - 1);
         int ntr = n - 2;
         Triangle[] tr = new Triangle[ntr];
         Tools2D.triangulate(p, tr);
         initgr();

         for (int j=0; j<ntr; j++)
         {  g.setColor(new Color(rand(), rand(), rand()));
            int[] x = new int[3], y = new int[3];
            x[0] = iX(tr[j].a.x); y[0] = iY(tr[j].a.y);
            x[1] = iX(tr[j].b.x); y[1] = iY(tr[j].b.y);
            x[2] = iX(tr[j].c.x); y[2] = iY(tr[j].c.y);
            g.fillPolygon(x, y, 3);
         }
      }
      g.setColor(Color.black);
      super.paint(g);
   }

   int rand(){return (int)(Math.random() * 256);}

   static boolean ccw(Point2D[] p)
   {  int n = p.length, k = 0;
      for (int i=1; i<n; i++)
         if (p[i].x <= p[k].x && (p[i].x < p[k].x || p[i].y < p[k].y))
            k = i;
      // p[k] is a convex vertex.
      int prev = k - 1, next = k + 1;
      if (prev == -1) prev = n - 1;
      if (next == n) next = 0;
      return Tools2D.area2(p[prev], p[k], p[next]) > 0;
   }
}
```

The canvas class *CvPolyTria* is a subclass of *CvDefPoly* so that the construction of a polygon with vertices specified by the user is done in the same way as in Section 1.5. In this subclass, we call the method *triangulate* to construct the array *tr* of triangles. These are then displayed in colors generated with a random number generator, so that we can clearly distinguish them. The result on the screen is much better than Figure 2.13, because the latter shows only shades of gray instead of the real colors.

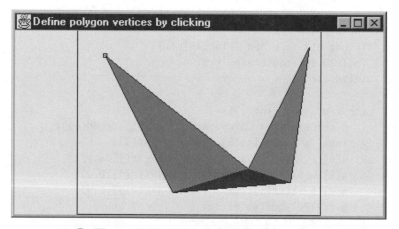

Figure 2.13: Triangulation of a polygon

EXERCISES

2.1   Write a program that draws a square ABCD. The points A and B are arbitrarily specified by the user by clicking the mouse button. The orientation of the points A, B, C and D should be counter-clockwise.

2.2   Write a program that, for four points A, B, C and P,
- draws a triangle formed by ABC and a small cross showing the position of P; and
- displays a line of text indicating which of the following three cases applies: P lies (a) inside ABC, (b) outside ABC, or (c) on an edge of ABC.

The user will specify the four points by clicking.

2.3 The same as Exercise 2.2, but, instead of displaying a line of text, the program computes the distances from P to the (infinite) lines AB, BC and CA, and draws the shortest possible line that connects P with the nearest of those three lines.

2.4 Write a program that computes the intersection point of two (infinite) lines AB and CD. The user will specify the points A, B, C and D by clicking. Draw a small circle around the intersection point. If the two lines AB and CD do not have a unique intersection point (because they are parallel or coinciding), display a line of text indicating this.

2.5 Write a program that constructs the bisector of the angle ABC (which divides the angle at B into two equal angles). After the user has specified the points A, B and C by clicking, the program should compute the intersection point D of this bisector with the opposite side AC, and draw both triangle ABC and bisector BD.

2.6 Write a program that draws the *circumscribed circle* (also known as the *circumcircle*) of a given triangle ABC; this circle passes through the points A, B and C. These points will be specified by the user by clicking the mouse button. Remember, the three perpendicular bisectors of the three edges of a triangle all pass through one point, the *circumcenter*, which is the center of the circumscribed circle.

2.7 Write a program that, for three given points P, Q and R specified by the user, draws a circular arc, starting at P, passing through Q and ending at R (see also Exercise 2.6).

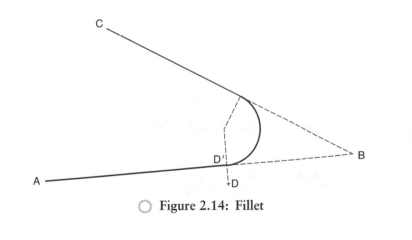

○ **Figure 2.14: Fillet**

2.8   Construct a fillet to replace a sharp corner with a rounded one, as illustrated by the solid lines and the arc in Figure 2.14. The four points A, B, C and D are specified by the user by clicking. Point D may or may not lie on AB; if it does not, it is projected onto AB, giving D', as Figure 2.14 illustrates. The arc starts at point D'.

2.9   Construct the *inscribed circle* (or *incircle*) of a given triangle ABC. The center of this circle lies on the point of intersection of the (internal) bisectors of the three angles A, B and C. Draw also the three *excircles*, which, like the incircle, are tangent to the sides of the triangle, as shown in Fig. 2.15. The centers of the excircles lie on the points of intersection of the external bisectors of the angles A, B and C.

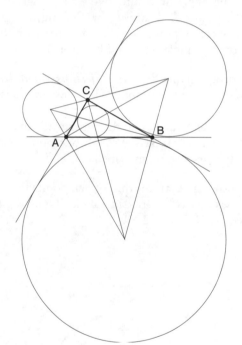

○ **Figure 2.15: Incircle and excircles of triangle ABC**

2.10   Write a program that draws a tree of Pythagoras as shown in Figure 2.16. Two vertices A and B, the basis of the tree, are specified by the user by clicking. Then both a square ABCD and an isosceles,

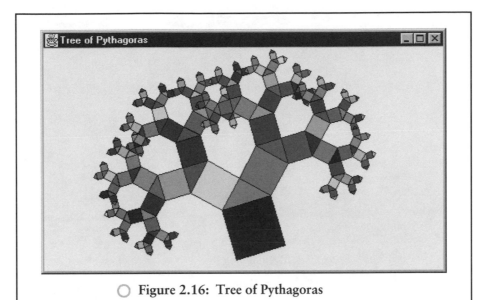

○ **Figure 2.16: Tree of Pythagoras**

right-angled triangle DCE, with right angle E, are constructed. The orientation of both ABCD and DCE is counter-clockwise. Finally, the points D and E form the basis of another tree of Pythagoras, and so do the points E and C. Use a recursive method, which does nothing at all if the two supplied basis points are closer together than some limit.

Chapter 3

Geometrical Transformations

To understand perspective projection, which we will discuss in Chapter 5, we need to be familiar with 3D rotations. These and other transformations will be discussed in this chapter. They are closely related to matrix multiplication, which is the subject we start with.

3.1 MATRIX MULTIPLICATION

A *matrix* (plural *matrices*) is a rectangular array of numbers enclosed in brackets (or parentheses). For example,

$$\begin{bmatrix} 2 & 0 & 0.1 & 3 \\ 1 & 4 & 2 & 10 \end{bmatrix}$$

is a 2×4 matrix: it consists of two rows and four columns. If a matrix consists of only one row, we call it a *row matrix* or *row vector*. In the same way, we use the term *column matrix* or *column vector* for a matrix that has only one column.

If A and B are matrices and the number of columns of A is equal to the number of rows of B, we can compute the *matrix product AB*. This product is another matrix, which has as many rows as A and as many columns as B. We will discuss this in detail for a particular case with regard to the dimensions of A and B: we will use a 2×3 matrix A and a 3×4 matrix B. Then the product $C = AB$ exists and is a 2×4 matrix. It will be clear that the matrix product AB can be computed for A and B of other dimensions in a similar way, provided the number of columns of A is equal to the number of rows of B.

Writing

$$A = \begin{bmatrix} a_{11} & a_{12} & a_{13} \\ a_{21} & a_{22} & a_{23} \end{bmatrix}$$

and similar expressions for both the matrix B and the product matrix $C = AB$, we have

$$\begin{bmatrix} a_{11} & a_{12} & a_{13} \\ a_{21} & a_{22} & a_{23} \end{bmatrix} \begin{bmatrix} b_{11} & b_{12} & b_{13} & b_{14} \\ b_{21} & b_{22} & b_{23} & b_{24} \\ b_{31} & b_{32} & b_{33} & b_{34} \end{bmatrix} = \begin{bmatrix} c_{11} & c_{12} & c_{13} & c_{14} \\ c_{21} & c_{22} & c_{23} & c_{23} \end{bmatrix}$$

Each element c_{ij} (found in row i and column j of the product matrix C) is equal to the dot product of the ith row of A and the jth column of B. For example, to find c_{23}, we need the numbers a_{21}, a_{22} and a_{23} in the second row of A and b_{13}, b_{23} and b_{33} in the third column of B. Using these two sequences as vectors, we can compute their dot product, finding

$$c_{23} = (a_{21}, a_{22}, a_{23}) \cdot (b_{13}, b_{23}, b_{33}) = (a_{21}b_{13} + a_{22}b_{23} + a_{23}b_{33})$$

In general, the elements of the above matrix C are computed as follows:

$$c_{ij} = (a_{i1}, a_{i2}, a_{i3}) \cdot (b_{1j}, b_{2j}, b_{3j}) = a_{i1}b_{1j} + a_{i2}b_{2j} + a_{i3}b_{3j}$$

3.2 LINEAR TRANSFORMATIONS

A transformation T is a mapping

$$\mathbf{v} \to T\mathbf{v} = \mathbf{v}'$$

such that each vector $\mathbf{v}$ (in the vector space we are dealing with) is assigned its unique image $\mathbf{v}'$. Let us begin with the xy-plane and associate with each vector $\mathbf{v}$ the point P, such that

$$\mathbf{v} = \mathbf{OP}$$

Then the transformation T is also a mapping

$$\mathbf{P} \to \mathbf{P}'$$

for each point P in the xy-plane, where $\mathbf{OP}' = \mathbf{v}'$.

A transformation is said to be *linear* if the following is true for any two vectors $\mathbf{v}$ and $\mathbf{w}$ and for any real number λ:

$$T(\mathbf{v} + \mathbf{w}) = T(\mathbf{v}) + T(\mathbf{w})$$
$$T(\lambda\mathbf{v}) = \lambda T(\mathbf{v})$$

By using $\lambda = 0$ in the last equation, we find that, for any linear transformation, we have

$$T(\mathbf{0}) = \mathbf{0}$$

We can write any linear transformation as a matrix multiplication. For example, consider the following linear transformation:

$$\begin{cases} x' = 2x \\ y' = x + y \end{cases}$$

We can write this as the matrix product

$$\begin{bmatrix} x' \\ y' \end{bmatrix} = \begin{bmatrix} 2 & 0 \\ 1 & 1 \end{bmatrix} \begin{bmatrix} x \\ y \end{bmatrix} \tag{3.1}$$

or as the following:

$$\begin{bmatrix} x' & y' \end{bmatrix} = \begin{bmatrix} x & y \end{bmatrix} \begin{bmatrix} 2 & 1 \\ 0 & 1 \end{bmatrix} \tag{3.2}$$

The notation of (3.1) is normally used in standard mathematics textbooks; in computer graphics and other applications in which transformations are combined, the notation of (3.2) is also popular because it avoids a source of mistakes, as we will see in a moment. We will therefore adopt this notation, using row vectors.

It is interesting to note that, in (3.2), the rows of the 2×2 transformation matrix are the images of the unit vectors $(1, 0)$ and $(0, 1)$, respectively, while these images are the columns in (3.1). You can easily verify this by substituting [1 0] and [0 1] for [x y] in (3.2), as the bold matrix elements below illustrate:

$$[\ \mathbf{2}\quad \mathbf{1}\ ] = [\ 1\quad 0\ ] \begin{bmatrix} 2 & 1 \\ 0 & 1 \end{bmatrix}$$

$$[\ \mathbf{0}\quad \mathbf{1}\ ] = [\ 0\quad 1\ ] \begin{bmatrix} 2 & 1 \\ 0 & 1 \end{bmatrix}$$

This principle also applies to other linear transformations. It provides us with a convenient way of finding the transformation matrices.

3.2.1 Rotation

To rotate all points in the xy-plane about O through the angle φ, we can now easily write the transformation matrix, using the rule we have just been discussing. We simply find the images of the unit vectors (1, 0) and (0, 1). As we know from elementary trigonometry, rotating the points P(1, 0) and Q(0, 1) about O through the angle φ gives $P'(\cos\varphi, \sin\varphi)$ and $Q'(-\sin\varphi, \cos\varphi)$. It follows that $(\cos\varphi, \sin\varphi)$ and $(-\sin\varphi, \cos\varphi)$ are the desired images of the unit vectors (1, 0) and (0, 1), as Figure 3.1 illustrates.

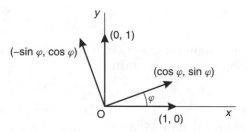

○ **Figure 3.1: Rotation of unit vectors**

Then all we need to do is to write these two images as the rows of our rotation matrix:

$$[\ x'\quad y'\ ] = [\ x\quad y\ ] \begin{bmatrix} \cos\varphi & \sin\varphi \\ -\sin\varphi & \cos\varphi \end{bmatrix} \tag{3.3}$$

3.2.2 A Programming Example

To see rotation in action, let us rotate an arrow about the origin O. Before this rotation, the arrow is vertical, points upward and can be found to the right of O. We will rotate this angle through 120° about the origin O, which is the center of the canvas. Figure 3.2 shows the coordinate axes (intersecting at O) and the arrow before and after the rotation.

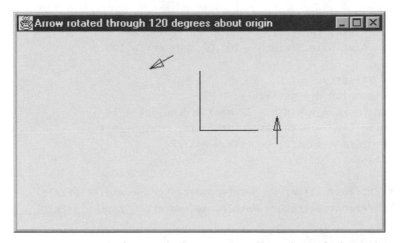

○ **Figure 3.2: Arrow before and after rotation through 120° about the origin**

If we change the dimensions of the window, the origin remains in the center and the sizes of the arrows and of the circle on which they lie change accordingly, while this circle remains a circle. Recall that we also placed the origin at the center of the canvas in the *Isotrop.java* program in Section 1.4, when dealing with the isotropic mapping mode. The following program also uses this mapping mode and contains the same methods *iX* and *iY* for the conversion from logical to device coordinates:

```
// Arrow.java: Arrow rotated through 120 degrees about the logical
//             origin O, which is the center of the canvas.
import java.awt.*;
import java.awt.event.*;

public class Arrow extends Frame
{  public static void main(String[] args){new Arrow();}

   Arrow()
   {  super("Arrow rotated through 120 degrees about origin");
      addWindowListener(new WindowAdapter()
         {public void windowClosing(WindowEvent e){System.exit(0);}});
      setSize (400, 300);
      add("Center", new CvArrow());
      show();
   }
}
```

```java
class CvArrow extends Canvas
{  int centerX, centerY, currentX, currentY;
   float pixelSize, rWidth = 100.0F, rHeight = 100.0F;

   void initgr()
   {  Dimension d = getSize();
      int maxX = d.width - 1, maxY = d.height - 1;
      pixelSize = Math.max(rWidth/maxX, rHeight/maxY);
      centerX = maxX/2; centerY = maxY/2;
   }

   int iX(float x){return Math.round(centerX + x/pixelSize);}
   int iY(float y){return Math.round(centerY - y/pixelSize);}

   void moveTo(float x, float y)
   {  currentX = iX(x); currentY = iY(y);
   }

   void lineTo(Graphics g, float x, float y)
   {  int x1 = iX(x), y1 = iY(y);
      g.drawLine(currentX, currentY, x1, y1);
      currentX = x1; currentY = y1;
   }

   void drawArrow(Graphics g, float[]x, float[]y)
   {  moveTo(x[0], y[0]);
      lineTo(g, x[1], y[1]);
      lineTo(g, x[2], y[2]);
      lineTo(g, x[3], y[3]);
      lineTo(g, x[1], y[1]);
   }

   public void paint(Graphics g)
   {  float r = 40.0F;
      float[] x = {r, r, r-2, r+2},
              y = {-7, 7, 0, 0};
      initgr();
      // Show coordinate axes:
      moveTo (30, 0); lineTo(g, 0, 0); lineTo(g, 0, 30);
      // Show initial arrow:
      drawArrow(g, x, y);
      float phi = (float)(2 * Math.PI / 3),
          c = (float)Math.cos(phi), s = (float)Math.sin(phi),
```

```
        r11 = c, r12 = s, r21 = -s, r22 = c;
     for (int j=0; j<4; j++)
     {  float xNew = x[j] * r11 + y[j] * r21,
              yNew = x[j] * r12 + y[j] * r22;
        x[j] = xNew; y[j] = yNew;
     }
     // Arrow after rotation:
     drawArrow(g, x, y);
  }
}
```

The logical coordinates of the four relevant points of the arrow are stored in the arrays x and y, and the variables $r11$, $r12$, $r21$ and $r22$ denote the elements of the rotation matrix. When programming rotations, we should be careful with two points. First, with a constant angle φ, we should compute $\cos\varphi$ and $\sin\varphi$ only once, even though they occur twice in the rotation matrix. Second, a serious and frequently occurring error is modifying $x[j]$ too early, that is, while we still need the old value for the computation of $y[j]$, as the following, incorrect fragment shows:

```
x[j] = x[j] * r11 + y[j] * r21; // ???
y[j] = x[j] * r12 + y[j] * r22;
```

There is no such problem if we use temporary variables *xNew* and *yNew* (although only the former is really required), as is done in the program.

3.2.3 Scaling

Suppose that we want to perform scaling with scale factors s_x for x and s_y for y and with point O remaining at the same place; the latter is also expressed by referring to O as a *fixed point* or by a *scaling with reference to* O. This can obviously be written as

$$\begin{cases} x' = s_x x \\ y' = s_y y \end{cases}$$

which can also be written as a very simple matrix multiplication:

$$[\, x' \quad y' \,] = [\, x \quad y \,] \begin{bmatrix} s_x & 0 \\ 0 & s_y \end{bmatrix}$$

There are some important special cases:

$s_x = s_y = -1$ gives a reflection about O;
$s_x = 1, s_y = -1$ gives a reflection about the x-axis;
$s_x = -1, s_y = 1$ gives a reflection about the y-axis.

3.2.4 Shearing

Consider the linear transformation given by

$$(1, 0) \rightarrow (1, 0)$$
$$(0, 1) \rightarrow (a, 1)$$

Since the images of the unit vectors appear as the rows of the transformation matrix, we can write this transformation, known as *shearing*, as

$$[\; x' \quad y' \;] = [\; x \quad y \;] \begin{bmatrix} 1 & 0 \\ a & 1 \end{bmatrix}$$

or

$$\begin{cases} x' = x + ay \\ y' = y \end{cases}$$

This set of equations expresses that each point (x, y) moves a distance ay to the right, which has the effect of shearing along the x-axis, as illustrated in Figure 3.3. We can use this transformation to turn regular characters into italic ones; for example, L becomes *L*.

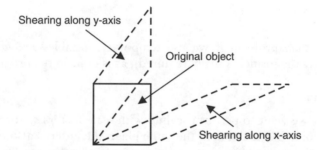

Shearing along y-axis

Original object

Shearing along x-axis

Figure 3.3: Shearing effects (dashed lines) on a square object (solid lines)

Shearing along the y-axis, also depicted in Figure 3.3, can be similarly expressed as

$$[\; x' \quad y' \;] = [\; x \quad y \;] \begin{bmatrix} 1 & b \\ 0 & 1 \end{bmatrix}$$

or

$$\begin{cases} x' = x \\ y' = bx + y \end{cases}$$

3.3 TRANSLATIONS

Shifting all points in the xy-plane a constant distance in a fixed direction is referred to as a *translation*. This is another transformation, which we can write as:

$$x' = x + a$$
$$y' = y + b$$

We refer to the number pair (a, b) as the *shift vector*, or *translation vector*. Although this transformation is a very simple one, it is not linear, as we can easily see by the fact that the image of the origin $(0, 0)$ is (a, b), while this can only be the origin itself with linear transformations. Consequently, we cannot obtain the image (x', y') by multiplying (x, y) by a 2×2 transformation matrix T, which prevents us from combining such a matrix with other transformation matrices to obtain composite transformations. Fortunately, there is a solution to this problem as described in the following section.

3.4 HOMOGENEOUS COORDINATES

To express all the transformations introduced so far as matrix multiplications in order to combine various transformation effects, we add one more dimension. As illustrated in Figure 3.4, the extra dimension W makes any point $P = (x, y)$ of normal coordinates have a whole family of homogeneous coordinate representations (wx, wy, w) for any value of w except 0. For example, $(3, 6, 1)$, $(0.3, 0.6, 0.1)$, $(6, 12, 2)$, $(12, 24, 4)$ and so on, represent the same point in two-dimensional space. Similarly, 4-tuples of coordinates represent points in

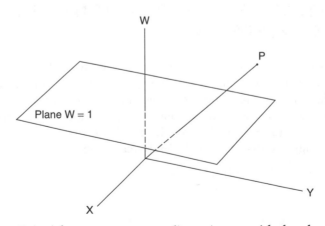

⚪ **Figure 3.4: A homogeneous coordinate system with the plane $W = 1$**

three-dimensional space. When a point is mapped onto the $W = 1$ plane, in the form $(x, y, 1)$, it is said to be *homogenized*. In the above example, point $(3, 6, 1)$ is homogenized, and the numbers 3, 6 and 1 are *homogeneous coordinates*. In general, to convert a point from normal coordinates to homogeneous coordinates, add a new dimension to the right with value 1. To convert a point from homogeneous coordinates to normal coordinates, divide all the dimension values by the rightmost dimension value, and then discard the rightmost dimension.

Having introduced homogeneous coordinates, we are able to describe a translation by a matrix multiplication using a 3×3 instead of a 2×2 matrix. Using a shift vector (a, b), we can write the translation of Section 3.3 as the following matrix product:

$$[\; x' \quad y' \quad 1 \;] = [\; x \quad y \quad 1 \;] \begin{bmatrix} 1 & 0 & 0 \\ 0 & 1 & 0 \\ a & b & 1 \end{bmatrix} \qquad (3.4)$$

Since we cannot multiply a 3×3 by a 2×2 matrix, we will also add a row and a column to linear transformation matrices if we want to combine these with translations (and possibly with other non-linear transformations). These additional rows and columns simply consist of zeros followed by a one at the end. For example, we can use the following equation instead of 3.3 (in Section 3.2) for a rotation about O through the angle φ:

$$[\; x' \quad y' \quad 1 \;] = [\; x \quad y \quad 1 \;] \begin{bmatrix} \cos\varphi & \sin\varphi & 0 \\ -\sin\varphi & \cos\varphi & 0 \\ 0 & 0 & 1 \end{bmatrix} \qquad (3.5)$$

3.5 INVERSE TRANSFORMATIONS AND MATRIX INVERSION

A linear transformation may or may not be reversible. For example, if we perform a rotation about the origin through an angle φ and follow this by another rotation, also about the origin but through the angle $-\varphi$, these two transformations cancel each other out. Let us denote the rotation matrix of Equation (3.3) (in Section 3.2) by R. It follows that the inverse rotation, through the angle $-\varphi$ instead of φ, is described by the equation

$$[\; x' \quad y' \;] = [\; x \quad y \;] R^{-1}$$

where

$$R^{-1} = \begin{bmatrix} \cos(-\varphi) & \sin(-\varphi) \\ -\sin(-\varphi) & \cos(-\varphi) \end{bmatrix} = \begin{bmatrix} \cos\varphi & -\sin\varphi \\ \sin\varphi & \cos\varphi \end{bmatrix}$$

The second equality in this equation is based on

$$\cos -\varphi = \cos \varphi$$
$$\sin -\varphi = -\sin \varphi$$

Matrix R^{-1} is referred to as the *inverse* of matrix R. In general, if a matrix A has an inverse, this is written A^{-1} and we have

$$AA^{-1} = A^{-1}A = I$$

where I is the identity matrix, consisting of zero elements except for the main diagonal, which contains elements one. For example, in the case of a rotation through φ, followed by one through $-\varphi$, we have

$$RR^{-1} = \begin{bmatrix} \cos \varphi & \sin \varphi \\ -\sin \varphi & \cos \varphi \end{bmatrix} \begin{bmatrix} \cos \varphi & -\sin \varphi \\ \sin \varphi & \cos \varphi \end{bmatrix} = \begin{bmatrix} 1 & 0 \\ 0 & 1 \end{bmatrix} = I$$

The identity matrix clearly maps each point to itself, that is,

$$[\ x \quad y\ ]I = [\ x \quad y\ ]$$

Not all linear transformations are reversible. For example, the one that projects each point onto the x-axis is not. This transformation is described by

$$\begin{cases} x' = x \\ y' = 0 \end{cases}$$

which we can also write as

$$[\ x' \quad y'\ ] = [\ x \quad y\ ] \begin{bmatrix} 1 & 0 \\ 0 & 0 \end{bmatrix}$$

The 2×2 matrix in this equation has no inverse. This corresponds to the impossibility of reversing the linear transformation in question: since any two point $P_1(x, y_1)$ and $P_2(x, y_2)$ have the same image $P'(x, 0)$, it is impossible to find a unique point P of which P' is the image.

A (square) matrix has an inverse if and only if its determinant is non-zero. Recall that we have discussed determinants in Section 2.3. For example, the determinant

$$\begin{vmatrix} \cos \varphi & \sin \varphi \\ -\sin \varphi & \cos \varphi \end{vmatrix}$$

is equal to $\cos \varphi \times \cos \varphi - (-\sin \varphi \times \sin \varphi) = \cos^2 \varphi + \sin^2 \varphi = 1$. Since this value is non-zero for any angle φ, the corresponding matrix

$$\begin{bmatrix} \cos \varphi & \sin \varphi \\ -\sin \varphi & \cos \varphi \end{bmatrix}$$

has an inverse.

Exercise 3.4 shows how to compute the inverse of any 2×2 matrix that has a non-zero determinant. A useful application of this follows in Exercise 3.5.

3.6 ROTATION ABOUT AN ARBITRARY POINT

So far we have only performed rotations about the origin O. A rotation about any point other than O is not a linear transformation, since it does not map the origin onto itself. It can nevertheless be described by a matrix multiplication, provided we use homogeneous coordinates. A rotation about the point $C(x_C, y_C)$ through the angle φ can be performed in three steps:

1. A translation from C to O, described by $[x' \quad y' \quad 1] = [x \quad y \quad 1]T^{-1}$, where

$$
T^{-1} = \begin{bmatrix} 1 & 0 & 0 \\ 0 & 1 & 0 \\ -x_C & -y_C & 1 \end{bmatrix}
$$

2. A rotation about O through the angle φ described by $[x' \quad y' \quad 1] = [x \quad y \quad 1]R_O$, where

$$
R_O = \begin{bmatrix} \cos\varphi & \sin\varphi & 0 \\ -\sin\varphi & \cos\varphi & 0 \\ 0 & 0 & 1 \end{bmatrix}
$$

3. A translation from O to C, described by $[x' \quad y' \quad 1] = [x \quad y \quad 1]T$, where

$$
T = \begin{bmatrix} 1 & 0 & 0 \\ 0 & 1 & 0 \\ x_C & y_C & 1 \end{bmatrix}
$$

Note that we deliberately use the notations T^{-1} and T, since these two matrices are each other's inverse. This is understandable, since the operations of translating from C to O and then back from O to C cancel each other out.

The purpose of listing the above three matrices is that we can combine them by forming their product. Therefore, the desired rotation about point C through the angle φ can be described by

$$
[\, x' \quad y' \quad 1 \,] = [\, x \quad y \quad 1 \,]R
$$

where

$$
\begin{aligned}
R &= T^{-1}R_O T \\
&= \begin{bmatrix} 1 & 0 & 0 \\ 0 & 1 & 0 \\ -x_C & -y_C & 1 \end{bmatrix} \begin{bmatrix} \cos\varphi & \sin\varphi & 0 \\ -\sin\varphi & \cos\varphi & 0 \\ 0 & 0 & 1 \end{bmatrix} \begin{bmatrix} 1 & 0 & 0 \\ 0 & 1 & 0 \\ x_C & y_C & 1 \end{bmatrix} \\
&= \begin{bmatrix} \cos\varphi & \sin\varphi & 0 \\ -\sin\varphi & \cos\varphi & 0 \\ -x_C\cos\varphi + y_C\sin\varphi + x_C & -x_C\sin\varphi - y_C\cos\varphi + y_C & 1 \end{bmatrix}
\end{aligned} \tag{3.6}
$$

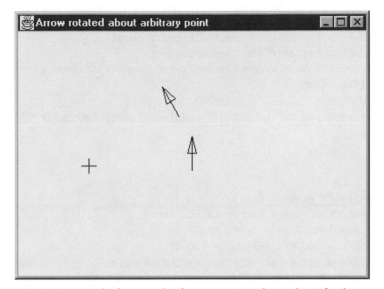

○ **Figure 3.5: Arrow before and after rotation through 30° about a point
    selected by the user**

3.6.1 An Application

To see this general type of rotation in action, we will now discuss a program
which rotates an arrow through 30° about a point selected by the user. Initially,
one arrow, pointing vertically upward, appears in the center of the canvas. As
soon as the user clicks a mouse button, a second arrow appears. This is the
image of the first one, resulting from a rotation through an angle of 30° about
the cursor position. This position is displayed as a crosshair cursor in Figure 3.5.

This action can be done repeatedly, in such a way that the most recently rotated
arrow is again rotated when the user clicks, and this last rotation is performed
about the most recently selected point. Since the rotation is counter-clockwise,
the new arrow would have appeared below the old one in Figure 3.5 if the user
had selected a point to the right instead of to the left of the first arrow. Program
ArrowPt.java shows how this rotation is computed.

```
// ArrowPt.java: Arrow rotated through 30 degrees
//    about a point selected by the user.
import java.awt.*;
import java.awt.event.*;

public class ArrowPt extends Frame
{  public static void main(String[] args){new ArrowPt();}
```

```
    ArrowPt()
    {  super("Arrow rotated about arbitrary point");
       addWindowListener(new WindowAdapter()
           {public void windowClosing(WindowEvent e){System.exit(0);}});
       setSize (400, 300);
       add("Center", new CvArrowPt());
       setCursor(Cursor.getPredefinedCursor(Cursor.CROSSHAIR_CURSOR));
       show();
    }
}

class CvArrowPt extends Canvas
{  int centerX, centerY, currentX, currentY;
   float pixelSize, xP = 1e9F, yP,
      rWidth = 100.0F, rHeight = 100.0F;
   float[] x = {0, 0, -2, 2}, y = {-7, 7, 0, 0};

   CvArrowPt()
   {  addMouseListener(new MouseAdapter()
      {  public void mousePressed(MouseEvent evt)
         {  xP = fx(evt.getX()); yP = fy(evt.getY());
            repaint();
         }
      });
   }
   void initgr()
   {  Dimension d = getSize();
      int maxX = d.width - 1, maxY = d.height - 1;
      pixelSize = Math.max(rWidth/maxX, rHeight/maxY);
      centerX = maxX/2; centerY = maxY/2;
   }

   int iX(float x){return Math.round(centerX + x/pixelSize);}
   int iY(float y){return Math.round(centerY - y/pixelSize);}

   float fx(int x){return (x - centerX) * pixelSize;}
   float fy(int y){return (centerY - y) * pixelSize;}

   void moveTo(float x, float y)
   {  currentX = iX(x); currentY = iY(y);
   }
```

```
void lineTo(Graphics g, float x, float y)
{  int x1 = iX(x), y1 = iY(y);
   g.drawLine(currentX, currentY, x1, y1);
   currentX = x1; currentY = y1;
}

void drawArrow(Graphics g, float[]x, float[]y)
{  moveTo(x[0], y[0]);
   lineTo(g, x[1], y[1]);
   lineTo(g, x[2], y[2]);
   lineTo(g, x[3], y[3]);
   lineTo(g, x[1], y[1]);
}


public void paint(Graphics g)
{  initgr();
   // Show initial arrow:
   drawArrow(g, x, y);
   if (xP > 1e8F) return;
   float phi = (float)(Math.PI / 6),
      c = (float)Math.cos(phi), s = (float)Math.sin(phi),
      r11 = c, r12 = s,
      r21 = -s, r22 = c,
      r31 = -xP * c + yP * s + xP, r32 = -xP * s - yP * c + yP;
   for (int j=0; j<4; j++)
   {  float xNew = x[j] * r11 + y[j] * r21 + r31,
            yNew = x[j] * r12 + y[j] * r22 + r32;
      x[j] = xNew; y[j] = yNew;
   }
   // Arrow after rotation:
   drawArrow(g, x, y);
   }
}
```

In contrast to program *Arrow.java* of Section 3.2, this new program *ArrowPt.java* uses the 3×3 rotation matrix displayed in Equation (3.6), as you can see in the fragment

```
float xNew = x[j] * r11 + y[j] * r21 + r31,
      yNew = x[j] * r12 + y[j] * r22 + r32;
```

The matrix elements r_{31} and r_{32} of the third row of the matrix depend on the point (x_P, y_P), selected by the user and acting as the center $C(x_C, y_C)$ in our previous discussion. As in program *Isotrop.java* of Section 1.4, the device coordinates of the selected point P are converted to logical coordinates by the methods *fx* and *fy*.

3.7 CHANGING THE COORDINATE SYSTEM

In the preceding sections, we have used a fixed coordinate system and applied transformations to points given by their coordinates for that system, using certain computations. We can use exactly the same computations for a different purpose, leaving the points unchanged but changing the coordinate system. It is important to bear in mind that the direction in which the coordinate system moves is opposite to that of the point movement. We can see this very clearly in the case of a translation. In Figure 3.6(a) we have a normal translation with any point P(x, y) mapped to its image P′(x′, y′), where

$$x' = x + a$$
$$y' = y + b$$

which can be written in matrix form as shown in Equation (3.4) (in Section 3.4). In Figure 3.6(b) we do not map the point P to another point but we express the position of this point in the x′y′-coordinate system, while coordinates x and y are given. As you can see, a translation upward and to the right in (a), corresponds with a movement of the coordinate system downward and to the left in (b): these two directions are exactly each other's opposite. It follows that the inverse translation matrix would have applied if, in (b), we had moved the axes in the same direction as that of the point translation. The same principle applies to other transformations, such as rotations, for which the inverse of the transformation matrix exists. We will use this principle in the next section.

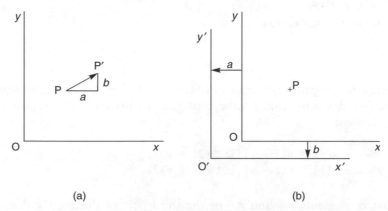

(a)   (b)

○ **Figure 3.6: (a) Translation; (b) change of coordinates**

3.8 ROTATIONS ABOUT 3D COORDINATE AXES

Let us use a right-handed three-dimensional coordinate system, with the positive x-axis pointing toward us, the y-axis pointing to the right and the z-axis pointing upward, as shown in Figure 3.7.

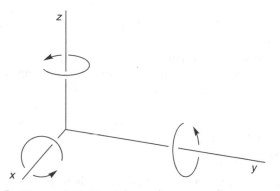

○ **Figure 3.7: Rotations about coordinate axes**

This figure also shows what we mean by rotations about the axes. A rotation about the z-axis through a given angle implies a rotation of all points in the xy-plane through that angle. For example, if this angle is $90°$, the image of all points of the positive x-axis will be those of the positive y-axis. In the same way, a rotation about the x-axis implies a similar rotation of the yz-plane and a rotation about the y-axis implies a similar rotation of the zx-plane. Note that we deliberately write zx in that order: when we are dealing with the x-, y- and z-axes in a cyclic way, x follows z. It is important to remember this when we have to write down the transformation matrices for the rotations about the x-, y- and z-axis through the angle φ:

$$R_x = \begin{bmatrix} 1 & 0 & 0 \\ 0 & \cos\varphi & \sin\varphi \\ 0 & -\sin\varphi & \cos\varphi \end{bmatrix}$$

$$R_y = \begin{bmatrix} \cos\varphi & 0 & -\sin\varphi \\ 0 & 1 & 0 \\ \sin\varphi & 0 & \cos\varphi \end{bmatrix}$$

$$R_z = \begin{bmatrix} \cos\varphi & \sin\varphi & 0 \\ -\sin\varphi & \cos\varphi & 0 \\ 0 & 0 & 1 \end{bmatrix}$$

These matrices are easy to construct. Matrix R_z is derived in a trivial way from the well-known 2×2 rotation matrix of Equation (3.3) (in Section 3.2). If you check this carefully, you will not find the other two matrices difficult. First, there is a 1 on the main diagonal in the position that corresponds to the axis of rotation (1 for x, 2 for y and 3 for z). The other elements in the same row or column as this matrix element 1 are equal to 0. Second, we use the elements of the 2×2 matrix just mentioned for the remaining elements of the 3×3 matrices, beginning just to the right and below the element 1, if that is possible; if not, we remember that x follows z. For example, in R_y, the first element, $\cos \varphi$, of this imaginary 2×2 matrix is placed in row 3 and column 3 because the element 1 has been placed in row 2 and column 2. Then, since we cannot place $\sin \varphi$ to the right of this element $\cos \varphi$ as we would like, we place it instead in column 1 of the same third row. In the same way, we cannot place $-\sin \varphi$ below $\cos \varphi$, as it occurs in Equation (3.3), so instead we put it in the first row of the same third column, and so on.

We should remember that the above matrices should be applied to row vectors. For example, using the above matrix R_x, we write

$$[\ x' \quad y' \quad z' \ ] = [\ x \quad y \quad z \ ] \, R_x$$

to obtain the image (x', y', z') of point (x, y, z) when the latter is subjected to a rotation about the x-axis through an angle φ.

3.9 ROTATION ABOUT AN ARBITRARY AXIS

To prepare for a three-dimensional rotation about an arbitrary axis, let us first perform such a rotation about an axis through the origin O. Actually, the rotation will take place about a vector, so that we can define its orientation, as illustrated by Figure 3.8.

If a point is rotated about the vector v through a positive angle α, this rotation will be such that it corresponds to a movement in the direction of the vector in the same way as turning a (right-handed) screw corresponds to its forward movement.

Instead of its Cartesian coordinates (v_1, v_2, v_3), we will use the angles θ and φ to specify the direction of the vector v. The length of this vector is irrelevant to our present purpose. As you can see in Figure 3.8, θ is the angle between the positive x-axis and the projection of v in the xy-plane and φ is the angle between the positive z-axis and the vector v. If v_1, v_2 and v_3 are given and we want to find θ and φ, we can compute them in Java in the following way, writing *theta* for θ and *phi* for φ:

```
theta = Math.atan2(v2, v1);
phi = Math.atan2(Math.sqrt(v1 * v1 + v2 * v2), v3);
```

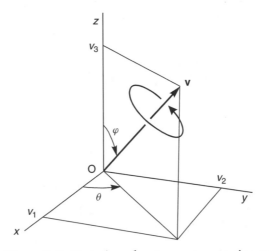

$\bigcirc$ **Figure 3.8: Rotation about a vector starting at O**

We will now derive a rather complicated 3×3 rotation matrix, which describes the rotation about the vector **v** through an angle α. First, we will change the coordinate system such that **v** will lie on the positive z-axis. This can be done in two steps:

1. A rotation of the coordinate system about the z-axis, such that the horizontal component of **v** lies on the new x-axis.
2. A rotation of the coordinate system about the new y-axis though the angle φ.

As discussed at the end of the previous section, coordinate transformations require the inverses of the matrices that we would use for normal rotations of points. Referring to Section 3.8, we now have to use the following matrices R_z^{-1} and R_y^{-1} for the above steps 1 and 2, respectively:

$$R_z^{-1} = \begin{bmatrix} \cos\theta & -\sin\theta & 0 \\ \sin\theta & \cos\theta & 0 \\ 0 & 0 & 1 \end{bmatrix}$$

$$R_y^{-1} = \begin{bmatrix} \cos\varphi & 0 & \sin\varphi \\ 0 & 1 & 0 \\ -\sin\varphi & 0 & \cos\varphi \end{bmatrix}$$

To combine these two coordinate transformations, we have to use the product of these two matrices. Before doing this matrix multiplication, let us first find the matrices of some more operations that are required.

Now that the new positive z-axis has the same direction as the vector **v**, the desired rotation about **v** through the angle α is also a rotation about the z-axis through that angle, so that, expressed in the new coordinates, we have the following rotation matrix:

$$R_v = \begin{bmatrix} \cos\alpha & \sin\alpha & 0 \\ -\sin\alpha & \cos\alpha & 0 \\ 0 & 0 & 1 \end{bmatrix}$$

Although this may seem to be the final operation, we must bear in mind that we want to express the image point P' of an original point P in terms of the original coordinate system. This implies that the first two of the above three transformations are to be followed by their inverse transformations, in reverse order. Therefore, in this order, we have to use the following two matrices after the three above:

$$R_y = \begin{bmatrix} \cos\varphi & 0 & -\sin\varphi \\ 0 & 1 & 0 \\ \sin\varphi & 0 & \cos\varphi \end{bmatrix}$$

$$R_z = \begin{bmatrix} \cos\theta & \sin\theta & 0 \\ -\sin\theta & \cos\theta & 0 \\ 0 & 0 & 1 \end{bmatrix}$$

The resulting matrix R, to be used in the equation

$$[\; x' \quad y' \quad z' \;] = [\; x \quad y \quad z \;]R$$

to perform a rotation about $\mathbf{v}$ through the angle α, can now be found as follows:

$$R = R_z^{-1}R_y^{-1}R_vR_yR_z = \begin{bmatrix} r_{11} & r_{12} & r_{13} \\ r_{21} & r_{22} & r_{23} \\ r_{31} & r_{32} & r_{33} \end{bmatrix}$$

where the matrix elements r_{ij} are rather complicated expressions in φ, θ and α. Before discussing how to compute these, let us first turn to the original problem, which was the same as the above, except that we want to use any point $A(a_1, a_2, a_3)$ as the start point of vector $\mathbf{v}$. We can do this by performing, in this order:

- a translation that shifts the point A to the origin O;
- the desired rotation using the above matrix R;
- the inverse of the translation just mentioned.

As discussed in Sections 3.4 and 3.6, we need to use homogeneous coordinates in order to describe translations by matrix multiplications. Since we use 3×3 matrices for linear transformations in three-dimensional space, we have to use 4×4 matrices in connection with these homogenous coordinates. Based on the coordinates a_1, a_2 and a_3 of the point A on the axis of rotation, the following matrix describes the translation from A to O:

$$T^{-1} = \begin{bmatrix} 1 & 0 & 0 & 0 \\ 0 & 1 & 0 & 0 \\ 0 & 0 & 1 & 0 \\ -a_1 & -a_2 & -a_3 & 1 \end{bmatrix}$$

After this translation, we perform the rotation about the vector **v**, which starts at point A, using the above matrix R, which we write as R^* after adding an additional row and column in the usual way:

$$R^* = \begin{bmatrix} r_{11} & r_{12} & r_{13} & 0 \\ r_{21} & r_{22} & r_{23} & 0 \\ r_{31} & r_{32} & r_{33} & 0 \\ 0 & 0 & 0 & 1 \end{bmatrix}$$

Finally, we use a translation from O back to A:

$$T = \begin{bmatrix} 1 & 0 & 0 & 0 \\ 0 & 1 & 0 & 0 \\ 0 & 0 & 1 & 0 \\ a_1 & a_2 & a_3 & 1 \end{bmatrix}$$

Writing R_{GEN} for the desired general (4×4) rotation matrix, we have

$$R_{GEN} = T^{-1} R^* T$$

Since R_{GEN} is a 4×4 matrix, we use it as follows:

$$[\; x' \quad y' \quad z' \quad 1 \;] = [\; x \quad y \quad z \quad 1 \;] R_{GEN}$$

3.9.1 Implementation

Since we are now dealing with points in three-dimensional space, let us begin by defining the following class to represent such points:

```
// Point3D.java: Representation of a point in 3D space.
class Point3D
{  float x, y, z;
   Point3D(double x, double y, double z)
   {  this.x = (float)x;
      this.y = (float)y;
      this.z = (float)z;
   }
}
```

As we normally have a great many points that are to be rotated, it is worthwhile to compute the matrix R_{GEN} beforehand. Although this could be done numerically, it is also possible to make our program slightly faster by doing this symbolically, that is, by expressing all matrix elements r_{ij} of R_{GEN} in six constant values for the rotation: the angles φ, θ and α and the coordinates a_1, a_2 and a_3 of point A on the axis of rotation. Instead of writing these matrix elements here in the usual mathematical formulas (which would be quite complicated), we may as well immediately present the resulting Java code. This has been done in the class *Rotate3D* below.

The actual rotation is performed by the *rotate* method, which is called as many times as there are relevant points (usually the vertices of polyhedra). Prior to this, the method *initRotate* is called only once, to build the above matrix R_{GEN}. There are actually two methods *initRotate*, of which we can choose one as we like. The first accepts two points A and B to specify the directed axis of rotation AB and computes the angles θ and φ. The second accepts these two angles themselves instead of point B:

```
// Rota3D.java: Class used in other program files
//      for rotations about an arbitrary axis.
// Uses: Point3D (discussed above).
class Rota3D
{   static double r11, r12, r13, r21, r22, r23,
                  r31, r32, r33, r41, r42, r43;

/* The method initRotate computes the general rotation matrix

            | r11   r12   r13   0 |
      R =   | r21   r22   r23   0 |
            | r31   r32   r33   0 |
            | r41   r42   r43   1 |

to be used as [x1  y1  z1  1] = [x  y  z  1] R
by the method 'rotate'.
Point (x1, y1, z1) is the image of (x, y, z).
The rotation takes place about the directed axis
AB and through the angle alpha.
*/
   static void initRotate(Point3D a, Point3D b,
      double alpha)
   {  double v1 = b.x - a.x,
             v2 = b.y - a.y,
             v3 = b.z - a.z,
         theta = Math.atan2(v2, v1),
         phi = Math.atan2(Math.sqrt(v1 * v1 + v2 * v2), v3);
```

```
        initRotate(a, theta, phi, alpha);
}

static void initRotate(Point3D a, double theta,
    double phi, double alpha)
{   double cosAlpha, sinAlpha, cosPhi, sinPhi,
    cosTheta, sinTheta, cosPhi2, sinPhi2,
    cosTheta2, sinTheta2, pi, c,
    a1 = a.x, a2 = a.y, a3 = a.z;
    cosPhi = Math.cos(phi); sinPhi = Math.sin(phi);
    cosPhi2 = cosPhi * cosPhi; sinPhi2 = sinPhi * sinPhi;
    cosTheta = Math.cos(theta);
    sinTheta = Math.sin(theta);
    cosTheta2 = cosTheta * cosTheta;
    sinTheta2 = sinTheta * sinTheta;
    cosAlpha = Math.cos(alpha);
    sinAlpha = Math.sin(alpha);
    c = 1.0 - cosAlpha;
    r11 = cosTheta2 * (cosAlpha * cosPhi2 + sinPhi2)
          + cosAlpha * sinTheta2;
    r12 = sinAlpha * cosPhi + c * sinPhi2 * cosTheta * sinTheta;
    r13 = sinPhi * (cosPhi * cosTheta * c - sinAlpha * sinTheta);
    r21 = sinPhi2 * cosTheta * sinTheta * c - sinAlpha * cosPhi;
    r22 = sinTheta2 * (cosAlpha * cosPhi2 + sinPhi2)
          + cosAlpha * cosTheta2;
    r23 = sinPhi * (cosPhi * sinTheta * c + sinAlpha * cosTheta);
    r31 = sinPhi * (cosPhi * cosTheta * c + sinAlpha * sinTheta);
    r32 = sinPhi * (cosPhi * sinTheta * c - sinAlpha * cosTheta);
    r33 = cosAlpha * sinPhi2 + cosPhi2;
    r41 = a1 - a1 * r11 - a2 * r21 - a3 * r31;
    r42 = a2 - a1 * r12 - a2 * r22 - a3 * r32;
    r43 = a3 - a1 * r13 - a2 * r23 - a3 * r33;
}

static Point3D rotate(Point3D p)
{   return new Point3D(
        p.x * r11 + p.y * r21 + p.z * r31 + r41,
        p.x * r12 + p.y * r22 + p.z * r32 + r42,
        p.x * r13 + p.y * r23 + p.z * r33 + r43);
}
}
```

Note that the actual rotation of points is done very efficiently in the method *rotate* at the end of this class. This is important because it will be called for each relevant point of the object to be rotated. Remember, the more time-consuming method *initRotate* is called only once.

Let us now see this class *Rota3D* in action. Although it can be used for any rotation axis and any angle of rotation, it is used here only in a very simple way so that we can easily check the result, even without graphics output. As Figure 3.9 shows, we have chosen the axis AB parallel to the diagonals 0–2 and 4–6 of the cube. The cube has a height 1 and point A has coordinates (0, 0, 2).

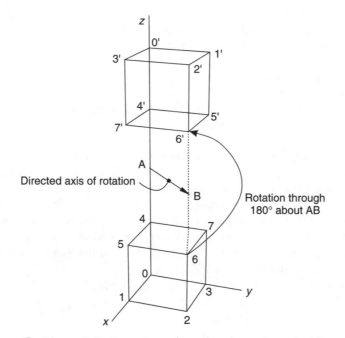

Figure 3.9: Rotation of a cube about the axis AB

The following program uses the above classes *Point3D* and *Rota3D* to perform the rotation shown in Figure 3.9:

```
// Rota3DTest.java: Rotating a cube about an axis
//     parallel to a diagonal of its top plane.
//     Uses: Point3D, Rota3D (discussed above).
public class Rota3DTest
{  public static void main(String[] args)
```

```
{ Point3D a = new Point3D (0, 0, 1), b = new Point3D (1, 1, 1);
  double alpha = Math.PI;
  // Specify AB as directed axis of rotation
  // and alpha as the rotation angle:
  Rota3D.initRotate(a, b, alpha);
  // Vertices of a cube; 0, 1, 2, 3 at the bottom,
  // 4, 5, 6, 7 at the top. Vertex 0 at the origin O:
  Point3D[] v = {
      new Point3D (0, 0, 0), new Point3D (1, 0, 0),
      new Point3D (1, 1, 0), new Point3D (0, 1, 0),
      new Point3D (0, 0, 1), new Point3D (1, 0, 1),
      new Point3D (1, 1, 1), new Point3D (0, 1, 1)};
  System.out.println(
      "Cube rotated through 180 degrees about line AB,");
  System.out.println(
      "where A =  (0, 0, 1)  and B =  (1, 1, 1) ");
  System.out.println("Vertices of cube:");
  System.out.println(
      "    Before rotation    After rotation");
  for (int i=0; i<8; i++)
  { Point3D p - v[i];
    // Compute P1, the result of rotating P:
    Point3D p1 = Rota3D.rotate(p);
    System.out.println(i + ":   " +
        p.x + " " + p.y + " " + p.z + "          " +
        f(p1.x) + " " + f(p1.y) + " " + f(p1.z));
  }
}

static double f(double x){return Math.abs(x) < 1e-10 ? 0.0 : x;}
}
```

Since we have not yet discussed how to produce perspective views, we produce only text output in this program, as listed below:

```
Cube rotated through 180 degrees about line AB,
where A =  (0, 0, 2)  and B =  (1, 1, 2)
Vertices of cube:
    Before rotation    After rotation
0:  0.0 0.0 0.0        0.0 0.0 4.0
1:  1.0 0.0 0.0        0.0 1.0 4.0
2:  1.0 1.0 0.0        1.0 1.0 4.0
3:  0.0 1.0 0.0        1.0 0.0 4.0
```

4:	0.0 0.0 1.0	0.0 0.0 3.0
5:	1.0 0.0 1.0	0.0 1.0 3.0
6:	1.0 1.0 1.0	1.0 1.0 3.0
7:	0.0 1.0 1.0	1.0 0.0 3.0

EXERCISES

3.1   In Section 3.2 we discussed scaling with reference to the origin O, that is, with O as a fixed point. It is also possible to use a different fixed point, say $C(x_C, y_C)$, but, for such a scaling in two-dimensional space, we need a 3×3 matrix M (and homogenous coordinates), writing

$$[\; x' \quad y' \quad 1 \;] = [\; x \quad y \quad 1 \;]M$$

Using scale factors s_x and s_y for x and y again, find this matrix M. Hint: You can perform a translation from C to O, followed by a scaling as discussed in Section 3.2, but described by a 3×3 matrix, followed by a translation back from O to C. Alternatively, you can start with the following system of equations, which shows very clearly what actually happens:

$$\begin{cases} x' - x_C = s_x(x - x_C) \\ y' - y_C = s_y(y - y_C) \end{cases}$$

3.2   Describe scaling in three-dimensional space with reference to a point C and three scale factors s_x, s_y and s_z. Find the 4×4 matrix (similar to matrix M of Exercise 3.1) for this transformation.

3.3   How can you apply shearing with reference to a point other than O (such that this point will remain at the same place)? Write a program that draws a square and an approximate circle, both before and after shearing, setting the constant a used at the end of Section 3.2 equal to 0.5. Apply shearing to these two figures with reference to their centers; in other words, the center of the square will remain at the same place and so will the center of the circle.

3.4   (This exercise prepares for the next one.) If the determinant $D = a_{11}a_{22} - a_{12}a_{21}$ of the matrix

$$A = \begin{bmatrix} a_{11} & a_{12} \\ a_{21} & a_{22} \end{bmatrix}$$

is non-zero, then the matrix

$$A^{-1} = \begin{bmatrix} \dfrac{a_{22}}{D} & -\dfrac{a_{12}}{D} \\ -\dfrac{a_{21}}{D} & \dfrac{a_{11}}{D} \end{bmatrix}$$

is the inverse of A, that is, $AA^{-1} = A^{-1}A = I = \begin{bmatrix} 1 & 0 \\ 0 & 1 \end{bmatrix}$. Prove this.

3.5   Our way of testing whether a given point P lies in a triangle ABC, discussed in Section 2.8, resulted in the method *insideTriangle*, which assumes that A, B and C are counter-clockwise. Develop a different method for the same purpose, based on the vectors $\mathbf{a} = (a_1, a_2) = \mathbf{CA}$ and $\mathbf{b} = (b_1, b_2) = \mathbf{CB}$ (see Figure 2.6 in Section 2.5). Let us write

$$\mathbf{CP} = \mathbf{p} = (p_1, p_2) = \lambda\mathbf{a} + \mu\mathbf{b}$$

or, in the form of a matrix product,

$$\begin{bmatrix} p_1 & p_2 \end{bmatrix} = \begin{bmatrix} \lambda & \mu \end{bmatrix} \begin{bmatrix} a_1 & a_2 \\ b_1 & b_2 \end{bmatrix} \tag{3.7}$$

Since we saw in Exercise 3.4 how to compute the inverse of a 2×2 matrix, we can now compute λ and μ as follows:

$$\begin{bmatrix} \lambda & \mu \end{bmatrix} = \begin{bmatrix} p_1 & p_2 \end{bmatrix} \begin{bmatrix} a_1 & a_2 \\ b_1 & b_2 \end{bmatrix}^{-1} \tag{3.8}$$

The point P lies in triangle ABC (or on one of its edges) if and only if $\lambda \geq 0$, $\mu \geq 0$ and $\lambda + \mu \leq 1$. Write the class *TriaTest*, which we can use as follows:

```
Point2D a, b, c, p;
TriaTest tt = new TriaTest(a, b, c);
if (tt.area2() != 0 && tt.insideTriangle(p)) ...
   // Point P within triangle ABC.
```

As in Section 2.5, the method *area2* returns twice the area of triangle ABC, preceded by a minus sign if ABC is clockwise. This return value is also equal to the determinant of the 2×2 matrix in Equation (3.7). We must not call the *TriaTest* method *insideTriangle* if this determinant is zero, since in that case the inverse matrix of Equation (3.8) does not exist (see Exercise 3.4).

Chapter 4

Some Classic Algorithms

Although programming is a very creative activity, often requiring entirely new (little) problems to be solved, we can sometimes benefit from well-known algorithms, published by others and usually providing more efficient or more elegant solutions than those we would have been able to invent ourselves. This is no different in computer graphics. This chapter is about some well-known graphics algorithms for (a) computing the coordinates of pixels that comprise lines and circles, (b) clipping lines and polygons, and (c) drawing smooth curves. These are the most primitive operations in computer graphics and should be executed as fast as possible. Therefore, the algorithms in this chapter ought to be optimized to avoid time-consuming executions, such as multiplication, division, and calculations on floating point numbers.

4.1 BRESENHAM'S ALGORITHM FOR LINE DRAWING

We will now discuss how to draw lines by placing pixels on the screen. Although, in Java, we can simply use the method *drawLine* without bothering about pixels, it would be unsatisfactory if we had no idea how this method works. We will be using integer coordinates, but when discussing the slope of a line it would be very inconvenient if we had to use a *y*-axis pointing downward, as is the case with the Java device coordinate system. Therefore, in accordance with mathematical usage, the positive *y*-axis will point upward in our discussion.

Unfortunately, Java lacks a method with the sole purpose of putting a pixel on the screen, so that we define the following, rather strange method to achieve this:

```
void putPixel(Graphics g, int x, int y)
{  g.drawLine(x, y, x, y);
}
```

We will now develop a *drawLine* method of the form

```
void drawLine(Graphics g, int xP, int yP, int xQ, int yQ)
{ ...
}
```

which only uses the above *putPixel* method for the actual graphics output.

Figure 4.1 shows a line segment with endpoints P(1, 1) and Q(12, 5), as well as the pixels that we have to compute to approximate this line.

To draw the line of Figure 4.1, we then write

```
drawLine(g, 1, 1, 12, 5);
```

Let us first solve the problem for situations such as Figure 4.1, in which point Q lies to the right and not lower than point P. More precisely, we will be dealing with the special case

$$x_P < x_Q$$
$$y_P \leq y_Q \qquad\qquad (4.1)$$
$$y_Q - y_P \leq x_Q - x_P$$

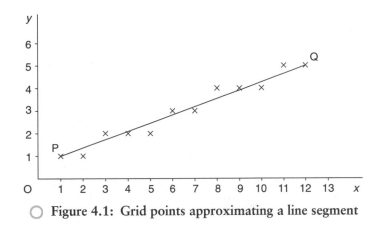

○ **Figure 4.1: Grid points approximating a line segment**

where the last condition expresses that the angle of inclination of line PQ is not greater than 45°. We then want to find exactly one integer y for each of the integers

$$x_P, x_P + 1, x_P + 2, \ldots, x_Q$$

Except for the first and the last (which are given as y_P and y_Q) the most straightforward way of computing these y-coordinates is by using the slope

$$m = \frac{y_Q - y_P}{x_Q - x_P} \tag{4.2}$$

so that, for each of the given integer x-coordinates, we can find the desired integer y-coordinate by rounding the value

$$y_{\text{exact}} = y_P + m(x - x_P)$$

to the nearest integer. Since two such successive x-coordinates differ by 1, the corresponding difference of two successive values of y_{exact} is equal to m. Figure 4.2 shows this interpretation of m, as well as that of the 'error'

$$d = y_{\text{exact}} - y \tag{4.3}$$

Since d is the error we make by rounding y_{exact} to the nearest integer, we can require d to satisfy the following condition:

$$-0.5 \le d < +0.5 \tag{4.4}$$

The following first version of the desired *drawLine* method is based on this observation:

```
void drawLine1(Graphics g, int xP, int yP, int xQ, int yQ)
{  int x = xP, y = yP;
   float d = 0, m = (float)(yQ - yP)/(float)(xQ - xP);
```

```
for (;;)
{  putPixel(g, x, y);
   if (x == xQ) break;
   x++;
   d += m;
   if (d >= 0.5){y++; d--;}
}
}
```

This version is easy to understand if we pay attention to Figure 4.2. Since the first call to *putPixel* applies to point P, we begin with the error $d = 0$. In each step of the loop, x is increased by 1. Assuming for the moment that y will not change, it follows from Equation (4.3) that the growth of d will be the same as that of y_{exact}, which explains why d is increased by m. We then check the validity of this assumption in the following if-statement. If d is no longer less than 0.5, this violates Equation (4.4), so that we apply a correction, consisting of increasing y and decreasing d by 1. The latter action makes Equation (4.4) valid again. By doing these two actions at the same time, Equation (4.3) also remains valid.

We use *drawLine*1 as a basis for writing a faster version, which no longer uses type *float*. This is possible because the slope variable m represents a rational number, that is, an integer numerator divided by an integer denominator, as Equation (4.2) shows. Since the other float variable, d, starts with the value zero and is altered only by adding m and -1 to it, it is also a rational number. In view of both the denominator $x_Q - x_P$ of these rational numbers and the constant 0.5 used in the if-statement, we will apply the scaling factor

$$c = 2(x_Q - x_P)$$

to m, to d and to this constant 0.5, introducing the *int* variables M and D instead of the *float* variables m and d. We will also use Δx instead of the constant 0.5.

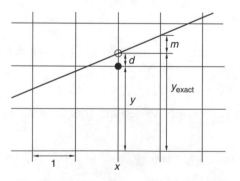

Figure 4.2: Slope m and error d

These new values M, D and Δx are c times as large as m, d and 0.5, respectively:

$$M = cm = 2(y_Q - y_P)$$
$$D = cd$$
$$\Delta x = x_Q - x_P = c \times 0.5$$

In this way we obtain the following integer version, which is very similar to the previous one and equivalent to it but faster. In accordance with the Java naming conventions for variables, we write m and d again instead of M and D, and dx instead of Δx:

```
void drawLine2(Graphics g, int xP, int yP, int xQ, int yQ)
{  int x = xP, y = yP, d = 0, dx = xQ - xP, c = 2 * dx,
      m = 2 * (yQ - yP);
   for (;;)
   {  putPixel(g, x, y);
      if (x == xQ) break;
      x++;
      d += m;
      if (d >= dx){y++; d -= c;}
   }
}
```

Having dealt with this special case, with points P and Q satisfying Equation (4.1), we now turn to the general problem, without any restrictions with regard to the relative positions of P and Q. To solve this, we have several symmetric cases to consider. As long as

$$|y_Q - y_P| \le |x_Q - x_P|$$

we can again use x as the independent variable, that is, we can increase or decrease this variable by one in each step of the loop. In the opposite case, with lines that have an angle of inclination greater than $45°$, we have to interchange the roles of x and y to prevent the selected pixels from lying too far apart. All this is realized in the general line-drawing method *drawLine* below. We can easily verify that this version plots exactly the same points approximating line PQ as version *drawLine2* if the coordinates of P and Q satisfy Equation (4.1).

```
void drawLine(Graphics g, int xP, int yP, int xQ, int yQ)
{  int x = xP, y = yP, d = 0, dx = xQ - xP, dy = yQ - yP,
      c, m, xInc = 1, yInc = 1;
   if (dx < 0){xInc = -1; dx = -dx;}
   if (dy < 0){yInc = -1; dy = -dy;}
   if (dy <= dx)
   {  c = 2 * dx; m = 2 * dy;
```

```
        if (xInc < 0) dx++;
        for (;;)
        { putPixel(g, x, y);
          if (x == xQ) break;
          x += xInc;
          d += m;
          if (d >= dx){y += yInc; d -= c;}
        }
    }
    else
    { c = 2 * dy; m = 2 * dx;
      if (yInc < 0) dy++;
      for (;;)
      { putPixel(g, x, y);
        if (y == yQ) break;
        y += yInc;
        d += m;
        if (d >= dy){x += xInc; d -= c;}
      }
    }
  }
}
```

Just before executing one of the above two for-statements, an if-statement is executed in the cases that *x* or *y* decreases instead of increases, which is required to guarantee that drawing PQ always plots exactly the same points as drawing QP.

The idea of drawing sloping lines by means of only integer variables was first realized by *Bresenham*; his name is therefore associated with this algorithm.

The above *drawLine* method is very easy to use if we are dealing with the floating-point logical-coordinate system used so far. For example, in Section 4.5, there will be a program *ClipPoly.java*, in which the following method occurs:

```
void drawLine(Graphics g, float xP, float yP, float xQ, float yQ)
{ g.drawLine(iX(xP), iY(yP), iX(xQ), iY(yQ));
}
```

Here our own method *drawLine* calls the Java method *drawLine* of the class *Graphics*. If, instead, we want to use our own method *drawLine* with four int arguments, listed above, we can replace the last three program lines with

```
void drawLine(Graphics g, float xP, float yP, float xQ, float yQ)
{ drawLine(g, iX(xP), iY(yP), iX(xQ), iY(yQ)); // int coordinates
}
```

provided that we also add the method *putPixel*, listed at the beginning of this section. This may at first be confusing because there are now two *drawLine* methods of our own. As the comment after the above call to *drawLine* indicates, the Java compiler will select our Bresenham method *drawLine* because there is an argument *g*, followed by four arguments of type *int*. It is also interesting to note that the direction of the positive *y*-axis in our discussion causes no practical problem.

4.2 DOUBLING THE LINE-DRAWING SPEED

As one of the primitive graphics operations, line drawing should be performed as rapidly as possible. In fact, graphics hardware is typically benchmarked by the speed in which it generates lines. Bresenham's line algorithm is simple and efficient in generating lines. The algorithm works incrementally by computing the position of the next pixel to be drawn. Hence it iterates as many times as the number of pixels in the line it generates. The double-step line-drawing algorithm by Rokne, Wyvill, and Wu (1990) aims at reducing the number of iterations by half, by computing the positions of the next *two* pixels.

Let us again start with the lines within the slope range of [0, 1] and consider the general case of any slopes later (as Exercise 4.2). For a line PQ, starting from P, we increment the *x*-coordinate by two pixels instead of one as in Bresenham's algorithm. All the possible positions of the two pixels in the above slope range form four patterns, expressed in a 2×2 mesh illustrated in Figure 4.3. It has been mathematically proven that patterns 1 and 4 would never occur on the same line, implying that a line would possibly involve patterns 1, 2 and 3, or patterns 2, 3 and 4, depending the slope of the line. The lines within the slope range of [0, 1/2) involve patterns 1, 2 and 3, and lines within the slope range of (1/2, 1] involve patterns 2, 3 and 4. At the exact slope of 1/2, the line involves either pattern 2 or 3, not 1 or 4.

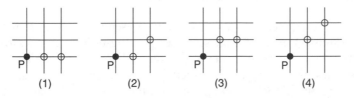

(1)   (2)   (3)   (4)

○ **Figure 4.3: Four double-step patterns when $0 \leq$ slope ≤ 1**

Figure 4.4 shows four sloping lines, all passing through the same point at a distance *d* above the point A. By approximating this common point of the four lines we make an error $d = y_{\text{exact}} - y$, which should not be greater than 0.5.

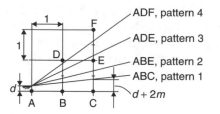

⭕ **Figure 4.4: Choice of patterns based on initial error d and slope m**

Since the slope of a line is equal to m, the exact y-coordinate of that line is equal to $d + m$ at its point of intersection with BD, and $d + 2m$ at its point of intersection with CF, as indicated in Figure 4.4 for the lowest of the four lines. With these two points of intersection lying closer to BC than to DE, it is clear that this lowest sloping line should be approximated by the points A, B, C, that is, by pattern 1 of Figure 4.3. Thus we have

if $d + 2m < 0.5$, we use pattern 1(ABC)

Otherwise, we use point E instead of C if E is the best approximation of the point where the sloping line intersects CF, that is, if $0.5 \leq d + 2m \leq 1.5$. However, we should now also pay attention to the point where the sloping line intersects BD. Comparing $d + m$ with 0.5 determines whether B or D should be taken. More precisely,

if $0.5 \leq d + 2m < 1.5$(so that point E is to be used), we choose B or D as follows:
if $d + m < 0.5$, we use pattern 2(ABE)
if $d + m \geq 0.5$, we use pattern 3(ADE)

Finally, there is this remaining case:

if $d + 2m \geq 1.5$, we use pattern 4(ADF).

As in the previous section when discussing Bresenham's algorithm, we begin with a preliminary method that still uses floating-point variables to make it easier to understand, so it is not yet optimized for speed. This version also works for lines drawn from right to left, that is, when $x_Q < x_P$, as well as for lines with negative slope. However, the absolute value of the slope should not be greater than 1. So *doubleStep*1 applies only to endpoints P and Q that satisfy the following conditions:

$$x_Q \neq x_P$$
$$|y_Q - y_P| \leq |x_Q - x_P|$$

It is wise to begin with the simplest case

$$x_P < x_Q$$
$$0 \le y_Q - y_P \le x_Q - x_P$$

when you read the following code for the first time:

```
void doubleStep1(Graphics g, int xP, int yP, int xQ, int yQ)
{  int dx, dy, x, y, yInc;
   if (xP >= xQ)
   {  if (xP == xQ) // Not allowed because we divide by dx (= xQ - xP)
         return;
      // xP > xQ, so swap the points P and Q
      int t;
      t = xP; xP = xQ; xQ = t;
      t = yP; yP = yQ; yQ = t;
   }
   // Now xP < xQ
   if (yQ >= yP){yInc = 1; dy = yQ - yP;}  // Normal case, yP < yQ
   else          {yInc = -1; dy = yP - yQ;}
   dx = xQ - xP;  // dx > 0, dy > 0
   float d = 0,                  // Error d = yexact - y
         m = (float)dy/(float)dx; //  m <= 1, m = | slope |
   putPixel(g, xP, yP);
   y = yP;
   for (x=xP; x<xQ-1;)
   {  if (d + 2 * m < 0.5) // Pattern 1:
      {  putPixel(g, ++x, y);
         putPixel(g, ++x, y);
         d += 2 * m; // Error increases by 2m, since y remains
                     // unchanged and yexact increases by 2m
      }
      else
      if (d + 2 * m < 1.5) // Pattern 2 or 3
      {  if (d + m < 0.5)  // Pattern 2
         {  putPixel(g, ++x, y);
            putPixel(g, ++x, y += yInc);
            d += 2 * m - 1; // Because of ++y, the error is now
                            // 1 less than with pattern 1
         }
         else  // Pattern 3
         {  putPixel(g, ++x, y += yInc);
            putPixel(g, ++x, y);
            d += 2 * m - 1;  // Same as pattern 2
```

```
          }
        }
        else  // Pattern 4:
        {  putPixel(g, ++x, y += yInc);
           putPixel(g, ++x, y += yInc);
           d += 2 * m - 2;   // Because of y += 2, the error is now
                             // 2 less than with pattern 1
        }
     }
     if (x < xQ)    // x = xQ - 1
        putPixel(g, xQ, yQ);
  }
```

Before the above for-loop is entered, there is a call to *putPixel* for $x = x_P$. The loop terminates as soon as the test

$$x < x_Q - 1$$

fails. This test is executed for the following values of x:

$x_P, \ x_P + 2, \ x_P + 4,$ and so on.

If it succeeds, *putPixel* is called for the next two values of x, not for the value of x used in the test. There are two cases to consider. If $x_Q - x_P$ is even, the test still succeeds when $x = x_Q - 2$, and *putPixel* is executed for both $x = x_Q - 1$ and $x = x_Q$, after which we are done and the next test, with $x = x_Q$, fails. On the other hand, if $x_Q - x_P$ is odd, the test succeeds when $x = x_Q - 3$, and *putPixel* is called for both $x = x_Q - 2$ and $x = x_Q - 1$, after which the test fails with $x = x_Q - 1$. Then, after loop termination, the remaining call to *putPixel* is executed in the following if-statement:

```
if (x < xQ)
   putPixel(g, xQ, yQ);
```

We will now derive a fast, integer version from the above method *doubleStep*1. Let us use the notation

$$\Delta x = x_Q - x_P$$
$$\Delta y = y_Q - y_P$$

so that slope $m = \Delta y / \Delta x$. We now want to introduce an *int* variable v, in such a way that the test

$$d + 2m < 0.5 \tag{4.5}$$

reduces to

$$v < 0 \tag{4.6}$$

To achieve this, we start writing (4.5) as $d + 2m - 0.5 < 0$ and, since this inequality contains the two fractions $m = \Delta y/\Delta x$ and 0.5, we multiply both sides of it by $2\Delta x$, obtaining

$$2d\Delta x + 4\Delta y - \Delta x < 0$$

Therefore, instead of the floating-point error variable $d = y_{\text{exact}} - y$, we will use the integer variable v, which relates to d as follows:

$$v = 2d\Delta x + 4\Delta y - \Delta x \tag{4.7}$$

We can now replace the test (4.5) with the more efficient one (4.6). It follows from (4.7) that increasing d by $2m$ is equivalent to increasing v by $2\Delta x \times 2m$, which is equal to $4\Delta y$. This explains both the test $v < 0$ and adding $dy4$ to v in the for-loop below. These operations on the variable v are marked by comments of the form //*Equivalent to . . .*, as are some others, which are left to the reader to verify.

```
void doubleStep2(Graphics g, int xP, int yP, int xQ, int yQ)
{  int dx, dy, x, y, yInc;
   if (xP >= xQ)
   {  if (xP == xQ) // Not allowed because we divide by (dx = xQ - xP)
         return;
      int t;          // xP > xQ, so swap the points P and Q
      t = xP; xP = xQ; xQ = t;
      t = yP; yP = yQ; yQ = t;
   }
   // Now xP < xQ
   if (yQ >= yP){yInc = 1; dy = yQ - yP;}
   else          {yInc = -1; dy = yP - yQ;}
   dx = xQ - xP;
   int dy4 = dy * 4, v = dy4 - dx, dx2 = 2 * dx, dy2 = 2 * dy,
       dy4Minusdx2 = dy4 - dx2, dy4Minusdx4 = dy4Minusdx2 - dx2;
   putPixel(g, xP, yP);
   y = yP;
   for (x=xP; x<xQ-1;)
   {  if (v < 0)                       // Equivalent to d + 2 * m < 0.5
      {  putPixel(g, ++x, y);          // Pattern 1
         putPixel(g, ++x, y);
         v += dy4;                      // Equivalent to d += 2 * m
      }
      else
```

```
        if (v < dx2)                        // Equivalent to d + 2 * m < 1.5
        {  // Pattern 2 or 3
           if (v < dy2)                      // Equivalent to d + m < 0.5
           { putPixel(g, ++x, y);        // Pattern 2
             putPixel(g, ++x, y += yInc);
             v += dy4Minusdx2;              // Equivalent to d += 2 * m - 1
            }
           else
           { putPixel(g, ++x, y += yInc); // Pattern 3
             putPixel(g, ++x, y);
             v += dy4Minusdx2;              // Equivalent to d += 2 * m - 1
            }
        }
        else
        { putPixel(g, ++x, y += yInc); // Pattern 4
          putPixel(g, ++x, y += yInc);
          v += dy4Minusdx4;                // Equivalent to d += 2 * m - 2
        }
     }
     if (x < xQ)
        putPixel(g, xQ, yQ);
}
```

Remember, the above method *doubleStep*2 works only if $|y_Q - y_P| \le |x_Q - x_P|$. In Exercise 4.2 the reader is asked to generalize the method to work for any line.

Like Bresenham's line algorithm, the above double-step algorithm computes on integers only. For long lines, it outperforms Bresenham's algorithm by a factor of almost two. One can further optimize the algorithm to achieve another factor of two of speed-up by taking advantage of the symmetry around the midpoint of the given line. We leave this as an exercise for interested readers. The double-step algorithm can in fact be generalized to draw circles, which will be left for readers to explore by consulting the papers by Wu and Rokne (1987) and Rokne, Wyvill, and Wu (1990) listed in the Bibliography. Adapting Bresenham's algorithm for circles will be the topic of the next section.

4.3 CIRCLES

In this section we will ignore the normal way of drawing a circle in Java by a call of the form

```
g.drawOval(xC - r, yC - r, 2 * r, 2 * r);
```

since it is our goal to construct such a circle, with center $C(x_C, y_C)$ and radius r ourselves, where the coordinates of C and the radius are given as integers.

If speed is not a critical factor, we can apply the method *drawLine* to a great many neighboring points (x, y), computed as

$$x = x_C + r \cos \varphi$$
$$y = y_C + r \sin \varphi$$

where

$$\varphi = i \times \frac{2\pi}{n} (i = 0, 1, 2, \ldots, n - 1)$$

for some large value of n.

Instead of the above two ways of drawing a circle, we will develop a method of the form

```
void drawCircle(Graphics g, int xC, int yC, int r)
{   ...
}
```

which uses only the method *putPixel* of the previous section as a graphics 'primitive', and which is an implementation of *Bresenham's algorithm for circles*. The circle drawn in this way will be exactly same as that produced by the above call to *drawOval*. In both cases, x will range from $x_C - r$ to $x_C + r$, including these two values, so that $2r + 1$ different values of x will be used.

As in the previous sections, we begin with a simple case: we use the origin of the coordinate system as the center of the circle, and, dividing the circle into eight arcs of equal length, we restrict ourselves to one of these, the arc PQ. The points $P(0, r)$ and $Q(r/\sqrt{2}, r/\sqrt{2})$ are shown in Figure 4.5.

The equation of this circle is

$$x^2 + y^2 = r^2 \qquad\qquad (4.8)$$

Figure 4.6 shows the situation, including the grid of pixels, for the case $r = 8$. Beginning at the top at point P, with $x = 0$ and $y = r$, we will use a loop in which we increase x by 1 in each step; as in the previous section, we need some test to decide whether we can leave y unchanged. If not, we have to decrease y by 1.

Since, just after increasing x by 1, we have to choose between (x, y) and $(x, y - 1)$, we could simply compute both

$$x^2 + y^2 \qquad \text{and} \qquad x^2 + (y - 1)^2$$

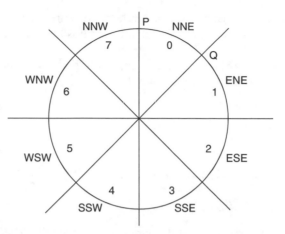

Figure 4.5: Arc PQ in sector O of a circle with origin O and radius r

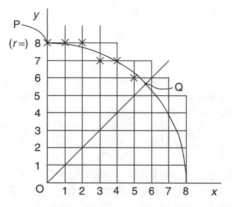

Figure 4.6: Pixels that approximate the arc PQ

to see which lies closer to r^2. Note that this can be done by using only integer arithmetic, so that in principle our problem is solved. To make our algorithm faster, we will avoid computing the squares x^2 and y^2, by introducing the three new, non-negative integer variables u, v and E denoting the differences between two successive squares and the 'error':

$$u = (x + 1)^2 - x^2 = 2x + 1 \tag{4.9}$$

$$v = y^2 - (y - 1)^2 = 2y - 1 \tag{4.10}$$

$$E = x^2 + y^2 - r^2 \tag{4.11}$$

Initially, we have $x = 0$ and $y = r$, so that $u = 1$, $v = 2r - 1$ and $E = 0$. In each step in the loop, we increase x by 1, as previously discussed. Since, according to

Equation (4.9), this will increase the value of x^2 by u, we also have to increase E by u to satisfy Equation (4.11). We can also see from Equation (4.9) that increasing x by 1 implies that we have to increase u by 2. We now have to decide whether or not to decrease y by 1. If we do, Equation (4.10) indicates that the square y^2 decreases by v, so that according to Equation (4.11) E also has to decrease by v. Since we want the absolute value of the error E to be as small as possible, the test we are looking for can be written

$$|E - v| < |E| \tag{4.12}$$

We will decrease y by 1 if and only if this test succeeds. It is interesting that we can write the condition (4.12) in a simpler form, by first replacing it with the equivalent test

$$(E - v)^2 < E^2$$

which can be simplified to

$$v(v - 2E) < 0$$

Since v is positive, we can simplify this further to

$$v < 2E$$

On the basis of the above discussion, we can now write the following method to draw the arc PQ (in which we write e instead of E):

```
void arc8(Graphics g, int r)
{  int x = 0, y = r, u = 1, v = 2 * r - 1, e = 0;
   while (x <= y)
   {  putPixel(g, x, y);
      x++; e += u; u += 2;
      if (v < 2 * e){y--; e -= v; v -= 2;}
   }
}
```

Equations (4.10) and (4.11) show that in the case of decreasing y by 1, we have to decrease E by v and v by 2, as implemented in the if-statement. Note the symmetry between the three actions (related to y) in the if-statement and those (related to x) in the preceding program line.

The method *arc8* is the basis for our final method, *drawCircle*, listed below. Besides drawing a full circle, it is also more general than *arc8* in that it allows an arbitrary point C to be specified as the center of the circle. The comments in this method indicate directions of the compass. For example, *NNE* stands for north-north-east, which we use to refer to the arc between the north and the north-east directions (see Figure 4.5). As usual, we think of the y-axis pointing upward, so that $y = r$ corresponds to north:

```
void drawCircle(Graphics g, int xC, int yC, int r)
{  int x = 0, y = r, u = 1, v = 2 * r - 1, e = 0;
   while (x < y)
   {  putPixel(g, xC + x, yC + y); // NNE
      putPixel(g, xC + y, yC - x); // ESE
      putPixel(g, xC - x, yC - y); // SSW
      putPixel(g, xC - y, yC + x); // WNW
      x++; e += u; u += 2;
      if (v < 2 * e){y--; e -= v; v -= 2;}
      if (x > y) break;
      putPixel(g, xC + y, yC + x); // ENE
      putPixel(g, xC + x, yC - y); // SSE
      putPixel(g, xC - y, yC - x); // WSW
      putPixel(g, xC - x, yC + y); // NNW
   }
}
```

This version has been programmed in such a way that *putPixel* will not visit the same pixel more than once. This is important if we want to use the XOR paint mode, writing

```
g.setXORMode(Color.white);
```

before the call to *drawCircle*. Setting the paint mode in this way implies that black pixels are made white and vice versa, so that we can remove a circle in the same way as we draw it. It is then essential that a single call to *drawCircle* does not put the same pixel twice on the screen, for then it would be erased the second time. To prevent pixels from being used twice, the eight calls to *putPixel* in the loop are divided into two groups of four: those in the first group draw the arcs 0, 2, 4 and 6 (see Figure 4.5), which include the starting points $(0, r)$, $(r, 0)$, $(0, -r)$ and $(-r, 0)$. The arcs 1, 3, 5 and 7 of the second group do not include these starting points because these calls to *putPixel* take place after x has been increased. As for the endpoint of each arc, we take care (a) that x is not greater than y for any call to *putPixel*, and (b) that the situation $x = y$ is covered by at most one of these two groups of *putPixel* calls. This situation will occur, for example, if $r = 6$; in this case the following eight points (relative to the center of the circle) are selected in this order, as far as the north-east quadrant of the circle (*NNE* and *ENE*) is concerned: $(0, 6)$, $(6, 1)$, $(1, 6)$, $(6, 2)$, $(2, 6)$, $(5, 3)$, $(3, 5)$, $(4, 4)$. In this situation the test after *while* terminates the loop. In contrast, the situation $x = y$ will not occur if $r = 8$, since in this case the eleven points $(0, 8)$, $(8, 1)$, $(1, 8)$, $(8, 2)$, $(2, 8)$, $(7, 3)$, $(3, 7)$, $(7, 4)$, $(4, 7)$, $(6, 5)$, $(5, 6)$ are chosen, in that order. The loop now terminates because the break-statement in the middle of it is executed.

4.4 COHEN–SUTHERLAND LINE CLIPPING

In this section we will discuss how to draw line segments only as far as they lie within a given rectangle. For example, given a point P inside and a point Q outside a rectangle. It is then our task to draw only the line segment PI, where I is the point of intersection of PQ and the rectangle, as shown in Figure 4.7. The rectangle is given by the four numbers $x_{min}, x_{max}, y_{min}$ and y_{max}. These four values and the coordinates of P and Q are floating-point logical coordinates, as usual.

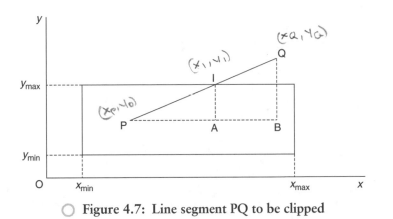

○ **Figure 4.7: Line segment PQ to be clipped**

Since PQ intersects the upper edge of the rectangle in I, we have

$$y_I = y_{max}$$

As the triangles PAI and PBQ are similar, we can write

$$\frac{x_I - x_P}{y_I - y_P} = \frac{x_Q - x_P}{y_Q - y_P}$$

After replacing y_I with y_{max} and multiplying both sides of this equation by $y_{max} - y_P$, we easily obtain

$$x_I = x_P + \frac{(y_{max} - y_P)(x_Q - x_P)}{(y_Q - y_P)}$$

so that we can draw the desired line segment PI.

This easy way of computing the coordinates of point I is based on several facts that apply to Figure 4.7, but that must not be relied on in a general algorithm. For example, if Q lies farther to the right, it may not be immediately clear whether the point of intersection lies on the upper edge $y = y_{max}$ or on the right edge $x = x_{max}$. In general, there are many more cases to consider. The logical decisions needed to find out which actions to take make line clipping an interesting topic from an algorithmic point of view. The Cohen–Sutherland algorithm solves this problem in an elegant and efficient way. We will express this algorithm in Java.

The four lines $x = x_{min}, x = x_{max}, y = y_{min}, y = y_{max}$ divide the xy-plane into nine regions. With any point P(x, y) we associate a four-bit code

$$b_3 b_2 b_1 b_0$$

identifying that region, as Figure 4.8 shows.

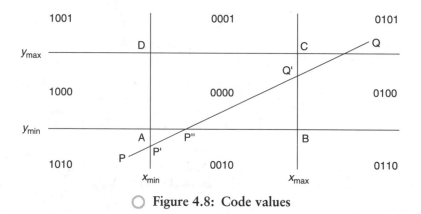

Figure 4.8: Code values

For any point (x, y), the above four-bit code is defined as follows:

$b_3 = 1$ if and only if $x < x_{min}$
$b_2 = 1$ if and only if $x > x_{max}$
$b_1 = 1$ if and only if $y < y_{min}$
$b_0 = 1$ if and only if $y > y_{max}$

Based on this code, the Cohen–Sutherland algorithm replaces the endpoints P and Q of a line segment, if they lie outside the rectangle, with points of intersection of PQ and the rectangle, that is, if there are such points of intersection. This is done in a few steps. For example, in Figure 4.8, the following steps are taken:

1. Since P lies to the left of the left rectangle edge, it is replaced with P′ (on $x = x_{min}$), so that only P′Q remains to be dealt with.

2. Since P′ lies below the lower rectangle edge, it is replaced with P″ (on $y = y_{min}$), so that P″Q remains to be dealt with.

3. Since Q lies to the right of the right rectangle edge, it is replaced with Q′ (on $x = x_{max}$), so that P″Q′ remains to be dealt with.

4. Line segment P″Q′ is drawn.

Steps 1, 2 and 3 are done in a loop, which can terminate in two ways:

- If the four-bit codes of P (or P′ or P″, which we again refer to as P in the program) and of Q are equal to zero; the (new) line segment PQ is then drawn.

- If the two four-bit codes contain a 1-bit in the same position; this implies that P and Q are on the same side of a rectangle edge, so that nothing has to be drawn.

The method *clipLine* in the following program shows this in greater detail:

```java
// ClipLine.java: Cohen-Sutherland line clipping.
import java.awt.*;
import java.awt.event.*;
import java.util.*;

public class ClipLine extends Frame
{  public static void main(String[] args){new ClipLine();}

   ClipLine()
   {  super("Click on two opposite corners of a rectangle");
      addWindowListener(new WindowAdapter()
         {public void windowClosing(WindowEvent e){System.exit(0);}});
      setSize (500, 300);
      add("Center", new CvClipLine());

      setCursor(Cursor.getPredefinedCursor(Cursor.CROSSHAIR_CURSOR));
      show();
   }
}

class CvClipLine extends Canvas
{  float xmin, xmax, ymin, ymax,
      rWidth = 10.0F, rHeight = 7.5F, pixelSize;
   int maxX, maxY, centerX, centerY, np=0;

   CvClipLine()
   {  addMouseListener(new MouseAdapter()
      {  public void mousePressed(MouseEvent evt)
```

```
            {  float x = fx(evt.getX()), y = fy(evt.getY());
               if (np == 2) np = 0;
               if (np == 0){xmin = x; ymin = y;}
               else
               {  xmax = x; ymax = y;
                  if (xmax < xmin)
                  {  float t = xmax; xmax = xmin; xmin = t;
                  }
                  if (ymax < ymin)
                  {  float t = ymax; ymax = ymin; ymin = t;
                  }
               }
               np++;
               repaint();
            }
      });
   }

   void initgr()
   {  Dimension d = getSize();
      maxX = d.width - 1; maxY = d.height - 1;
      pixelSize = Math.max(rWidth/maxX, rHeight/maxY);
      centerX = maxX/2; centerY = maxY/2;
   }

   int iX(float x){return Math.round(centerX + x/pixelSize);}
   int iY(float y){return Math.round(centerY - y/pixelSize);}
   float fx(int x){return (x - centerX) * pixelSize;}
   float fy(int y){return (centerY - y) * pixelSize;}

   void drawLine(Graphics g, float xP, float yP,
      float xQ, float yQ)
   {  g.drawLine(iX(xP), iY(yP), iX(xQ), iY(yQ));
   }

   int clipCode(float x, float y)
   {  return
         (x < xmin ? 8 : 0) | (x > xmax ? 4 : 0) |
         (y < ymin ? 2 : 0) | (y > ymax ? 1 : 0);
   }

   void clipLine(Graphics g,
      float xP, float yP, float xQ, float yQ,
```

```
         float xmin, float ymin, float xmax, float ymax)
{  int cP = clipCode(xP, yP), cQ = clipCode(xQ, yQ);
   float dx, dy;
   while ((cP | cQ) != 0)
   {  if ((cP & cQ) != 0) return;
      dx = xQ - xP; dy = yQ - yP;
      if (cP != 0)
      {  if ((cP & 8) == 8){yP += (xmin-xP) * dy / dx; xP = xmin;}
         else
         if ((cP & 4) == 4){yP += (xmax-xP) * dy / dx; xP = xmax;}
         else
         if ((cP & 2) == 2){xP += (ymin-yP) * dx / dy; yP = ymin;}
         else
         if ((cP & 1) == 1){xP += (ymax-yP) * dx / dy; yP = ymax;}
         cP = clipCode(xP, yP);
      }
      else
      if (cQ != 0)
      {  if ((cQ & 8) == 8){yQ += (xmin-xQ) * dy / dx; xQ = xmin;}
         else
         if ((cQ & 4) == 4){yQ += (xmax-xQ) * dy / dx; xQ = xmax;}
         else
         if ((cQ & 2) == 2){xQ += (ymin-yQ) * dx / dy; yQ = ymin;}
         else
         if ((cQ & 1) == 1){xQ += (ymax-yQ) * dx / dy; yQ = ymax;}
         cQ = clipCode(xQ, yQ);
      }
   }
   drawLine(g, xP, yP, xQ, yQ);
}
public void paint(Graphics g)
{  initgr();
   if (np == 1)
   {  // Draw horizontal and vertical lines through
      // first defined point:
      drawLine(g, fx (0) , ymin, fx(maxX), ymin);
      drawLine(g, xmin, fy (0) , xmin, fy(maxY));
    } else
   if (np == 2)
   {  // Draw rectangle:
      drawLine(g, xmin, ymin, xmax, ymin);
      drawLine(g, xmax, ymin, xmax, ymax);
      drawLine(g, xmax, ymax, xmin, ymax);
```

```
      drawLine(g, xmin, ymax, xmin, ymin);

      // Draw 20 concentric regular pentagons, as
      // far as they lie within the rectangle:
      float rMax = Math.min(rWidth, rHeight)/2,
         deltaR = rMax/20, dPhi = (float)(0.4 * Math.PI);

      for (int j=1; j<=20; j++)
      {  float r = j * deltaR;
         // Draw a pentagon:
         float xA, yA, xB = r, yB = 0;

         for (int i=1; i<=5; i++)
         {  float phi = i * dPhi;
            xA = xB; yA = yB;
            xB = (float)(r * Math.cos(phi));
            yB = (float)(r * Math.sin(phi));
            clipLine(g, xA, yA, xB, yB, xmin, ymin, xmax, ymax);
         }
      }
   }
}
```

The program draws 20 concentric (regular) pentagons, as far as these lie within a rectangle, which the user can define by clicking on any two opposite corners. When he or she clicks for the third time, the situation is the same as at the beginning: the screen is cleared and a new rectangle can be defined, in which again parts of 20 pentagons appear, and so on. As usual, if the user changes the window dimensions, the size of the result is changed accordingly. Figure 4.9 shows the situation just after the pentagons are drawn.

If we look at the while-loop in the method *clipLine*, it seems that this code is somewhat inefficient because of the divisions dy/dx and dx/dy inside that loop while dx and dy are not changed in it. However, we should bear in mind that dx or dy may be zero. The if-statements in the loop guarantee that no division by dx or dy will be performed if that variable is zero. Besides, this loop is different from most other program loops in that the inner part is usually executed only once or not at all, and rarely more than once.

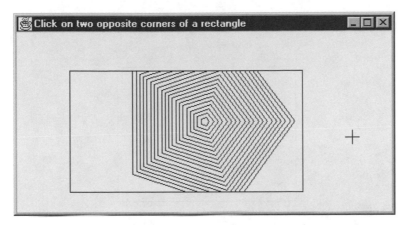

○ Figure 4.9: Demonstration of program *ClipLine.java*

4.5 SUTHERLAND–HODGMAN POLYGON CLIPPING

In contrast to line clipping, discussed in the previous section, we will now deal with polygon clipping, which is different in that it converts one polygon into another within a given rectangle, as Figures 4.10 and 4.11 illustrate.

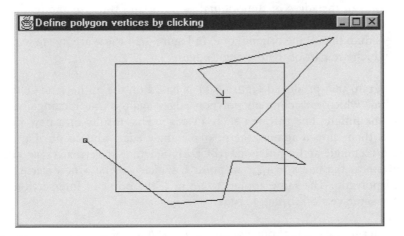

○ Figure 4.10: Nine polygon vertices defined; final edge not yet drawn

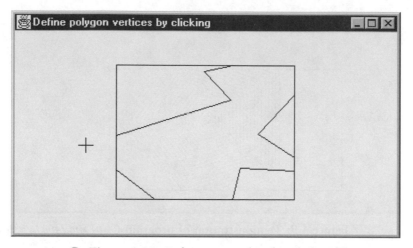

○ **Figure 4.11: Polygon completed and clipped**

The program that we will discuss draws a fixed rectangle and enables the user to specify the vertices of a polygon by clicking, in the same way as discussed in Section 1.5. As long as the first vertex, in Figure 4.10 on the left, is not selected for the second time, successive vertices are connected by polygon edges. As soon as the first vertex is selected again, the polygon is clipped, as Figure 4.11 shows. Some vertices of the original polygon do not belong to the clipped one. On the other hand, the latter polygon has some new vertices, which are all points of intersection of the edges of the original polygon and those of the rectangle. In general, the number of vertices of the clipped polygon can be greater than, equal to or less than that of the original one. In Figure 4.11 there are five new polygon edges, which are part of the rectangle edges.

The program that produced Figure 4.11 is based on the Sutherland–Hodgman algorithm, which first clips all polygon edges against one rectangle edge, or rather, the infinite line through such an edge. This results in a new polygon, which is then clipped against the next rectangle edge, and so on. Figure 4.12 shows a rectangle and a polygon, ABCDEF. Starting at vertex A, we find that AB intersects the line $x = x_{max}$ in point I, which will be a new vertex of the clipped polygon. The same applies to point J, the point of intersection of DE with the same vertical rectangle edge.

Let us refer to the original polygon as the *input polygon* and the new one as the *output polygon*. We represent each polygon by a sequence of successive vertices. Let us start with the right rectangle edge and treat it as an infinite clipping line, which can be expressed as $x = x_{max}$, and see how to clip the polygon against this line. In general, when working on one clipping line, we ignore all

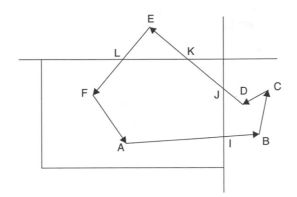

○ **Figure 4.12: The Sutherland–Hodgman algorithm**

other rectangle edges. Initially, the output polygon is empty. When following all successive polygon edges such as AB, we focus on the endpoint, B, and decide as follows which points will belong to the output polygon:

> If A and B lie on different sides of the clipping line, the point of intersection, I, is added to the output polygon. Regardless of this being the case, B is added to the output polygon if and only if it lies on the same side of the clipping line as the rectangle.

Starting with the directed edge AB in Figure 4.12, point I is the first to be added to the output polygon. Vertex B is not added because it is not on the same side of the clipping line as the rectangle, and the same applies to the endpoints of the following directed edges, BC and CD. When dealing with edge DE, we first add J and then E to the output polygon since they are both on the same side of the clipping line as the rectangle. The endpoints of the next two edges, EF and FA, lie on the same side of the clipping line as the rectangle and are therefore added to the output polygon. In this way we obtain the vertices I, J, E, F and A, in that order. We then use this output polygon as the input polygon to clip against the top rectangle edge. Using the same method as described above on the right edge, we obtain the vertices I, J, K, L, F and A, which forms the output polygon IJKLFA. Although in this example IJKLFA is the desired clipped polygon, it will in general be necessary to use the output polygon as input for working with another rectangle edge. The program below shows an implementation in Java:

```
// ClipPoly.java: Clipping a polygon.
// Uses: Point2D (Section 1.5).
import java.awt.*;
import java.awt.event.*;
import java.util.*;
```

```java
public class ClipPoly extends Frame
{  public static void main(String[] args){new ClipPoly();}

   ClipPoly()
   {  super("Define polygon vertices by clicking");
      addWindowListener(new WindowAdapter()
         {public void windowClosing(WindowEvent e)
                  {System.exit(0);}});
      setSize (500, 300);
      add("Center", new CvClipPoly());

      setCursor(Cursor.getPredefinedCursor
                  (Cursor.CROSSHAIR_CURSOR));
      show();
   }
}

class CvClipPoly extends Canvas
{  Poly poly = null;
   float rWidth = 10.0F, rHeight = 7.5F, pixelSize;
   int x0, y0, centerX, centerY;
   boolean ready = true;

   CvClipPoly()
   {  addMouseListener(new MouseAdapter()
      {  public void mousePressed(MouseEvent evt)
         {  int x = evt.getX(), y = evt.getY();
            if (ready)
            {  poly = new Poly();
               x0 = x; y0 = y;
               ready = false;
            }
            if (poly.size() > 0 &&
               Math.abs(x - x0) < 3 && Math.abs(y - y0) < 3)
               ready = true;
            else
               poly.addVertex(new Point2D(fx(x), fy(y)));
            repaint();
         }
      });
   }
```

```
void initgr()
{  Dimension d = getSize();
   int maxX = d.width - 1, maxY = d.height - 1;
   pixelSize = Math.max(rWidth/maxX, rHeight/maxY);
   centerX = maxX/2; centerY = maxY/2;
}

int iX(float x){return Math.round(centerX + x/pixelSize);}
int iY(float y){return Math.round(centerY - y/pixelSize);}
float fx(int x){return (x - centerX) * pixelSize;}
float fy(int y){return (centerY - y) * pixelSize;}

void drawLine(Graphics g, float xP, float yP, float xQ,
                 float yQ)
{  g.drawLine(iX(xP), iY(yP), iX(xQ), iY(yQ));
}

void drawPoly(Graphics g, Poly poly)
{  int n = poly.size();
   if (n == 0) return;
   Point2D a = poly.vertexAt(n - 1);
   for (int i=0; i<n; i++)
   {  Point2D b = poly.vertexAt(i);
      drawLine(g, a.x, a.y, b.x, b.y);
      a = b;
   }
 }

public void paint(Graphics g)
{  initgr();
   float xmin = -rWidth/3, xmax = rWidth/3,
         ymin = -rHeight/3, ymax = rHeight/3;
   // Draw clipping rectangle:
   g.setColor(Color.blue);
   drawLine(g, xmin, ymin, xmax, ymin);
   drawLine(g, xmax, ymin, xmax, ymax);
   drawLine(g, xmax, ymax, xmin, ymax);
   drawLine(g, xmin, ymax, xmin, ymin);
   g.setColor(Color.black);
   if (poly == null) return;
   int n = poly.size();
   if (n == 0) return;
   Point2D a = poly.vertexAt (0);
```

```
          if (!ready)
          {  // Show tiny rectangle around first vertex:
             g.drawRect(iX(a.x)-2, iY(a.y)-2, 4, 4);
             // Draw incomplete polygon:
             for (int i=1; i<n; i++)
             {  Point2D b = poly.vertexAt(i);
                drawLine(g, a.x, a.y, b.x, b.y);
                a = b;
             }
          }  else
          {  poly.clip(xmin, ymin, xmax, ymax);
             drawPoly(g, poly);
          }
       }
   }
}
class Poly
{  Vector v = new Vector();
   void addVertex(Point2D p){v.addElement(p);}
   int size(){return v.size();}

   Point2D vertexAt(int i)
   {  return (Point2D)v.elementAt(i);
   }

   void clip(float xmin, float ymin, float xmax, float ymax)
   {  // Sutherland-Hodgman polygon clipping:
      Poly poly1 = new Poly();
      int n;
      Point2D a, b;
      boolean aIns, bIns; // whether A or B is on the same
                          //           side as the rectangle

      // Clip against x == xmax:
      if ((n = size()) == 0) return;
      b = vertexAt(n-1);
      for (int i=0; i<n; i++)
      {  a = b; b = vertexAt(i);
         aIns = a.x <= xmax; bIns = b.x <= xmax;
         if (aIns != bIns)
            poly1.addVertex(new Point2D(xmax, a.y +
            (b.y - a.y) * (xmax - a.x)/(b.x - a.x)));
         if (bIns) poly1.addVertex(b);
      }
```

```
    v = poly1.v; poly1 = new Poly();

    // Clip against x == xmin:
    if ((n = size()) == 0) return;
    b = vertexAt(n-1);
    for (int i=0; i<n; i++)
    {   a = b; b = vertexAt(i);
        aIns = a.x >= xmin; bIns = b.x >= xmin;
        if (aIns != bIns)
            poly1.addVertex(new Point2D(xmin, a.y +
            (b.y - a.y) * (xmin - a.x)/(b.x - a.x)));
        if (bIns) poly1.addVertex(b);
    }
    v = poly1.v; poly1 = new Poly();

    // Clip against y == ymax:
    if ((n = size()) == 0) return;
    b = vertexAt(n-1);
    for (int i=0; i<n; i++)
    {   a = b; b = vertexAt(i);
        aIns = a.y <= ymax; bIns = b.y <= ymax;
        if (aIns != bIns)
            poly1.addVertex(new Point2D(a.x +
            (b.x - a.x) * (ymax - a.y)/(b.y - a.y), ymax));
        if (bIns) poly1.addVertex(b);
    }
    v = poly1.v; poly1 = new Poly();

    // Clip against y == ymin:
    if ((n = size()) == 0) return;
    b = vertexAt(n-1);
    for (int i=0; i<n; i++)
    {   a = b; b = vertexAt(i);
        aIns = a.y >= ymin;
        bIns = b.y >= ymin;
        if (aIns != bIns)
            poly1.addVertex(new Point2D(a.x +
            (b.x - a.x) * (ymin - a.y)/(b.y - a.y), ymin));
        if (bIns) poly1.addVertex(b);
    }
    v = poly1.v; poly1 = new Poly();
  }
}
```

The Sutherland–Hodgman algorithm can be adapted for clipping regions other than rectangles and for three-dimensional applications.

4.6 BÉZIER CURVES

There are many algorithms for constructing curves. A particularly elegant and practical one is based on specifying four points that completely determine a curve segment: two endpoints and two control points. Curves constructed in this way are referred to as *(cubic) Bézier curves*. In Figure 4.13, we have the endpoints P_0 and P_3, the control points P_1 and P_2, and the curve constructed on the basis of these four points.

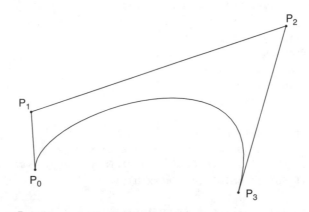

Figure 4.13: Bézier curve based on four points

Writing a method to draw this curve is surprisingly easy, provided we use recursion. As Figure 4.14 shows, we compute six midpoints, namely:

- A, the midpoint of $P_0 P_1$
- B, the midpoint of $P_2 P_3$
- C, the midpoint of $P_1 P_2$
- A_1, the midpoint of AC
- B_1, the midpoint of BC
- C_1, the midpoint of $A_1 B_1$

After this, we can divide the original task of drawing the Bézier curve $P_0 P_3$ (with control points P_1 and P_2) into two simpler tasks:

- drawing the Bézier curve $P_0 C_1$, with control points A and A_1
- drawing the Bézier curve $C_1 P_3$, with control points B_1 and B

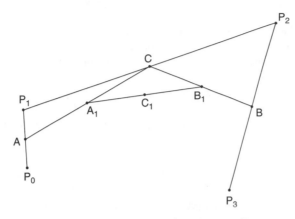

○ **Figure 4.14: Constructing points for two smaller curve segments**

All this needs to be done only if the original points P_0 and P_3 are further apart than some small distance, say, ε. Otherwise, we simply draw the straight line P_0P_3. Since we are using pixels on a raster, we can also base the test just mentioned on device coordinates: we will simply draw a straight line from P_0 to P_3 if and only if the corresponding pixels are neighbors or identical, writing

```
if (Math.abs(x0 - x3) <= 1 && Math.abs(y0 - y3) <= 1)
     g.drawLine(x0, y0, x3, y3);
else ...
```

The recursive method *bezier* in the following program shows an implementation of this algorithm. The program expects the user to specify the four points P_0, P_1, P_2 and P_3, in that order, by clicking the mouse. After the fourth point, P_3, has been specified, the curve is drawn. Any new mouse clicking is interpreted as the first point, P_0, of a new curve; the previous curve simply disappears and another curve can be constructed in the same way as the first one, and so on.

```
// Bezier.java: Bezier curve segments.
// Uses: Point2D (Section 1.5).

import java.awt.*;
import java.awt.event.*;
import java.util.*;

public class Bezier extends Frame
{  public static void main(String[] args){new Bezier();}
```

```
    Bezier()
    {  super("Define endpoints and control points of curve segment");
       addWindowListener(new WindowAdapter()
           {public void windowClosing(WindowEvent e){System.exit(0);}});
       setSize (500, 300);
       add("Center", new CvBezier());

       setCursor(Cursor.getPredefinedCursor(Cursor.CROSSHAIR_CURSOR));
       show();
    }
}

class CvBezier extends Canvas
{  Point2D[] p = new Point2D[4];
   int np = 0, centerX, centerY;
   float rWidth = 10.0F, rHeight = 7.5F, eps = rWidth/100F, pixelSize;

   CvBezier()
   {  addMouseListener(new MouseAdapter()
        {  public void mousePressed(MouseEvent evt)
           {  float x = fx(evt.getX()), y = fy(evt.getY());
              if (np == 4) np = 0;
              p[np++] = new Point2D(x, y);
              repaint();
           }
        });
   }

   void initgr()
   {  Dimension d = getSize();
      int maxX = d.width - 1, maxY = d.height - 1;
      pixelSize = Math.max(rWidth/maxX, rHeight/maxY);
      centerX = maxX/2; centerY = maxY/2;
   }

   int iX(float x){return Math.round(centerX + x/pixelSize);}
   int iY(float y){return Math.round(centerY - y/pixelSize);}
   float fx(int x){return (x - centerX) * pixelSize;}
   float fy(int y){return (centerY - y) * pixelSize;}
   Point2D middle(Point2D a, Point2D b)
   {  return new Point2D((a.x + b.x)/2, (a.y + b.y)/2);
   }
```

```
void bezier(Graphics g, Point2D p0, Point2D p1,
   Point2D p2, Point2D p3)
{  int x0 = iX(p0.x), y0 = iY(p0.y),
      x3 = iX(p3.x), y3 = iY(p3.y);
   if (Math.abs(x0 - x3) <= 1 && Math.abs(y0 - y3) <= 1)
      g.drawLine(x0, y0, x3, y3);
   else
   {  Point2D a = middle(p0, p1), b = middle(p3, p2),
         c = middle(p1, p2), a1 = middle(a, c),
         b1 = middle(b, c), c1 = middle(a1, b1);
      bezier(g, p0, a, a1, c1);
      bezier(g, c1, b1, b, p3);
   }
}

public void paint(Graphics g)
{  initgr();
   int left = iX(-rWidth/2), right = iX(rWidth/2),
      bottom = iY(-rHeight/2), top = iY(rHeight/2);
   g.drawRect(left, top, right - left, bottom - top);

   for (int i=0; i<np; i++)
   {  // Show tiny rectangle around point:
      g.drawRect(iX(p[i].x)-2, iY(p[i].y)-2, 4, 4);
      if (i > 0)
         // Draw line p[i-1]p[i]:
         g.drawLine(iX(p[i-1].x), iY(p[i-1].y),
                 iX(p[i].x), iY(p[i].y));
   }
   if (np == 4) bezier(g, p[0], p[1], p[2], p[3]);
}
}
```

Since this program uses the isotropic mapping mode with logical coordinate ranges 0–10.0 for x and 0–7.5 for y, we should only use a rectangle whose height is 75 % of its width. As in Sections 1.4 and 1.5, we place this rectangle at the center of the screen and make it as large as possible. It is shown in Figure 4.15; if the four points for the curve are chosen within this rectangle, they will be visible regardless of how the size of the window is changed by the user. The same applies to the curve, which is automatically scaled, in the same way as we did in Sections 1.4 and 1.5.

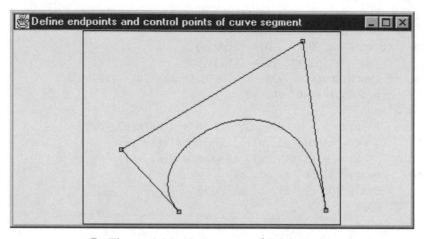

○ Figure 4.15: A constructed Bézier curve

This way of constructing a Bézier curve may look like magic. To understand what is going on, we must be familiar with the notion of *parametric representation*, which, in 2D, we can write as

$$\begin{cases} x = f(t) \\ y = g(t) \end{cases}$$

where t is a parameter, which we may think of as *time*. Variable t ranges from 0 to 1: as if we move from P_0 to P_3 with constant velocity, starting at $t = 0$ and finishing at $t = 1$. At time $t = 0.5$ we are half-way. With cubic Bézier curves, both $f(t)$ and $g(t)$ are third degree polynomials in t.

Before we proceed, let us pay some attention to expressions such as

$$A = \tfrac{1}{2}(P_0 + P_1)$$

to compute the midpoint A of line segment P_0P_1. The points in such expressions actually denote vectors, which enables us to form their sum and to multiply them by a scalar. Without this shorthand notation, we would have to write

$$\mathbf{OA} = \tfrac{1}{2}(\mathbf{OP_0} + \mathbf{OP_1})$$

which would be rather awkward. Let us write each P_i as the column vector

$$P_i = \begin{pmatrix} P[i].x \\ P[i].y \end{pmatrix}$$

(where we have taken the liberty of mixing mathematical and programming notations). In the same way, we combine the above functions $f(t)$ and $g(t)$, writing

$$B(t) = \begin{pmatrix} x \\ y \end{pmatrix} = \begin{pmatrix} f(t) \\ g(t) \end{pmatrix}$$

Then the cubic Bézier curve is defined as follows:

$$B(t) = (1-t)^3 P_0 + 3t(1-t)^2 P_1 + 3t^2(1-t)P_2 + t^3 P_3 \qquad (4.13)$$

Substituting 0 and 1 for t, we find $B(0) = P_0$ and $B(1) = P_3$. Before discussing the relation between this definition and the recursive midpoint construction, let us see this definition in action. It enables us to replace the recursive method *bezier* with the following non-recursive one:

```
void bezier1(Graphics g, Point2D[] p)
{  int n = 200;
   float dt = 1.0F/n, x = p[0].x, y = p[0].y, x0, y0;
   for (int i=1; i<=n; i++)
   {  float t = i * dt, u = 1 - t,
         tuTriple = 3 * t * u,
         c0 = u * u * u,
         c1 = tuTriple * u,
         c2 = tuTriple * t,
         c3 = t * t * t;
      x0 = x; y0 = y;
      x = c0*p[0].x + c1*p[1].x + c2*p[2].x + c3*p[3].x;
      y = c0*p[0].y + c1*p[1].y + c2*p[2].y + c3*p[3].y;
      g.drawLine(iX(x0), iY(y0), iX(x), iY(y));
   }
}
```

This method produces the same curve as that produced by *bezier*, provided we also replace the call to *bezier* with this one:

```
bezier1(g, P);
```

We will discuss a more efficient non-recursive method, *bezier2*, equivalent to *bezier1*, at the end of this section.

Since $B(t)$ denotes the position at time t, the derivative $B'(t)$ of this function (which is also a column vector depending on t) can be regarded as the *velocity*. After some algebraic manipulation and differentiating, we find

$$B'(t) = -3(t-1)^2 P_0 + 3(3t-1)(t-1)P_1 - 3t(3t-2)P_2 + 3t^2 P_3 \quad (4.14)$$

which gives

$$B'(0) = 3(P_1 - P_0)$$
$$B'(1) = 3(P_3 - P_2)$$

These two results are velocity vectors at the starting point P_0 and the endpoint P_3. They show that the direction we move at on these points is along the vectors $P_0 P_1$ and $P_2 P_3$, as Figure 4.16 illustrates.

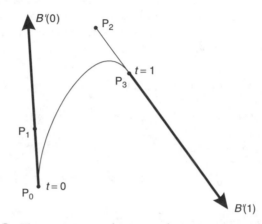

○ **Figure 4.16: Velocity at the points P_0 and P_3**

We have been discussing two entirely different ways to construct a curve between the points P_0 and P_3, and, without an experiment, it is not clear that these curves are identical. For the time being, we will distinguish between the two curves and refer to them as

- the *midpoint curve*, constructed by a recursive process of computing mid-points, and implemented in the method *bezier*;
- the *analytical curve*, given by Equation (4.13) and implemented in the method *bezier*1.

Although both methods are based on the four points P_0, P_1, P_2 and P_3, the ways we compute hundreds of curve points (to connect them by tiny straight lines) are very different. It would be unsatisfactory if it remained a mystery why these curves are identical. Let us therefore briefly discuss a way to prove this fact.

Using the function $B(t)$ of Equation (4.13), we find

$$B(0.5) = \tfrac{1}{8}(P_0 + 3P_1 + 3P_2 + P_3)$$

Since point C_1 in Figure 4.14 was used to divide the whole midpoint curve into two smaller curves, we might suspect that C_1 and $B(0.5)$ are two different expressions for the same point. We verify this by expressing C_1 in terms of the four given points, using Figure 4.14. Because C_1 is the midpoint of A_1B_1 and both A_1 and B_1 are also midpoints, and so on, we find

$$A = \tfrac{1}{2}(P_0 + P_1) \tag{4.15}$$
$$B = \tfrac{1}{2}(P_2 + P_3)$$
$$C = \tfrac{1}{2}(P_1 + P_2)$$
$$A_1 = \tfrac{1}{2}(A + C) = \tfrac{1}{4}(P_0 + 2P_1 + P_2) \tag{4.16}$$
$$B_1 = \tfrac{1}{2}(C + B) = \tfrac{1}{4}(P_1 + 2P_2 + P_3)$$
$$C_1 = \tfrac{1}{2}(A_1 + B_1) = \tfrac{1}{8}(P_0 + 3P_1 + 3P_2 + P_3) \tag{4.17}$$

which is indeed the expression that we found for $B(0.5)$. This proves that point C_1, which obviously belongs to the midpoint curve, also lies on the analytical curve. Besides P_0 and P_3, there is now only one point, C_1, which we have proved lies on both curves, so it seems we are still far away from the proof that these curves are identical. However, we can now apply the same argument recursively, which would enable us to find as many points that lie on both curves as we like. Restricting ourselves to the first half of each curve, we focus on the points P_0, A, A_1 and C_1, which we can again use to construct both midpoint and analytical curves. For the latter we use the following equation, which is similar to Equation (4.13):

$$b(u) = (1 - u)^3 P_0 + 3u(1 - u)^2 A + 3u^2(1 - u)A_1 + u^3 C_1 \tag{4.18}$$

It is then obvious that $b(0) = P_0$, $b(1) = C_1$ and $b(0.5)$ is identical with a midpoint (between P_0 and C_1) used in the recursive process, in the same way as $B(0.5)$ is identical with the midpoint C_1. There is one remaining difficulty: is the analytical curve given by Equation (4.18) really the same as the first part of that given by Equation (4.13)? We will show that this is indeed the case. Using $u = 2t$ (since $u = 1$ and $t = 0.5$ at point C_1) we have

$$b(u) = B(t)$$

To verify this, note that, according to Equation (4.18), we have

$$b(u) = b(2t) = (1 - 2t)^3 P_0 + 6t(1 - 2t)^2 A + 12t^2(1 - 2t)A_1 + 8t^3 C_1$$

Using Equations (4.15), (4.16) and (4.17), we can write the last expression as

$$(1 - 2t)^3 P_0 + 3t(1 - 2t)^2 (P_0 + P_1) + 3t^2(1 - 2t)(P_0 + 2P_1 + P_2)$$
$$+ t^3(P_0 + 3P_1 + 3P_2 + P_3)$$

Rearranging this formula, we find that it is equal to the expression for $B(t)$ in Equation (4.13), which is what we had to prove.

4.6.1 Building Smooth Curves from Curve Segments

Suppose that we want to combine two Bézier curve segments, one based on the four points P_0, P_1, P_2, P_3 and the other on Q_0, Q_1, Q_2 and Q_3, in such a way that the endpoint P_3 of the first segment coincides with the starting point Q_0 of the second. Then the combined curve will be smoothest if the final velocity $B'(1)$ (see Figure 4.16) of the first segment is equal to the initial velocity $B'(0)$ of the second. This will be the case if the point $P_3(= Q_0)$ lies exactly at the middle of the line segment P_2Q_1. The high degree of smoothness obtained in this way is referred to as second-order continuity. It implies not only that the two segments have the same tangent at their common point $P_3 = Q_0$, but also that the curvature is continuous at this point. By contrast, we have first-order continuity if P_3 lies on the line segment P_2Q_1 but not at the middle of it. In this case, although the curve looks reasonably smooth because both segments have the same tangent in the common point $P_3 = Q_0$, there is a discontinuity in the curvature at this point.

4.6.2 Matrix Notation

It will be clear that we can write Equation (4.13) as follows:

$$B(t) = [\ (1-t)^3 \quad 3t(1-t)^2 \quad 3t^2(1-t) \quad t^3\ ] \begin{bmatrix} P_0 \\ P_1 \\ P_2 \\ P_3 \end{bmatrix} \qquad (4.19)$$

Since the row vector in this matrix product is equal to

$$[\ -t^3 + 3t^2 - 3t + 1 \quad 3t^3 - 6t^2 + 3t \quad -3t^3 + 3t^2 \quad t^3\ ]$$

we can also write it as the product of a simpler row vector, $[t^3 \quad t^2 \quad t \quad 1]$, and a 4×4 matrix, obtaining the following result for the Bézier curve:

$$B(t) = [\ t^3 \quad t^2 \quad t \quad 1\ ] \begin{bmatrix} -1 & 3 & -3 & 1 \\ 3 & -6 & 3 & 0 \\ -3 & 3 & 0 & 0 \\ 1 & 0 & 0 & 0 \end{bmatrix} \begin{bmatrix} P_0 \\ P_1 \\ P_2 \\ P_3 \end{bmatrix} \qquad (4.20)$$

As we know, any matrix product ABC of three matrices is equal to both $(AB)C$ and $A(BC)$. If we do the first matrix multiplication first, as in $(AB)C$, Equation (4.20) reduces to Equation (4.19). On the other hand, if we do the second first, as in $A(BC)$, we obtain the following result:

$$B(t) = (-P_0 + 3P_1 - 3P_2 + P_3)t^3 + 3(P_0 - 2P_1 + P_3)t^2 - 3(P_1 - P_0)t + P_0$$

This is interesting because it provides us with a very efficient way of drawing a Bézier curve segment, as the following improved method shows:

```
void bezier2(Graphics g, Point2D[] p)
{  int n = 200;
   float dt = 1.0F/n,
   cx3 = -p[0].x + 3 * (p[1].x - p[2].x) + p[3].x,
   cy3 = -p[0].y + 3 * (p[1].y - p[2].y) + p[3].y,
   cx2 = 3 * (p[0].x - 2 * p[1].x + p[2].x),
   cy2 = 3 * (p[0].y - 2 * p[1].y + p[2].y),
   cx1 = 3 * (p[1].x - p[0].x),
   cy1 = 3 * (p[1].y - p[0].y),
   cx0 = p[0].x,
   cy0 = p[0].y,
   x = p[0].x, y = p[0].y, x0, y0;
   for (int i=1; i<=n; i++)
   {  float t = i * dt;
      x0 = x; y0 = y;
      x = ((cx3 * t + cx2) * t ı cx1) * t + cx0;
      y = ((cy3 * t + cy2) * t + cy1) * t + cy0;
      g.drawLine(iX(x0), iY(y0), iX(x), iY(y));
   }
}
```

The above computation of x and y is an application of *Horner's rule,* according to which we can efficiently compute polynomials by using the right-hand rather than the left-hand side of the following equation:

$$a_3t^3 + a_2t^2 + a_1t + a_0 = ((a_3t + a_2)t + a_1)t + a_0$$

Although *bezier2* does not look simpler than *bezier1*, it is much more efficient because of the reduced number of arithmetic operations in the for-loop. With a large number of steps, such as $n = 200$ in these versions of *bezier1* and *bezier2*, it is the number of operations inside the loop that counts, not the preparatory actions that precede the loop.

4.6.3 3D Curves

Although the curves discussed here are two-dimensional, three-dimensional curves can be generated in the same way. We simply add a z-component to $B(t)$ and to the control points, and compute this in the same way as the x- and y-components are computed. The possibility of generating curves that do not lie in a plane is related to the degree of the polynomials we have been discussing. If the four given points do not lie in the same plane, the generated cubic curve segment does not either. By contrast, quadratic curves are determined by only three points, which uniquely define a plane (unless they are collinear); the quadratic curve through those three points lies in that plane. In other words, polynomial curves can be non-planar only if they are at least of degree 3.

4.7 B-SPLINE CURVE FITTING

Besides the techniques discussed in the previous section, there are other ways of generating curves $x = f(t)$, $y = g(t)$, where f and g are polynomials in t of degree 3. A popular one, known as *B-splines*, has the characteristic that the generated curve will normally not pass through the given points. We will refer to all these points as *control points*. A single segment of such a curve, based on four control points A, B, C and D, looks rather disappointing in that it seems to be related only to B and C. This is shown in Figure 4.17, in which, from left to right, the points A, B, C and D are again marked with tiny squares.

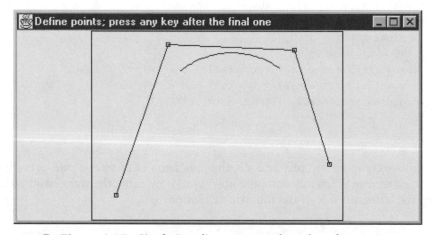

Define points; press any key after the final one

○ **Figure 4.17: Single B-spline segment, based on four points**

However, a strong point in favor of B-splines is that this technique makes it easy to draw a very smooth curve consisting of many curve segments. To avoid confusion, note that each curve segment consists of many straight-line segments. For example, Figure 4.17 shows one curve segment which consists of 50 line segments. Since four control points are required for a single curve segment, we have

number of control points = number of curve segments + 3

in this case. This equation also applies if there are several curve segments. At first sight, Figure 4.18 seems to violate this rule, since there are five curve segments, and it looks as if there are only six control points. However, two of these were used twice. This curve was constructed by clicking first on the lower-left vertex (= point 0), followed by clicking on the upper-left one (= point 1), then the upper-right one (= point 2), and so on, following the polygon clockwise. Altogether, the eight control points 0, 1, 2, 3, 4, 5, 0, 1 were selected, in that order. If after this, a key on the keyboard is pressed, only the curve is redrawn, not the control points and the lines that connect them.

If we had clicked on yet another control point (point 2, at the top, right), we would have had a closed curve. In general, to produce a closed curve, there must be three overlapping vertices, that is, two overlapping polygon edges. As you can see in Figure 4.18, the curve is very smooth indeed: we have second-order continuity, as discussed in the previous section. Recall that this implies that even the curvature is continuous in the points where two adjacent curve segments meet. As the part of the curve near the lower-right corner shows, we can make the distance between a curve and the given points very small by supplying several points close together.

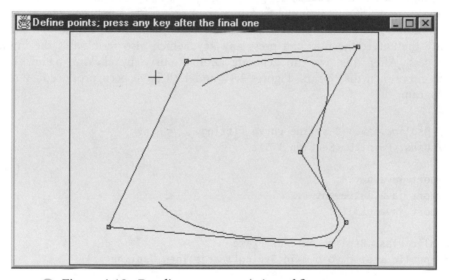

⭕ **Figure 4.18: B-spline curve consisting of five curve segments**

The mathematics of B-splines can be expressed by the following matrix equation, similar to Equation (4.20):

$$B(t) = \tfrac{1}{6} \begin{bmatrix} t^3 & t^2 & t & 1 \end{bmatrix} \begin{bmatrix} -1 & 3 & -3 & 1 \\ 3 & -6 & 3 & 0 \\ -3 & 0 & 3 & 0 \\ 1 & 4 & 1 & 0 \end{bmatrix} \begin{bmatrix} P_0 \\ P_1 \\ P_2 \\ P_3 \end{bmatrix} \qquad (4.21)$$

If we have n control points P_0, P_1, ..., P_{n-1} ($n \geq 4$) then, strictly speaking, Equation (4.21) applies only to the first curve segment. For the second, we have to replace the points P_0, P_1, P_2 and P_3 in the column vector with P_1, P_2, P_3 and P_4, and so on. As with Bézier curves, the variable t ranges from 0 to 1 for each curve segment. Multiplying the above 4×4 matrix by the column vector that follows it, we obtain

$$B(t) = \frac{1}{6} [\ t^3 \quad t^2 \quad t \quad 1\ ] \begin{bmatrix} -P_0 + 3P_1 - 3P_2 + P_3 \\ 3P_0 - 6P_1 + 3P_2 \\ -3P_0 + 3P_2 \\ P_0 + 4P_1 + P_2 \end{bmatrix}$$

or

$$B(t) = \frac{1}{6}(-P_0 + 3P_1 - 3P_2 + P_3)t^3 + \frac{1}{2}(P_0 - 2P_1 + P_2)t^2 + \frac{1}{2}(-P_0 + P_2)t$$
$$+ \frac{1}{6}(P_0 + 4P_1 + P_2)$$

The following program is based on this equation. The user can click any number of points, which are used as the points $P_0, P_1, \ldots, P_{n-1}$. The first curve segment appears immediately after the fourth control point, P_3, has been defined, and each additional control point causes a new curve segment to appear. To show only the curve, the user can press any key, which also terminates the input process. After this, we can generate another curve by clicking again. The old curve then disappears. Figures 4.17 and 4.18 have been produced by this program:

```
// Bspline.java: B-spline curve fitting.
// Uses: Point2D (Section 1.5).

import java.awt.*;
import java.awt.event.*;
import java.util.*;

public class Bspline extends Frame
{  public static void main(String[] args){new Bspline();}

   Bspline()
   {  super("Define points; press any key after the final one");
      addWindowListener(new WindowAdapter()
         {public void windowClosing(WindowEvent e){System.exit(0);}});
      setSize (500, 300);
      add("Center", new CvBspline());

      setCursor(Cursor.getPredefinedCursor(Cursor.CROSSHAIR_CURSOR));
      show();
   }
}

class CvBspline extends Canvas
```

```
{  Vector V = new Vector();
   int np = 0, centerX, centerY;
   float rWidth = 10.0F, rHeight = 7.5F, eps = rWidth/100F, pixelSize;
   boolean ready = false;

   CvBspline()
   {  addMouseListener(new MouseAdapter()
      {  public void mousePressed(MouseEvent evt)
         {  float x = fx(evt.getX()), y = fy(evt.getY());
            if (ready)
            {  V.removeAllElements();
               np = 0;
               ready = false;
            }
            V.addElement(new Point2D(x, y));
            np++;
            repaint();
         }
      });

      addKeyListener(new KeyAdapter()
      {  public void keyTyped(KeyEvent evt)
         {  evt.getKeyChar();
            if (np >= 4) ready = true;
            repaint();
         }
      });
   }

   void initgr()
   {  Dimension d = getSize();
      int maxX = d.width - 1, maxY = d.height - 1;
      pixelSize = Math.max(rWidth/maxX, rHeight/maxY);
      centerX = maxX/2; centerY = maxY/2;
   }
   int iX(float x){return Math.round(centerX + x/pixelSize);}
   int iY(float y){return Math.round(centerY - y/pixelSize);}
   float fx(int x){return (x - centerX) * pixelSize;}
   float fy(int y){return (centerY - y) * pixelSize;}

   void bspline(Graphics g, Point2D[] p)
   {  int m = 50, n = p.length;
      float xA, yA, xB, yB, xC, yC, xD, yD,
```

```
         a0, a1, a2, a3, b0, b1, b2, b3, x=0, y=0, x0, y0;
      boolean first = true;
      for (int i=1; i<n-2; i++)
      { xA=p[i-1].x; xB=p[i].x; xC=p[i+1].x; xD=p[i+2].x;
        yA=p[i-1].y; yB=p[i].y; yC=p[i+1].y; yD=p[i+2].y;
        a3=(-xA+3*(xB-xC)+xD)/6; b3=(-yA+3*(yB-yC)+yD)/6;
        a2=(xA-2*xB+xC)/2;       b2=(yA-2*yB+yC)/2;
        a1=(xC-xA)/2;            b1=(yC-yA)/2;
        a0=(xA+4*xB+xC)/6;       b0=(yA+4*yB+yC)/6;
        for (int j=0; j<=m; j++)
        { x0 = x;
          y0 = y;
          float t = (float)j/(float)m;
          x = ((a3*t+a2)*t+a1)*t+a0;
          y = ((b3*t+b2)*t+b1)*t+b0;
          if (first) first = false;
          else
             g.drawLine(iX(x0), iY(y0), iX(x), iY(y));
        }
      }
   }

   public void paint(Graphics g)
   { initgr();
     int left = iX(-rWidth/2), right = iX(rWidth/2),
         bottom = iY(-rHeight/2), top = iY(rHeight/2);
     g.drawRect(left, top, right - left, bottom - top);
     Point2D[] p = new Point2D[np];
     V.copyInto(p);
     if (!ready)
     { for (int i=0; i<np; i++)
       { // Show tiny rectangle around point:
         g.drawRect(iX(p[i].x)-2, iY(p[i].y)-2, 4, 4);
         if (i > 0)
            // Draw line p[i-1]p[i]:
            g.drawLine(iX(p[i-1].x), iY(p[i-1].y),
                       iX(p[i].x), iY(p[i].y));
       }
     }
     if (np >= 4) bspline(g, p);
   }
}
```

To see why B-splines are so smooth, you should differentiate $B(t)$ twice and verify that, for any curve segment other than the final one, the values of $B(1)$, $B'(1)$ and $B''(1)$ at the endpoints of these segments are equal to the values $B(0)$, $B'(0)$ and $B''(0)$ at the start point of the next curve segment. For example, for the continuity of the curve itself we find

$$B(1) = \tfrac{1}{6}(-P_0 + 3P_1 - 3P_2 + P_3) + \tfrac{1}{2}(P_0 - 2P_1 + P_2) + \tfrac{1}{2}(-P_0 + P_2)$$
$$+ \tfrac{1}{6}(P_0 + 4P_1 + P_2)$$
$$= \tfrac{1}{6}(P_1 + 4P_2 + P_3)$$

for the first curve segment, based on P_0, P_1, P_2 and P_3, while we can immediately see that we obtain exactly this value if we compute $B(0)$ for the second curve segment, based on P_1, P_2, P_3 and P_4.

EXERCISES

4.1 Replace the *drawLine* method based on Bresenham's algorithm and listed near the end of Section 4.1 with an even faster version that benefits from the symmetry of the two halves of the line. For example, with endpoints P and Q satisfying Equation (4.1), and using the integer value x_{Mid} halfway between x_P and x_Q, we can let the variable x run from x_P to x_{Mid} and also use a variable x_2, which at the same time runs backward from x_Q to x_{Mid}. In each iteration of the loop, x is increased by 1 and x_2 is decreased by 1. Note that there will be either one point or two points in the middle of the line, depending on the number of pixels to be plotted being odd or even. Be sure that no pixel of the line is omitted and that no pixel is put twice on the screen. To test the latter, you can use XOR mode so that writing the same pixel twice would have the same effect as omitting a pixel.

4.2 Generalize the method *doubleStep2* (of Section 4.2), to make it work for any lines.

4.3 Since normal pixels are very small, they do not show very clearly which of them are selected by Bresenham's algorithms. Use a grid to simulate a screen with a very low resolution. Demonstrate both the method *drawLine* (with g as its first argument) of Section 4.1 and the method *drawCircle* of Section 4.3. Only the gridpoints of your grid are to be used as the centers of 'superpixels'. The method *putPixel* is to draw a small circle with such a center and the distance *dGrid* of

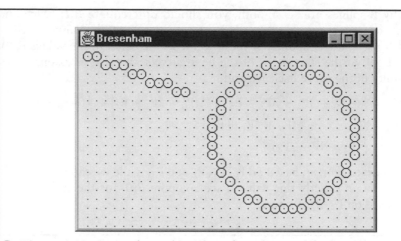

○ **Figure 4.19: Bresenham algorithms for a line and for a circle (see also Figures 4.1 and 4.6)**

two neighboring gridpoints as its diameter. Do not change the methods *drawLine* and *drawCircle* that we have developed, but use *dGrid*, just mentioned, in a method *putPixel* that is very different from the one shown at the beginning of Section 4.1. Figure 4.19 shows a grid (with $dGrid = 10$) and both a line and a circle drawn in this way. As in Figure 4.1, the line shown here has the endpoints P(1, 1) and Q(12, 5) but this time the positive *y*-axis points downward and the origin is the upper-left corner of the drawing rectangle. The circle has radius $r = 8$, and is approximated by the same pixels as shown in Figure 4.6 for one eighth of this circle. The line and circle were produced by the following calls to the methods *drawLine* and *drawCircle* of Sections 4.1 and 4.3 (but with a different method *putPixel*):

```
drawLine(g, 1, 1, 12, 5);   // g, xP, yP, xQ, yQ
drawCircle(g, 23, 10, 8);   // g, xC, yC, r
```

4.4   In the *Bezier.java* program we constructed only one curve segment, using the points P_0, P_1, P_2 and P_3. Extend this program to enable the user to draw very smooth curves consisting of more than one segment. After the first segment has been drawn, the second one is based on these points Q_0, Q_1, Q_2 and Q_3 (similar to P_0, P_1, P_2 and P_3):
• Q_0 is identical with P_3; clicking on P_3 acts as a signal that we want to start another curve segment.

- Q_1 is not specified by the user, but is automatically constructed by reflecting P_2 about P_3; in other words, P_3 (= Q_0) will be the midpoint of P_2Q_1. This principle will make the curve very smooth.
- Q_2 and Q_3 are defined in the usual way, that is, by clicking on these points.

It should also be possible to specify a third curve segment by starting at Q_3, and so on. When the curve (consisting of an arbitrary number of segments) is completed, the user clicks on a point other than the final one of the last segment. This will be the starting point (similar to P_0) of an entirely new curve (to be drawn in addition to the previous one), unless, after this, the user clicks on this new point once again: this clicking twice on the same point will be the signal that the drawing is ready. As soon as a curve is completed, it is to be drawn without displaying any straight lines connecting control points and without any little squares marking these points.

4.5 Extend the program *Bspline.java* of Section 4.7. Supply a grid, with visible gridpoints lying, say, 10 pixels apart, horizontally and vertically. Any control point specified by the user using the mouse should be pulled to the nearest gridpoint. This makes it easier for the user to specify two or more points that lie on the same horizontal or vertical line. Apart from using a grid, your program will also be different from *Bspline.java* in that it must be able to store several B-spline curves instead of only one. The following characters are to be interpreted as commands:

+ Increase the distance between gridpoints by one.
− Decrease the distance between gridpoints by one.
n After this command, start with a new curve, retaining the previous ones.
d Delete the last curve.
g Change the visibility status of gridpoints (visible/invisible).
c Show only the curves, without any control points or lines connecting these.

4.6 Implement a restricted version of Bresenham's line-drawing algorithm as a demonstration. The purpose of the exercise is to visualize how this algorithm works by showing its stepwise execution on an exaggerated screen area as a 10×10 grid. Draw the grid on the left half of the drawing space and the main body of method *drawLine2* (listed

in Section 4.1) on the right half with text font size of 14. At the bottom
of the drawing space, add both a button labeled *Step* and a small space
for displaying the values of the program variables dx, c, m, d, x and
y. When the user clicks on two intersection points P and Q, satisfying
Equations (4.1), on the grid, a thin line is drawn and the initial values
of the program variables d and m are displayed. Just after the definition
of point Q, the call to *putPixel* is highlighted (by coloring or boxing
the statement), indicating that this program line is next to be executed.
Then whenever the user clicks on *Step*, the highlighted program line
is executed, the next program line in the right half is highlighted, and
the values of d, x and y are updated. Each time *putPixel* is executed, a
filled circle is drawn on the appropriate grid intersection (representing
a pixel on the line).

Chapter 5

Perspective

We now turn to the exciting subject of 3D graphics. As soon as we know how to compute the perspective image of a single point, we can easily produce more interesting images. To obtain the perspective image of a straight line, we simply connect the images of its endpoints, using the fact that the image of a straight line is also a straight line. In this chapter, the computation of the perspective image of a point is done in two steps: a viewing transformation followed by a perspective transformation.

5.1 INTRODUCTION

In Figure 5.1 a two-dimensional representation of a cube is shown along with some auxiliary lines. Although AB is a horizontal edge, it is not a horizontal line in the picture. Lines that in 3D space are horizontal and parallel meet in the picture in a so-called *vanishing point*. All these vanishing points lie on the same line, which is called the *horizon*. The horizon and vanishing points refer to the 2D image space, not to the 3D object space. For many centuries these concepts have been used by artists to draw realistic images of three-dimensional objects. This way of representing three-dimensional objects is usually referred to as *perspective*.

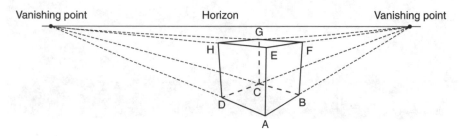

Figure 5.1: **Vanishing points on the horizon**

The invention of photography offered a new (and easier) way of producing images in perspective. There is a strong analogy between a camera used in photography and the human eye. Our eye is a very sophisticated instrument of which a camera is an imitation. In the following discussion the word *eye* may be replaced with *camera* if we want to emphasize that a two-dimensional hard copy is desired.

It is obvious that the image will depend upon the position of the eye. An important aspect is the distance between the eye and the object, since the effect of perspective will be inversely proportional to this distance. If the eye is close to the object, the effect of perspective is strong, as shown in Figure 5.2(a). Here we can very clearly see that in the image the extensions of parallel line segments meet.

Besides the classical and the photographic method, there is a way of producing perspective images which is based on analytical geometry. Let us write X and Y for 2D and x, y and z for 3D coordinates.

If we want to produce a drawing in perspective, we are given a great many points $P(x, y, z)$ of the object and we want their images $P'(X, Y)$ in the picture.

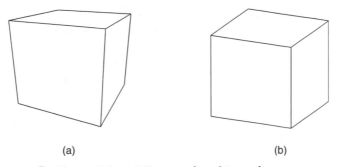

(a)   (b)

Figure 5.2: (a) Eye nearby; (b) eye far away

Thus all we need is a mapping from the *world coordinates* (x, y, z) of a point P
to the *screen coordinates* (X, Y) of its central projection P′. We imagine a screen
between the object and the eye E. For every point P of the object the line PE
intersects the screen at point P′. It is convenient to perform this mapping in two
stages. The first is called a *viewing transformation*; point P is left at its place,
but we change from world coordinates to so-called *eye coordinates*. The second
stage is called a *perspective transformation*. This is a proper transformation from
P to P′, combined with a transition from the three-dimensional eye coordinates
to the two-dimensional screen coordinates:

World coordinates (x_w, y_w, z_w)

Viewing transformation

Eye coordinates (x_e, y_e, z_e)

Perspective transformation

Screen coordinates (X, Y)

5.2 THE VIEWING TRANSFORMATION

To perform the viewing transformation we must be given not only an object
but also a viewpoint E. Let us require that the world-coordinate system be
right-handed. It is convenient if its origin O lies more or less centrally in the
object; we then view the object from E to O. We will assume this to be the
case; in practice this might require a coordinate transformation consisting of
decreasing the original world coordinates by the coordinates of the central

object point. We will include this very simple coordinate transformation in our program, without writing it down in mathematical notation.

Let the viewpoint E be given by its spherical coordinates $\rho(= rho)$, $\theta(= theta)$, $\varphi(= phi)$, relative to the world-coordinate system. Thus its world-coordinates are

$$x_E = \rho \sin \varphi \cos \theta$$
$$y_E = \rho \sin \varphi \sin \theta \qquad\qquad (5.1)$$
$$z_E = \rho \cos \varphi$$

as shown in Figure 5.3.

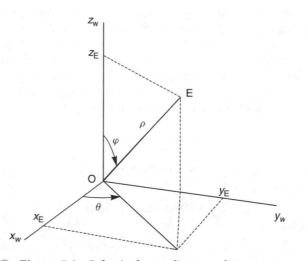

Figure 5.3: Spherical coordinates of viewpoint E

The direction of vector $\mathbf{EO}(= -\mathbf{OE})$ is said to be the viewing direction. From our eye at E we can only see points within some cone whose axis is EO and whose apex is E. If the Cartesian coordinates x_E, y_E, z_E of viewpoint E were given, we could derive the spherical coordinates from them as follows:

```
rho = Math.sqrt(xE * xE + yE * yE + zE * zE);
theta = Math.atan2(yE, xE);
phi = Math.acos(zE/rho);
```

Our final objective will be to compute the screen coordinates X, Y, where we have an X-axis and a Y-axis, lying in a screen between E and O and perpendicular to the viewing direction EO. This is why the eye-coordinate system will have its x_e-axis and y_e-axis perpendicular to EO, leaving the z_e-axis in the direction of OE. The origin of the eye-coordinate system is viewpoint E, as shown in Figure 5.4. Viewing from E to O, we find the positive x_e-axis pointing to the right and the positive y_e-axis upwards. These directions will enable us later to establish screen axes in the same directions. We could have used a positive z_e-axis pointing from E to O; on the one hand this is attractive because it makes the z_e-coordinates of all object points positive, but, on the other hand, it would have required a left-handed eye-coordinate system. In this book we will use a right-handed eye-coordinate system (as shown in Figure 5.4) to avoid confusion with regard to the use of the cross product, taking the minus sign of z_e-coordinates into the bargain.

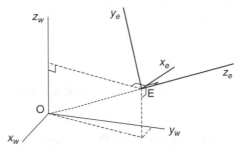

Figure 5.4: Eye-coordinate system

The viewing transformation can be written as a matrix multiplication, for which we need the 4×4 *viewing matrix* V:

$$[x_e \quad y_e \quad z_e \quad 1] = [x_w \quad y_w \quad z_w \quad 1]V \tag{5.2}$$

To find V, we imagine this transformation to be composed of three elementary ones, for which the matrices can easily be written down. Matrix V will be the product of these three matrices. Each of the three transformations is in fact a change of coordinates and has therefore a matrix which is the inverse of the matrix for an equivalent point transformation.

(1) Moving the origin from O to E

We perform a translation of the coordinate system such that viewpoint E becomes the new origin. The matrix for this change of coordinates is

$$T = \begin{bmatrix} 1 & 0 & 0 & 0 \\ 0 & 1 & 0 & 0 \\ 0 & 0 & 1 & 0 \\ -x_E & -y_E & -z_E & 1 \end{bmatrix} \tag{5.3}$$

(Do not confuse x_E, y_E, z_E, the world coordinates of viewpoint E, with x_e, y_e, z_e, the eye coordinates of any point.) The new coordinate system is shown in Figure 5.5.

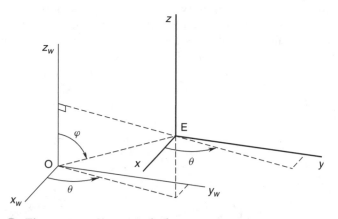

○ **Figure 5.5: Situation before rotation about the z-axis**

(2) Rotating the coordinate system about the z-axis

Starting with Figure 5.5 we rotate the coordinate system about the z-axis through the angle $\theta + 90°$, so the new x-axis points to the right and is perpendicular to the vertical plane through E and O. The matrix for this change of coordinates is the same as that for a rotation of points through the angle $-(\theta + 90°)$, which equals $-\theta - 90°$. We obtain the 4×4 matrix R_z for this rotation by including a 2×2 matrix, as discussed in Section 3.2, and adding the third and fourth columns and rows of a 4×4 unit matrix:

$$R_z = \begin{bmatrix} \cos(-\theta - 90°) & \sin(-\theta - 90°) & 0 & 0 \\ -\sin(-\theta - 90°) & \cos(-\theta - 90°) & 0 & 0 \\ 0 & 0 & 1 & 0 \\ 0 & 0 & 0 & 1 \end{bmatrix}$$

$$= \begin{bmatrix} -\sin\theta & -\cos\theta & 0 & 0 \\ \cos\theta & -\sin\theta & 0 & 0 \\ 0 & 0 & 1 & 0 \\ 0 & 0 & 0 & 1 \end{bmatrix} \tag{5.4}$$

If you find the simplifications

$$\cos(-\theta - 90°) = -\sin\theta \quad \text{and} \quad \sin(-\theta - 90°) = -\cos\theta$$

difficult, it will be helpful to plot the two angles of this formula in a unit circle for some value of θ, as Figure 5.6 illustrates.

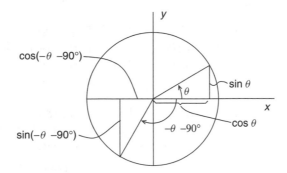

○ **Figure 5.6: Relating the sine and cosine of $-\theta - 90°$ to those of θ**

After applying the above matrix R_z, the new position of the x-, y- and z-axes is as shown in Figure 5.7.

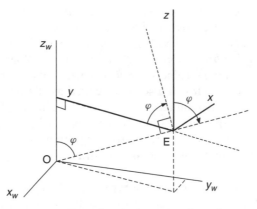

○ **Figure 5.7: Situation before rotation about x-axis**

(3) Rotating the coordinate system about the x-axis

Since the z-axis is to have the direction **OE**, we now rotate the coordinate system about the x-axis through the angle φ. The dashed line near the positive z-axis in Figure 5.7 indicates the new y-axis after this rotation. A rotation about the x-axis is said to be *positive* if the y-axis goes towards the z-axis (through an angle of 90°). It corresponds to the turning of a normal, right-handed screw which moves forward in the direction of the positive x-axis. However, since we are performing a coordinate transformation instead of rotating points, we have to use $-\varphi$ instead of φ as the angle of rotation, so that we obtain the following rotation matrix:

$$R_x = \begin{bmatrix} 1 & 0 & 0 & 0 \\ 0 & \cos(-\varphi) & \sin(-\varphi) & 0 \\ 0 & -\sin(-\varphi) & \cos(-\varphi) & 0 \\ 0 & 0 & 0 & 1 \end{bmatrix} = \begin{bmatrix} 1 & 0 & 0 & 0 \\ 0 & \cos\varphi & -\sin\varphi & 0 \\ 0 & \sin\varphi & \cos\varphi & 0 \\ 0 & 0 & 0 & 1 \end{bmatrix}$$

$$(5.5)$$

After this final rotation, we have obtained the eye-coordinate system with x_e-, y_e- and z_e-axes, which we have already seen in Figure 5.4. Multiplying the above matrices T, R_z and R_x, we obtain the desired viewing matrix:

$$V = TR_z R_x = \begin{bmatrix} -\sin\theta & -\cos\varphi\cos\theta & \sin\varphi\cos\theta & 0 \\ \cos\theta & -\cos\varphi\sin\theta & \sin\varphi\sin\theta & 0 \\ 0 & \sin\varphi & \cos\varphi & 0 \\ 0 & 0 & -\rho & 1 \end{bmatrix}$$

$$(5.6)$$

Recall that we use this matrix in Equation (5.2), to compute the eye coordinates x_e, y_e and z_e from the given world coordinates x_w, y_w and z_w.

The viewing transformation described above is to be followed by the perspective transformation to be discussed in the next section. However, we could also use the eye coordinates x_e and y_e, simply ignoring z_e. In that case we have a so-called *orthographic projection*. Every point P of the object is then projected into a point P′ by drawing a line from P, perpendicular to the plane through the x-axis and the y-axis. It can also be regarded as the perspective image we obtain if the viewpoint is infinitely far away. An example of such a picture is the cube in Figure 5.2(b). Parallel lines remain parallel in pictures obtained by orthographic projection. Such pictures are very often used in practice because with conventional methods they are easier to draw than real perspective images.

On the other hand, bringing some perspective into the picture will make it much more realistic. Our viewing transformation will therefore be followed by the perspective transformation, which will involve surprisingly little computation.

5.3 THE PERSPECTIVE TRANSFORMATION

You might have the impression that we are only half-way, and that in this section we will need as much mathematics as in Section 5.2. However, most of the work has already been done. Since we will not use world coordinates in this section, there will be no confusion if we denote eye coordinates simply by (x, y, z) instead of (x_e, y_e, z_e).

In Figure 5.8 we have chosen a point Q, whose eye coordinates are $(0, 0, -d)$ for some positive value d.

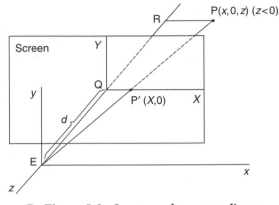

◯ **Figure 5.8: Screen and eye coordinates**

Our screen will be the plane $z = -d$, that is, the plane through Q and perpendicular to the z-axis. Then the screen-coordinate system has Q as its origin, and its X- and Y-axes are parallel to the x- and y-axes. For every object point P, the image point P$'$ is the intersection of line PE and the screen. To keep Figure 5.8 simple, we consider a point P whose y-coordinate is zero. However, the following equations to compute its screen coordinate X are also valid for other y-coordinates. In Figure 5.8 the triangles EPR and EP$'$Q are similar. Hence

$$\frac{P'Q}{EQ} = \frac{PR}{ER}$$

so we have

$$\frac{X}{d} = \frac{x}{-z}$$

(Recall that z-coordinates of object points are negative, so that $-z$ is a positive value.) In other words,

$$X = -d \cdot \frac{x}{z} \tag{5.7}$$

In the same way we can derive

$$Y = -d \cdot \frac{y}{z} \tag{5.8}$$

At the beginning of Section 5.2 we chose the origin O of the world-coordinate system to be a central point of the object. The origin Q of the screen-coordinate system will be central in the image because the z-axis of the eye-coordinate system is a line through E and O, which intersects the screen at Q. We must bear in mind that Equations (5.7) and (5.8) can be used in this form only if the origin Q of the screen coordinate system (with X- and Y-axes) lies in the center of the screen. If this origin lies instead in the lower-left corner of the screen

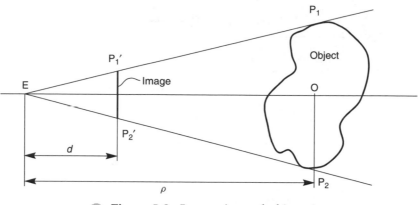

○ **Figure 5.9: Image size and object size**

and the screen has width w and height h, we have to add $w/2$ and $h/2$ to the Equations (5.7) and (5.8), respectively.

We still have to specify the distance d between viewpoint E and the screen. Roughly speaking, we have

$$\frac{d}{\rho} = \frac{\text{image size}}{\text{object size}}$$

which follows from the similarity of the triangles $EP_1'P_2'$ and EP_1P_2 in Figure 5.9. Thus we have

$$d = \rho \cdot \frac{\text{image size}}{\text{object size}} \tag{5.9}$$

This equation should be applied to both the horizontal and the vertical directions. It should be interpreted only as a means to obtain an indication about an appropriate value for d, for the three-dimensional object may have a complicated shape, and it may not be clear how its size is to be measured. We then use a rough estimation of the object size, such as the maximum of its length, width and height. The image size in Equation (5.9) should be taken somewhat smaller than the screen.

5.4 A CUBE IN PERSPECTIVE

We will now discuss a complete Java program, which draws a perspective representation of a cube, as shown in Figure 5.10. Such representations, with all edges visible, are called *wire-frame* models.

To specify this cube in a program, we assign numbers to its vertices, as shown in Figure 5.11. The center of the cube coincides with the origin O and its edges

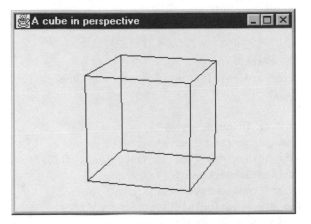

○ **Figure 5.10: Output of program *CubePers.java***

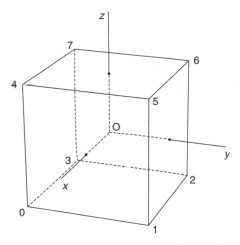

○ **Figure 5.11: Vertex numbers and coordinate axes**

have length 2, which implies that the x-, y- and z-coordinates of its eight vertices are equal to $+1$ or -1.

The following program produces the wire-frame model of Figure 5.10. We store the world, eye and screen coordinates for each of the eight vertices of the cube in the class *Obj*:

```
// CubePers.java: A cube in perspective.
// Uses: Point2D (Section 1.5), Point3D (Section 3.9).
```

```java
import java.awt.*;
import java.awt.event.*;

public class CubePers extends Frame
{  public static void main(String[] args){new CubePers();}

   CubePers()
   {  super("A cube in perspective");
      addWindowListener(new WindowAdapter()
         {public void windowClosing(WindowEvent e){System.exit(0);}});
      setLayout(new BorderLayout());
      add("Center", new CvCubePers());
      Dimension dim = getToolkit().getScreenSize();
      setSize(dim.width/2, dim.height/2);
      setLocation(dim.width/4, dim.height/4);
      show();
   }
}

class CvCubePers extends Canvas
{  int centerX, centerY;
   Obj obj = new Obj();

   int iX(float x){return Math.round(centerX + x);}
   int iY(float y){return Math.round(centerY - y);}

   void line(Graphics g, int i, int j)
   {  Point2D p = obj.vScr[i], q = obj.vScr[j];
      g.drawLine(iX(p.x), iY(p.y), iX(q.x), iY(q.y));
   }

   public void paint(Graphics g)
   {  Dimension dim = getSize();
      int maxX = dim.width - 1, maxY = dim.height - 1,
          minMaxXY = Math.min(maxX, maxY);
      centerX = maxX/2; centerY = maxY/2;
      obj.d = obj.rho * minMaxXY / obj.objSize;
      obj.eyeAndScreen();
      // Horizontal edges at the bottom:
      line(g, 0, 1); line(g, 1, 2); line(g, 2, 3); line(g, 3, 0);
      // Horizontal edges at the top:
      line(g, 4, 5); line(g, 5, 6); line(g, 6, 7); line(g, 7, 4);
      // Vertical edges:
```

```
      line(g, 0, 4); line(g, 1, 5); line(g, 2, 6); line(g, 3, 7);
   }
}

class Obj // Contains 3D object data
{  float rho, theta=0.3F, phi=1.3F, d, objSize,
         v11, v12, v13, v21, v22, v23, v32, v33, v43;
                    // Elements of viewing matrix V
   Point3D[] w;      // World coordinates
   Point2D[] vScr;  // Screen coordinates
   Obj()
   {  w = new Point3D[8];
      vScr = new Point2D[8];
      // Bottom surface:
      w[0] = new Point3D( 1, -1, -1);
      w[1] = new Point3D( 1,  1, -1);
      w[2] = new Point3D(-1,  1, -1);
      w[3] = new Point3D(-1, -1, -1);
      // Top surface:
      w[4] = new Point3D( 1, -1,  1);
      w[5] = new Point3D( 1,  1,  1);
      w[6] = new Point3D(-1,  1,  1);
      w[7] = new Point3D(-1, -1,  1);
      objSize = (float)Math.sqrt (12F);
         // = sqrt(2 * 2 + 2 * 2 + 2 * 2)
         // = distance between two opposite vertices.
      rho = 5 * objSize; // For reasonable perspective effect
   }

   void initPersp()
   {  float costh = (float)Math.cos(theta),
            sinth = (float)Math.sin(theta),
            cosph = (float)Math.cos(phi),
            sinph = (float)Math.sin(phi);
      v11 = -sinth; v12 = -cosph * costh; v13 = sinph * costh;
      v21 = costh;  v22 = -cosph * sinth; v23 = sinph * sinth;
                    v32 = sinph;          v33 = cosph;
                                          v43 = -rho;
   }

   void eyeAndScreen()
   {  initPersp();
      for (int i=0; i<8; i++)
```

```
    {  Point3D p = w[i];
       float x = v11 * p.x + v21 * p.y,
             y = v12 * p.x + v22 * p.y + v32 * p.z,
             z = v13 * p.x + v23 * p.y + v33 * p.z + v43;
       vScr[i] = new Point2D(-d * x/z, -d * y/z);
    }
  }
}
```

As discussed in Section 5.3 (see point Q in Figure 5.8), the perspective transformation is simplest if we use a coordinate system with the origin in the center of the screen and with a *y*-axis pointing upward. To convert such (floating-point) coordinates to device coordinates of type *int*, we again use the methods *iX* and *iY*. As usual, these are based on the values of the fields *centerX*, *centerY* and *maxY*, which are computed in the *paint* method before this method uses *iX* and *iY*.

The *paint* method also computes the screen distance *d* (stored in *obj*), using Equation (5.9). After calling the *Obj* method *eyeAndScreen* to compute eye and screen coordinates, we use our method *line* to draw all 12 cube edges.

In the class *Obj*, the arrays *w* and *vScr* contain the world and the screen coordinates, respectively, of the cube vertices. Recall that we use the matrix multiplication of Equation (5.2) to compute the eye coordinates from the given world coordinates stored in *w*. We then use these eye coordinates to compute the screen coordinates for the array *vScr*. Figure 5.11 is helpful in specifying the coordinate values in the array *w* and the vertex numbers in calls to the *line* method.

5.5 SOME USEFUL CLASSES

To avoid duplication of code, we now present some classes (*Input*, *Obj3D*, *Tria*, *Polygon3D*, *Canvas3D* and *Fr3D*) that we will frequently use later.

5.5.1 *Input*: A Class for File Input Operations

The first class we will discuss is *Input*. It is not really specific for computer graphics, but useful for any programming task that involves reading data from a textfile in a simple way. We will use it to read data for 3D objects, specified in a particular format. There is an *Input* constructor that accepts the name of an input file as an argument, as well as a constructor without any arguments to read data from the keyboard. To demonstrate how easy it is to use this class, let us suppose we are given a textfile containing only numbers and we want to write a program to read this file and compute the sum of these numbers. For example, this textfile, say, *example.txt*, may have the following contents:

```
2.5     6
200     100
```

Then the desired program is shown below:

```java
// Sum.java: Demonstrating the class Input by computing the sum
//    of all numbers in the textfile example.txt (which contains
//    only numbers and whitespace characters).
public class Sum
{  public static void main(String[] args)
   {  float x, s=0;
      Input inp = new Input("example.txt");
      for (;;)
      {  x = inp.readFloat();
         if (inp.fails())
            break;
         s += x;
      }
      System.out.println("The computed sum is " + s);
   }
}
```

After compiling and executing this program in a directory that also contains the files *Input.java* and *example.txt*, the following output line is displayed:

```
The computed sum is 308.5
```

This example demonstrates the use of the *Input* constructor and of the methods *readFloat* and *fails*. The complete class *Input*, listed below, shows that it contains some other useful methods as well:

```java
// Input.java: A class to read numbers and characters from textfiles.
// Methods of this class, available for other program files:
//    Input(fileName) (constructor; open input file)
//    Input()         (constructor; prepare for input from keyboard)
//    readInt()       (read an integer)
//    readFloat()     (read a float number)
//    readChar()      (read a character)
```

```
//   readString()    (read a string between double quotes)
//   skipRest()      (skip all remaining characters of current line)
//   fails()         (input operation failed)
//   eof()           (failure because of end of file)
//   clear()         (reset error flag)
//   close()         (close input file)
//   pushBack(ch)    (push character ch back into the input stream)
import java.io.*;

class Input
{  private PushbackInputStream pbis;
   private boolean ok = true;
   private boolean eoFile = false;

   Input(){pbis = new PushbackInputStream(System.in);}

   Input(String fileName)
   {  try
      {  InputStream is = new FileInputStream(fileName);
         pbis = new PushbackInputStream(is);
      }
      catch(IOException ioe){ok = false;}
   }

   int readInt()
   {  boolean neg = false;
      char ch;
      do {ch = readChar();}while (Character.isWhitespace(ch));
      if (ch == '-'){neg = true; ch = readChar();}
      if (!Character.isDigit(ch))
      {  pushBack(ch);
         ok = false;
         return 0;
      }
      int x = ch - '0';
      for (;;)
      {  ch = readChar();
         if (!Character.isDigit(ch)){pushBack(ch); break;}
         x = 10 * x + (ch - '0');
      }
      return (neg ? -x : x);
   }
```

```
float readFloat()
{   char ch;
    int nDec = -1;
    boolean neg = false;
    do
    {   ch = readChar();
    }   while (Character.isWhitespace(ch));
    if (ch == '-'){neg = true; ch = readChar();}
    if (ch == '.'){nDec = 1; ch = readChar();}
    if (!Character.isDigit(ch)){ok = false; pushBack(ch); return 0;}
    float x = ch - '0';
    for (;;)
    {   ch = readChar();
        if (Character.isDigit(ch))
        {   x = 10 * x + (ch - '0');
            if (nDec >= 0) nDec++;
        }
        else
        if (ch == '.' && nDec == -1) nDec = 0;
        else break;
    }
    while (nDec > 0){x *= 0.1; nDec--;}
    if (ch == 'e' || ch == 'E')
    {   int exp = readInt();
        if (!fails())
        {   while (exp < 0){x *= 0.1; exp++;}
            while (exp > 0){x *= 10; exp--;}
        }
    }
    else pushBack(ch);
    return (neg ? -x : x);
}

char readChar()
{   int ch=0;
    try
    {   ch = pbis.read();
        if (ch == -1) {eoFile = true; ok = false;}
    }
    catch(IOException ioe){ok = false;}
    return (char)ch;
}
```

```
String readString()  // Read first string between quotes (").
{  String str = " ";
   char ch;
   do ch = readChar(); while (!(eof() || ch == '"'));
                                       // Initial quote
   for (;;)
   {  ch = readChar();
      if (eof() || ch == '"') // Final quote (end of string)
         break;
      str += ch;
   }
   return str;
}

void skipRest()  // Skip rest of line
{  char ch;
   do ch = readChar(); while (!(eof() || ch == '\n'));
}

boolean fails(){return !ok;}
boolean eof(){return eoFile;}
void clear(){ok = true;}

void close()
{  if (pbis != null)
   try {pbis.close();}catch(IOException ioe){ok = false;}
}

void pushBack(char ch)
{  try {pbis.unread(ch);}catch(IOException ioe){}
}
}
```

Using a call to *readChar* immediately after *readInt* or *readFloat* causes the character immediately after the number to be read. To realize this, we use the standard Java class *PushbackInputStream*, which enables us to push back, or 'unread' the last character that we have read and that does not belong to the number we are reading.

After an attempt to read a number by using *readInt* or *readFloat*, we can call the *fails* method to check whether that attempt was successful. If *fails* returns *true*, a non-numeric character, such as a period in the second part of our input files, may have been read. It is then still possible to read that character by using *readChar*. The *clear* method resets the error flag, so that we can resume input, using *fails* again. The method *fails* also returns *true* if an input operation fails because the end of the file is encountered during a call to one of the methods *readInt*, *readFloat* and *readChar*. In that case, the *eof* method also returns *true*. We can use the method *readString* to read a string surrounded by double quotes (”), as we will do in Chapter 8. To skip all remaining characters of the current input line, we use the method *skipRest*.

5.5.2 *Obj3D*: A Class to Store 3D Objects

Let us now discuss the way the above class *Input* is used in the method *readObject* of the class *Obj3D*. Suppose we have an input file such as the one shown below:

```
1   0   0       0
2   0  100.5    0
3   0   0      1.5e2
Faces:
1 2 3.
3 2 1.
```

We will often use files of this type, which will be described in more detail in the next chapter. This example defines a 3D object that has only three vertices, with numbers 1, 2 and 3. The *x*-, *y*- and *z*-coordinates are given after each of these vertex numbers. The object has two faces, which are the two sides of the triangle with these three vertices. The first line following the word *Faces* indicates the side where we view the vertices 1, 2 and 3, in that order, counter-clockwise, while the last line denotes the other side. Obviously, which of these two triangle sides we can see depends on the point of view.

A simplified version of the *Obj3D* method *readObject* is shown below. It shows how the class *Input* can be used to read data files such as the one shown above. In this fragment three dots (. . .) denote code that is not relevant in this discussion because it does not perform any input operations:

```java
private boolean readObject(Input inp)
{  for (;;)
   {  int i = inp.readInt();
      if (inp.fails()){inp.clear(); break;}
      ...
      float x = inp.readFloat(),
            y = inp.readFloat(),
            z = inp.readFloat();
```

```
   addVertex(i, x, y, z);
}
...
do   // Skip the line "Faces:"
{  ch = inp.readChar(); count++;
}  while (!inp.eof() && ch != '\n');
...
// Build polygon list:
for (;;)
{  Vector vnrs = new Vector();
   for (;;)
   {  int i = inp.readInt();
      if (inp.fails()){inp.clear(); break;}
      ...
      vnrs.addElement(new Integer(i));
   }
   ch = inp.readChar();
   if (ch != '.') break;
   // Ignore input lines with only one vertex number:
   if (vnrs.size() >= 2)
      polyList.addElement(new Polygon3D(vnrs));
}
inp.close();
return true;
}
```

The above fragment is a simplified version of the method *readObject* of the class *Obj3D*, which we will now discuss in more detail. We will use this class to store all data of 3D objects, along with their 2D representations, in such a way that this data is easy to use in our programs. We store three representations of vertices:

'Vector' *w* of *Point*3D elements: world coordinates
Array *e* of *Point*3D elements: eye coordinates
Array *vScr* of *Point*2D elements: screen coordinates

Recall the classes *Point*2D and *Point*3D discussed in Sections 1.5 and 3.9. Since we read the world coordinates from an input file without knowing in advance how many vertices there will be, we use a Java *Vector* for them. This is different with the eye and screen coordinates. Since we compute these ourselves after we have read the world coordinates of all vertices, we know the size of the arrays *e* and *vScr*, so that we can allocate memory for them. We use the vertex numbers to indicate the positions in *w*, *e*, and *vScr*. In other words, with an input line of the form

$$i \quad x \quad y \quad z$$

we can find these world coordinates x, y and z of vertex i in the *Point3D* object

```
(Point3D)w.elementAt(i)
```

We use the *Obj3D* method *eyeAndScreen* to compute the corresponding eye coordinates and store them in the *Point3D* object

```
e[i]
```

This method also computes the corresponding screen coordinates and stores them in the *Point2D* object

```
vScr[i]
```

It follows that *w.size()*, *e.length* and *vScr.length* will be one higher than the highest vertex number that is in use.

We will use the accessor methods *getE()* and *getVScr()* for access to the arrays *e* and *vScr*. The *Vector* object *w* will not be used at all outside the class *Obj3D*.

Another useful method of *Obj3D* is *planeCoeff*. For each face (or polygon) of the object, it computes the coefficients a, b, c and h of the equation

$$ax + by + cz = h \tag{5.10}$$

which describes the plane where this face lies. Using the first three vertices A, B and C of a polygon, we compute the normal vector $\mathbf{n} = (a, b, c)$ of the plane as the vector product $\mathbf{AB} \times \mathbf{AC}$ (see Section 2.4), scaled such that

$$a^2 + b^2 + c^2 = 1$$

Using the inner product (see Section 2.2) of $\mathbf{n}$ and a vector $\mathbf{x} = \mathbf{EP}$ for any point P in the plane, we can write (5.10) as

$$\mathbf{n} \cdot \mathbf{x} = h$$

in which h is positive if the sequence A, B and C is clockwise, that is, if ABC is a back face. On the other hand, if ABC is not a back face, h is negative and the sequence A, B and C is counter-clockwise. Recall that the positive z-axis (in the eye-coordinate system) points towards us, as is more or less the case with the normal vector $\mathbf{n}$ of a visible face. However, the vector $\mathbf{x}$ points away from us, which implies that the inner product $\mathbf{n} \cdot \mathbf{x} = h$ will be negative for a visible face and positive for a back face. The absolute value of h is the distance between the eye E and the plane in question (see Exercise 7.1). We will use the coefficients a, b, c and h on several occasions. In the class *Obj3D*, the method *planeCoeff* computes these coefficients, after which they are stored in *Polygon3D* objects, as we will see shortly. This method *planeCoeff* also computes the maximum and minimum values of an inner product used to determine which color is to be assigned to each face, as we will discuss in Section 7.2.

Since the file *Obj3D.java* is considerably larger than the program files we have seen so far, it is not listed here but you can find it in Appendix C. Here is a summary of all methods of this class that we can use outside it:

```
boolean read(String fName)  // Reads a 3D object file, if possible.
Vector getPolyList()        // Returns polyList, the list of faces.
String getFName()           // File name of current object.
Point3D[] getE()            // Eye coordinates e of vertices.
Point2D[] getVScr()         // Screen coordinates vScr of vertices.
Point2D getImgCenter()      // Center of image in screen coordinates.
float getRho()              // Rho, the viewing distance.
float getD()                // d, scaling factor, also screen distance.
float eyeAndScreen          // Computes eye and screen coordinates and
                            // returns maximum screen-coordinate range.
void planeCoeff()           // Computes the coefficients a, b, c, h
                            // for all faces.
boolean vp(Canvas cv, float dTheta, float dPhi, float fRho)
                            // Changes the viewpoint.
int colorCode(double a, double b, double c)
                            // Computes the color code of a face.
```

We will discuss the method *colorCode* in detail in Section 7.2. The public *Obj3D* method *read* calls the private method *readObject*, discussed above, as the following fragment shows:

```
boolean read(String fName)
{  Input inp = new Input(fName);
   ...
   return readObject(inp); // Read from inp into obj
}
```

As we have seen in the simplified version of *readObject*, this method starts by repeatedly reading four numbers, i, x, y and z, and calls the method *addVertex*, which keeps track of the minimum and maximum values of x, y and z. The loop in which the four numbers are read terminates when an attempt to read a vertex number i fails because of the word *Faces*. The minimum and maximum coordinate values just mentioned are required for a call to the private method *shiftToOrigin*, which reduces all world coordinates such that the origin of the coordinate center will coincide with the center of the bounding box of the object.

After skipping the rest of the line on which we encounter the word *Faces*, we enter a loop to read vertex-number sequences representing polygons. Vertex numbers in these sequences may be preceded by a minus sign, as we will discuss in Chapter 6, so that the vertex numbers are actually the absolute values of the integers that we read.

Since we will often refer to the class *Obj3D*, let us have a look at a simplified version of it:

```
// Obj3D.java: A 3D object and its 2D representation.
// Uses: Point2D (Section 1.5), Point3D (Section 3.9),
//       Polygon3D, Input (Section 5.5).
...
class Obj3D
{  ...
   private Vector w = new Vector();        // World coordinates
   private Point3D[] e;                    // Eye coordinates
   private Point2D[] vScr;                 // Screen coordinates
   private Vector polyList = new Vector(); // Polygon3D objects
   ...
   private void addVertex(int i, float x, float y, float z)
   {  ...
   }
   ...
}
```

Recall that the complete version is listed in Appendix C.

5.5.3 *Tria*: A Class to Store Triangles by Their Vertex Numbers

We will often store large sets of triangles, the vertices of which have numbers in the same way as letters normally used in geometry. Since several triangles may share some vertices, it would not be efficient to store the coordinates of each vertex separately for every triangle. For example, suppose in 3D space we have a triangle with vertices 1, 2 and 3 and another with vertices 1, 4 and 2. It will then be efficient to set up a table with the x-, y- and z-coordinates of the four vertices 1, 2, 3 and 4, and denote the triangles only by their vertex numbers. The following class represents triangles in this way:

```
// Tria.java: Triangle represented by its vertex numbers.
class Tria
{   int iA, iB, iC;
    Tria(int i, int j, int k){iA = i; iB = j; iC = k;}
}
```

If there had been no 3D programs in this book other than that for wire-frame models, as discussed in Section 5.6, it would not have been necessary to store polygons, let alone triangles. We could then have restricted ourselves to the edges of 3D objects, that is, to line segments. We will nevertheless store the polygonal faces of the objects even in this chapter, to prepare for some more interesting programs where hidden lines or faces are not displayed.

5.5.4 *Polygon3D*: A Class to Store 3D Polygons

Almost at the end of the *Obj3D* method *readObject* you may have noticed the following statement:

```
polyList.addElement(new Polygon3D(vnrs));
```

Here a new *Polygon3D* object is created to store the vertex numbers of a polygon. This object is then added to the *Vector* object *polyList*, a private variable of the class *Obj3D*. The class *Polygon3D* contains a number of methods that we will not use in this chapter. These are related to triangles resulting from polygons and will be useful in the next two chapters, in which we will be dealing with algorithms to eliminate hidden lines and faces. Thanks to the above class *Tria*, the coordinates of the vertices of each triangle are not duplicated. Since they are stored in arrays that are data members of the *Obj3D* class, we only need to store the numbers *iA*, *iB* and *iC* of the vertices here. Although, in Section 2.13, we have already used a method *triangulate* to divide a polygon into triangles, we will need a slightly different one that represents vertices by numbers referring to the *Obj3D* class. This special method for triangulation is part of the class *Polygon3D*, listed below:

```
// Polygon3D.java: Polygon in 3D, represented by vertex numbers
//                 referring to coordinates stored in an Obj3D object.
import java.util.*;
```

```
class Polygon3D
{  private int[] nrs;
   private double a, b, c, h;
   private Tria[] t;
   Polygon3D(Vector vnrs)
   {  int n = vnrs.size();
      nrs = new int[n];
      for (int i=0; i<n; i++)
         nrs[i] = ((Integer)vnrs.elementAt(i)).intValue();
   }

   int[] getNrs(){return nrs;}
   double getA(){return a;}
   double getB(){return b;}
   double getC(){return c;}
   double getH(){return h;}
   void setAbch(double a, double b, double c, double h)
   {  this.a = a; this.b = b; this.c = c; this.h = h;
   }
   Tria[] getT(){return t;}

   void triangulate(Obj3D obj)
   // Successive vertex numbers (CCW) in vector nrs.
   // Resulting triangles will be put in array t.
   {  int n = nrs.length;          // n > 2 is required
      int[] next = new int[n];
      t = new Tria[n - 2];
      Point2D[] vScr = obj.getVScr();
      int iA=0, iB, iC;
      int j = n - 1;
      for (int i=0; i<n; i++){next[j] = i; j = i;}
      for (int k=0; k<n-2; k++)
      {  // Find a suitable triangle, consisting of two edges
         // and an internal diagonal:
         Point2D a, b, c;
         boolean found = false;
         int count = 0, nA = -1, nB = 0, nC = 0, nj;
         while (!found && ++count < n)
         {  iB = next[iA]; iC = next[iB];
            nA = Math.abs(nrs[iA]); a = vScr[nA];
            nB = Math.abs(nrs[iB]); b = vScr[nB];
            nC = Math.abs(nrs[iC]); c = vScr[nC];
```

```
            if (Tools2D.area2(a, b, c) >= 0)
            {  // Edges AB and BC; diagonal AC.
               // Test to see if no vertex (other than A,
               // B, C) lies within triangle ABC:
               j = next[iC]; nj = Math.abs(nrs[j]);
               while (j != iA &&
                       (nj == nA || nj == nB || nj == nC ||
                        !Tools2D.insideTriangle(a, b, c, vScr[nj])))
                  {  j = next[j]; nj = Math.abs(nrs[j]);
                  }
               if (j == iA)
               {  // Triangle found:
                  t[k] = new Tria(nA, nB, nC);
                  next[iA] = iC;
                  found = true;
               }
            }
            iA = next[iA];
         }
         if (count == n)
         {  // Degenerated polygon, possibly with all
            // vertices on one line.
            if (nA >= 0) t[k] = new Tria(nA, nB, nC);
            else
            { System.out.println("Nonsimple polygon");
              System.exit(1);
            }
         }
      }
   }
}
```

The vertex numbers of the given polygon are available in the array *nrs*, while those of each resulting triangle are stored in an element of the array *t*. The most difficult part of this class is the method *triangulate*, which is the 3D equivalent of the *Tools2D* method with the same name, discussed in Section 2.13 and not used in this chapter.

5.5.5 *Canvas3D*: An Abstract Class to Adapt the Java Class *Canvas*

The canvas classes we will be using will contain the methods *getObj* and *setObj*, to retrieve and store a reference to an *Obj3D* object. In view of a separate frame class, *Fr3D*, we need to define the following abstract class:

```
// Canvas3D.java: Abstract class.
import java.awt.*;

abstract class Canvas3D extends Canvas
{   abstract Obj3D getObj();
    abstract void setObj(Obj3D obj);
}
```

Remember, abstract classes are only useful to create subclasses, not to define objects. Any (non-abstract) subclass of *Canvas3D* is simply a subclass of the standard class *Canvas*, except that it is guaranteed to define the methods *getObj* and *setObj*. For example, in the next section we will discuss a class *CvWireframe* of which the first line reads

```
class CvWireframe extends Canvas3D
```

By writing here *Canvas3D* instead of *Canvas*, we are obliged to define the methods *getObj* and *setObj* in this *CvWireframe* class, and in return we are allowed to call these two methods for any object of class *CvWireframe*. We will clarify the use of the abstract class *Canvas3D* further at the end of this section.

5.5.6 *Fr3D*: A Frame Class for 3D Programs

The class *Fr3D* will be used in four non-trivial 3D programs of this book, *Wireframe.java* (Section 5.6), *HLines.java* (Chapter 6), *Painter.java* (Section 7.3) and *ZBuf.java* (Section 7.4). Since these programs will have the same menus, it makes sense to let them share the file *Fr3D.java*, listed below, in which much of the code is related to these menus. The Java compiler accepts the calls *cv.getObj()* and *cv.setObj(obj)* in this file because, as *Canvas3D* is an abstract class, the actual type of *cv* can only be a subclass of it. As we have just seen, this implies that this subclass will define the methods *getObj* and *setObj*:

```
// Fr3D.java: Frame class to deal with menu commands and other
//    user actions.
import java.awt.*;
import java.awt.event.*;
import java.util.*;

class Fr3D extends Frame implements ActionListener
{   protected MenuItem open, exit, eyeUp, eyeDown, eyeLeft, eyeRight,
        incrDist, decrDist;
    protected String sDir;
```

```
protected Canvas3D cv;
protected Menu mF, mV;

Fr3D(String argFileName, Canvas3D cv, String textTitle)
{ super(textTitle);
  addWindowListener(new WindowAdapter()
      {public void windowClosing(WindowEvent e){System.exit(0);}});
  this.cv = cv;
  MenuBar mBar = new MenuBar();
  setMenuBar(mBar);
  mF = new Menu("File");
  mV = new Menu("View");
  mBar.add(mF); mBar.add(mV);

  open = new MenuItem("Open",
      new MenuShortcut(KeyEvent.VK_O));
  eyeDown = new MenuItem("Viewpoint Down",
      new MenuShortcut(KeyEvent.VK_DOWN));
  eyeUp = new MenuItem("Viewpoint Up",
      new MenuShortcut(KeyEvent.VK_UP));
  eyeLeft = new MenuItem("Viewpoint to Left",
      new MenuShortcut(KeyEvent.VK_LEFT));
  eyeRight = new MenuItem("Viewpoint to Right",
      new MenuShortcut(KeyEvent.VK_RIGHT));

  incrDist = new MenuItem("Increase viewing distance",
      new MenuShortcut(KeyEvent.VK_INSERT));
  decrDist = new MenuItem("Decrease viewing distance",
      new MenuShortcut(KeyEvent.VK_DELETE));
  exit = new MenuItem("Exit",
      new MenuShortcut(KeyEvent.VK_Q));
  mF.add(open); mF.add(exit);
  mV.add(eyeDown); mV.add(eyeUp);
  mV.add(eyeLeft); mV.add(eyeRight);
  mV.add(incrDist); mV.add(decrDist);
  open.addActionListener(this);
  exit.addActionListener(this);
  eyeDown.addActionListener(this);
  eyeUp.addActionListener(this);
  eyeLeft.addActionListener(this);
  eyeRight.addActionListener(this);
  incrDist.addActionListener(this);
  decrDist.addActionListener(this);
```

```
    add("Center", cv);
    Dimension dim = getToolkit().getScreenSize();
    setSize(dim.width/2, dim.height/2);
    setLocation(dim.width/4, dim.height/4);
    if (argFileName != null)
    {  Obj3D obj = new Obj3D();
       if (obj.read(argFileName)){cv.setObj(obj); cv.repaint();}
    }
    cv.setBackground(new Color (180, 180, 255) );
    show();
}

void vp(float dTheta, float dPhi, float fRho) // Viewpoint
{  Obj3D obj = cv.getObj();
   if (obj == null || !obj.vp(cv, dTheta, dPhi, fRho))
      Toolkit.getDefaultToolkit().beep();
}

public void actionPerformed(ActionEvent ae)
{  if (ae.getSource() instanceof MenuItem)
   {  MenuItem mi = (MenuItem)ae.getSource();
      if (mi == open)
      {  FileDialog fDia = new FileDialog(Fr3D.this,
            "Open", FileDialog.LOAD);
         fDia.setDirectory(sDir);
         fDia.setFile("*.dat");
         fDia.show();
         String sDir1 = fDia.getDirectory();
         String sFile = fDia.getFile();
         String fName = sDir1 + sFile;
         Obj3D obj = new Obj3D();
         if (obj.read(fName))
         {  sDir = sDir1;
            cv.setObj(obj);
            cv.repaint();
         }
      }
      else
      if (mi == exit) System.exit(0); else
      if (mi == eyeDown) vp(0, .1F, 1); else
      if (mi == eyeUp) vp(0, -.1F, 1); else
      if (mi == eyeLeft) vp(-.1F, 0, 1); else
      if (mi == eyeRight) vp(.1F, 0, 1); else
```

```
        if (mi == incrDist) vp (0, 0, 2); else
        if (mi == decrDist) vp(0, 0, .5F);
    }
  }
}
```

Notice the use of the abstract class *Canvas3D* in the line

```
Fr3D(String argFileName, Canvas3D cv, String textTitle)
```

almost at the beginning of class *Fr3D*. We cannot replace *Canvas3D* with *Canvas* here because the compiler would not accept the statement

```
cv.setObj(obj);
```

in the if-statement near the end of the *Fr3D* constructor. After all, *setObj* is not a method of the standard Java class *Canvas*. Since, in the next section we will actually be using the class *CvWireframe*, of which *setObj* is really a method, it is tempting to write *CvWireframe* instead of *Canvas3D*. This would indeed work, but then we would not be able to use the class *Fr3D* also in programs with canvas classes other than *CvWireframe*, as we will do in Chapters 6 and 7. We now see that the abstract class *Canvas3D* is very useful. It is general enough to be used in several of our programs and yet less general than the standard *Canvas* class in that it 'promises' an implementation of the methods *setObj* and *getObj*. We will discuss some aspects of the class *Fr3D* in Chapter 7 when using it.

5.6 A GENERAL PROGRAM FOR WIRE-FRAME MODELS

It is now time to see the classes of the previous section in action. A relatively simple way of displaying 3D objects, bounded by polygons, is by drawing all the edges of these polygons, as we did for a cube in Section 5.4. The classes we have just seen enable us to write a general program *Wireframe.java*, which reads input files through a menu command *Open* and enables the user to view the object from any reasonable viewpoint, by using either menu commands or the keyboard. The comment lists all classes that *Wireframe.java* directly or indirectly uses.

```
// Wireframe.java: Perspective drawing using an input file that lists
//     vertices and faces.
```

```
// Uses: Point2D (Section 1.5),
//       Triangle, Tools2D (Section 2.13),
//       Point3D (Section 3.9),
//       Input, Obj3D, Tria, Polygon3D, Canvas3D, Fr3D (Section 5.5),
//       CvWireframe (Section 5.6).
import java.awt.*;

public class Wireframe extends Frame
{  public static void main(String[] args)
   {  new Fr3D(args.length > 0 ? args[0] : null, new CvWireframe(),
        "Wire-frame model");
   }
}
```

This rather simple program file accepts an optional program argument, which
may be supplied to specify the name of the input file. This is what the first
argument, a conditional expression, of the *Fr3D* constructor is about. The
second argument of this constructor generates an object of class *CvWireframe*,
which does almost all the work. Finally, the third argument specifies the text,
Wire-frame model, that we want to appear in the title bar of the window. The
class *CvWireframe* is listed below:

```
// CvWireframe.java: Canvas class for class Wireframe.
import java.awt.*;
import java.util.*;

class CvWireframe extends Canvas3D
{  private int maxX, maxY, centerX, centerY;
   private Obj3D obj;
   private Point2D imgCenter;

   Obj3D getObj(){return obj;}
   void setObj(Obj3D obj){this.obj = obj;}
   int iX(float x){return Math.round(centerX + x - imgCenter.x);}
   int iY(float y){return Math.round(centerY - y + imgCenter.y);}

   public void paint(Graphics g)
   {  if (obj == null) return;
      Vector polyList = obj.getPolyList();
      if (polyList == null) return;
      int nFaces = polyList.size();
      if (nFaces == 0) return;
```

```
Dimension dim = getSize();
maxX = dim.width - 1; maxY = dim.height - 1;
centerX = maxX/2; centerY = maxY/2;
// ze-axis towards eye, so ze-coordinates of
// object points are all negative.
// obj is a java object that contains all data:
// - Vector w        (world coordinates)
// - Array e         (eye coordinates)
// - Array vScr      (screen coordinates)
// - Vector polyList (Polygon3D objects)

// Every Polygon3D value contains:
// - Array 'nrs' for vertex numbers
// - Values a, b, c, h for the plane ax+by+cz=h.
// (- Array t (with nrs.length-2 elements of type Tria))

obj.eyeAndScreen(dim);
      // Computation of eye and screen coordinates.

imgCenter = obj.getImgCenter();
obj.planeCoeff();     // Compute a, b, c and h.
Point3D[] e = obj.getE();
Point2D[] vScr = obj.getVScr();

g.setColor(Color.black);

for (int j=0; j<nFaces; j++)
{ Polygon3D pol = (Polygon3D)(polyList.elementAt(j));
  int nrs[] = pol.getNrs();
  if (nrs.length < 3)
    continue;
  for (int iA=0; iA<nrs.length; iA++)
  { int iB = (iA + 1) % nrs.length;
    int na = Math.abs(nrs[iA]), nb = Math.abs(nrs[iB]);
    // abs in view of minus signs discussed in Section 6.4.
    Point2D a = vScr[na], b = vScr[nb];
    g.drawLine(iX(a.x), iY(a.y), iX(b.x), iY(b.y));
  }
}
   }
}
```

Thanks to the other classes discussed in the previous section, this program file is rather small. However, due to the object-oriented character of Java, the flow of control of the whole program may not be immediately clear. In particular, you may wonder how starting the program leads to reading a 3D object file and displaying the desired image. Let us begin with the *main* method in the file *Wireframe.java*. Here an *Fr3D* object is created by calling its constructor, and a *CvWireframe* object is created at the same time in the second argument of this constructor call. As we have seen in the previous section, the first line of class *Fr3D* reads

```
class Fr3D extends Frame implements ActionListener
```

which indicates that this class contains a method *actionPerformed*. This method is called when a menu command is given. In particular, the *Open* command in the *File* menu triggers the execution of a fragment that causes a standard dialog box for 'Open file' to appear, as you can see in the method *actionPerformed* at the end of Section 5.5. This fragment contains the following:

```
Obj3D obj = new Obj3D();
if (obj.read(fName))
{   sDir = sDir1;
    cv.setObj(obj);
    cv.repaint();
}
```

Here we see that the *Obj3D* method *read* is called, with the file name supplied by the user as an argument, so that this method can read any 3D object provided by the user. We also find here a call to *setObj*, a method defined in the above class *CvWireframe* as

```
void setObj(Obj3D obj){this.obj = obj;}
```

As a result, the *CvWireframe* class gets access to the *Obj3D* object that contains all data for the real 3D object. The above if-statement also contains a call to the standard Java *Canvas* method *repaint*, which calls the method *paint* of our *CvWireframe* class. The actual computation and display of the image are done in this method *paint*, although much of the computation work is delegated to methods of other classes. An example of this is the statement

```
obj.eyeAndScreen(dim);
```

which calls the *Obj3D* method *eyeAndScreen* to compute the eye and screen coordinates of the object.

5.6.1 A Demonstration

It is now time to see the program *Wireframe.java* in action. For example, let us use the object with vertices $1, 2, \ldots, 6$, shown in Figure 5.12.

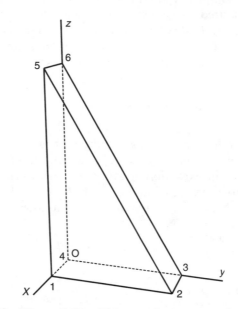

○ **Figure 5.12: Object and vertex numbers**

With dimensions 1, 3 and 5 for the thickness, the width and the height, respectively, the following data file specifies this object:

```
1    1 0 0
2    1 3 0
3    0 3 0
4    0 0 0
5    1 0 5
6    0 0 5
Faces:
1 2 5.
3 4 6.
2 3 6 5.
1 5 6 4.
1 4 3 2.
```

When running program *Wireframe.java* and opening the above input file, a window as shown in Figure 5.13 appears.

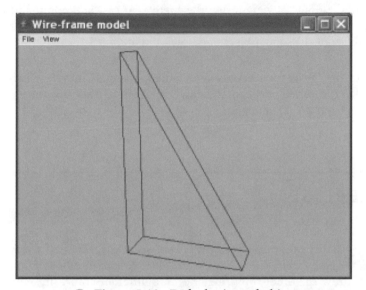

○ **Figure 5.13: Default view of object**

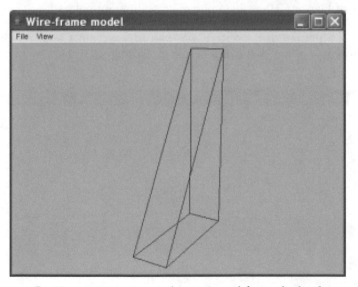

○ **Figure 5.14: Same object viewed from the back**

By moving the point of view, using the *Viewpoint to Right* command from the *View* menu or its shortcut *Ctrl+Arrow right* a number of times, we obtain a different view of the same object, as shown in Figure 5.14.

Note that the program chooses a default viewing distance which is quite reasonable. If desired we can increase or decrease this distance using two commands from the *View* menu.

EXERCISES

5.1   Modify program *CubePers.java* of Section 5.4 in such a way that, *with the given viewpoint*, only the visible edges are drawn as solid black lines; draw the other, invisible lines in a different color, or, as usually in mechanical engineering, as dashed lines (see Exercise 1.5).

5.2   Use a *fillPolygon* method to display only the top, right and front faces of Figure 5.10 as filled polygons of different colors.

5.3   To prepare for Exercise 5.5, extend program *CubePers.java* of Section 5.4 so that two cubes beside each other are generated.

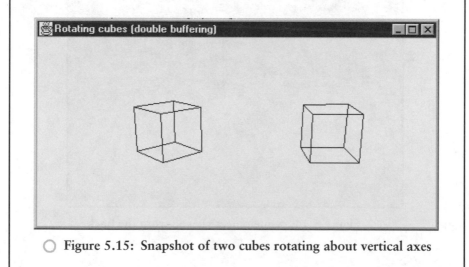

○ **Figure 5.15: Snapshot of two cubes rotating about vertical axes**

5.4   Use the class *Rota3D* of Section 3.9 to apply *animation with double buffering* to the cube of Section 5.4, using a rotation about some line, say, 0–6 (see Figure 5.11) through some small angle. If you are unfamiliar with animation in Java or with the Java class *Image*, required for double buffering, you will find the program *Anim.java* in Appendix F helpful.

5.5   As Exercise 5.4, but the rotation is to be applied to the two cubes of Exercise 5.3. Use different axes of rotation and increase the rotation angles for the two cubes by different amounts, so that the cubes seem to rotate independently of each other, with different speeds. Figure 5.15 shows a snapshot of the two cubes, each rotating about one of its vertical edges.

Chapter 6

Hidden–Line Elimination

Traditionally, engineers who want to display three-dimensional objects use line drawings, with black lines on white paper. Although line drawings might look rather dull compared with colored representations of such objects, there are many technical applications for which they are desired. We will now produce exactly the set of line segments that appear in the final result, so we will not put any pixels on the screen that we overwrite later, as we will do in Chapter 7. An advantage of this approach is that this set can also be used for output on a printer or a plotter. Since each of these line segments will be specified only by its endpoints, the possibly limited resolution of our computer screen does not affect the representation of the lines on the printer or plotter; in other words, these lines are of high quality. By using HP-GL (short for Hewlett-Packard Graphics Language) as our file format, we will be able to import the files we produce in text processors such as Microsoft Word. Still better, we can use drawing programs such as CorelDraw to read these files and then enhance the graphics results, for example, by adding text and changing the line type and thickness, before we import them into our documents. In this book, most line drawings of 3D objects have been produced in this way.

6.1 LINE SEGMENTS AND TRIANGLES

Although the faces of the objects we are dealing with can be polygons with any number of vertices, we will triangulate these polygons and use the resulting triangles instead. Suppose we are given a set of line segments PQ and a set of triangles ABC in terms of the eye and screen coordinates of all points P, Q, A, B and C. It will then be our task to draw each line segment PQ as far as none of the triangles ABC obscures them. A line segment (or *line*, for short) may be completely visible, completely invisible or partly visible. For example, in Figure 6.1, line 1 is completely visible because it lies in front of the triangle on the left and is unrelated to the other two triangles. In contrast, line 2 lies behind the triangle in the middle and is therefore completely invisible. Finally, lines 3 and 4 are not completely visible, but some parts of them are.

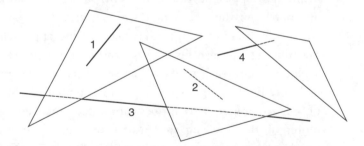

○ **Figure 6.1: Triangles and line segments**

There is another important case: since the edges of the triangles are also line segments, it will frequently occur that a line segment is an edge of the triangle

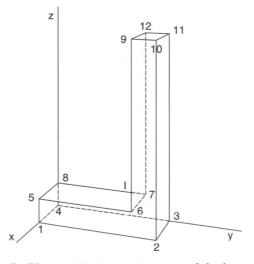

○ **Figure 6.2: A non-convex polyhedron**

under consideration. Such line segments are to be considered visible, as far as that triangle is concerned. For example, consider the letter L in Figure 6.2. Here the only line segment that is partly visible and partly invisible is the line 7–8, which intersects the face 1-2-10-9-6-5, or rather one of the triangles (6-10-9, for example) of which this face consists. In the image, the line 7–8 intersects the edge 6–9 of that triangle in point I, which divides this line into the visible part 8-I and the invisible one I-7.

6.2 TESTS FOR VISIBILITY

On the basis of the given faces of the object, we build a set of triangles and a set of line segments. Then for each line segment PQ, we call a method *lineSegment*, which has the task to draw any parts of PQ that are visible. This method is recursive and can be represented in the flowchart in Figure 6.3, where the numbered tests performed in different steps will be individually discussed in this section and the boxes with double edges denote recursive calls.

This flowchart is equivalent to the following pseudocode, in which I and J are points (between P and Q) of line segment PQ. On the screen we view I and J as intersecting points of PQ with edges of triangle ABC:

```
void lineSegment(line PQ, set s of triangles)
{  In set s, try to find a triangle ABC that obscures PQ (or part of it)
```

If no such triangle found,
    Draw PQ
Else
{ If triangle ABC leaves part PI of PQ visible
    lineSegment(PI, the remaining triangles of *s*);   // Recursive call
   If triangle ABC leaves JQ of PQ visible
    lineSegment(JQ, the remaining triangles of *s*);   // Recursive call
}
}

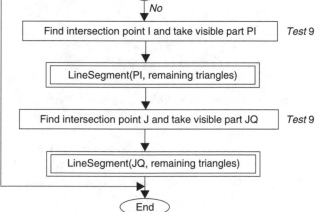

○ **Figure 6.3: Flowchart for** *lineSegment* **method**

According to both the flowchart and this pseudocode, the loop that searches the set of triangles terminates as soon as a triangle ABC is found that obscures PQ.

If ABC obscures PQ completely, no other action is required. If ABC obscures PQ partly, the parts that are possibly visible are dealt with recursively, using the remaining triangles. Note that in these cases the remaining triangles of the current loop are not applied to the whole line segment PQ anymore. The line PQ is drawn only if none of the triangles obscures it, that is, after the loop is completed.

To make the above algorithm as fast as we can, we should be careful with the order in which we perform several tests when we are looking for a triangle that obscures PQ. Tests that take little computing time and are likely to succeed are good candidates for being performed as soon as possible. Sometimes these aspects are contradictory. For example, in the sequence of tests that we will be discussing, the second is not very likely to succeed but it nevertheless deserves its position in this sequence because it is very inexpensive. The inner part of the loop that searches the set of triangles is discussed in greater detail below. Since we have to be careful with small numerical errors due to the finite precision of floating-point computations, we sometimes use small positive real numbers $\varepsilon = eps$ as tolerances, as these examples show:

Mathematical expression	Implementation in program
$x \leq a$	x < a + eps
$x < b$	x < b − eps
$y \geq c$	y > c − eps
$y > d$	y > d + eps

In the second column, it does not make any significant difference if we replace < with <=, and > with >=. We should take some care in choosing the value of *eps*, since this should preferably be related to the magnitude of the numbers we are comparing. You can find details of such tolerance values ε in the program file *HLines.java*, but they are omitted in the discussion below for the sake of clarity.

6.2.1 Test 1 (2D; Figure 6.4)

If neither P nor Q lies to the right of the leftmost one of the three vertices A, B and C (of triangle *t*) the triangle does not obscure PQ. This type of test is known as a *minimax* test: we compare the maximum of all *x*-coordinates of PQ with the minimum of all those of triangle *t*. Loosely speaking, we have now covered the case that PQ lies completely to the left of triangle *t*. In the same way, we deal with PQ lying completely to the right of *t*. Similar tests are performed for the minimum and maximum *y*-coordinates.

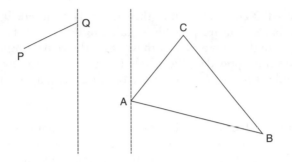

○ Figure 6.4: Test 1: both P and Q on the left of A, B and C

6.2.2 Test 2 (3D; Figure 6.5)

If PQ (in 3D space) is identical with one of the edges of triangle t, this triangle does not obscure PQ. This test is done very efficiently by using the vertex numbers of P, Q, A, B and C. As we will see in a moment, in recursive calls, P or Q may be a computed point, which has no vertex number. It is therefore not always possible to perform this test.

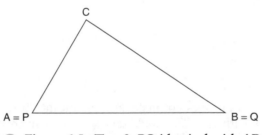

○ Figure 6.5: Test 2: PQ identical with AB

6.2.3 Test 3 (3D; Figure 6.6)

If neither P nor Q is further away than the nearest of the three vertices A, B and C of triangle t, this triangle does not obscure PQ. This is a minimax test, like Test 1, but this time applied to the z-coordinates. Since the positive z-axis points to the left in Figure 6.6, the greater the z-coordinate of a point, the nearer this point is. Therefore, triangle ABC does not obscure PQ if the minimum of z_P and z_Q is greater than or equal to the maximum of z_A, z_B and z_C.

6.2.4 Test 4 (2D; Figure 6.7)

If, on the screen, the points P and Q lie on one side of the line AB while the third triangle vertex C lies on the other, triangle ABC does not obscure PQ.

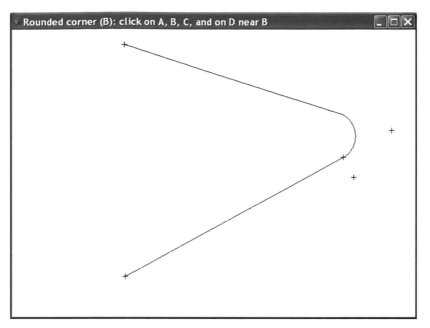

Plate 1. Fillet or rounded corner, Exercise 2.8

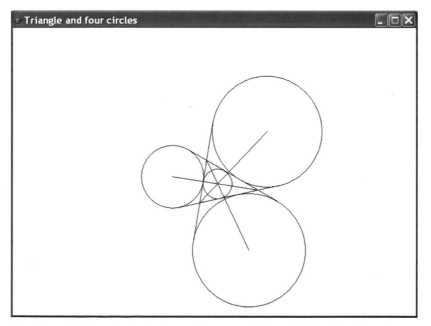

Plate 2. Inscribed circle and three excircles of triangle, Exercise 2.9

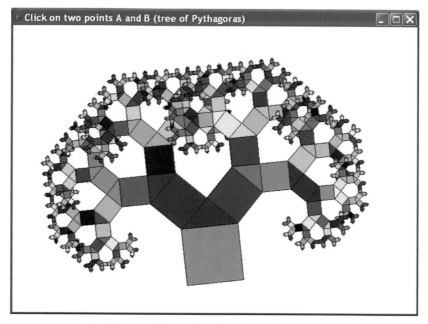

Plate 3. Tree of Pythagoras, Exercise 2.10

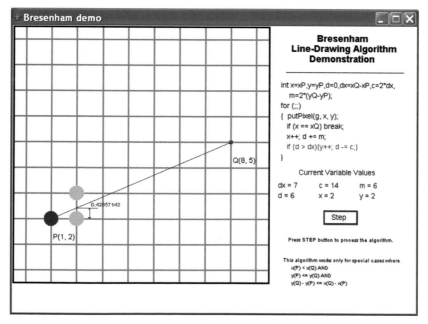

Plate 4. Demonstration of Bresenham's algorithm, Exercise 4.6

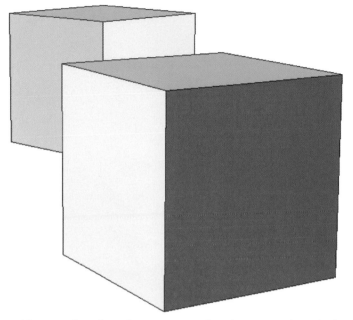

Plate 5. Two colored cubes, captured when rotating independently, Exercise 7.3

Plate 6. Three beams partly hiding each other, see Sections 6.7, 7.3 and 7.4

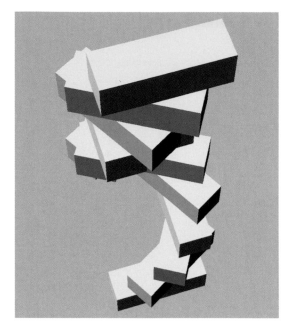

Plate 7. Beams in a spiral, see Section E4, Appendix E

Plate 8. An open book, see Exercise 6.5

○ Plate 9. Solid letter A as an object with a hole, see Section 6.4

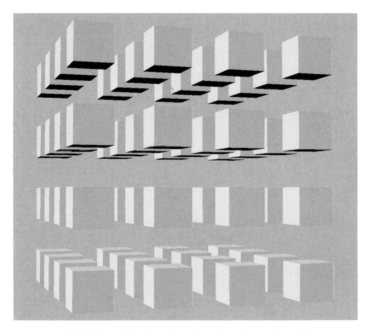

○ Plate 10. A cube of cubes, Exercise 6.8

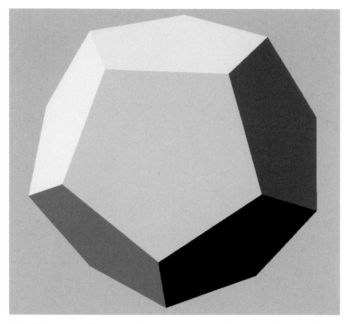

Plate 11. Dodecahedron, see Section E1, Appendix E

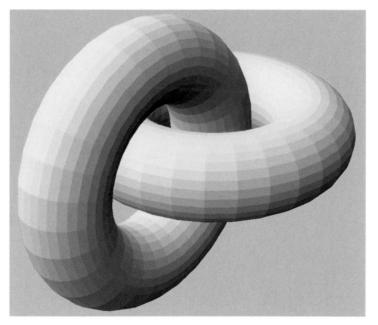

Plate 12. Two tori, Exercise 6.9

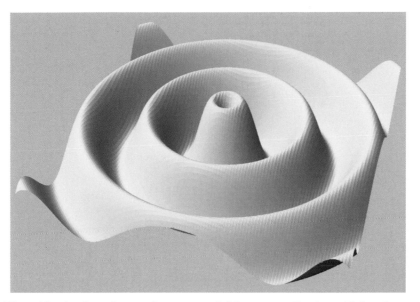

Plate 13. A function of two variables, see Section E.5, Appendix E. The expression $10^* \sin(\text{pow}(x^*x + y^*y, 0.5))/(1 + \text{pow}(x^*x + y^*y, 0.2))$ was supplied to program *Func.java*, with ranges and step sizes for x and y specified as $-15(0.25)15$

Plate 14. Tree with green leaves, Exercise 8.4

○ Plate 15. Sample output of program *MandelbrotZoom.java*, see Section 8.4

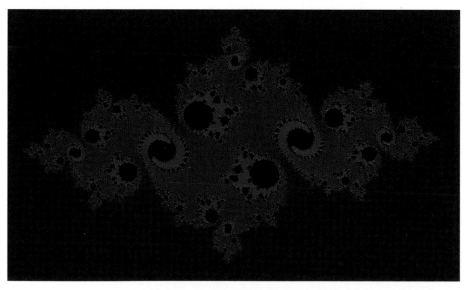

○ Plate 16. Julia set, as discussed at the end of Section 8.4

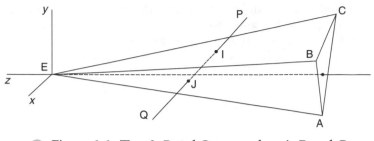

Figure 6.6: Test 3: P and Q nearer than A, B and C

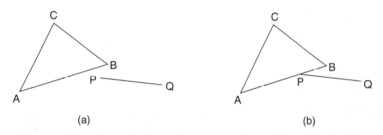

(a)   (b)

Figure 6.7: Test 4: P and Q on a side of AB different from that of C

The lines BC and CA are dealt with similarly. This test is likely to succeed, but we perform it only after the previous three tests because it is rather expensive. Since the vertices A, B and C are counter-clockwise, the points P and C are on different sides of AB if and only if the point sequence ABP is clockwise. As we have seen in Section 2.5, this implies that we can use the static method *area*2 of class *Tools2D*. With *Point2D* objects *AScr*, *BScr*, *CScr* for the points A, B and C, the left-hand side in the comparison

```
Tools2D.area2(AScr, BScr, PScr) <= 0
```

is equal to twice the area of triangle ABP, preceded by a minus sign if (and only if) the sequence ABP is clockwise. This value is negative if P and C lie on different sides of AB, and it is zero if A, B and P lie on a straight line. If this comparison succeeds and the same applies to

```
Tools2D.area2(AScr, BScr, QScr) <= 0
```

then the whole line PQ and point C lie on different sides of the line AB, so that triangle ABC does not obscure line segment PQ. After this test for the triangle edge AB, we use similar tests for edges BC and CA.

Note that P and Q can both lie outside triangle ABC, while PQ intersects this triangle. This explains the above test, which at first may look quite complicated. Unfortunately, the current test does not cover all cases in which PQ lies outside triangle ABC, as you can see in Figure 6.8.

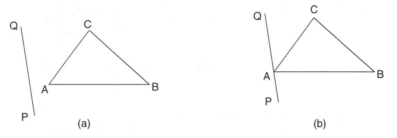

Figure 6.8: Test 5: triangle ABC on one side of PQ

6.2.5 Test 5 (2D; Figure 6.8)

Triangle ABC does not obscure PQ if the points A, B and C lie on the same side of the infinite line through P and Q. We determine if this is the case using a test that is similar to the previous one:

$$(PQA \leq 0 \text{ and } PQB \leq 0 \text{ and } PQC \leq 0) \text{ or}$$
$$(PQA \geq 0 \text{ and } PQB \geq 0 \text{ and } PQC \geq 0)$$

where PQA, obtained as

```
double PQA = Tools2D.area2(PScr, QScr, AScr);
```

denotes twice the area of triangle PQA, preceded by a minus sign if the point sequence P, Q, A is clockwise. The variables PQB and PQC have similar meanings.

6.2.6 Test 6 (3D; Figure 6.9)

If neither P nor Q lies behind the plane through A, B and C, triangle ABC does not obscure PQ. This test deals with those line segments PQ for which Test 3 failed because the further one of the points P and Q does *not* lie nearer than the nearest of A, B, C, while P and Q nevertheless lie on the same side of the (infinite) plane ABC as the viewpoint E. Figure 6.9 illustrates this situation.

We now benefit from the fact that we have stored the normal vector $\mathbf{n} = (a, b, c)$ of plane ABC and the distance h between E and this plane. The equation of this plane is

$$ax + by + cz = h$$

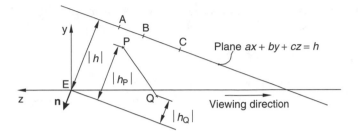

○ **Figure 6.9: Test 6: neither P nor Q behind plane ABC**

We compute

$$h_P = \mathbf{n} \cdot \mathbf{EP}$$
$$h_Q = \mathbf{n} \cdot \mathbf{EQ}$$

to perform the following test, illustrated by Figure 6.9:

$$|h_P| \leq |h| \text{ and } |h_Q| \leq |h|$$

Since **n**, when starting at E, points away from the plane, the values of h_P, h_Q, like that of h, are negative, so that this test is equivalent to the following:

$$h_P \geq h \text{ and } h_Q \geq h$$

6.2.7 Test 7 (2D; Figure 6.10)

If (on the screen) neither P nor Q lies outside the triangle ABC, and the previous tests were indecisive, PQ lies behind this triangle and is therefore completely invisible. The *Tools2D* method *insideTriangle*, discussed in Section 2.8, makes this test easy to program:

```
boolean pInside = Tools2D.insideTriangle(aScr, bScr, cScr, pScr);
boolean qInside = Tools2D.insideTriangle(aScr, bScr, cScr, qScr);
if (pInside && qInside) return;
```

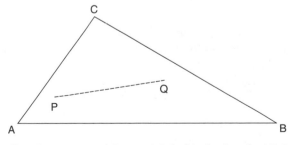

○ **Figure 6.10: Test 7: PQ behind triangle ABC**

The partial results of this test, stored in the boolean variables *pInside* and *qInside*, will be useful in Tests 8 and 9 in the case that this test fails.

6.2.8 Test 8 (3D; Figure 6.11)

If P is nearer than the plane of triangle ABC and, on the screen, P lies inside triangle ABC, this triangle does not obscure PQ. The same is true for Q.

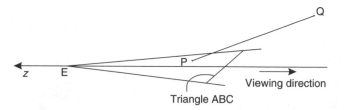

○ **Figure 6.11: Test 8: P nearer than plane ABC**

This test relies on the fact that no line segment PQ intersects any triangle. This test is easy to perform since the variables h_P and h_Q, computed in Test 6, and *pInside* and *qInside*, computed in Test 7, are now available. Using also the abbreviations *pNear* for $h_P > h$ and *qNear* for $h_Q > h$, we conclude that triangle ABC does not obscure PQ if the following is true:

```
pNear && pInside || qNear && qInside
```

6.2.9 Test 9 (3D; Figure 6.12)

Although it might seem that, after Test 8, all cases with PQ not being obscured have been dealt with, this is not the case, as Figure 6.12 illustrates. In this example, Q lies behind the plane ABC, and, on the screen, PQ intersects ABC in the points I and J, but PQ is nevertheless completely visible (as far as triangle ABC is concerned). This is because both points of intersection, I and J, lie in front of (that is, nearer than) triangle ABC. We take three steps to deal with this situation:

1. We compute (the 2D projections of) I and J on the screen.
2. We compute the *z*-values of I and J by linear interpolation of $1/z$ (see Section 7.4 and Appendix A).
3. To determine if I and J lie in front of the plane ABC, we compute how far I and J lie away in the direction towards this plane.

We will now discuss these three steps in more detail, starting with step 1, which we deal with as a 2D problem, writing, for example, P for what is actually the projection P′ of P on the screen.

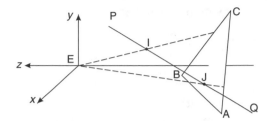

○ **Figure 6.12: Test 9: I and J in front of plane ABC**

Since we do not know in advance which of the three triangle edges AB, BC and CA may intersect PQ, we try all three by rotating the points A, B and C. Here we deal only with AB. Suppose that, on the screen, the infinite line PQ intersects the infinite line AB in point I, where

$$\mathbf{PI} = \lambda\mathbf{PQ} \qquad\qquad (6.1)$$

$$\mathbf{AI} = \mu\mathbf{AB} \qquad\qquad (6.2)$$

Then point I belongs to the line *segments* PQ and AB if and only if

$$0 \le \lambda \le 1 \text{ and } 0 \le \mu \le 1$$

While rotating A, B and C, we may find two points of intersection, with λ and μ satisfying these restrictions. We then denote the values λ of these points by λ_{min} and λ_{max}, and the corresponding points with I and J, so that we have

$$0 \le \lambda_{min} < \lambda_{max} \le 1$$

$$\mathbf{PI} = \lambda_{min}\mathbf{PQ}$$

$$\mathbf{PJ} = \lambda_{max}\mathbf{PQ}$$

As for the actual computation of λ and μ, let us use the vectors $\mathbf{u} = \mathbf{PQ}$ and $\mathbf{v} = \mathbf{AB}$. It then follows from Equations (6.1) and (6.2) that we can express point I as the left- and right-hand sides of the following equation:

$$\mathbf{P} + \lambda\mathbf{u} = \mathbf{A} + \mu\mathbf{v}$$

Writing $\mathbf{w} = \mathbf{PA}(= \mathbf{A} - \mathbf{P})$, we can replace this with

$$\lambda\mathbf{u} - \mu\mathbf{v} = \mathbf{w}$$

As usual, we write $\mathbf{u} = (u_1, u_2)$ and so on, which expands this vector equation to the following set of simultaneous linear equations:

$$u_1\lambda - v_1\mu = w_1$$

$$u_2\lambda - v_2\mu = w_2$$

Solving this system of equations, we obtain

$$\lambda = \frac{v_1\,w_2 - v_2\,w_1}{u_2 v_1 - u_1 v_2}$$
$$\mu = \frac{u_1 w_2 - u_2 w_1}{u_2 v_1 - u_1 v_2}$$

It goes without saying that this applies only if the denominators in these expressions are non-zero; otherwise PQ and AB are parallel, so that there are no points of intersection.

Having found the points I and J on the screen, we turn to step 2, to compute their z-coordinates. We do this by linear interpolation of $1/z$ on the segment PQ. Using the values λ_{min} and λ_{max}, which we have just found, and referring to Equation (6.1), we can write

$$\frac{1}{z_I} = \frac{1}{z_P} + \lambda_{min}\left(\frac{1}{z_Q} - \frac{1}{z_P}\right) = \frac{\lambda_{min}}{z_Q} + \frac{1 - \lambda_{min}}{z_P}$$
$$\frac{1}{z_J} = \frac{1}{z_P} + \lambda_{max}\left(\frac{1}{z_Q} - \frac{1}{z_P}\right) = \frac{\lambda_{max}}{z_Q} + \frac{1 - \lambda_{max}}{z_P}$$

Refer to the discussion in Section 7.4 and Appendix A about the reason why we should use $1/z$ instead of simply z in this type of linear interpolation.

Finally, we proceed to step 3, to determine whether or not the points I and J lie in front of the plane through the points A, B and C. Recall that the equation of this plane is

$$ax + by + cz = h$$

where h is negative, and that its normal vector (with length 1) is

$$\mathbf{n} = (a, b, c)$$

We compute the value h_I, which is similar to h_P, discussed in Test 6 and illustrated by Figure 6.9, as

$$h_I = \mathbf{EI} \cdot \mathbf{n} = ax_I + by_I + cz_I$$

After computing h_J similarly, we can now test if I and J lie in front of the plane ABC (so that triangle ABC does not obscure PQ) in the following way:

$$h_I > h \text{ and } h_J > h$$

In the above discussion, we considered two distinct points I and J in which, on the screen, PQ intersects edges of triangle ABC. As we have seen, PI and JQ were visible, as far as triangle ABC is concerned, but IJ may be obscured by triangle ABC. Actually, there may be only one point, I or J, to deal with. If, again on the screen, P lies outside triangle ABC and Q inside it, there is only point

I to consider. In this case triangle ABC may obscure part IQ of line segment PQ. If it does, the remaining triangles are only to be applied to PI. Similarly, if, on the screen, P lies inside and Q outside triangle ABC, this triangle may obscure part PJ of PQ, and, if so, the remaining triangles are only to be applied to JQ.

6.2.10 Recursive Calls

If all the above tests fail, the most interesting (and time consuming) case applies: PQ is neither completely visible nor completely hidden. Fortunately, we have just computed the points of intersection I and J, and we know that triangle ABC obscures the segment IJ, while the other two segments, PI and QJ are visible, as far as triangle ABC is concerned. We therefore apply the method *lineSegment* recursively to the latter two segments. Actually, the recursive call for PI applies only to the case that, on the screen, P lies outside triangle ABC and λ_{min} (see Test 9) is greater than zero. Analogously, the recursive call for QJ applies only if Q lies outside that triangle and λ_{max} is less than 1.

6.2.11 The Arguments of the *lineSegment* Method

In the *paint* method of the class *CvHLines*, we may be inclined to write the call to the method *lineSegment* in a very simple form, such as

```
lineSegment(g, iP, iQ);
```

where *g* is the graphics context and *iP* and *iQ* are the vertex numbers of the vertices P and Q. However, in the recursive calls just discussed, we have two new points I and J, for which there are no vertex numbers, so that this does not work. On the other hand, omitting the vertex numbers altogether would deprive us of Test 2 in its current efficient form, in which we determine if PQ is one of the edges of triangle ABC. We therefore decide to supply P and Q both as *Point3D* objects (containing the eye coordinates of P and Q) and as vertex numbers if this is possible; if it is not, we use −1 instead of a vertex number. When we recursively call *lineSegment*, the screen coordinates of P and Q are available. If we did not supply these as arguments, it would be necessary to compute them inside *lineSegment* once again. To avoid such superfluous actions, we also supply the screen coordinates of P and Q as arguments as *Point2D* objects. Finally, it would be a waste of time if the recursive calls would again be applied to all triangles. After all, we know that PI and PJ are not obscured by the triangles that we have already dealt with. We therefore also use the parameter *iStart*, indicating the start position in the array of triangles that is to be used. This explains that the method *lineSegment* has as many as eight parameters, as its heading shows:

```
void lineSegment(Graphics g, Point3D p, Point3D q,
   Point2D PScr, Point2D QScr, int iP, int iQ, int iStart)
```

The complete method *lineSegment* can be found in class *CvHLines*, listed in Appendix D.

6.3 SPECIFICATION AND REPRESENTATION OF 3D OBJECTS

From now on, we will no longer restrict ourselves to cubes, as we did in the previous chapter, but rather accept input files that define objects bounded by polygons (which may contain holes, as we will see in Section 6.4). These input files consist of two parts: a list of vertices, each in the form of a positive vertex number followed by three real numbers, the world coordinates of that vertex. The second part consists of an input line of the form

```
Faces:
```

followed by sequences of vertex numbers, each sequence followed by a period (.). Each such sequence denotes a polygon of the object. For each polygon, when viewed from outside the object, the vertex sequence must be counter-clockwise. This orientation must also apply to the first three vertices of each sequence; in other words, the second number of each sequence must denote a convex vertex. For example, the following input file, say, *letterL.dat*, describes the solid letter *L* of Figure 6.2:

```
 1   20    0    0
 2   20   50    0
 3    0   50    0
 4    0    0    0
 5   20    0   10
 6   20   40   10
 7    0   40   10
 8    0    0   10
 9   20   40   80
10   20   50   80
11    0   50   80
12    0   40   80
Faces:
1  2  10  9  6  5.
3  4  8  7  12  11.
```

```
2   3   11   10.
7   6   9   12.
4   1   5   8.
9   10   11   12.
5   6   7   8.
1   4   3   2.
```

The first line after *Faces* specifies the front face. We might have used a different vertex-number sequence for this face, such as

```
10   9   6   5   1   2.
```

However, the following sequences would be incorrect:

```
2   1   5   6   9   10.    (invalid: clockwise)
9   6   5   1   2   10.    (invalid: 6 is not a convex vertex)
```

Although the sequence

```
3   4   8   7   12   11.
```

seems to be clockwise, it is really counter-clockwise when the face in question is viewed from outside the object, that is, from the back. As we will see in Section 7.1, we use this phenomenon in our programs to detect back faces.

In the first part of the input file, it is not required that the vertex numbers are consecutive and in ascending order. For example, the following input file (defining a pyramid similar to those in Egypt) is also acceptable. It also shows that the vertex coordinates need not be integers:

```
10    -1.5 -1.5   0
30     1.5 -1.5   0
20     1.5  1.5   0
12    -1.5  1.5   0
5      0    0     3
Faces:
30 20 5.
20 12 5.
12 10 5.
10 30 5.
30 10 12 20.
```

We will use the extension *.dat* for these input files.

6.4 HOLES AND INVISIBLE LINE SEGMENTS

The above way of specifying the boundary faces of objects does not work for polygons that contain holes. For example, consider the solid letter A of Figure 6.13, the front face of which is not a proper polygon because there is a triangular hole in it. The same applies to the (identical) face on the back. Each vertex i of the front face is connected with vertex $i + 10$ of the back face $(1 \leq i \leq 10)$.

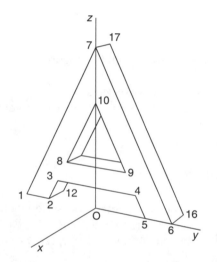

○ **Figure 6.13: Solid letter A**

We can turn the front face into a polygon by introducing a very narrow gap, say, between the vertices 7 and 10, as shown in Figure 6.14. After doing this, we could try to specify this new polygon as

1 2 3 4 5 6 7 10 9 8 10 7.

Note that this requires the gap (7, 10) to have width zero, so that there is only one vertex (7) at the top. On the other hand, only a real gap makes it clear that the vertex numbers (10, 9, 8) occur in that order in the above input line: just follow the vertices in Figure 6.14, starting at vertex 1.

If we really specified the front face in the above way, the line (7, 10) would be regarded as a polygon edge and therefore appear in our result. This is clearly undesirable. To prevent this from happening, we adopt the convention of writing a minus sign in front of the second vertex of a pair, indicating that

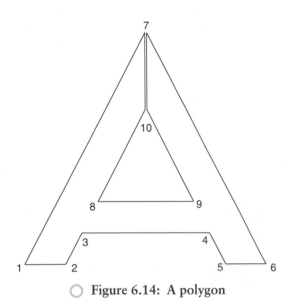

○ **Figure 6.14: A polygon**

this pair denotes a line segment that is not to be drawn. We do this with the ordered pairs (7, 10) and (10, 7) in the above input line, writing (7, −10) and (10, −7), so that we use the following input line instead of the above one:

1 2 3 4 5 6 7 -10 9 8 10 -7.

The solid letter A of Figure 6.13 is therefore obtained by using the following input file, in which the extra minus signs occur in the first two lines after the word *Faces*:

```
1     0 -30   0
2     0 -20   0
3     0 -16   8
4     0  16   8
5     0  20   0
6     0  30   0
7     0   0  60
8     0 -12  16
9     0  12  16
10    0   0  40
11  -10 -30   0
12  -10 -20   0
13  -10 -16   8
14  -10  16   8
```

```
15 -10  20   0
16 -10  30   0
17 -10   0  60
18 -10 -12  16
19 -10  12  16
20 -10   0  40
Faces:
1 2 3 4 5 6 7 -10 9 8 10 -7.
11 17 -20 18 19 20 -17 16 15 14 13 12.
2 12 13 3.
3 13 14 4.
15 5 4 14.
8 9 19 18.
8 18 20 10.
19 9 10 20.
6 16 17 7.
11 1 7 17.
11 12 2 1.
15 16 6 5.
```

(Note that this use of minus signs applies only to vertex numbers in the second part of an input file. In the first part, minus signs can only occur in coordinate values, where they have their usual meaning.)

Implementing this idea is very simple. For example, because of the minus sign that precedes vertex number 10 in

```
... 7   -10 ...
```

we do not store line segment (7, 10) in the data structure that will be discussed in Section 6.5. In other respects, we simply ignore these minus signs. Therefore the set of triangles resulting from the above complete set of input data (for the solid letter A) is the same as when there had been no minus signs in front of any vertex numbers.

Besides for holes, we can also use these minus signs for the approximation for curved surfaces, as discussed in Section E.5 of Appendix E.

6.5 INDIVIDUAL FACES AND LINE SEGMENTS

Although we usually draw polygons that are boundary faces of solid objects, we sometimes want to draw very thin (finite) planes, here also called *faces*.

Examples are sheets of paper and a cube made of very thin material, of which the top face is removed, as shown in Figure 6.15.

Since such faces have two visible sides, we specify each face twice: counter-clockwise for the side we are currently viewing and clockwise for the side that is currently invisible but may become visible when we change the viewpoint. For example, the front face of the cube of Figure 6.15 is specified twice in the input file:

```
1 2 3 4.
4 3 2 1.
```

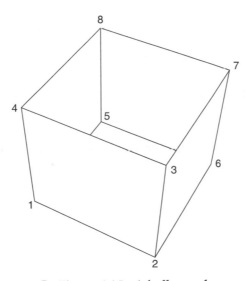

○ **Figure 6.15: A hollow cube**

Although the user supplies polygons in input files as object faces, we deal primarily with line segments, referred to as PQ in the previous section. Besides the polygons and the triangles resulting from them, we also store the edges of the polygons as line segments. It is also desirable to be able to draw line segments that are not edges of polygons.

Examples of such 'loose', individual line segments are the axes of a 3D coordinate system. Sometimes we want to define the edges of polygons as individual line segments, to prevent such polygons from obscuring other line segments, displaying objects as wire-frame models. An example of this is shown in Figure 6.16. Here we have a solid pyramid fitting into a cube. Obviously, the pyramid would not be visible if the cube was solid; we therefore prefer the latter

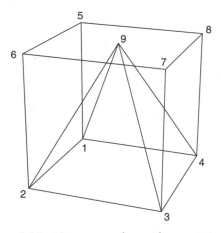

○ **Figure 6.16: Solid pyramid in wire-frame cube**

to be displayed as a wire-frame model. To provide an input file for this pyramid, we begin by assigning vertex numbers, as shown in Figure 6.17.

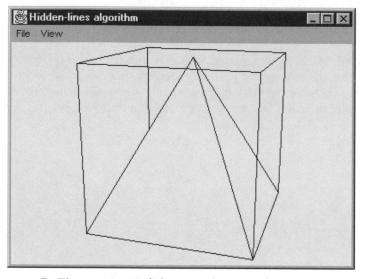

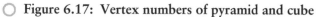

○ **Figure 6.17: Vertex numbers of pyramid and cube**

These vertex numbers occur in the following input file:

```
1  0 0 0
2  2 0 0
```

```
3  2 2 0
4  0 2 0
5  0 0 2
6  2 0 2
7  2 2 2
8  0 2 2
9  1 1 2
Faces:
1 4 3 2.
1 2 9.
2 3 9.
3 4 9.
4 1 9.
1 5.
2 6.
3 7.
4 8.
5 6.
6 7.
7 8.
8 5.
```

After the word *Faces*, we begin with the square bottom face and the four triangular faces of the pyramid. After this, four vertical and four horizontal cube edges follow, each specified by its two endpoints. It follows that the word *Faces* in our input files should not be taken too literally: this *Faces* section may include pairs of vertex numbers, which are not faces at all but line segments not necessarily belonging to faces.

Since line segments can occur not only as edges of faces but also individually, we have to design and implement a special data structure to store them in our program. This also provides us with the opportunity to store them only once. For example, the edge 3–9 of the pyramid of Figure 6.17 is part of the faces 2-3-9 and 3-4-9, but it would be inefficient to draw it twice. By using a special data structure for line segments, we can ensure that this edge is stored only once.

Our data structure for line segments will be based on an array of arrays, as shown on the left in Figure 6.18.

An array element *connect*[i] referring to an array containing the integer j implies that there is a line segment (i, j) to be drawn. By requiring that i is less than j, we ensure that each line segment is stored only once. For example, *connect*[1] refers to the array containing the integers 2, 4, 9 and 5. This indicates that the

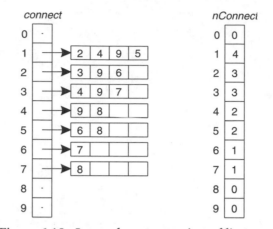

○ **Figure 6.18: Internal representation of line segments**

following line segments start at vertex 1 (each ending at a vertex that has a number higher than 1): 1–2, 1–4, 1–9 and 1–5, which is in accordance with Figure 6.17. The next element, *connect*[2] refers to three vertex numbers, 3, 9 and 6. Although, besides 2–3, 2–9 and 2–6, there is also a line segment 2–1 (see Figure 6.17), this is not included here because 2 is greater than 1 and this segment has already been stored as line segment 1–2. You may wonder why in Figure 6.18 there are only boxes that give room for at most four vertex numbers. Actually, the sizes of these boxes will always be a multiple of some *chunk size*, here arbitrarily chosen as 4. In other words, if there are five line segments (i, j) with the same i and all with i less than j, the box size would be increased from 4 to 8 and so on. Since increasing the box size requires memory reallocation and copying, we should not choose the chunk size too small. On the other hand, the larger the chunk size, the more memory will be wasted, since they will normally not be completely filled. To indicate how many vertex numbers are actually stored in each box, we use another array, *nConnect*, as shown in Figure 6.18 on the right. For example, *nConnect*[1] = 4 because *connect*[1] refers to four vertex numbers.

6.6 AUTOMATIC GENERATION OF OBJECT SPECIFICATION

As long as 3D objects do not have too many vertices and the vertex coordinates are easily available, it is not difficult to create 3D specifications as input files by entering all data manually, using a text editor. This is the case, for example, with the solid letter A, discussed in Section 6.4. If there are many vertices, which is normally the case if we approximate curved surfaces, we had better generate 3D data files by special programs. This section explains how to automatically generate 3D specifications through an example. The generated specification files are accepted by the programs *Painter.java*, *ZBuf.java* (for hidden-face elimination, described in Chapter 7) and *HLines.java* (for hidden-line elimination, described in the next two sections). Most illustrations in this chapter have been obtained by using *HLines.java* for this purpose.

Many 3D objects are bounded by curved surfaces. We can approximate these by a set of polygons. An example is a hollow cylinder as shown in Figure 6.19 on the right. Both representations of hollow cylinders (or rather, hollow prisms) of Figure 6.19 were obtained by running the program *Cylinder.java*, which we will be discussing, followed by the execution of program *HLines.java*. HP-GL files exported by the latter program were combined by CorelDraw, after which the result was imported into this book. Although the object shown on the left in Figure 6.19 is a (hollow) *prism*, not a cylinder, we will consistently use the term *cylinder* in this discussion.

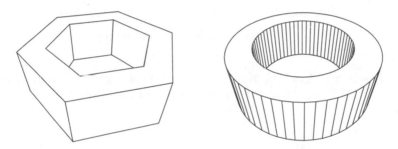

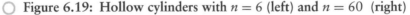

Figure 6.19: Hollow cylinders with $n = 6$ (left) and $n = 60$ (right)

The user will be able to enter the diameters of both the (outer) cylinder and the (inner) cylindrical hole. If the latter, smaller diameter is zero, our program will produce a solid cylinder instead of a hollow one. For simplicity, we will ignore this special case, with only half the number of vertices, in our discussion below, but simply implement it in the program.

For some sufficiently large integer n (not less than 3), we choose n equidistant points on the outer circle (with radius R) of the top face, and we choose n similar points on the bottom face. Then we approximate the outer cylinder by a prism whose vertices are these $2n$ points. The inner circle (of the cylindrical hole) has radius r ($< R$). The hollow cylinder has height h. Let us use the z-axis of our coordinate system as the cylinder axis. The cylindrical hole is approximated by rectangles in the same way as the outer cylinder. The bottom face lies in the plane $z = 0$ and the top face in the plane $z = h$. A vertex of the bottom face lies on the positive x-axis. Let us set $h = 1$. Then for given values n, R and r, the object to be drawn and its position are then completely determined. We shall first deal with the case $n = 6$ and generalize this later for arbitrary n. We number the vertices as shown in Figure 6.20.

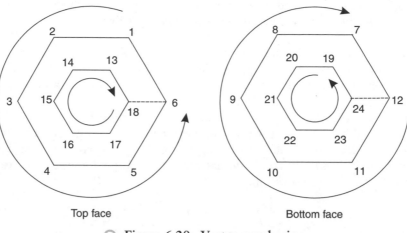

Top face   Bottom face

○ **Figure 6.20: Vertex numbering**

For each vertex i of the top face there is a vertical edge that connects it with vertex $i + 6$. We can specify the top face by the following sequence:

```
1 2 3 4 5 6 -18 17 16 15 14 13 18 -6.
```

Here the pairs $(6, -18)$ and $(18, -6)$ denote an artificial edge, as discussed in Section 6.4. The bottom face on the right is viewed here from the positive z-axis, but in reality only the other side is visible. The orientation of this bottom face is therefore opposite to what we see in Figure 6.20 on the right, so that we can specify this face as

```
12 11 10 9 8 7 -19 20 21 22 23 24 19 -7.
```

Since $n = 6$, we have $12 = 2n$, $18 = 3n$ and $24 = 4n$, so the above sequences are special cases of

$$1 \quad 2 \ldots n \quad -3n \quad 3n-1 \quad 3n-2 \quad \ldots \quad 2n+1 \quad 3n \quad -n.$$

and

$$2n \quad 2n-1 \quad \ldots \quad n+1 \quad -(3n+1) \quad 3n+2 \quad 3n+3 \quad \ldots \quad 4n$$
$$3n+1 \quad -(n+1).$$

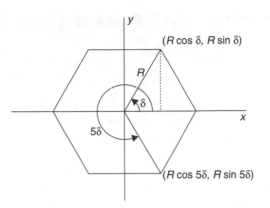

○ **Figure 6.21: Calculating vertex coordinates**

Let us define

$$\delta = \frac{2\pi}{n}$$

Since, in Figure 6.20, on the left, vertex 6 lies on the positive x-axis and according to geometry in Figure 6.21 (outer circle), the Cartesian coordinates of the vertices on the top face are as follows:

$$x_i = R \cos i\delta$$
$$y_i = R \sin i\delta \qquad (i = 1, \ldots, n; \text{ outer circle})$$
$$z_i = h$$
$$x_i = r \cos(i - 2n)\delta$$
$$y_i = r \sin(i - 2n)\delta \qquad (i = 2n + 1, \ldots, 3n; \text{ inner circle})$$
$$z_i = h$$

For the bottom face we have

$$x_i = x_{i-n}$$
$$y_i = y_{i-n} \qquad (i = n + 1, \ldots, 2n, 3n + 1, \ldots, 4n)$$
$$z_i = 0$$

A program based on the above analysis can be written in any programming language. Using Java for this purpose, we can choose between an old-fashioned, text-line oriented solution and a graphical user interface with, for example, a dialog box with text fields and a button as shown in Figure 6.22.

This dialog box contains a title bar, and seven so-called *components*: three *labels* (that is, static text in the gray area), three text fields in which the user can enter data, and an OK button. Programming the layout of a dialog box in Java

┌───┐
│ ▩ Cylinder (possibly hollow); height = 1   ☒ │
│   │
│   Number of vertices on outer circle: [60]   │
│   │
│   Diameters D and d (cylinder is hollow if d > 0): [3]   [2]   │
│   │
│   │
│   Generate 3D object file?   [OK]   │
└───┘

◯ **Figure 6.22: Dialog box for (possibly hollow) cylinder**

can be done in several ways, none of which is particularly simple. Here we do this by using three *panels*:

- Panel *p*1 at the top, or *North*, for both the label *Number of vertices on outer circle* and a text field in which this number is to be entered.
- Panel *p*2 in the middle, or *Center*, for the label *Diameters D and d (cylinder is hollow if d > 0)* and two text fields for these diameters.
- Panel *p*3 at the bottom, or *South*, for the label *Generate 3D object file?* and an OK button.

Since there are only a few components in each panel, we can use the default *FlowLayout* layout manager for the placements of these components in the panels. By contrast, the panels are placed above one another by using *Border-Layout*, as the above words *North*, *Center* and *South*, used in the program as character strings, indicate. As in many other graphics programs in this book, we use two classes in this program, but this time there is a dialog class instead of a canvas class. Another difference is that we do not display the frame, but restrict the graphical output to the dialog box. (We cannot omit the frame class altogether because the *Dialog* constructor requires a 'parent frame' as an argument.) Recall that we previously used calls to *setSize*, *setLocation* and *show* in the constructor of the frame class. We simply omit these calls to prevent the frame from appearing on the screen. Obviously, we must not omit such calls in the constructor of our dialog class, called *DlgCylinder* in the program. As for the generation of the hollow cylinder itself, as discussed above, this can be found in the method *genCylinder*, which follows this constructor:

```
// Cylinder.java: Generating an input file for a
//                (possibly hollow) cylinder.
import java.awt.*;
import java.awt.event.*;
import java.io.*;

public class Cylinder extends Frame
```

```
{  public static void main(String[] args){new Cylinder();}
   Cylinder(){new DlgCylinder(this);}
}

class DlgCylinder extends Dialog
{  TextField tfN = new TextField (5);
   TextField tfOuterDiam = new TextField (5);
   TextField tfInnerDiam = new TextField (5);
   Button button = new Button("  OK  ");
   FileWriter fw;

   DlgCylinder(Frame fr)
   {  super(fr, "Cylinder (possibly hollow); height = 1", true);
      addWindowListener(new WindowAdapter()
      {  public void windowClosing(WindowEvent e)
         {  dispose();
            System.exit(0);
         }
      });
      Panel p1 = new Panel(), p2 = new Panel(), p3 = new Panel();
      p1.add(new Label("Number of vertices on outer circle: "));
      p1.add(tfN);
      p2.add(new Label(
         "Diameters D and d (cylinder is hollow if d > 0): "));
      p2.add(tfOuterDiam); p2.add(tfInnerDiam);
      p3.add(new Label("Generate 3D object file?"));
      p3.add(button);
      setLayout(new BorderLayout());
      add("North", p1);
      add("Center", p2);
      add("South", p3);

      button.addActionListener(new ActionListener()
      {  public void actionPerformed(ActionEvent ae)
         {  int n=0;
            float dOuter=0, dInner=0;
            try
            {  n = Integer.valueOf(tfN.getText()).intValue();
               dOuter =
                  Float.valueOf(tfOuterDiam.getText()).floatValue();
               dInner =
                  Float.valueOf(tfInnerDiam.getText()).floatValue();
               if (dInner < 0) dInner = 0;
```

```
            if (n < 3 || dOuter <= dInner)
               Toolkit.getDefaultToolkit().beep();
            else
            { try
               { genCylinder(n, dOuter/2, dInner/2);
               }
               catch (IOException ioe){}
               dispose();
               System.exit(0);
            }
         }
         catch (NumberFormatException nfe)
         { Toolkit.getDefaultToolkit().beep();
         }
      }
   });
   Dimension dim = getToolkit().getScreenSize();
   setSize(3 * dim.width/4, dim.height/4);
   setLocation(dim.width/8, dim.height/8);
   show();
}

void genCylinder(int n, float rOuter, float rInner)
   throws IOException
{  int n2 = 2 * n, n3 = 3 * n, n4 = 4 * n;
   fw = new FileWriter("Cylinder.dat");
   double delta = 2 * Math.PI / n;
   for (int i=1; i<=n; i++)
   {  double alpha = i * delta,
         cosa = Math.cos(alpha), sina = Math.sin(alpha);
      for (int inner=0; inner<2; inner++)
      {  double r = (inner == 0 ? rOuter : rInner);
         if (r > 0)
         for (int bottom=0; bottom<2; bottom++)
         {  int k = (2 * inner + bottom) * n + i;
            // Vertex numbers for i = 1:
            // Top:       1 (outer)   2n+1 (inner)
            // Bottom: n+1 (outer)   3n+1 (inner)
            wi(k); // w = write, i = int, r = real
            wr(r * cosa); wr(r * sina); // x and y
            wi(1 - bottom); // bottom: z = 0; top: z = 1
            fw.write("\r\n");
         }
```

```java
      }
   }
   fw.write("Faces:\r\n");
   // Top boundary face:
   for (int i=1; i<=n; i++) wi(i);
   if (rInner > 0)
   {  wi(-n3); // Invisible edge, see Section 7.5
      for (int i=n3-1; i>=n2+1; i--) wi(i);
      wi(n3); wi(-n); // Invisible edge again.
   }
   fw.write(".\r\n");

   // Bottom boundary face:
   for (int i=n2; i>=n+1; i--) wi(i);
   if (rInner > 0)
   {  wi(-(n3+1));
      for (int i=n3+2; i<=n4; i++) wi(i);
      wi(n3+1); wi(-(n+1));
   }
   fw.write(".\r\n");
   // Vertical, rectangular faces:
   for (int i=1; i<=n; i++)
   {  int j = i % n + 1;
      // Outer rectangle:
      wi(j); wi(i); wi(i + n); wi(j + n); fw.write(".\r\n");
      if (rInner > 0)
      {  // Inner rectangle:
         wi(i + n2); wi(j + n2); wi(j + n3); wi(i + n3);
         fw.write(".\r\n");
      }
   }
   fw.close();
}

void wi(int x)
   throws IOException
{  fw.write(" " + String.valueOf(x));
}

void wr(double x)
   throws IOException
{  if (Math.abs(x) < 1e-9) x = 0;
   fw.write(" " + String.valueOf((float)x));
```

```
        // float instead of double to reduce the file size
    }
}
```

The number 60 entered in the top text field of Figure 6.22 refers to the hollow cylinder shown in Figure 6.19 on the right. The hollow prism shown on the left in this figure is obtained by replacing 60 with 6. In that case the following file is generated:

```
1 0.75 1.299038 1
7 0.75 1.299038 0
13 0.5 0.8660254 1
19 0.5 0.8660254 0
2 -0.75 1.299038 1
8 -0.75 1.299038 0
14 -0.5 0.8660254 1
20 -0.5 0.8660254 0
3 -1.5 0.0 1
9 -1.5 0.0 0
15 -1.0 0.0 1
21 -1.0 0.0 0
4 -0.75 -1.299038 1
10 -0.75 -1.299038 0
16 -0.5 -0.8660254 1
22 -0.5 -0.8660254 0
5 0.75 -1.299038 1
11 0.75 -1.299038 0
17 0.5 -0.8660254 1
23 0.5 -0.8660254 0
6 1.5 0.0 1
12 1.5 0.0 0
18 1.0 0.0 1
24 1.0 0.0 0
Faces:
1 2 3 4 5 6 -18 17 16 15 14 13 18 -6.
12 11 10 9 8 7 -19 20 21 22 23 24 19 -7.
2 1 7 8.
13 14 20 19.
3 2 8 9.
14 15 21 20.
4 3 9 10.
15 16 22 21.
5 4 10 11.
```

```
16 17 23 22.
 6  5 11 12.
17 18 24 23.
 1  6 12  7.
18 13 19 24.
```

Recall that we have already discussed the first two lines that follow the word *Faces*. More interesting examples on generating input files for different 3D objects can be found in Appendix E.

6.7 HIDDEN-LINE ELIMINATION WITH HP-GL OUTPUT

Besides graphics output on the screen, it is sometimes desired to produce output files containing the same results. An easy way to realize this for line drawings is by using the file format known as HP-GL, which stands for Hewlett-Packard Graphics Language. We will use only a very limited number of HP-GL commands:

IN: Initialize
SP: Set pen
PU: Pen up
PD: Pen down
PA: Plot absolute

We think of drawing by moving a pen, which can be either on or above a sheet of paper. These two cases are distinguished by the commands *PD* and *PU*. The *PA* command is followed by a coordinate pair x, y, each as a four-digit integer in the range 0000–9999. This coordinate pair indicates a point that the pen will move to. The origin (0000, 0000) lies in the bottom-left corner. For example, the following HP-GL file draws a capital letter X in italic, shown in Figure 6.23:

```
IN;SP1;
PU;PA5000,2000;PD;PA5000,8000;
PU;PA3000,2000;PD;PA7000,8000;
```

This file format is easy to understand and it is accepted by many well-known packages, such as Microsoft Word and CorelDraw. The latter enables us to enhance the drawing after importing the HP-GL file, as was done to add text, resulting in Figure 6.23.

We will see how to implement this in the next section.

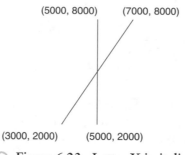

(5000, 8000)   (7000, 8000)

(3000, 2000)   (5000, 2000)

○ **Figure 6.23: Letter X in italic**

The program *HLines.java* is listed in Appendix D. First, *HLines.java* can generate HP-GL files (Figure 6.24 illustrates a menu item for exporting HP-GL files); second, it can display individual lines, and third, printing and photocopying the resulting images can be done in black and white without loss of quality. On the contrary, these line drawings, obtained via HP-GL files and produced by a printer, look better than those on the screen.

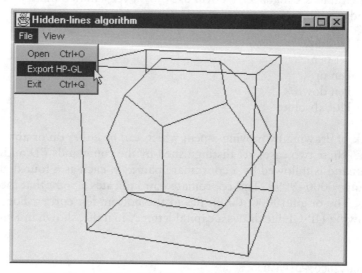

○ **Figure 6.24: The Export HP-GL menu item**

This example also shows the use of individual line segments, as discussed in Section 6.5. The solid inside the wire-frame cube is a dodecahedron, which is discussed in greater detail in Section E.1 of Appendix E.

The statement

```
cv.setHPGL(new HPGL(obj));
```

in the class *MenuCommands* (at the end of the file *HLines.java*) creates an object of class *HPGL*, and the variable *hpgl* of the class *CvHLines* is made to refer to it. The fact that *hpgl* is no longer equal to *null* will be interpreted as an indication that an HP-GL file is to be written. The class *HPGL* can be found at the end of Appendix D. The *write* method of this class is used in the *drawLine* method of the class *CvHLines*, that is, if the variable *hpgl* is unequal to *null*, as discussed above. After we have written an HP-GL file, we set *hpgl* equal to *null* again (at the end of the *paint* method) to avoid that every call to *paint* should automatically produce HP-GL output. If this is again desired, the user must use the *Export HP-GL* command of the *File* menu once again. The class *CvHLines* is defined in the file *HLines.java* (see Appendix D).

Figure 6.25 shows that our hidden-line algorithm can correctly render the three beams that we will use to demonstrate the Z-buffer algorithm for hidden-face elimination. As we will see in Section 7.3, the painter's algorithm fails in this case.

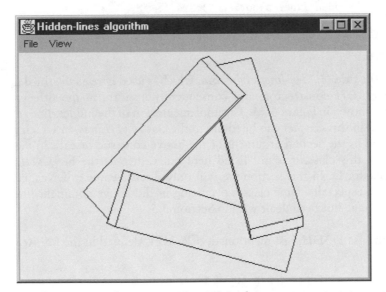

○ **Figure 6.25: Three beams**

6.8 IMPLEMENTATION

The program *HLines.java* has much in common with *Wireframe.java*, discussed at the end of Chapter 5. We will therefore benefit as much as possible from the code that we have already developed in Section 5.5. Unfortunately, since we now have an extra menu item, *Export HPGL*, in the *File* menu, we cannot use the existing frame class *Fr3D* directly, but we will use an extended version, that is, a subclass of it. The name of this subclass, *Fr3DH*, occurs in the *main* method of the following file:

```
// HLines.java: Perspective drawing with hidden-line elimination.
// When you compile this program, the .class or the .java files of the
// following classes should also be in your current directory:
//      CvHLines, Fr3D, Fr3DH, Polygon3D, Obj3D, Input, Canvas3D,
//      Point3D, Point2D, Triangle, Tria, Tools2D, HPGL.
import java.awt.*;
import java.awt.event.*;
import java.util.*;

public class HLines extends Frame
{  public static void main(String[] args)
   {  new Fr3DH(args.length > 0 ? args[0] : null, new CvHLines(),
        "Hidden-lines algorithm");
   }
}
```

Notice the title *Hidden-lines algorithm*, which is used here as the third argument of the *Fr3DH* constructor, and consequently appears in the title bar of the window shown in Figure 6.25. The implementation of the hidden-lines algorithm discussed in this chapter can be found in the class *CvHLines*, of which an object is created in the second argument of the above constructor call. In view of the extent of this class, it is not listed here but rather as the file *CvHLines.java* in Appendix D. In this section we will only discuss some other aspects of the program, especially some classes occurring in the above comment lines, as far as these have not been dealt with in Section 5.5.

The subclass *Fr3DH*, just mentioned, of *Fr3D* is defined in the following file:

```
// Fr3DH.java: Frame class for HLines.java.
// This class extends Fr3D to enable writing HP-GL output files.
import java.awt.*;
import java.awt.event.*;
import java.util.*;

class Fr3DH extends Fr3D
{  private MenuItem exportHPGL;
   CvHLines cv;
```

```
Fr3DH(String argFileName, CvHLines cv, String textTitle)
{  super(argFileName, cv, textTitle);
   exportHPGL = new MenuItem("Export HP-GL");
   mF.add(exportHPGL);
   exportHPGL.addActionListener(this);
   this.cv = cv;
}

public void actionPerformed(ActionEvent ae)
{  if (ae.getSource() instanceof MenuItem)
   {  MenuItem mi = (MenuItem)ae.getSource();
      if (mi == exportHPGL)
      {  Obj3D obj = cv.getObj();
         if (obj != null)
         {  cv.setHPGL(new HPGL(obj));
            cv.repaint();
         }
         else
            Toolkit.getDefaultToolkit().beep();
      }
      else
         super.actionPerformed(ae);
   }
}
}
```

At the start of the class, the variable *exportHPGL* is declared to implement the additional menu item that we need. The method *actionPerformed* overrides the method with the same name of the super class *Fr3D*. When any menu command is used, a test is executed to see if this command is *Export HPGL*. If this is not the case, the method *actionPerformed* of the super class is called to deal with other menu commands. If it is the case, the statement

```
cv.setHPGL(new HPGL(obj));
```

is executed, which makes a variable *hpgl* of the class *CvHlines* point to an *HPGL* object, generated here as an argument of *setHPGL*. By making this variable *hpgl* unequal to *null*, any call of the *CvHLines* method *drawLine* will perform the desired HP-GL output, as you can see in the following lines, copied from Appendix D.

```
private void drawLine(Graphics g, float x1, float y1,
```

```
        float x2, float y2)
{   if (x1 != x2 || y1 != y2)
    {   g.drawLine(iX(x1), iY(y1), iX(x2), iY(y2));
        if (hpgl != null)
        {   hpgl.write("PU;PA" + hpx(x1) + "," + hpy(y1));
            hpgl.write("PD;PA" + hpx(x2) + "," + hpy(y2) + "\n");
        }
    }
}
```

To clarify both the use of the *HPGL* constructor in the above call of *setHPGL* and this method *drawLine*, we will also have a look at the way the class *HPGL* is defined:

```
// HPGL.java: Class for export of HP-GL files.
import java.io.*;

class HPGL
{   FileWriter fw;
    HPGL(Obj3D obj)
    {   String plotFileName = "", fName = obj.getFName();
        for (int i=0; i<fName.length(); i++)
        {   char ch = fName.charAt(i);
            if (ch == '.') break;
            plotFileName += ch;
        }
        plotFileName += ".plt";
        try
        {   fw = new FileWriter(plotFileName);
            fw.write("IN;SP1;\n");
        }
        catch (IOException ioe){}
    }

    void write(String s)
    {   try {fw.write(s); fw.flush();}catch (IOException ioe){}
    }
}
```

Apart from the extra code to generate HP-GL output and the obvious greater complexity of the canvas class due to hidden-line elimination, the structure of program *HLines.java* is very similar to *Wireframe.java* discussed at the end of the previous chapter.

EXERCISES

6.1   Use a normal editor or text processor to create a data file, to be used with program *HLines.java*, for the object consisting of both a horizontal square and a vertical line through its center, as shown twice in Figure 6.26. On the left the viewpoint is above the square (as it is by default), while the situation on the right, with the viewpoint below the square, has been obtained by using the *Viewpoint Down* command of the *View* menu (or by pressing Ctrl+↓).

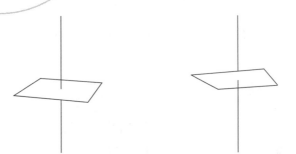

Figure 6.26: Line passing through the center of a square

6.2   Hidden-line elimination works correctly for the problem in Exercise 6.1 because the vertical line passes through edges of the triangles produced by triangulation of the square. Change the horizontal square to a horizontal triangle and use *HLines.java* to display the object with the same vertical line through the triangle. The object may not be displayed properly like those in Figure 6.26. Explain why and find a simple solution.

6.3   The same as Exercise 6.1 for Figure 6.27, which shows two very thin square rings. Again, the object is shown twice to demonstrate that there are four potentially visible faces.

6.4   Write a program *HLinesDashed.java* similar to *HLines.java* but instead of omitting hidden lines, draw them as dashed lines. For example, when applied to the file *letterL.dat* of Section 6.3, it produces the result of Figure 6.28 (after changing the viewpoint). An easy way of doing this is by letting the method *lineSegment* in your class *CvHLinesDashed* first draw the whole line PQ as a dashed line, so these dashed lines, or parts of them, will later be overwritten by normally drawn

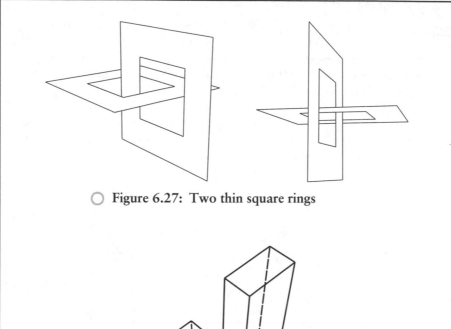

○ **Figure 6.27: Two thin square rings**

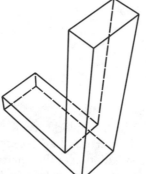

○ **Figure 6.28: Hidden lines represented by dashed lines**

lines if the line segments in question happen to be visible. Note that this should happen only for calls to *lineSegment* from the *paint* method, not for recursive calls. You can use a method *dashedLine* similar to the one of Exercise 1.5. This call to *dashedLine* can be followed by a fragment of the form

```
if (hpgl != null)
{  hpgl.write("LT4 1;\n");
   ...
   hpgl.write("LT;\n");
}
```

where ... denotes two lines similar to those for HP-GL output in the method *drawLine*. This will make dashed lines also appear in HP-GL output when the user uses the *Export HP-GL* command. The two HP-GL commands *LT* shown here will switch from normally drawn to dashed lines, and back to normal lines.

For each of Exercises 6.5–6.10, you are to write a program that generates a 3D object file in the format discussed in Sections 6.3–6.5. You may refer to Appendix E for more relevant examples. The files generated by your program can be read by not only the program *HLines.java*, but also the programs *Painter.java* and *ZBuf.java* described in Chapter 7.

6.5 Write a program *BookView.java* that can generate a data file for an open book. Enable the user to supply the number of sheets, the page width and height, and the name of the output file as program arguments. For example, the files *bookv*4. *dat* and *bookv*150. *dat* for the books shown in Figure 6.29 were obtained by executing the following commands:

```
java BookView 4 15 20 bookv4.dat
java BookView 150 15 20 bookv150.dat
```

Apply the program *HLines.java* to it to generate HP-GL files. Import these files into a text processor or drawing program, as was done twice for Figure 6.29.

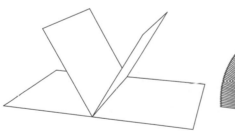

◯ **Figure 6.29: Two open books; number of sheets: 4 on the left and 150 on the right**

6.6 Write a program to generate a globe model of a sphere, as shown in Figure E.4 of Appendix E. Enable the user to supply *n* (see Section E.2) as a program argument.

6.7 Write a program to generate a semi-sphere, as shown in Figure 6.30.

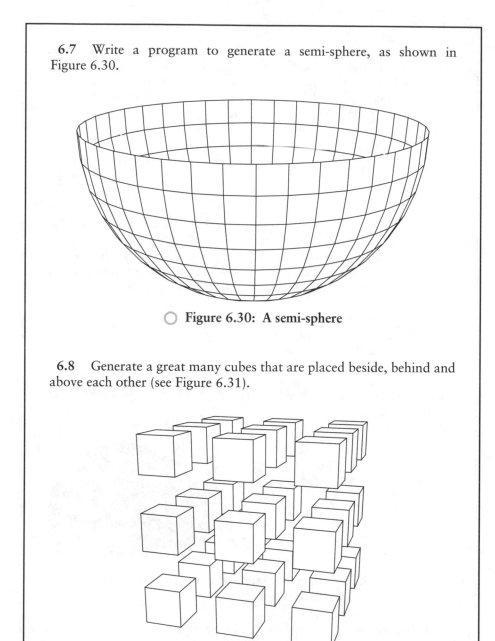

○ **Figure 6.30: A semi-sphere**

6.8 Generate a great many cubes that are placed beside, behind and above each other (see Figure 6.31).

○ **Figure 6.31: A cube of cubes**

6.9 Generate a data file for two tori (the plural of torus), as shown in Figure 6.32.

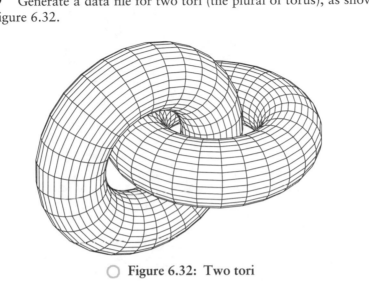

○ **Figure 6.32: Two tori**

6.10 Write a program to generate a spiral staircase, as shown in Figure 6.33.

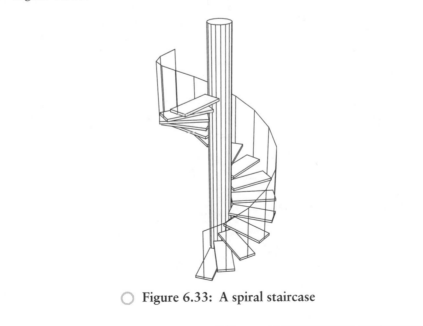

○ **Figure 6.33: A spiral staircase**

Chapter 7

Hidden-Face Elimination

In the previous two chapters we have discussed the wireframe model and how to remove hidden-lines of 3D objects. For example, a realistic looking cube is displayed by simply drawing all the visible edges of the cube. Instead, we can construct a polygon for each of the six faces. If we display only the visible faces, we obtain a more realistic image of a cube. In Exercise 5.2 this was done by displaying only the top, right and front faces, taking the chosen viewpoint into account. Recall that we used $\theta = 0.3$ and $\varphi = 1.3$ (both in radians) at the beginning of class *Obj* in program *CubePers.java*. The solution of Exercise 5.2 will fail, for example, if we use $\theta = -0.3$ because then the left instead of the right face of the cube (see Figure 5.10) should be displayed as a filled polygon. In this chapter, the viewpoint will be taken care of automatically, so that the invisible faces of a cube, also known as *back faces*, are omitted regardless of the chosen viewpoint. Besides, a face may be only partly visible, which is the case, for example, if we have two cubes, with the nearer one partly hiding the farther one. The problem of displaying only the visible portions of faces will also be solved in this chapter. Finally, instead of taking just some colors, we will assume that there is a source of light, such as the sun, to determine the brightness or darkness of a face. Except for Section 7.1, we will display all faces of 3D objects in shades of yellow, against a blue background.

7.1 BACK-FACE CULLING

It is not difficult to determine which faces of a cube are invisible because they are at the back. Such faces, known as *back faces*, can be detected by investigating the orientation of their vertices. To begin with, we specify each face counter-clockwise, when viewed from outside the object. For example, we denote the top face of the cube of Figure 5.11 as the counter-clockwise vertex sequence 4, 5, 6, 7, or, for example, 6, 7, 4, 5, but not 6, 5, 4, 7, for that would be clockwise. In contrast, we can specify the bottom face of the cube as the sequence 0, 3, 2, 1, which is counter-clockwise when this face is viewed from the outside but clockwise in our perspective image. Here we see that the orientation of the bottom face in the image is different from that in 3D space, when the object is viewed from the outside (that is, from below). This is because this bottom face is a back face. We use this principle to tell back faces from visible faces. The method *area*2, discussed in Section 2.7, will now be very useful, so that we will again use the class *Tools*2D, in which this method occurs. Recall that the complete version of class *Tools*2D can be found in Section 2.13.

Note that we should use screen coordinates in the test we have just been discussing. If we used the x_e- and y_e-coordinates instead (ignoring the z_e-coordinate; see Figure 5.4), this test about the orientation of the vertices would be equivalent to testing whether the normal vector, perpendicular to the face in question and pointing outward, would point more or less towards us or away from us, that is, whether that vector would have a positive or a negative z_e-component. This test would be correct with orthographic (or parallel) projection but not necessarily with central projection, which we are using. Exercise 7.1 deals with this subject in greater detail.

This time we will use the *Graphics* methods *setColor* and *fillPolygon*, to display each face, if it is visible, in a color that is unique for that face. Just before we do this (in the *paint* method) we test whether the face we are dealing with is visible; if it is not, it is a back face so that we can ignore it. To demonstrate that this really works, we will modify the viewpoint (by altering the angles θ and φ) each time the user presses a mouse button:

```java
// Backface.java: A cube in perspective with back-face culling.
// Uses: Point2D (Section 1.5), Point3D (Section 3.9),
//       Tools2D (Section 2.13).

import java.awt.*;
import java.awt.event.*;

public class Backface extends Frame
{  public static void main(String[] args){new Backface();}

   Backface()
   {  super("Press mouse button ...");
      addWindowListener(new WindowAdapter()
         {public void windowClosing(WindowEvent e){System.exit(0);}});
      add("Center", new CvBackface());
      Dimension dim = getToolkit().getScreenSize();
      setSize(dim.width/2, dim.height/2);
      setLocation(dim.width/4, dim.height/4);
      show();
   }
}


class CvBackface extends Canvas
{  int centerX, centerY;
   ObjFaces obj = new ObjFaces();
   Color[] color = {Color.blue, Color.green, Color.cyan,
                    Color.magenta, Color.red, Color.yellow};
   float dPhi = 0.1F;
   CvBackface()
   {  addMouseListener(new MouseAdapter()
        { public void mousePressed(MouseEvent evt)
           { obj.theta += 0.1F;
             obj.phi += dPhi;
```

```
            if (obj.phi > 2 || obj.phi < 0.3) dPhi = -dPhi;
            repaint();
         }
      });
   }

   int iX(float x){return Math.round(centerX + x);}
   int iY(float y){return Math.round(centerY - y);}

   public void paint(Graphics g)
   {  Dimension dim = getSize();
      int maxX = dim.width - 1, maxY = dim.height - 1,
         minMaxXY = Math.min(maxX, maxY);
      centerX = maxX/2;
      centerY = maxY/2;
      obj.d = obj.rho * minMaxXY / obj.objSize;
      obj.eyeAndScreen();
      Point2D[] p = new Point2D[4];
      for (int j=0; j<6; j++)
      {  Polygon pol = new Polygon();
         Square sq = obj.f[j];
         for (int i=0; i<4; i++)
         {  int vertexNr = sq.nr[i];
            p[i] = obj.vScr[vertexNr];
            pol.addPoint(iX(p[i].x), iY(p[i].y));
         }
         g.setColor(color[j]);
         if (Tools2D.area2(p[0], p[1], p[2]) > 0)
            g.fillPolygon(pol);
      }
   }
}

class ObjFaces // Contains 3D object data of cube faces
{  float rho, theta=0.3F, phi=1.3F, d;
   Point3D[] w;      // World coordinates
   Point3D[] e;      // Eye coordinates
                     // (e = wV where V is a 4 x 4 matrix)
   Point2D[] vScr;  // Screen coordinates
   Square[] f;      // The six (square) faces of a cube.
   float v11, v12, v13, v21, v22, v23,
      v32, v33, v43, // Elements of viewing matrix V.
      xe, ye, ze, objSize;
```

```
ObjFaces()
{  w = new Point3D[8];
   e = new Point3D[8];
   vScr = new Point2D[8];
   f = new Square[6];
   // Bottom surface:
   w[0] = new Point3D( 1, -1, -1);
   w[1] = new Point3D( 1,  1, -1);
   w[2] = new Point3D(-1,  1, -1);
   w[3] = new Point3D(-1, -1, -1);
   // Top surface:
   w[4] = new Point3D( 1, -1,  1);
   w[5] = new Point3D( 1,  1,  1);
   w[6] = new Point3D(-1,  1,  1);
   w[7] = new Point3D(-1, -1,  1);
   f[0] = new Square (0, 1, 5, 4); // Front
   f[1] = new Square (1, 2, 6, 5); // Right
   f[2] = new Square (2, 3, 7, 6); // Back
   f[3] = new Square (3, 0, 4, 7); // Left
   f[4] = new Square (4, 5, 6, 7); // Top
   f[5] = new Square (0, 3, 2, 1); // Bottom
   objSize = (float)Math.sqrt (12F);
      // distance between two opposite vertices.
   rho = 3 * objSize; // For reasonable perspective effect
}


void initPersp()
{  float
   costh = (float)Math.cos(theta), sinth = (float)Math.sin(theta),
   cosph = (float)Math.cos(phi), sinph = (float)Math.sin(phi);
   v11 = -sinth;   v12 = -cosph * costh;   v13 = sinph * costh;
   v21 = costh;    v22 = -cosph * sinth;   v23 = sinph * sinth;
                   v32 = sinph;            v33 = cosph;
                                           v43 = -rho;

}


void eyeAndScreen()
{  initPersp();
   for (int i=0; i<8; i++)
   {  Point3D p = w[i];
      float x = v11 * p.x + v21 * p.y;
      float y = v12 * p.x + v22 * p.y + v32 * p.z;
      float z = v13 * p.x + v23 * p.y + v33 * p.z + v43;
```

```
            Point3D Pe = e[i] = new Point3D(x, y, z);
            vScr[i] = new Point2D(-d * Pe.x/Pe.z, -d * Pe.y/Pe.z);
      }
   }
}

class Square
{  int nr[];
   Square(int iA, int iB, int iC, int iD)
   {  nr = new int[4];
      nr[0] = iA; nr[1] = iB; nr[2] = iC; nr[3] = iD;
   }
}
```

If you do not use the Java *classpath* variable, you should make sure that the files *Point2D.class*, *Point3D.class* and *Tools2D.class* (or the corresponding *.java* files) are in the same directory as this program. We now obtain images of a cube in bright colors, so the result on the screen looks much better than Figure 7.1. Initially, the top face of the cube is visible, but after we have clicked the mouse button several times the cube shows its bottom face, as is the case in this illustration.

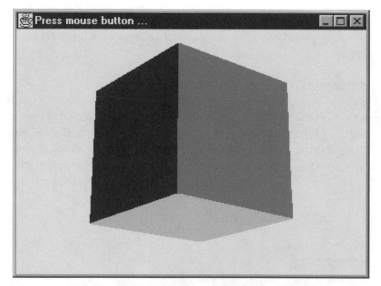

○ **Figure 7.1: Result of back-face culling**

We will use back-face culling in the programs that follow. This technique is worthwhile because it drastically reduces the number of polygons that may be visible and it is inexpensive compared with some more time-consuming algorithms to be discussed later in this chapter. However, using only back-face culling is not sufficient, since it does not work for non-convex solids. As Figure 6.12 illustrates, the solid letter L is not convex, since the line that connects, for example, vertices 1 and 11 does not lie completely inside the object. In that example, the rectangle 5-6-7-8 is not a back face, but it is only partly visible.

7.2 COLORING INDIVIDUAL FACES

Let us now decide on the color to be used for each polygon (and for all triangles of which it consists) based on its orientation in relation to the light source. For a polygon in a plane with equation

$$ax + by + cz = h,$$

we can obtain a color code by calling the method *colorCode* of the class *Obj3D* as follows:

```
int cCode = obj.colorCode(a, b, c);
```

(Note that we use the name *colorCode* both for an array and for a method.) This color code, stored in the variable *cCode*, will later be used as follows:

```
g.setColor(new Color(cCode, cCode, 0));
```

Using integers in the range 0–255 for *cCode*, we obtain shades of yellow in this way. For a given polygon, we will associate the values in this range with the inner product (see Section 2.2) between the following two vectors:

$\mathbf{s} = (1/\sqrt{3})(-1, 1, 1)$:   vector directed from the object to the sun;
$\mathbf{n} = (a, b, c)$:   normal vector, perpendicular to the polygon and pointing away from the object (more or less towards the viewpoint E).

Note that these vectors have length 1 and are expressed in eye coordinates x_e, y_e and z_e. The signs of the triple elements -1, 1, 1 imply that the light comes from the left, from above and from the front, as Figure 7.2 illustrates.

Since we know the range of the color codes, we can convert inner-product values to color codes, if we also know the range of all possible inner products that can occur. This range

$$inprodRange = inprodMax - inprodMin$$

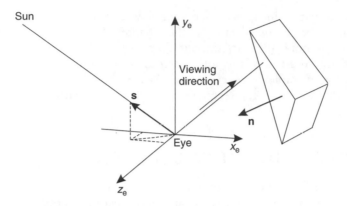

○ **Figure 7.2: Vector s, pointing to the sun, and normal vector n of a face**

is found in the method *planeCoeff* of the class *Obj3D* simply by computing all those inner products, as soon as *a*, *b* and *c* are computed.

The following method of *Obj3D.java* shows how an inner product $n \cdot s$, discussed above, is computed and how the above values *inprodMin* and *inprodRange* are used to derive a color code in the range 0–255:

```
int colorCode(double a, double b, double c)
{   double inprod = a * sunX + b * sunY + c * sunZ;
    return (int)Math.round(((inprod - inprodMin)/inprodRange) * 255);
}
```

The method *colorCode* needs to be called for every polygon, or face, to be colored. It is usually placed in the method *paint*, along with its color code and its distance, as demonstrated in the example program of the next section.

7.3 PAINTER'S ALGORITHM

It is an attractive idea to solve the hidden-face problem by displaying all polygons in a specific order, namely first the most distant one, then the second furthest, and so on, finishing with the one that is closest to the viewpoint. Painters sometimes follow the same principle, particularly when working with oil paintings. They typically start with the background and paint a new layer for objects on the foreground later, so that the overlapped parts of objects in the background, painted previously, are covered by the current layer and thus become invisible. This algorithm is therefore known as the *painter's algorithm*. It is based on the assumption that each triangle can be assigned a z_e-coordinate,

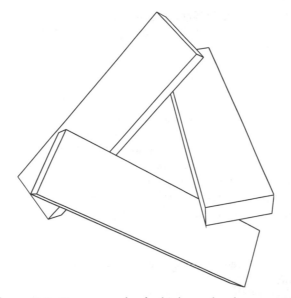

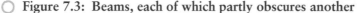

Figure 7.3: Beams, each of which partly obscures another

which we can use to sort all triangles. One way of obtaining such a z_e-coordinate for a triangle ABC is by computing the average of the three z_e-coordinates of A, B and C. However, there is a problem, which is clarified by Figure 7.3. For each of the three beams, a large rectangle is partly obscured by another, so we cannot satisfactorily place them (or the triangles in which these rectangles are divided) in the desired order, that is, from back to front (see also Figures 7.8 and 7.9). Consequently, the naïve approach just suggested will fail in this case. Surprisingly enough, it gives good results in many other cases, such as the solid letter L in Figure 6.2 and the sphere and cone in Figure 7.5. It is also very fast.

The program *Painter.java* is listed below. If you compile and run this program, all classes defined in the program files *Point2D.java*, *Point3D.java*, *Obj3D.java*, etc., must be available, as the comment below indicates. Recall our discussion of this subject at the end of Chapter 1.

```
// Painter.java: Perspective drawing using an input file that lists
//    vertices and faces. Based on the Painter's algorithm.
// Uses: Fr3D (Section 5.5) and CvPainter (Section 7.3),
//       Point2D (Section 1.5), Point3D (Section 3.9),
//       Obj3D, Polygon3D, Tria, Fr3D, Canvas3D (Section 5.5).
import java.awt.*;

public class Painter extends Frame
```

```
{  public static void main(String[] args)
   {  new Fr3D(args.length > 0 ? args[0] : null, new CvPainter(),
         "Painter");
   }
}
```

In the above *Fr3D* constructor call, the first argument is a conditional expression to check if the user has used the option of specifying an input file as a program argument in the command line. (This is not required, since the user can also use the *File* menu to open input files). Recall that this is similar to what we did in Sections 5.6 and 6.8. The second argument of the constructor call just mentioned creates an object of class *CvPainter*, which is listed below in the separate file *CvPainter.java*. The third argument specifies the window title *Painter* that will appear.

```
// CvPainter.java: Used in the file Painter.java.
import java.awt.*;
import java.util.*;

class CvPainter extends Canvas3D
{  private int maxX, maxY, centerX, centerY;
   private Obj3D obj;
   private Point2D imgCenter;

   Obj3D getObj(){return obj;}
   void setObj(Obj3D obj){this.obj = obj;}
   int iX(float x){return Math.round(centerX + x - imgCenter.x);}
   int iY(float y){return Math.round(centerY - y + imgCenter.y);}

   void sort(Tria[] tr, int[] colorCode, float[] zTr, int l, int r)
   {  int i = l, j = r, wInt;
      float x = zTr[(i + j)/2], w;
      Tria wTria;
      do
      {  while (zTr[i] < x) i++;
         while (zTr[j] > x) j--;
         if (i < j)
         {  w = zTr[i]; zTr[i] = zTr[j]; zTr[j] = w;
            wTria = tr[i]; tr[i] = tr[j]; tr[j] = wTria;
            wInt = colorCode[i]; colorCode[i] = colorCode[j];
            colorCode[j] = wInt;
            i++; j--;
         } else
```

```
         if (i == j) {i++; j--;}
      } while (i <= j);
      if (l < j) sort(tr, colorCode, zTr, l, j);
      if (i < r) sort(tr, colorCode, zTr, i, r);
   }

public void paint(Graphics g)
{  if (obj == null) return;
   Vector polyList = obj.getPolyList();
   if (polyList == null) return;
   int nFaces = polyList.size();
   if (nFaces == 0) return;

   Dimension dim = getSize();
   maxX = dim.width - 1; maxY = dim.height - 1;
   centerX = maxX/2; centerY = maxY/2;
   // ze-axis towards eye, so ze-coordinates of
   // object points are all negative.
   // obj is a java object that contains all data:
   // - Vector w         (world coordinates)
   // - Array e          (eye coordinates)
   // - Array vScr       (screen coordinates)
   // - Vector polyList (Polygon3D objects)

   // Every Polygon3D value contains:
   // - Array 'nrs' for vertex numbers
   // - Values a, b, c, h for the plane ax+by+cz=h.
   // - Array t (with nrs.length-2 elements of type Tria)

   // Every Tria value consists of the three vertex
   // numbers iA, iB and iC.
   obj.eyeAndScreen(dim);
        // Computation of eye and screen coordinates.

   imgCenter = obj.getImgCenter();
   obj.planeCoeff();     // Compute a, b, c and h.

   // Construct an array of triangles in
   // each polygon and count the total number
   // of triangles:
   int nTria = 0;
   for (int j=0; j<nFaces; j++)
   {  Polygon3D pol = (Polygon3D)(polyList.elementAt(j));
```

```
         if (pol.getNrs().length < 3 || pol.getH() >= 0)
            continue;
         pol.triangulate(obj);
         nTria += pol.getT().length;
      }
      Tria[] tr = new Tria[nTria];
      int[] colorCode = new int[nTria];
      float[] zTr = new float[nTria];
      int iTria = 0;
      Point3D[] e = obj.getE();
      Point2D[] vScr = obj.getVScr();

      for (int j=0; j<nFaces; j++)
      {  Polygon3D pol = (Polygon3D)(polyList.elementAt(j));
         if (pol.getNrs().length < 3 || pol.getH() >= 0) continue;
         int cCode =
            obj.colorCode(pol.getA(), pol.getB(), pol.getC());
         Tria[] t = pol.getT();
         for (int i=0; i< t.length; i++)
         {  Tria tri = t[i];
            tr[iTria] = tri;
            colorCode[iTria] = cCode;
            float zA = e[tri.iA].z, zB = e[tri.iB].z,
               zC = e[tri.iC].z;
            zTr[iTria++] = zA + zB + zC;
         }
      }

      sort(tr, colorCode, zTr, 0, nTria - 1);

      for (iTria=0; iTria<nTria; iTria++)
      {  Tria tri = tr[iTria];
         Point2D a = vScr[tri.iA],
                 b = vScr[tri.iB],
                 c = vScr[tri.iC];
         int cCode = colorCode[iTria];
         g.setColor(new Color(cCode, cCode, 0));
         int[] x = {iX(a.x), iX(b.x), iX(c.x)};
         int[] y = {iY(a.y), iY(b.y), iY(c.y)};
         g.fillPolygon(x, y, 3);
      }
   }
}
```

We use a special method, *sort*, to sort the triangles; it is based on the well-known and efficient quicksort algorithm, discussed in detail in Ammeraal (1996). Before calling *sort*, we build three arrays:

Array element	Type	Contains
tr[iTria]	*Tria*	the three vertex numbers of the triangle
colorCode[iTria]	*int*	value between 0 and 255
zTr[iTria]	*float*	value representing z_e-coordinate of triangle

For a given subscript value *iTria*, the three array elements in the first column of this table belong to the same triangle. We may regard them as members of the same record, of which *zTr* is the key. During sorting, whenever two elements *zTr[i]* and *zTr[j]* are swapped, we swap *tr[i]* and *tr[j]* as well as *colorCode[i]* and *colorCode[j]* at the same time. It seems reasonable to use the average of the three z_e-coordinates of a triangle's vertices as the z_e-coordinate of that triangle, but we may as well simply use the sum instead of the average. Recall that the positive z_e-axis points towards us, so that all z_e values that we use are negative: the more negative it is, the further away the triangle is. It follows that we have to paint the triangles in increasing order of their z_e-coordinates, or, equivalently, in decreasing order of their absolute values.

As the class *CvPainter* in the program *Painter.java* shows, there is a call to *colorCode* in the method *paint* for every polygon just before entering the loop. Within the loop, all the triangles of that polygon, their color code, and each triangle's distance, are stored in the three arrays *tr*, *colorCode* and *zTr*, discussed above. After this has been done for all polygons, the triangles are sorted on the basis of their distances stored in *zTr*, and then displayed in order of decreasing distance.

Next, we demonstrate the application of the painter's algorithm to some simple 3D objects, with the implementation of user operations. As Figure 7.4 shows, we will enable the user to change the viewpoint E, characterized by its spherical coordinates. Immediately after an input file has been opened, these coordinates have the following (default) values:

$\rho = 3 \times$ the distance between two opposite vertices of a box in which the objects fits

$\theta = 0.3$ radians ($\approx 17°$)

$\varphi = 1.3$ radians ($\approx 74°$)

If the user gives the menu command *Viewpoint Down* the value of φ is increased by 0.1 radians ($\approx 6°$). Similarly, *Viewpoint Up* decreases φ by 0.1 radians,

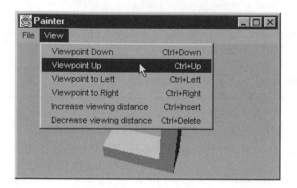

○ **Figure 7.4: Program *Painter.java* applied to file *letterL.dat***

while *Viewpoint Left* and *Viewpoint Right* decrease and increase θ by 0.1 radians, respectively. The same effects can be achieved by using one of the four arrow keys, ↓, ↑, ← and →, together with the Ctrl-key, as indicated in the menu. Figure 7.4 shows the screen when the input file *letterL.dat*, discussed in Section 6.3, has been read by program *Painter.java* and the user has used the *Viewpoint Up* command four times, so that we view the object from a higher viewpoint than in the initial situation.

The *File* menu, not shown in Figure 7.4, consists of the following commands:

```
Open    Ctrl+O
Exit    Ctrl+Q
```

If several input files are available, the user can switch to another object by using the *Open* command (or Ctrl+O), as usual. The simplicity of our file format makes it easy to generate such files by other programs, as we will discuss in the next two sections. In particular, mathematically well-defined solids, such as the sphere and the cone of Figure 7.5, are very suitable for this. Incidentally, this example demonstrates that what we call a 'three-dimensional object' may consist of several solids. Note, however, that the input-file format requires that all vertices, in this example of both the sphere and the cone, must be defined in the first part of the file and all faces in the second. In other words, the line with the word *Faces* must occur only once in the file. This example also shows that curved surfaces can be approximated by a great many flat faces. In this example, there are altogether 1804 vertices and 1920 faces. Here the command *Viewpoint Down* has been used four times and the command *Viewpoint Right* twice.

An object will normally appear with a reasonable perspective effect, but the user will be able to increase or decrease the viewing distance by using menu commands or their shortcuts, Ctrl+Insert and Ctrl+Delete, as Figure 7.4 shows.

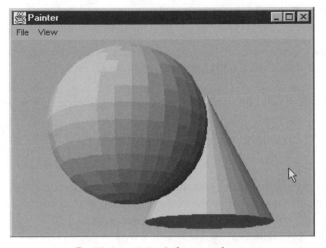

○ **Figure 7.5: Sphere and cone**

Although we can see only shades of gray in Figures 7.4 and 7.5, the situation looks much more interesting on the screen: the background is light blue like the sky and all faces of the object are yellow. The source of light is far away, at the top left, so that the upper and the left faces are bright yellow, while those on the right and on the bottom are much darker.

To start the program, we can supply the (initial) input file as a program argument, if we like. For example, if the first 3D object to be displayed is given by the file *letterL.dat*, we can start the program by entering

```
java Painter   letterL.dat
```

Alternatively, we can enter

```
java Painter
```

and use the *Open* command in the *File* menu (or Ctrl+O) to specify the input file *letterL.dat*. With both ways of starting the program, we can switch to another object by using this *Open* command.

As discussed at the beginning of this section, the painter's algorithm will fail in some cases, such as the three beams of Figure 7.3. We will therefore discuss another algorithm for hidden-face elimination in the next section.

7.4 Z-BUFFER ALGORITHM

If the images of two faces F_1 and F_2 overlap, we may consider two questions with regard to the correct representation of these faces:

1. Which pixels would be used for both F_1 and F_2 if each face were completely visible?
2. For each of these pixels, which of the corresponding points in F_1 and F_2 is nearer?

The Z-buffer algorithm deals with these questions in a general and elegant way. Recall that we are using an eye-coordinate system, with z-coordinates denoting the distance we are interested in. We consider points P in 3D space and their corresponding projections P′ in 2D space, where we use central projection with the viewpoint E as the center of projection. In other words, each line PE is a ray of light, intersecting the screen in P′. We are especially interested in such points P′ that are the centers of pixels.

The Z-buffer algorithm is based on a large two-dimensional array in which we store numbers that represent z-coordinates. Using the variable *dim* as the current canvas dimension, we define the following array, also known as a *Z-buffer*, for this purpose:

```
private float buf[][];
buf = new float[dim.width][dim.height];
```

We initialize array *buf* with values corresponding to points that are very far away. As before, we ignore back faces. For each of the remaining faces we compute all pixels and the z-values that correspond with these. For each pixel P′(*ix*, *iy*), we test whether the corresponding point P in 3D space is nearer than *buf*[*ix*][*iy*] indicates. If it is, we put this pixel on the screen, using the color for the face in question, computed as in the previous section, while, at the same time, updating *buf*[*ix*][*iy*]:

```
For each face F (and its image, consisting of a set of pixels):
    For each pixel P′(ix, iy), corresponding with a 3D point P of F:
        If P is nearer than the distance stored in buf[ix][iy],
        {   set pixel P′ to the color for face F
            update buf[ix][iy] so that it refers to the distance of P
        }
```

In this discussion, the words *distance* and *near* refer to the z-coordinates in the eye-coordinate system. (Since we use no other 3D coordinates here, we simply write z instead of z_e here.) There are two aspects that make the implementation of the above algorithm a bit tricky:

1. Since the z-axis points towards us, the larger z is, the shorter the distance.
2. It is necessary to use $1/z$ instead of z for linear interpolation.

Let us take a look at this rather surprising point 2. Suppose we are given the z_e-coordinates of two points A and B in 3D space and the central projections A′ and B′ of these points on the screen. Besides, some point P′ on the screen, lying on A′B′, is given and we have

$$x_{P'} = x_{A'} + \lambda(x_{B'} - x_{A'})$$
$$y_{P'} = y_{A'} + \lambda(y_{B'} - y_{A'})$$

where $x_{P'}$, and so on, are screen coordinates. We are then interested in the point P (in 3D space) of which P′ is the central projection. Since we want to know how far away P is, our goal is to compute z_P. (After this, we can also compute the 3D coordinates $x_P = -x_{P'}z_P/d$ and $y_P = -y_{P'}z_P/d$, using Equations (5.7) and (5.8) of Section 5.3, where we wrote X and Y instead of x' and y'.) Curiously enough, to compute this eye coordinate z_P by interpolation, we need to use the inverse values of the z-coordinates:

$$\frac{1}{z_P} = \frac{1}{z_A} + \lambda\left(\frac{1}{z_B} - \frac{1}{z_A}\right)$$

We will simply use this result here; it is discussed in more detail in Appendix A. Let us write

$$z_{Pi} = \frac{1}{z_P}$$

which we write as *zPi* (equal to $1/zP$) in the program. Using the same convention ($z_{Ai} = 1/zA$, etc.) for other variables and writing xA, yA etc. for screen coordinates, we compute the centroid $D(x_D, y_D)$ along with its inverse z-value z_{Di} for each triangle ABC as follows:

```
xD = (xA + xB + xC)/3;
yD = (yA + yB + yC)/3;
zDi = (zAi + zBi + zCi)/3;
```

This centroid will be the basis for computing z_i-values for other points of the triangle by linear interpolation. To do this, we are interested in how much z_{Pi} increases if P moves one pixel to the right. This quantity, which we may write as $\partial z_i/\partial x$ or simply as *dzdx* in the program, is constant for the whole triangle.

We will use this value, as well as its counterpart $dzdy = \partial z_i/\partial y$ indicating how much z_{Pi} increases if P moves one pixel upward, that is, if the screen coordinate y_P is increased by 1. It is useful to think of the triples x, y and z_i (where x and y are screen coordinates and $z_i = 1/z$) as points in a plane of an imaginary 3D space. We can then denote this plane as

$$ax + by + cz_i = k \tag{7.1}$$

Writing this in the form $z_i = (k - ax - by)/c$ and applying partial differentiation to z_i, we obtain

$$\frac{\partial z_i}{\partial x} = -\frac{a}{c} \tag{7.2}$$

$$\frac{\partial z_i}{\partial y} = -\frac{b}{c} \tag{7.3}$$

To find a, b and c, remember that (a, b, c) in Equation (7.1) is the normal vector of the plane of triangle ABC (in the imaginary space we are dealing with). We define the vectors

$$\mathbf{u} = \mathbf{AB} = (u_1, u_2, u_3)$$
$$\mathbf{v} = \mathbf{AC} = (v_1, v_2, v_3)$$

where

$$u_1 = x_B - x_A \qquad\qquad v_1 = x_C - x_A$$
$$u_2 = y_B - y_A \qquad\qquad v_2 = y_C - y_A$$
$$u_3 = z_{Bi} - z_{Ai} \qquad\qquad v_3 = z_{Ci} - z_{Ai}$$

Then the vector product

$$\mathbf{u} \times \mathbf{v} = \begin{vmatrix} \mathbf{i} & \mathbf{j} & \mathbf{k} \\ u_1 & u_2 & u_3 \\ v_1 & v_2 & v_3 \end{vmatrix}$$

(see Section 2.4) is also perpendicular to triangle ABC, so that we can compute the desired values a, b and c of (7.1), (7.2) and (7.3) as the coefficients of $\mathbf{i}$, $\mathbf{j}$ and $\mathbf{k}$, respectively, finding

$$a = u_2 v_3 - u_3 v_2$$
$$b = u_3 v_1 - u_1 v_3$$
$$c = u_1 v_2 - u_2 v_1$$

So much for the computation of $dzdx = \partial z_i/\partial x$ and $dzdy = \partial z_i/\partial y$, which we will use to compute z_{Pi} for each point P of triangle ABC, as we will see below.

To prepare for traversing all relevant *scan lines* for triangle ABC, such as LR in Figure 7.6, we compute the y-coordinates $yTop$ and $yBottom$ of the vertices at the top and the bottom of this triangle. For all pixels that comprise triangle ABC on the screen, we have to compute the z-coordinate of the corresponding point in 3D space. In view of the enormous number of those pixels, we should do this as efficiently as possible. Working from the bottom of the triangle to the top, when dealing with a scan line, we traverse all its pixels from left to right. Figure 7.6 shows a situation in which all pixels of triangle ABC below the scan line LR have already been dealt with.

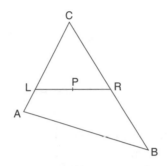

○ **Figure 7.6: Triangle ABC and scan line LR**

For each scan line at level y ($yBottom \leq y \leq yTop$), we find the points of intersection L and R with triangle ABC as follows. We introduce the points I, J and K, which are associated with the triangle edges BC, CA and AB, respectively. Initially, we set the program variables xI, xJ and xK to 10^{30}, and $xI1$, $xJ1$ and $xK1$ to -10^{30}. Then, if y lies between yB and yC or is equal to one of these values, we compute the point of intersection of the scan line with BC, and we assign the x-coordinate of this point to both xI and $xI1$. In the same way we possibly update xJ, $xJ1$ for CA and xK and $xK1$ for AB. After this, each of the variables xI, xJ and xK is equal either to its original value 10^{30} or to the x-coordinate of the scan line in question with BC, CA and AB, respectively. The same applies to the other three variables, except that these may still have a different original value, -10^{30}. We can now easily find xL and xR:

$$xL = \min(xI, xJ, xK)$$
$$xR = \max(xI1, xJ1, xK1)$$

So far, we have been using floating-point, logical coordinates y, xL and xR. Since we have to deal with pixels, we convert these to the (integer) device coordinates iY, iXL and iXR as follows:

```
int iy = iY(y), iXL = iX(xL+0.5), iXR = iX(xR-0.5);
```

By adding 0.5 to xL and subtracting 0.5 from xR, we avoid clashes between neighboring triangles of different colors: the pixel (iXR, y) belonging to triangle

ABC should preferably not also occur as a pixel (iXL, y) of the right-hand neighbor of this triangle, because it would then not be clear which color to use for this pixel. Before entering the loop for all pixels $iXL, iXL + 1, \ldots, iXR$ for the scan line on level y, we compute the inverse z value $zi = zLi$ for the pixel (iXL, y). Theoretically, this value is

$$z_{Li} = z_{Di} + (y - y_D)\frac{\partial z}{\partial y} + (x_L - x_D)\frac{\partial z}{\partial x}$$

In the program we modify this a little, giving a little more weight to the centroid D of the triangle:

```
double zi = 1.01 * zDi + (y - yD) * dzdy + (xL - xD) * dzdx;
```

This modification is useful in some special cases of which we will give an example at the end of this section.

Starting at the left end (iXL, y) of a scan line with the above z value $zi = z_{Li}$, we could now write the loop for this scan line as follows:

```
for (int x=iXL; x<=iXR; x++)
{  if (zi < buf[x][iy])    // '<' means 'nearer'
   {  g.drawLine(x, iy, x, iy);
      buf[x][iy] = (float)zi;
   }
   zi += dzdx;
}
```

Along a horizontal line LR, shown in Figure 7.6, we compute the inverse z-coordinate, zi. If this is less than the contents of the array element $buf[x][y]$, we put a pixel on the screen and update that array element.

The above test $zi < buf[x][y]$ may at first look confusing. Since the positive z-axis of the eye-coordinate system points towards us, we have:

• the *larger* the z-coordinate of a point, the nearer this point is to the eye.

However, we are using inverse values $zi = 1/z$, so that the above is equivalent to

• the *smaller* the zi-value of a point, the nearer it is to the eye.

A complicating factor is that we are using negative z-coordinates, but the above also applies to negative numbers. The following example for two points P and Q will make the situation clear:

P nearby		Q far away
$z_P = -10$	$>$	$z_Q = -20$
$zi_P = 1/z_P = -0.1$	$<$	$zi_Q = 1/z_Q = -0.05$

Another curious aspect of the above fragment is that putting a pixel on the screen is done here by drawing a line of only one pixel. It is strange that Java does not supply a more elementary routine, say, *putPixel*, for this purpose. However, we can do much better by delaying this '*putPixel*' operation until we know for how many adjacent pixels it is to be used; in other words, we build horizontal line segments in memory, storing their leftmost x values and displaying these segments if we can no longer extend it on the right. This implies that even if there were a *putPixel* method, we would not use it, but rather draw horizontal line segments, consisting of some pixels we have recently been dealing with. Instead of the above for-loop we will actually use an 'optimized' fragment which is equivalent to it, as we will discuss in a moment. The program *ZBuf.java* is listed below.

```
// ZBuf.java: Perspective drawing using an input file that
//     lists vertices and faces.
//     Z-buffer algorithm used for hidden-face elimination.
// Uses: Point2D (Section 1.5), Point3D (Section 3.9) and
//       Obj3D, Polygon3D, Tria, Fr3D, Canvas3D (Section 5.5).
import java.awt.*;

public class ZBuf extends Frame
{ public static void main(String[] args)
   { new Fr3D(args.length > 0 ? args[0] : null, new CvZBuf(),
       "ZBuf");
   }
}
```

The class *CvZBuf* is defined in the following separate file:

```
// CvZBuf.java: Canvas class for ZBuf.java.
import java.awt.*;
import java.util.*;

class CvZBuf extends Canvas3D
```

```
{   private int maxX, maxY, centerX, centerY, maxX0 = -1, maxY0 = -1;
    private float buf[][];
    private Obj3D obj;
    private Point2D imgCenter;

    int iX(float x){return Math.round(centerX + x - imgCenter.x);}
    int iY(float y){return Math.round(centerY - y + imgCenter.y);}

    Obj3D getObj(){return obj;}
    void setObj(Obj3D obj){this.obj = obj;}

    public void paint(Graphics g)
    {   if (obj == null) return;
        Vector polyList = obj.getPolyList();
        if (polyList == null) return;
        int nFaces = polyList.size();
        if (nFaces == 0) return;
        float xe, ye, ze;

        Dimension dim = getSize();
        maxX = dim.width - 1; maxY = dim.height - 1;
        centerX = maxX/2; centerY = maxY/2;
        // ze-axis towards eye, so ze-coordinates of
        // object points are all negative. Since screen
        // coordinates x and y are used to interpolate for
        // the z-direction, we have to deal with 1/z instead
        // of z. With negative z, a small value of 1/z means
        // a small value of |z| for a nearby point. We there-
        // fore begin with large buffer values 1e30:
        if (maxX != maxX0 || maxY != maxY0)
        {   buf = new float[dim.width][dim.height];
            maxX0 = maxX; maxY0 = maxY;
        }
        for (int iy=0; iy<dim.height; iy++)
            for (int ix=0; ix<dim.width; ix++)buf[ix][iy] = 1e30F;

        obj.eyeAndScreen(dim);
        imgCenter = obj.getImgCenter();
        obj.planeCoeff();      // Compute a, b, c and h.
        Point3D[] e = obj.getE();
        Point2D[] vScr = obj.getVScr();

        for (int j=0; j<nFaces; j++)
```

```
{  Polygon3D pol = (Polygon3D)(polyList.elementAt(j));
   if (pol.getNrs().length < 3 || pol.getH() >= 0)
      continue;
   int cCode =
      obj.colorCode(pol.getA(), pol.getB(), pol.getC());
   g.setColor(new Color(cCode, cCode, 0));

   pol.triangulate(obj);

   Tria[] t = pol.getT();
   for (int i=0; i<t.length; i++)
   {  Tria tri = t[i];
      int iA = tri.iA, iB = tri.iB, iC = tri.iC;
      Point2D a = vScr[iA], b = vScr[iB], c = vScr[iC];
      double zAi = 1/e[tri.iA].z, zBi = 1/e[tri.iB].z,
         zCi = 1/e[tri.iC].z;
      // We now compute the coefficients a, b and c
      // (written here as aa, bb and cc)
      // of the imaginary plane ax + by + czi = h,
      // where zi is 1/z (and x, y and z are
      // eye coordinates. Then we compute
      // the partial derivatives dzdx and dzdy:
      double u1 = b.x - a.x, v1 = c.x - a.x,
         u2 = b.y - a.y, v2 = c.y - a.y,
         cc = u1 * v2 - u2 * v1;
      if (cc <= 0) continue;
      double xA = a.x, yA = a.y,
         xB = b.x, yB = b.y,
         xC = c.x, yC = c.y,
         xD = (xA + xB + xC)/3,
         yD = (yA + yB + yC)/3,
         zDi = (zAi + zBi + zCi)/3,
         u3 = zBi - zAi, v3 = zCi - zAi,
         aa = u2 * v3 - u3 * v2,
         bb = u3 * v1 - u1 * v3,
         dzdx = -aa/cc, dzdy = -bb/cc,
         yBottomR = Math.min(yA, Math.min(yB, yC)),
         yTopR = Math.max(yA, Math.max(yB, yC));
      int yBottom = (int)Math.ceil(yBottomR),
         yTop = (int)Math.floor(yTopR);

      for (int y=yBottom; y<=yTop; y++)
      {  // Compute horizontal line segment (xL, xR)
```

```
                    // for coordinate y:
                    double xI, xJ, xK, xI1, xJ1, xK1, xL, xR;
                    xI = xJ = xK = 1e30;
                    xI1 = xJ1 = xK1 = -1e30;
                    if ((y - yB) * (y - yC) <= 0 && yB != yC)
                       xI = xI1 = xC + (y - yC)/(yB - yC) * (xB - xC);
                    if ((y - yC) * (y - yA) <= 0 && yC != yA)
                       xJ = xJ1 = xA + (y - yA)/(yC - yA) * (xC - xA);
                    if ((y - yA) * (y - yB) <= 0 && yA != yB)
                       xK = xK1 = xB + (y - yB)/(yA - yB) * (xA - xB);
                    // xL = xR = xI;
                    xL = Math.min(xI, Math.min(xJ, xK));
                    xR = Math.max(xI1, Math.max(xJ1, xK1));
                    int iy = iY((float)y), iXL = iX((float)(xL+0.5)),
                       iXR = iX((float)(xR-0.5));
                    double zi =  1.01 * zDi + (y - yD) * dzdy +
                                             (xL - xD) * dzdx;
                /*
                    for (int x=iXL; x<=iXR; x++)
                    { if (zi < buf[x][iy]) // < is nearer
                       { g.drawLine(x, iy, x, iy);
                          buf[x][iy] = (float)zi;
                       }
                       zi += dzdx;
                    }
                */
                    // The above comment fragment is optimized below:
                    // ---
                    boolean leftmostValid = false;
                    int xLeftmost = 0;
                    for (int ix=iXL; ix<=iXR; ix++)
                    { if (zi < buf[ix][iy])  // < means nearer
                       { if (!leftmostValid)
                          { xLeftmost = ix;
                             leftmostValid = true;
                          }
                          buf[ix][iy] = (float)zi;
                       }
                       else
                       if (leftmostValid)
                       { g.drawLine(xLeftmost, iy, ix-1, iy);
                          leftmostValid = false;
                       }
```

```
            zi += dzdx;
        }
        if (leftmostValid)
            g.drawLine(xLeftmost, iy, iXR, iy);
    // ---
        }
    }
    }
  }
}
```

Almost at the end of this program, the fragment between the two lines // --- is a more efficient version than the for-loop in the comment that precedes it. In that for-loop, each line LR is drawn pixel by pixel. In the more efficient version that follows, however, the line LR is drawn by one or more line segments depending on how much the line LR is blocked by the triangles that are nearer. In the best case, where no triangle is in front of the line, the line is drawn by a simple call to the *drawLine* method. Scanning through each horizontal line from left to right, we use a Boolean variable *leftmostValid* to record if we have found a leftmost point that is not blocked by any other triangle. If so, we keep scanning and updating the Z-buffer until we encounter the first point that is further away than the corresponding Z-buffer value, such as *I* in Figure 7.7. We then draw the line up to the point just before that blocked point (*I*). We meanwhile set *leftmostValid* to false, entering the line segment, such as *IJ* in Figure 7.7. Continuing scanning through until the first visible point, such as *J*, is found, we record *J* as the new leftmost point and set *leftmostValid* to true. This process continues to reach R, and the last line segment, such as *JR*, is drawn if it is not blocked.

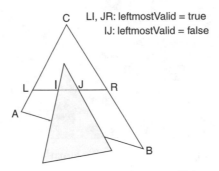

○ **Figure 7.7: Illustration of more efficient version**

Figure 7.8 demonstrates that the Z-buffer algorithm can also be used in cases in which the painter's algorithm fails. The latter is illustrated by Figure 7.9. (We have also seen these three beams in Figures 6.25 and 7.3.)

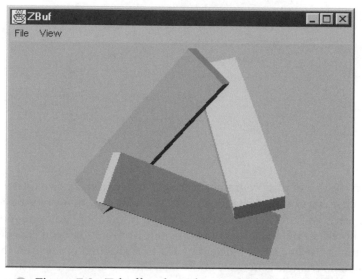

○ Figure 7.8: Z-buffer algorithm applied to three beams

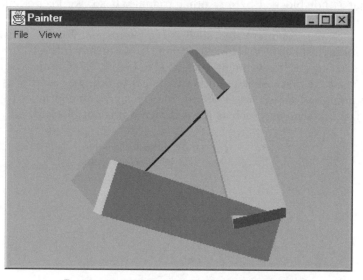

○ Figure 7.9: Painter's algorithm failing

In Appendix E (Section E.5) we will develop a program that enables us to display the surfaces of functions of two variables. Files generated by this program are also accepted by the program *ZBuf.java*, as Figure 7.10 demonstrates.

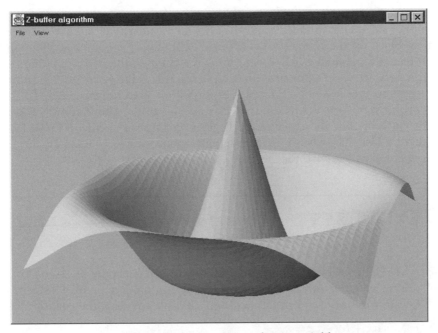

○ **Figure 7.10: Function of two variables**

Here we are using faces with two sides, as discussed in Section 6.5. The way these are used here requires a correction in the computation of zi. Recall that we have introduced the factor 1.01 in the following statement:

```
double zi =  1.01 * zDi + (y - yD) * dzdy + (xL - xD) * dzdx;
```

Without this factor, some incorrect dark pixels would appear on the boundary, also referred to as the *silhouette*, of the (yellow) object and the (light blue) background. To understand this, we note that in Figure 7.11 point P lies on the boundary of the triangles T_1 and T_2.

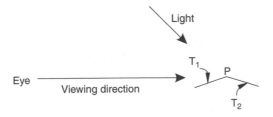

○ **Figure 7.11: Point P belonging to triangles of very different colors**

The nearer triangle, T_1, is visible and its color is bright yellow because it lies on the upper side of the surface. Triangle T_2 lies on the lower side and would appear almost black on the screen if it were not obscured by T_1. Point P, belonging to both triangles, is used twice to determine the color of the corresponding pixel on the basis of the zi value of P. In both cases, this value is the same or almost the same, so that it is not clear which color will be used for this pixel. To solve this problem, we use the factor 1.01 instead of 1 in the above computation of zi. Because of this, the zi value for P when taken as a point of T_1 will now be slightly less than when P is regarded as a point of T_2. As a result, the light yellow color will be used for the pixel in question.

EXERCISES

7.1   The problem of back-face culling cannot generally be solved by testing whether the z_e-component of the normal vector of a face in question is positive or negative. Recall that we are using the equation

$$ax + by + cz = h$$

for the plane of each face, in which $\mathbf{n} = (a, b, c)$ is the normal vector of that face, pointing outward. Using also the vector $\mathbf{x} = (x, y, z)$, we can write the above equation as

$$\mathbf{n} \cdot \mathbf{x} = h$$

Figure 7.12 shows the geometrical interpretation of $\mathbf{n}$, $\mathbf{x}$ and h. For a visible face, the inner product h is negative because $\mathbf{n}$ and $\mathbf{x}$ point in opposite directions. By contrast, h is positive for a back face.

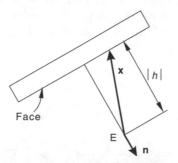

Figure 7.12: Geometrical interpretation of x, n and h, where h is negative

Although in most cases c, the third component of the vector **n**, is positive for a visible face and negative for a back face, there are situations in which this is not true. Give an example of such a situation, with a detailed explanation. How does back-face culling based on the signs of h and (incorrectly) of c relate to that based on the orientation of point sequences?

7.2 Apply animation with double buffering to a cube, as in Exercise 5.4, but use colored faces.

7.3 Apply animation to two colored cubes (see Exercises 5.5 and 7.2), but use colored faces. Even if they partly hide each other, this problem can be solved by back-face culling, provided the farther cube is drawn before the nearer one. This is demonstrated in Figure 7.13; here the *Graphics* methods *fillPolygon* and *drawPolygon* are applied to each visible face. By drawing the edges of such faces in black, we make sure that we can clearly distinguish the colored faces if shades of gray are used in black-and-white reproductions, such as Figure 7.13.

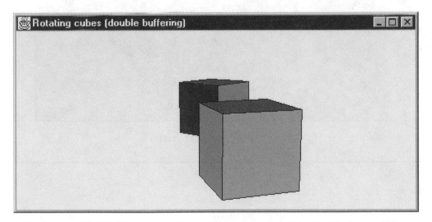

Figure 7.13: Two rotating cubes, generated by back-face culling

7.4 In the program file *Obj3D.java*, the direction of the light vector (*sunX*, *sunY*, *sunZ*) pointing to the source of light was arbitrarily chosen. Even without moving the object (by rotating it, for example), we can obtain an exciting effect by using animation to change this vector, so that the source of light rotates. Extend the program *Painter.java* to realize this. An easy way of doing this is by using spherical coordinates *sunTheta* and *sunPhi* and radius 1 for a light vector of unit length, similar to the spherical coordinates θ, φ and ρ, shown in Figure 5.1, and increasing, say, *sunTheta* by 0.02 radians every 50 ms.

7.5   Write a 3D data file (using a text editor) for the steps shown in Figure 7.14. Apply the programs *Painter.java* and *ZBuf.java* to it. Can you write a program to generate such data files? In such a program, the number of steps and the dimensions should preferably be variables.

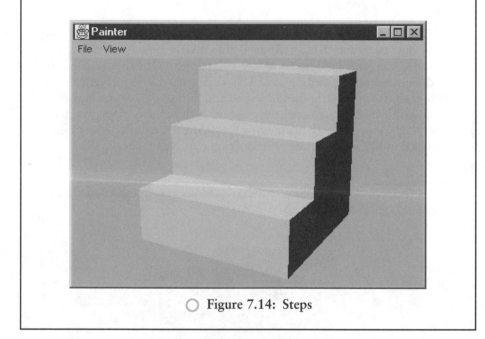

Figure 7.14: Steps

Chapter 8

Fractals

8.1 INTRODUCTION

There are many aspects in nature that are repeating and many cases of patterns similar at different scales. For example, when observing a pine tree, one may notice that the shape of a branch is very similar to that of the entire tree, and the shapes of sub-branches and the main branch are also similar. Such kind of self-similar structure that occurs at different levels of magnification can be modeled by a branch of mathematics called *Fractal geometry*. The term *fractal* was coined by Benoît Mandelbrot in 1975, and means *fractus* or *broken* in Latin. Fractal geometry studies the properties and behavior of fractals. It describes many situations which cannot be explained easily by classical geometry. Fractals can be used to model plants, weather, fluid flow, geologic activity, planetary orbits, human body rhythms, socioeconomic patterns, and music, just to name a few. They have been applied in science, technology, and computer generated art. For example, engineers use fractals to control fluid dynamics in order to reduce process size and energy use.

A fractal, typically expressed as curves, can be generated by a computer recursively or iteratively with a repeating pattern. Compared with human beings, computers are much better in processing long and repetitive information without complaint. Fractals are therefore particularly suitable for computer processing. This chapter introduces the basic concepts and program implementation of fractals. It starts with a simple type of fractal curves, then focuses on a grammar-based generic approach for generating different types of fractal images, and finally discusses the well-known Mandelbrot set.

8.2 KOCH CURVES

A simple example of self-similar curves is the Koch curve, discovered by the Swedish mathematician Helge von Koch in 1904. It serves a useful introduction to the concepts of fractal curves.

In Figure 8.1, K_0, K_1, and K_2 denote successive generations of the Koch curve. A straight line segment is called the zero-th generation. We can construct Koch curve as follows:

- Begin with a straight line and call it K_0;
- Divide each segment of K_n into three equal parts; and
- Replace the middle part by the two sides of an equilateral triangle of the same length as the part being removed.

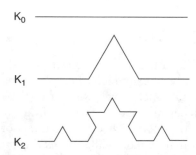

Figure 8.1: Three generations of the Koch curve

The last step ensures that every straight line segment of K_n becomes the shape of K_1 in a smaller scale in K_{n+1}.

Koch curves have the following interesting characteristics:

- Each segment is increased in length by a factor of 4/3. Therefore, K_{n+1} is 4/3 as long as K_n, and K_i has the total length of $(4/3)^i$.
- When n is getting large, the curve still appears to have the same shape and roughness.
- When n becomes infinite, the curve has an infinite length, while occupying a finite region in the plane.

The Koch curve can be easily implemented using the turtle graphics method. Originated in the Logo programming language, turtle graphics is a means of computer drawing using the concept of a turtle crawling over the drawing space with a pen attached to its underside. The drawing is always relative to the current position and direction of the turtle. Considering each straight line of K_{n-1} to be drawn as a K_1 in K_n in the next generation, we can write a recursive program to draw Koch curves as in the following pseudocode:

To draw K_n we proceed as follows:

```
If  (n == 0) Draw a straight line;
Else
{  Draw Kn-1;
   Turn left by 60°;
   Draw Kn-1;
   Turn right by 120°;
   Draw Kn-1;
   Turn left by 60°;
   Draw Kn-1;
}
```

To implement the above pseudocode in a Java program, we need to keep track of the turtle's current position and direction. The following program draws the Koch curve at the zero-th generation K_0. With each mouse click, it draws a higher generation replacing the previous generation. The program defines the origin of the coordinate system at the center of the screen. The turtle starts pointing to the right, and locating at half of the initial length to the left of the origin, that is, $(-200, 0)$ for the initial length of 400. The turtle moves from the current position at (x, y) to the next position at $(x1, y1)$ while changing its direction accordingly.

```
// Koch.java: Koch curves.
import java.awt.*;
import java.awt.event.*;
public class Koch extends Frame
{  public static void main(String[] args){new Koch();}
   Koch()
   {  super("Koch. Click the mouse button to increase the level");
      addWindowListener(new WindowAdapter()
         {public void windowClosing(
                WindowEvent e){System.exit(0);}});
      setSize (600, 500);
      add("Center", new CvKoch());
```

```
         show();
   }
}

class CvKoch extends Canvas
{  public float x, y;
   double dir;
   int midX, midY, level = 1;

   int iX(float x){return Math.round(midX+x);}
   int iY(float y){return Math.round(midY-y);}

   CvKoch()
   {  addMouseListener(new MouseAdapter()
      {  public void mousePressed(MouseEvent evt)
         {  level++; // each mouse click increases the level
            repaint();
         }
      });
   }

   public void paint(Graphics g)
   {  Dimension d = getSize();
      int maxX = d.width - 1, maxY = d.height - 1,
          length = 3 * maxX / 4;
      midX = maxX/2; midY = maxY/2;
      x = (float)(-length/2);          // Start point
      y = 0;
      dir = 0;
      drawKoch(g, length, level);
   }

   public void drawKoch(Graphics g, double len, int n)
   {  if (n == 0)
      {  double dirRad, xInc, yInc;
         dirRad = dir * Math.PI/180;
         xInc = len * Math.cos(dirRad);   // x increment
         yInc = len * Math.sin(dirRad);   // y increment
         float x1 = x + (float)xInc,
               y1 = y + (float)yInc;
         g.drawLine(iX(x), iY(y), iX(x1), iY(y1));
         x = x1;
         y = y1;
```

```
        }
    else
    {   drawKoch(g, len/=3, --n);
        dir += 60;
        drawKoch(g, len, n);
        dir-=120;
        drawKoch(g, len, n);
        dir += 60;
        drawKoch(g, len, n);
    }
    }
}
```

Joining three Koch curves together, we obtain the interesting Koch snowflake as shown in Figure 8.2. The length of a Koch snowflake is $3*(4/3)^i$ for the ith generation since the length of K_i is $(4/3)^i$. It increases infinitely as does i. The area of the Koch snowflake grows slowly and is indeed bounded. In fact, as i becomes very large, its shape and roughness appear to remain the same. Koch snowflakes can be easily drawn by connecting three Koch curves using a modified version of the program above (see Exercise 8.2).

○ **Figure 8.2: Koch snowflakes of generations 3, 5 and 7**

8.3 STRING GRAMMARS

As discussed above, Koch curves are drawn through a set of commands specifically defined for Koch curves. Many interesting curves could be drawn in a similar fashion but they would require a complete program for each different kind of curve. The approach in the above section is apparently not general for generating different kinds of curves.

Consider again the Koch curve. The pattern of the first generation repeats itself in smaller scales at higher generations.

Such a common pattern distinguishes Koch curves from other curves. Therefore, an approach that can encode the common pattern in a simple string of characters would be general enough to specify a variety of curves. Formally, the specification of a common pattern is called a *grammar*, and the grammar-based systems for drawing fractal curves are called *L-Systems* (invented by the Hungarian biologist Aristid Lindenmayer in 1968).

The string of characters defining a common pattern instructs the turtle to draw the pattern. Each character in the string serves as a command to perform an atomic operation. Given the distance D and turning angle α through which the turtle is supposed to move, let us now introduce the three most common commands:

- F - move forward the distance D while drawing in the current direction.
- + - turn right through the angle α.
- − - turn left through the angle α.

For example, given a string $F-F++F-F$ and angle $60°$, the turtle would draw the first generation of Koch curve K_1 as shown in Figure 8.1. It would however be tedious and error-prone to manually provide long strings for different curves. Fortunately, computers are best at performing repeated, long and tedious tasks without making mistakes. Using the same Koch curve example, to draw more generations, we define a *string production rule*

$$F \rightarrow F-F++F-F$$

The rule means that every occurrence of F (that is, the left-hand side of '$\rightarrow$') should be replaced by $F-F++F-F$ (that is, the right-hand side). Starting from an initial string F which is called the *axiom*, recursively applying this production rule would produce strings of increasing lengths. Interpreting any of the strings, the turtle would draw a corresponding generation of the Koch curve. Let us make the axiom the zero-th generation $K_0 = F$ and the first generation $K_1 = F-F++F-F$, then K_2 can be obtained by substituting every F character in K_1 by $F-F++F-F$, so that

$$K_2 = F-F++F-F-F-F++F-F++F-F++F-F-F-F++F-F$$

By interpreting this string, the turtle would draw a curve exactly the same as K_2 in Figure 8.1. This process can continue to generate the Koch curve at any higher generation.

In summary, to draw a fractal curve, such as the Koch curve, at any generation, we need to know at least the following three parameters:

1. The axiom from which the turtle starts.
2. The production rule for producing strings from the F character. We will call the right-hand side of this rule the *F-string*, which is sufficient to represent the rule.
3. The angle at which the turtle should turn.

Denoting these parameters in a template form (axiom, F-string, angle), we call this the *grammar* of the curve, and we can specify the Koch curve as $(F, F-F++F-F, 60)$.

To define more complex and interesting curves, we introduce three more production rules, obtaining grammars of six elements instead of three as above. We introduce an *X-string*, to be used to replace every occurrence of X when producing the next generation string. Similarly, there will be a *Y-string*, used to replace every occurrence of Y. Their replacement process is performed in the same fashion as for the F-string. In other words, all the three string types are treated equally during the string-production process. The X and Y characters are, however, different from the F character as they are simply ignored by the turtle when drawing the curve. The third new production rule, named *f-string*, will be discussed shortly. In the meantime, we reserve its position, but substitute *nil* for it to indicate that we do not use it. It follows that there are six parameters in the extended grammar template

(axiom, F-string, f-string, X-string, Y-string, angle).

The following grammars produce some more interesting curves:

Dragon curve: $(X, F, nil, X+YF+, -FX-Y, 90)$.

Hilbert curve: $(X, F, nil, -YF+XFX+FY-, +XF-YFY-FX+, 90)$.

Sierpinski: arrowhead$(YF, F, nil, YF+XF+Y, XF-YF-X, 60)$.

Figures 8.3, 8.4 and 8.5 illustrate some selected generations of the Dragon, Hilbert and Sierpinski curves that are generated based on their string grammars as defined above.

○ **Figure 8.3: Dragon curves: 1st, 2nd, 3rd, 4th, 5th and 11th generations**

It is remarkable that no Dragon curve intersects itself. There seems to be one such intersection in the 4th generation Dragon curve of Figure 8.3 and many more in those of higher generations. However, that is not really the case, as demonstrated by using rounded instead of sharp corners. Figure 8.4 illustrates this for an 8th generation Dragon curve.

It is interesting to note that all the curves we have seen so far share one common characteristic, that is, each curve reflects the exact trace of the turtle's movement

○ **Figure 8.4: Dragon curve of 8th generation, rounded corners**

○ **Figure 8.5: Hilbert curve (5th generation) and Sierpinski arrowhead (7th generation)**

and is drawn essentially as one long and curved line. This is because the turtle always moves forward and draws by executing the *F* character command.

8.3.1 Moving without drawing and f-strings

Sometimes, it is desirable to keep some of the curve components at proper distances from each other. This implies that such a curve is not connected. We therefore need to define a forward moving action for the turtle without drawing:

- *f* - move forward the distance *D* without drawing a line.

The f-string, for which we have already reserved a position (just after the F-string) indicates how each lower-case *f* is to be expanded. By using an f-string other than *nil*, we are able to generate an image with a combination of islands and lakes as shown in Figure 8.6, based on the following grammar:

$$(F+F+F+F, F+f-FF+F+FF+Ff+FF-f+FF-F-FF-Ff-FFF,$$
$$ffffff, nil, nil, 90)$$

Note that here the parameters X-string and Y-string are unused and therefore written as *nil*.

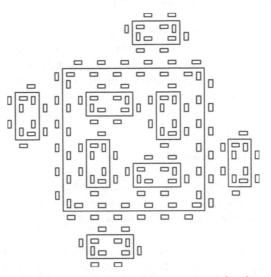

Figure 8.6: Second generation islands

To summarize, we have introduced the following six parameters into our string grammar:

1. The axiom from which the turtle starts;
2. The F-string for producing strings from *F* that instructs the turtle to move forward while drawing;
3. The f-string for producing strings from *f*, that instructs the turtle to move forward without drawing;
4. The X-string for producing strings from X, that does not affect the turtle;
5. The Y-string for producing strings from Y, that does not affect the turtle; and
6. The angle at which the turtle should turn.

In principle, more parameters may be introduced if the above six parameters cannot express new types of curves. On the other hand, a grammar does not have to use all the introduced parameters since, as we have seen, a *nil* can be used to represent an unused parameter.

8.3.2 Branching

With all the curves we have seen so far, one may observe the following phenomenon. The turtle is always moving forward along a curved line. It sometimes draws (seeing an *F* character) and sometimes does not draw (seeing an *f* character). The turtle never turns back to where it has visited before, since it cannot remember its previous positions. This implies that the turtle is unable to branch off from any of the previous curve positions and draw branching lines.

To make the turtle remember places that it has visited, we need to introduce the concept of the turtle's *state*. Let us call the turtle's current position together with its direction the *state* of the turtle. In other words, a state is defined by the values of a location in the drawing space and the angle at the location. To enhance the drawing power of string-production rules, we allow the turtle to keep its states and return to any of them later by introducing two more character commands:

- [- store the current state of the turtle
-] - restore the turtle's previously stored state

These two characters, however, do not form strings of their own and thus do not require new production rules. They merely participate in the F-, f-, X-, and Y-strings to instruct how the turtle should behave.

The most appropriate data structure to implement the store and restore operations is a stack. Upon meeting a [character, the turtle pushes its current state onto the stack. When encountering a] character, the turtle pops its previous state from the stack and starts from the previous position and direction to continues its journey. Having empowered the turtle with the capability of returning and restarting from its previous states, we are able to draw curves with branches, such as trees defined in the following string grammars:

$$\text{Tree1: } (F, F[+F]F[-F]F, nil, nil, nil, 25.7)$$
$$\text{Tree2: } (X, FF, nil, F[+X]F[-X]+X, nil, 20.0)$$
$$\text{Tree3: } (F, FF-[-F+F+F]+[+F-F-F], nil, nil, nil, 22.5)$$

These grammars were used to obtain the trees shown in Figure 8.7.

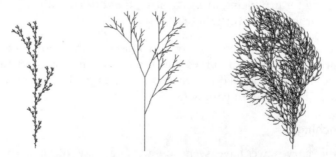

Figure 8.7: **Examples of fractal trees: Tree1 (4th generation), Tree2 (5th generation) and Tree3 (4th generation)**

If the line thickness of each branch is set in proportion to its distance from the root, and also a small fraction of randomness is applied to the turning angle, more realistic looking trees would be produced.

Most of the figures in this section were produced by the program below, with input files to be discussed after this program:

```java
// FractalGrammars.java
import java.awt.*;
import java.awt.event.*;

public class FractalGrammars extends Frame
{  public static void main(String[] args)
   {  if (args.length == 0)
         System.out.println("Use filename as program argument.");
      else
         new FractalGrammars(args[0]);
   }
   FractalGrammars(String fileName)
   {  super("Click left or right mouse button to change the level");
      addWindowListener(new WindowAdapter()
         {public void windowClosing(
                WindowEvent e){System.exit(0);}});
      setSize (800, 600);
      add("Center", new CvFractalGrammars(fileName));
      show();
   }
}


class CvFractalGrammars extends Canvas
{  String fileName, axiom, strF, strf, strX, strY;
   int maxX, maxY, level = 1;
   double xLast, yLast, dir, rotation, dirStart, fxStart, fyStart,
      lengthFract, reductFact;

   void error(String str)
   {  System.out.println(str);
      System.exit(1);
   }

   CvFractalGrammars(String fileName)
   {  Input inp = new Input(fileName);
      if (inp.fails())
         error("Cannot open input file.");
```

```
            axiom = inp.readString(); inp.skipRest();
            strF = inp.readString(); inp.skipRest();
            strf = inp.readString(); inp.skipRest();
            strX = inp.readString(); inp.skipRest();
            strY = inp.readString(); inp.skipRest();
            rotation = inp.readFloat(); inp.skipRest();
            dirStart = inp.readFloat(); inp.skipRest();
            fxStart = inp.readFloat(); inp.skipRest();
            fyStart = inp.readFloat(); inp.skipRest();
            lengthFract = inp.readFloat(); inp.skipRest();
            reductFact = inp.readFloat();
            if (inp.fails())
                error("Input file incorrect.");

            addMouseListener(new MouseAdapter()
            {   public void mousePressed(MouseEvent evt)
                {   if ((evt.getModifiers() & InputEvent.BUTTON3_MASK) != 0)
                    {   level--;        // Right mouse button decreases level
                        if (level < 1)
                            level = 1;
                    }
                    else
                        level++;        // Left mouse button increases level
                    repaint();
                }
            });

    }

    Graphics g;
    int iX(double x){return (int)Math.round(x);}
    int iY(double y){return (int)Math.round(maxY-y);}

    void drawTo(Graphics g, double x, double y)
    {   g.drawLine(iX(xLast), iY(yLast), iX(x) ,iY(y));
        xLast = x;
        yLast = y;
    }

    void moveTo(Graphics g, double x, double y)
    {   xLast = x;
        yLast = y;
    }
```

```
public void paint(Graphics g)
{  Dimension d = getSize();
   maxX = d.width - 1;
   maxY = d.height - 1;
   xLast = fxStart * maxX;
   yLast = fyStart * maxY;
   dir = dirStart;    // Initial direction in degrees
   turtleGraphics(g, axiom, level, lengthFract * maxY);
}

public void turtleGraphics(Graphics g, String instruction,
   int depth, double len)
{  double xMark=0, yMark=0, dirMark=0;
   for (int i=0;i<instruction.length();i++)
   {  char ch = instruction.charAt(i);
      switch(ch)
      {
      case 'F': // Step forward and draw
         // Start: (xLast, yLast), direction: dir, steplength: len
         if (depth == 0)
         {  double rad = Math.PI/180 * dir, // Degrees -> radians
               dx = len * Math.cos(rad), dy = len * Math.sin(rad);
            drawTo(g, xLast + dx, yLast + dy);
         }
         else
            turtleGraphics(g, strF, depth - 1, reductFact * len);
         break;
      case 'f': // Step forward without drawing
         // Start: (xLast, yLast), direction: dir, steplength: len
         if (depth == 0)
         {  double rad = Math.PI/180 * dir, // Degrees -> radians
               dx = len * Math.cos(rad), dy = len * Math.sin(rad);
            moveTo(g, xLast + dx, yLast + dy);
         }
         else
            turtleGraphics(g, strf, depth - 1, reductFact * len);
         break;
      case 'X':
         if (depth > 0)
            turtleGraphics(g, strX, depth - 1, reductFact * len);
         break;
      case 'Y':
         if (depth > 0)
```

```
                    turtleGraphics(g, strY, depth - 1, reductFact * len);
                break;
            case '+': // Turn right
                dir -= rotation; break;
            case '-': // Turn left
                dir += rotation; break;
            case '[': // Save position and direction
                xMark = xLast; yMark = yLast; dirMark = dir; break;
            case ']': // Back to saved position and direction
                xLast = xMark; yLast = yMark; dir = dirMark; break;
            }
        }
    }
}
```

The most essential input data consist of the grammar, for example,

$$(X, F, nil, X+YF+, -FX-Y, 90)$$

for the Dragon curve. In addition, the following five values would help in obtaining desirable results:

- The direction in which the turtle starts, specified as the angle, in degrees, relative to the positive x-axis.
- The distance between the left window boundary and the start point, expressed as a fraction of the window width.
- The distance between the lower window boundary and the start point, expressed as a fraction of the window height.
- The length of a single line segment in the first generation, expressed as a fraction of the window height.
- A factor to reduce the length in each next generation, to prevent the image from growing outside the window boundaries.

Setting the last two values can be regarded as tuning, so they were found experimentally. We supply all these data, that is, five strings and six real numbers, in a file, the name of which is supplied as a program argument. For example, to produce the Dragon curve, we can enter this command to start the program:

```
java FractalGrammars Dragon.txt
```

where the file *Dragon.txt* is listed below, showing the grammar $(X, F, X+YF+, -FX-Y, 90)$ followed by the five values just discussed:

```
"X"        // Axiom
"F"        // strF
""         // strf
```

```
"X+YF+"    // strX
"-FX-Y"    // strY
90         // Angle of rotation
0          // Initial direction of turtle (east)
0.5        // Start at x = 0.5 * width
0.5        // Start at y = 0.5 * height
0.6        // Initial line length is 0.6 * height
0.6        // Reduction factor for next generation
```

As you can see, strings are supplied between a pair of quotation marks, and comment is allowed at the end of each line. Instead of *nil*, we write the empty string "". Although the initial direction of the turtle is specified as east, the first line is drawn in the direction south. This is because of the axiom "*X*", which causes initially *strX* = "X+YF+" to be used, where *X* and *Y* are ignored. So actually "+F+" is executed by the turtle. As we know, the initial + causes the turtle to turn right before the first line is drawn due to *F*, so this line is drawn downward instead of from left to right.

The other curves were produced in a similar way. Both the grammars and the five additional parameter values, as discussed above, for these curves are listed in the following table:

Dragon	(X, F, *nil*, X+YF+, −FX−Y, 90)	0	0.5	0.5	0.6	0.6
Hilbert	(X, F, *nil*, −YF+XFX+FY−, +XF−YFY−FX+, 90)	0	0.25	0.25	0.8	0.47
Sier-pinski	(YF, F, *nil*, YF+XF+Y, XF−YF−X, 60).	0	0.33	0.5	0.38	0.51
Islands	(F+F+F+F, F+f−FF+F+ FF+Ff+FF − f+ FF−F−FF−Ff−FFF, *ffffff*, *nil*, *nil*, 90)	0	0.25	0.65	0.2	0.2
Tree1	(F, F[+F]F[-F]F, *nil*, *nil*, *nil*, 25.7)	90	0.5	0.05	0.7	0.34
Tree2	(X, FF, *nil*, F[+X]F[−X]+X, *nil*, 20.0)	90	0.5	0.05	0.45	0.5
Tree3	(F, FF−[−F+F+F]+ [+F−F−F], *nil*, *nil*, *nil*, 22.5)	90	0.5	0.05	0.25	0.5

When discussing the Tree examples with branches, we suggested that a stack would be used to push and pop states, while there seemed to be no stack structure in the program. However, there is a local variable *xMark* in the recursive method *turtleGraphics*, and for each recursive call a version of this variable is stored on a system stack. In other words, the use of a stack is implicit in this program.

8.4 MANDELBROT AND JULIA SETS

The *Mandelbrot set*, named after Polish-born French mathematician Benoît Mandelbrot, is a fractal. Recall that a fractal curve reveals small-scale details similar to the large-scale characteristics. Although the Mandelbrot set is self-similar at different scales, the small-scale details are not *identical* to the whole. Also, the Mandelbrot set is infinitely complex. Yet the process of generating it is based on an extremely simple equation involving complex numbers. The left part of Figure 8.8 shows a view of the Mandelbrot set. The outline is a fractal curve that can be zoomed in for ever on any part for a close-up view, as the right part of Figure 8.8 illustrates. Even parts of the image that appear quite smooth show a jagged outline consisting of many tiny copies of the Mandelbrot set. For example, as displayed in Figure 8.8, there is a large black region like a cardioid near the center with a circle joining its left-hand side. The region where the cardioid and the circle are joined together appears smooth. When the region is magnified, however, the detailed structure becomes apparent and shows many fascinating details that were not visible in the original picture. In theory, the zooming can be repeated for ever, since the border is 'infinitely complex'.

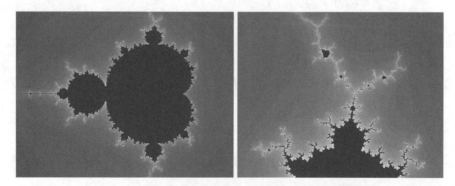

Figure 8.8: Mandelbrot set and magnified detail

The Mandelbrot set is a set M of complex numbers defined in the following way:

$$M = \{c \in C|\ \lim_{n \to \infty} z_n \neq \infty\}$$

where C is the set of all complex numbers and, for some constant c, the sequence $z_0, z_1, \ldots$ is defined as follows:

$$z_0 = 0$$
$$z_{n+1} = z_n^2 + c$$

That is, the Mandelbrot set is the set of all complex numbers which fulfill the condition described above. In other words, if the sequence $z_0, z_1, z_2, \ldots$ does not approach infinity, then c belongs to the set. Given a value c, the system generates a sequence of values called the *orbit* of the start value 0:

$$z_0 = 0$$
$$z_1 = z_0^2 + c = c$$
$$z_2 = z_1^2 + c = c^2 + c$$
$$z_3 = z_2^2 + c = (c^2 + c)^2 + c$$
$$z_4 = z_3^2 + c = ((c^2 + c)^2 + c)^2 + c$$

$$\ldots$$

As soon as an element of the sequence $\{z_n\}$ is at a distance greater than 2 from the origin, it is certain that the sequence tends to infinity. A proof of this goes beyond the scope of this book. If the sequence does not approach infinity and therefore remains at a distance of at most 2 from the origin for ever, then the point c is in the Mandelbrot set. If any z_n is farther than 2 from the origin, then the point c is not in the set.

Now let us consider how to generate a Mandelbrot image. Since the Mandelbrot set is a set of complex numbers, first we have to find these numbers that are part of the set. To do this we need a test that will determine if a given number is inside the set or outside. The test is applied to complex numbers z_n computed as $z_{n+1} = z_n^2 + c$. The constant c does not change during the testing process. As the number being tested, c is the point on the complex plane that will be plotted when the testing is complete. This plotting will be done in a color that depends on the test result. For some value n_{Max}, say 30, we start computing $z_1, z_2, \ldots$ until either we have computed z_n for $n = n_{\text{Max}}$, or we have found a point z_n ($n \leq n_{\text{Max}}$) whose distance from the origin O is greater than 2. In the former case, having computed n_{Max} elements of the sequence, none of which is farther than a distance 2 away from O, we give up, consider the point c belonging to the Mandelbrot set, and plot it in black. In the latter case, the point z_n going beyond the distance 2, we plot the point c in a color that depends on the value of n.

Let us now briefly discuss complex arithmetic, as far as we need it here, for those who are unfamiliar with this subject. Complex numbers are two-dimensional by nature. We may regard the complex number

$$z = x + yi$$

as the real number pair (x, y). It is customary to refer to x as the *real part* and to y as the *imaginary part* of z. We display z in the usual way, with x drawn along the horizontal axis and y along the vertical axis. Addition of two complex numbers is the same as that for vectors:

$$(x_1 + y_1 i) + (x_2 + y_2 i) = (x_1 + x_2) + (y_1 + y_2)i$$

By contrast, multiplication of complex numbers is rather complicated:

$$(x_1 + y_1 i)(x_2 + y_2 i) = (x_1 x_2 - y_1 y_2) + (x_1 y_2 + x_2 y_1)i$$

It follows that for

$$z = x + yi$$

we have

$$z^2 = (x^2 - y^2) + 2xyi$$

Although we do not need this for our purpose, we may as well note that by setting $x = 0$ and $y = 1$, giving $0 + 1 \times i = i$, we find

$$i^2 = (0^2 - 1^2) + 2 \times 0 \times 1 \times i = -1$$

which explains why the symbol i is often referred to as the square root of -1:

$$i = \sqrt{-1}$$

The distance of the complex number $z = x + yi$ from the origin O is called the *absolute value* or *modulus* of z and is denoted as $|z|$. It follows that

$$|z| = \sqrt{x^2 + y^2}$$

Remember, $|z|^2 = x^2 + y^2$, while $z^2 = (x^2 - y^2) + 2xyi$ so, in general, $|z|^2$ is unequal to z^2. This very brief introduction to complex numbers cannot replace a thorough treatment as found in mathematics textbooks, but it will be sufficient for our Mandelbrot subject.

In the algorithm for Mandelbrot fractals, when computing each successive value of z, we want to know if its distance from the origin exceeds 2. To calculate this distance, usually denoted as $|z|$, we add the square of its distance from the x-axis (the horizontal real axis) to the square of its distance from the y-axis (the vertical imaginary axis) and then take the square root of the result. The computation of the square root operation can be saved by just checking whether the sum of these squares is greater than 4. In other words, for

$$z = x + yi$$

we perform the test

$$|z|^2 > 4$$

which is expressed in terms of real numbers as

$$x^2 + y^2 > 4$$

Now to compute each new value of z using $z_{n+1} = z_n^2 + c$, let us write $Re(c)$ and $Im(c)$ for the real and imaginary parts of c. It then follows from

$$z^2 = (x + yi)^2 = (x^2 - y^2) + (2xy)i$$

that the real and imaginary parts of each element z_{n+1} are found as follows:

real part: $\quad x_{n+1} = x_n^2 - y_n^2 + Re(c)$

imaginary part: $y_{n+1} = 2x_n y_n + Im(c)$

As we increment n, the value of $|z_n|^2$ will either stay equal to or below 4 for ever, or eventually surpass 4. Once $|z_n|^2$ surpasses 4, it will increase for ever. In the former case, where the $|z_n|^2$ stays small, the number c being tested is part of the Mandelbrot set. In the latter case, when $|z_n|^2$ eventually surpasses 4, the number c is not part of the Mandelbrot set.

8.4.1 Implementation in Java

To display the whole Mandelbrot set image properly, we need some mapping

$$x_{\text{Pix}} \rightarrow x$$

$$y_{\text{Pix}} \rightarrow y$$

to convert the device coordinates $(x_{\text{Pix}}, y_{\text{Pix}})$ to the real and imaginary parts x and y of the complex number $c = x + yi$. In the program, the variables x_{Pix} and y_{Pix} are of type *int*, while x and y are of type *double*. We will use the following ranges for the device coordinates:

$$0 \leq x_{\text{Pix}} < w$$

$$0 \leq y_{\text{Pix}} < h$$

where we obtain the width w and height h of the drawing rectangle in the usual way:

```
w = getSize().width;
h = getSize().height;
```

For x and y we have

$$minRe \leq x \leq maxRe$$

$$minIm \leq y \leq maxIm$$

The user will be able to change these boundary variables *minRe*, *maxRe*, *minIm* and *maxIm* by dragging the left mouse button. Their default values are $minRe0 = -2, maxRe0 = +1, minIm0 = -1, maxIm0 = +1$, which will at any time be restored when the user clicks the right mouse button. Using the variable *factor*, computed in Java as

```
factor = Math.max((maxRe - minRe)/w, (maxIm - minIm)/h);
```

we can perform the above mapping from $(x_{\text{Pix}}, y_{\text{Pix}})$ to (x, y) by computing

$$x = minRe + factor \times x_{\text{Pix}}$$
$$y = minIm + factor \times y_{\text{Pix}}$$

For every device coordinate pair $(x_{\text{Pix}}, y_{\text{Pix}})$ of the window, the associated point $c = x + iy$ in the complex plane is computed in this way. Then, in up to n_{Max} iterations, we determine whether this point belongs to the Mandelbrot set. If it does, we display the original pixel $(x_{\text{Pix}}, y_{\text{Pix}})$ in black; otherwise, we plot this pixel in a shade of red that depends on n, the number of iterations required to decide that the point is outside the Mandelbrot set. The expression $100 + 155 * n/n_{\text{Max}}$ ensures that this color value will not exceed its maximum value 255. If n_{Max} is set larger than that in the program, program execution will take more time but the quality of the image would improve. The implementation of this can by found in the *paint* method at the bottom of the following program, after which we will discuss the implementation of cropping and zooming.

```
// MandelbrotZoom.java: Mandelbrot set, cropping and zooming in.
import java.awt.*;
import java.awt.event.*;

public class MandelbrotZoom extends Frame
{   public static void main(String[] args){new MandelbrotZoom();}
    MandelbrotZoom()
    {   super("Drag left mouse button to crop and zoom. " +
             "Click right mouse button to restore.");
        addWindowListener(new WindowAdapter()
          {public void windowClosing(
                  WindowEvent e){System.exit(0);}});
        setSize (800, 600);
        add("Center", new CvMandelbrotZoom());
        show();
    }
}
class CvMandelbrotZoom extends Canvas
{   final double minRe0 = -2.0, maxRe0 = 1.0,
                 minIm0 = -1.0, maxIm0 = 1.0;
    double minRe = minRe0, maxRe =  maxRe0,
                 minIm = minIm0, maxIm =  maxIm0, factor, r;
    int n, xs, ys, xe, ye, w, h;

    void drawWhiteRectangle(Graphics g)
    {   g.drawRect(Math.min(xs, xe), Math.min(ys, ye),
```

```
                         Math.abs(xe - xs), Math.abs(ye - ys));
}

boolean isLeftMouseButton(MouseEvent e)
{  return (e.getModifiers() & InputEvent.BUTTON3_MASK) == 0;
}

CvMandelbrotZoom()
{  addMouseListener(new MouseAdapter()
   {  public void mousePressed(MouseEvent e)
      {  if (isLeftMouseButton(e))
         {  xs = xe = e.getX(); // Left button
            ys = ye = e.getY();
         }
         else
         {  minRe = minRe0;      // Right button
            maxRe = maxRe0;
            minIm = minIm0;
            maxIm = maxIm0;
            repaint();
         }
      }

      public void mouseReleased(MouseEvent e)
      {  if (isLeftMouseButton(e))
         {  xe = e.getX(); // Left mouse button released
            ye = e.getY(); // Test if points are really distinct:
            if (xe != xs && ye != ys)
            {  int xS = Math.min(xs, xe), xE = Math.max(xs, xe),
                   yS = Math.min(ys, ye), yE = Math.max(ys, ye),
                   w1 = xE - xS, h1 = yE - yS, a = w1 * h1,
                   h2 = (int)Math.sqrt(a/r), w2 = (int)(r * h2),
                   dx = (w2 - w1)/2, dy = (h2 - h1)/2;
               xS -= dx; xE += dx;
               yS -= dy; yE += dy; // aspect ration corrected
               maxRe = minRe + factor * xE;
               maxIm = minIm + factor * yE;
               minRe += factor * xS;
               minIm += factor * yS;
               repaint();
            }
         }
      }
```

```
            });

        addMouseMotionListener(new MouseMotionAdapter()
        {  public void mouseDragged(MouseEvent e)
           {  if (isLeftMouseButton(e))
              {  Graphics g = getGraphics();
                 g.setXORMode(Color.black);
                 g.setColor(Color.white);
                 if (xe != xs || ye != ys)
                    drawWhiteRectangle(g); // Remove old rectangle:
                 xe = e.getX();
                 ye = e.getY();
                 drawWhiteRectangle(g);    // Draw new rectangle:
              }
           }
        });
     }

     public void paint(Graphics g)
     {  w = getSize().width;
        h = getSize().height;
        r = w/h; // Aspect ratio, used in mouseReleased
        factor = Math.max((maxRe - minRe)/w, (maxIm - minIm)/h);
        for(int yPix=0; yPix<h; ++yPix)
        {  double cIm = minIm + yPix * factor;
           for(int xPix=0; xPix<w; ++xPix)
           {  double cRe = minRe + xPix * factor, x = cRe, y = cIm;
              int nMax = 100, n;
              for (n=0; n<nMax; ++n)
              {  double x2 = x * x, y2 = y * y;
                 if (x2 + y2 > 4)
                    break;   // Outside
                 y = 2 * x * y + cIm;
                 x = x2 - y2 + cRe;
              }
              g.setColor(n == nMax ? Color.black        // Inside
                  : new Color(100 + 155 * n / nMax, 0, 0)); // Outside
              g.drawLine(xPix, yPix, xPix, yPix);
           }
        }
     }
}
```

As indicated in the title bar (implemented by a call to *super* at the beginning of the *MandelbrotZoom* constructor), the user can zoom in by using the left mouse button. By dragging the mouse with the left button pressed down, a rectangle appears, as shown in Figure 8.9, with one of its corners at the point first clicked and the opposite one denoting the current mouse position. This process is sometimes referred to as *rubber banding*.

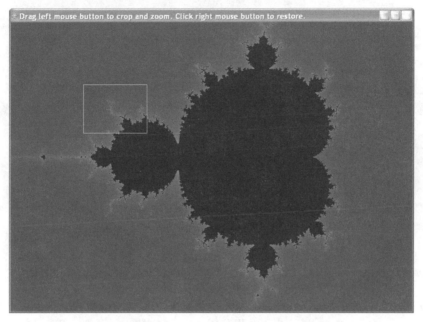

Figure 8.9: Cropping and zooming in

When the user releases the mouse button, the picture is cropped so that everything outside the rectangle is removed and the contents inside are enlarged and displayed in the full window. This cropping is therefore combined with zooming in, as Figure 8.10 illustrates. The user can continue zooming in by cropping in the same way for ever. It would be awkward if there were no way of either zooming out or returning to the original image. In program *MandelbrotZoom.java* the latter is possible by clicking the right mouse button.

To implement this cropping rectangle, we use two opposite corner points of it. The start point (xs, ys) is where the user clicks the mouse to start dragging, while the opposite corner is the endpoint (xe, ye). Three Java methods are involved:

mousePressed: to define both the start point (xs, ys) and initial
                     position of the endpoint (xe, ye);

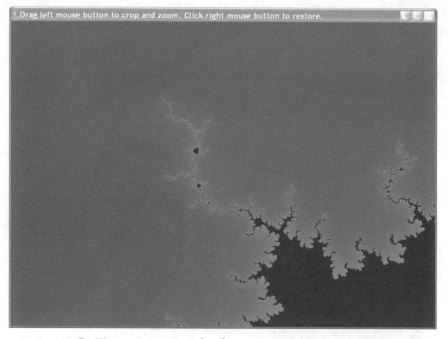

Figure 8.10: Result of cropping and zooming in

mouseDragged:	to update the endpoint (xe, ye), removing the old rectangle and drawing the new one;
mouseReleased:	to compute the logical boundary values *minRe*, *maxRe*, *minIm* and *maxIm* on the basis of (xs, ys) and (xe, ye).

In *mouseDragged*, drawing and removing the cropping rectangle is done using the XOR mode which was briefly discussed at the end of Section 4.3. Here we use two calls

```
g.setXORMode(Color.black);
g.setColor(Color.white);
```

after which we draw both the old and the new rectangles. In *mouseReleased*, some actions applied to the cropping rectangle require explanation. As we want the zooming to be isotropic, we have to pay attention to the cropping rectangle having an aspect ratio

$$r_1 = w_1 : h_1$$

different from the aspect ratio

$$r = w : h$$

of the (large) drawing rectangle. For example, the cropping rectangle may be in 'portrait' format (with $w_1 < h_1$), while the drawing rectangle has the 'landscape' characteristic (with $w > h$). The simplest way to deal with this case would be to cut off a portion of the cropping rectangle at the top or the bottom. However, that would lead to a result that may be unexpected and undesirable for the user. We will therefore replace the cropping rectangle with one that has the same center and the same area $a = w_1 h_1$, but an aspect ratio of r (mentioned above) instead of r_1. The dimensions of this new rectangle will be $w_2 \times h_2$ instead of $w_1 \times h_1$. To find w_2 and h_2 we solve

$$w_2 h_2 = a \quad (= \text{area of cropping rectangle defined by the user})$$
$$w_2 : h_2 = r \quad (= \text{aspect ratio } w/h \text{ of drawing rectangle})$$

giving

$$h_2 = \sqrt{\frac{a}{r}}$$
$$w_2 = r h_2$$

Then we add the correction term $\Delta x = 1/2(w_2 - w_1)$ to the x-coordinate xE of the right cropping-rectangle edge and subtract it from the x-coordinate xS of the corresponding left edge. After performing similar operations on yS and yE, the resulting new rectangle with top-left corner point (xS, yS) and bottom-right corner point (xE, yE) is about as large as the user-defined rectangle but in shape similar to the large drawing rectangle. We then have to compute the corresponding coordinates in the complex plane, using the mapping discussed earlier. Since the new logical right boundary values *maxRe* and *maxIm* should correspond to xE and yE, we compute

```
maxRe = minRe + factor * xE;
maxIm = minIm + factor * yE;
```

Similarly, to obtain the new left boundary values, we have to add *factor* $\times$ *xS* and *factor* $\times$ *yS* to the old values *minRe* and *minIm*, respectively, giving the slightly more cryptic statements

```
minRe += factor * xS;
minIm += factor * yS;
```

8.4.2 Julia sets

Associated with every point in the complex plane is a set somewhat similar to the Mandelbrot set called a *Julia set*, named after the French mathematician

Gaston Julia. To produce an image of a Julia set, we use the same iteration $z_{n+1} = z_n^2 + c$, this time with a constant value of c but with a starting value z_0 derived from the coordinates $(x_{\text{Pix}}, y_{\text{Pix}})$ of the pixel displayed on the screen. We obtain interesting Julia sets if we choose points near the boundaries of the Mandelbrot set as starting values z_0. For example, we obtained Figure 8.11 by taking $c = -0.76 + 0.084i$, which in the Mandelbrot set (Figure 8.8) is the point near the top of the circle on the left.

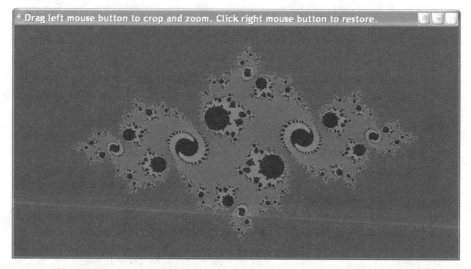

Figure 8.11: Julia set, obtained by using $c = -0.76 + 0.084i$

Since the Mandelbrot set can be used to select c for the Julia set, it is said to form an index into the Julia set. Such an interesting relationship is also evidenced by the following fact. A Julia set is either connected or disconnected. For values of z_0 chosen from within the Mandelbrot set, we obtain connected Julia sets. That is, all the black regions are connected. Conversely, those values of z_0 outside the Mandelbrot set give disconnected Julia sets. The disconnected sets are often called *dust*, consisting of individual points no matter what resolution they are viewed at. If, in the program *MandelbrotZoom.java*, we replace the *paint* method with the one below (preferably also replacing the name *Mandelbrot* with *Julia* throughout the program), and specify the dimensions $w = 900$ and $h = 500$ in the call to *setSize*, we obtain a program which initially produces Figure 8.11. Again, we can display all kinds of fascinating details by cropping and zooming. Note, in this program, c is a constant and the starting value z of the sequence is derived from the device coordinates (x_{Pix}, y_{Pix}).

```
public void paint(Graphics g)
{  Dimension d = getSize();
   w = getSize().width;
   h = getSize().height;
   r = w/h;
   double cRe = -0.76, cIm = 0.084;
   factor = Math.max((maxRe - minRe)/w, (maxIm - minIm)/h);
   for(int yPix=0; yPix<h; ++yPix)
   {  for(int xPix=0; xPix<w; ++xPix)
      {  double x = minRe + xPix * factor,
                y = minIm + yPix * factor;
         int nMax = 100, n;
         for (n=0; n<nMax; ++n)
         {  double x2 = x * x, y2 = y * y;
            if (x2 + y2 > 4)
               break;   // Outside
            y = 2 * x * y + cIm;
            x = x2 - y2 + cRe;
         }
         g.setColor(n == nMax ? Color.black                // Inside
               : new Color(100 + 155 * n / nMax, 0, 0)); // Outside
         g.drawLine(xPix, yPix, xPix, yPix);
      }
   }
}
```

EXERCISES

8.1   Write a program to produce Dragon curves with rounded corners, as shown in Figure 8.4.

8.2   Write a program to connect Koch curves, as shown in Figure 8.2.

8.3   To make bush curves (trees) appear more natural and pleasing, add randomness to the angles and lengths of the lines, and also draw lines with thickness. For example, the lower part of a tree is thicker than its upper part.

8.4   Further to Exercise 8.3, add green leaves to the branches and make the leaves oriented toward the same directions as the branches.

8.5   Apply the method of cropping and zooming used in *Mandel-brotZoom.java* to some other (non-trivial) graphics program of your own choice.

8.6   Write a program to draw the Mandelbrot set, and when clicked on the Mandelbrot image, a Julia set corresponding to the clicked point is drawn in a window beside the Mandelbrot window. The clicked point in the form of $z = x + yi$ should also be displayed in the side window.

Appendix A

Linear Interpolation of 1/z

We will now discuss why, with central projection, we can use linear interpolation of $1/z$, called zi in Chapter 7, and not simply z. For example, with two points $P_1(x_1', y_1', zi_1)$ and $P_2(x_2', y_2', zi_2)$, where x_1', y_1', x_2' and y_2' are logical screen coordinates, while $zi_1 = 1/z_1$ and $zi_2 = 1/z_2$, we can compute similar coordinates of the midpoint $M(x_M, y_M, zi_M)$ by using

$$x_M' = 0.5(x_1' + x_2')$$
$$y_M' = 0.5(y_1' + y_2')$$
$$zi_M = 0.5(zi_1 + zi_2)$$

In general we have

$$z_M \neq 0.5(z_1 + z_2)$$

Figure A.1 shows the eye-coordinate axes x and z and the screen $z = -d$. For simplicity, we ignore the y-axis. Recall that the position E of the eye is the origin of this coordinate system and that the negative z-axis points towards the center of the object. Point P lies on line l, which has the following equation:

$$\frac{x}{a} + \frac{z}{-b} = 1 \tag{A.1}$$

The ray of light PE intersects the screen in $P'(x', -d)$. Then all points (x, z) of this ray of light satisfy the equation

$$\frac{x}{x'} = \frac{z}{-d}$$

or

$$x = -\frac{x'z}{d}$$

To compute the point of intersection of this ray of light and line l, we substitute this result in (A.1), finding

$$-\frac{x'z}{ad} - \frac{z}{b} = 1$$

Dividing the left- and right-hand sides of this equation by z and swapping them, we obtain

$$\frac{1}{z} = -\frac{1}{ad}x' - \frac{1}{b} \tag{A.2}$$

which shows that $1/z$ is a linear function of x'.

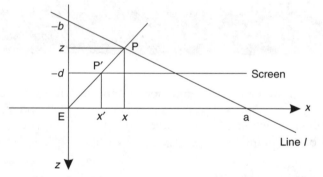

○ **Figure A.1: Central projection of point P on screen**

This is useful because it enables us to perform *linear interpolation*. This term is used to indicate that, with a linear function

$$f(x) = mx + c$$

and three values x_A, x_B and x_I satisfying

$$x_I = x_A + \lambda(x_B - x_A)$$

we can express $f(x_I)$ in $f(x_A)$ and $f(x_B)$ in the same way as x_I is expressed in x_A and x_B, that is,

$$f(x_I) = f(x_A) + \lambda\{f(x_B) - f(x_A)\}$$

Although this sounds very plausible, here is a proof for the sake of completeness:

$$f(x_I) = mx_I + c$$
$$= m\{x_A + \lambda(x_B - x_A)\} + c$$
$$= mx_A + c + \lambda(mx_B - mx_A)$$
$$= f(x_A) + \lambda\{(mx_B + c) - (mx_A + c)\}$$
$$= f(x_A) + \lambda\{f(x_B) - f(x_A)\}$$

As we have seen in Equation (A.2) that $1/z$ is a linear function of x', it follows that we can find the z-coordinate of a point I on a line AB in 3D space by using

$$\frac{1}{z_I} = \frac{1}{z_A} + \lambda\left(\frac{1}{z_B} - \frac{1}{z_A}\right) \qquad (A.3)$$

where λ indicates the position of the projection I$'$ relative to A$'$ and B$'$:

$$x_{I'} = x_{A'} + \lambda(x_{B'} - x_{A'})$$
$$y_{I'} = y_{A'} + \lambda(y_{B'} - y_{A'})$$

We have used Equation (A.3) in Chapters 6 and 7 to compute the z-coordinate of an unknown 3D point that is the original of a given 2D image point.

A different notation

In the preceding discussion we have written equations of the form

$$x_{I'} = x_{A'} + \lambda(x_{B'} - x_{A'})$$

in which the variable $x_{A'}$ occurs twice. We can instead use a different equation, in which each of the variables $x_{A'}$ and $x_{B'}$ occurs only once, at the price of using two occurrences of the parameter λ:

$$x_{I'} = (1 - \lambda)x_{A'} + \lambda x_{B'}$$

An example

Using $\lambda = 0.5$ in the above formulas, we obtain

$$x_{I'} = 0.5(x_{A'} + x_{B'})$$
$$y_{I'} = 0.5(y_{A'} + y_{B'})$$
$$\frac{1}{z_I} = 0.5\left(\frac{1}{z_A} + \frac{1}{z_B}\right)$$

Figure A.2 illustrates this. The object shown in (a) is a wire-frame model of a cube, containing an extra square between the front and back faces and passing through point I. The viewpoint indicated in (c) as *Eye* is used to obtain the perspective view (b). Here the projection I$'$ is the midpoint of A$'$B$'$, so that the first and second of the above three equations clearly apply. In 3D space, I is not

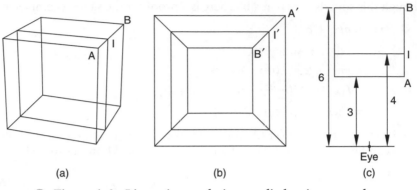

(a)   (b)   (c)

○ **Figure A.2: Linear interpolation applied to inverse values**

the midpoint of AB, but BI = 2AI, as (a) and (c) show. Since the negative z_e-axis points from the eye to the center of the object, the distances shown in (c) imply that

$$z_A = -3$$
$$z_I = -4$$
$$z_B = -6$$

These values satisfy the third of the above three equations.

Appendix B

A Note on Event Handling

A brief discussion of event handling in Java will be helpful to understand some related, rather cryptic program fragments in this book.

An event listener

For some component, say, a button *bt*, we can write

```
bt.addActionListener(x);
```

where *x* is an object of a class that implements the interface *ActionListener*. Since this implies that there is a method *actionPerformed* in this class, the above statement is in fact a means to provide the button *bt* with information about how to respond to the user clicking this button. For example, the above statement might be preceded by

```
ButtonAction x = new ButtonAction();
```

with *ButtonAction* defined as

```
class ButtonAction implements ActionListener
{  public void actionPerformed(ActionEvent ae)
   {  System.out.println("Button bt clicked.");
   }
}
```

The object *x* in the above example is referred to as an *event listener*.

Using *this* as an event listener

Instead of writing a special class, such as *ButtonAction*, for the event in question, we may as well use a class that also contains methods that are unrelated to it, provided that this class implements the interface *ActionListener*. In particular, we can use the very class in which we create the button and call the method *addActionListener*, writing

```
class MyFrame extends Frame implements ActionListener
{  MyFrame()
   {  ...
      bt.addActionListener(this);
      ...
   }
   public void actionPerformed(ActionEvent ae){ ... }
   ...
}
```

In contrast to our previous example, this method *actionPerformed* has access to all fields and methods of the class (*MyFrame*) in which the call to *addActionListener* occurs.

Inner classes

Instead of the previous, somewhat contrived solution, we can use a special class *ButtonAction* and yet have access to the fields and methods of another class. We simply define *ButtonAction* in that class. For example, in the following fragment the method *actionPerformed* has access to the fields and methods of *MyFrame*:

```
class MyFrame extends Frame
{  MyFrame()
   {  ...
      bt.addActionListener(new ButtonClass());
      ...
   }
   class ButtonClass implements ActionListener
   {  public void actionPerformed(ActionEvent ae){ ... }
   }
   ...
}
```

Anonymous classes

It is possible to define a class at the place where we need it, without giving it a name. For example, to create an object of such an anonymous subclass of, say, *Superclass*, we can write

```
Superclass y = new Superclass(){...};
```

Recall that a variable of type *Superclass* can also refer to objects of subclasses of *Superclass*. In the above statement, the part {...} can be identical to that which we would otherwise use in the more familiar form

```
class Subclass extends Superclass {...}
Superclass y = new Subclass();
```

Instead of a normal class *Superclass*, we can also use an interface here. This explains the following usage of an anonymous class for event handling:

```
class MyFrame extends Frame
{  MyFrame()
   {  ...
      bt.addActionListener(new ActionListener(){...});
      ...
   }
   ...
}
```

Since the anonymous class, defined on the program line in the middle of this fragment, implements *ActionListener*, the part {...} must contain the method *actionPerformed*. This very compact form is used, for example, in program *Cylinder.java* of Section 6.6.

Adapter classes

As you will know, an interface promises that a set of methods will be defined. For the *ActionListener* interface, this set consists of only one method, *action-Performed*. However, many more methods have to be defined for other event interfaces, such as *WindowListener* and *MouseListener*. For every frame, a call to *addWindowListener* is required to enable the user to close this frame. Unfortunately, the interface *WindowListener* requires as many as seven methods to be defined, even if we are interested in only one, *windowClosing*. The fragment below lists these seven methods, six of which are defined as do-nothing functions:

```
class MyFrame extends Frame
{  MyFrame()
   {  ...
      addWindowListener(new WindowListener()
      {  public void windowClosing(WindowEvent e){System.exit(0);}
         public void windowOpened(WindowEvent e){}
         public void windowIconified(WindowEvent e){}
         public void windowDeiconified(WindowEvent e){}
         public void windowClosed(WindowEvent e){}
         public void windowActivated(WindowEvent e){}
         public void windowDeactivated(WindowEvent e){}
      });
      ...
   }
   ...
}
```

To enable us to avoid such tedious program code, the designers of JDK1.1 have introduced a class *WindowAdapter*, which implements the interface *WindowListener* by providing seven do-nothing methods, so we can override only those we like. Therefore, instead of the above fragment, we will actually write

```
class MyFrame extends Frame
{  MyFrame()
   {  ...
      addWindowListener(new WindowAdapter()
         {public void windowClosing(WindowEvent e){System.exit(0);}});
      ...
   }
   ...
}
```

The two lines in the middle of this fragment occur in most programs in this book. Mouse events are similar: here we can use the class *MouseAdapter*, which implements the interface *MouseListener*. It is used, for example, in the following fragment, copied from program *Anisotr.java* of Section 1.4:

```
CvAnisotr()
{  addMouseListener(new MouseAdapter()
   {  public void mousePressed(MouseEvent evt)
      {  xP = fx(evt.getX()); yP = fy(evt.getY());
```

```
        repaint();
    }
  });
}
```

Note that the method *addMouseListener* is used here for a canvas, not for a frame.

Appendix C

File Obj3D.java

The following file is not a complete program. It is the code for a single class, *Obj3D*, which is discussed in Section 5.5 and used in the programs *Wireframe.java* of Chapter 5, *HLines.java* of Chapter 6, *Painter.java* of Section 7.3, and *ZBuf.java* of Section 7.4.

```java
// Obj3D.java: A 3D object and its 2D representation.
// Uses: Point2D (Section 1.5), Point3D (Section 3.9),
//       Polygon3D, Input (Section 5.5).
import java.awt.*;
import java.util.*;

class Obj3D
{  private float rho, d, theta=0.30F, phi=1.3F, rhoMin, rhoMax,
      xMin, xMax, yMin, yMax, zMin, zMax, v11, v12, v13, v21,
      v22, v23, v32, v33, v43, xe, ye, ze, objSize;
   private Point2D imgCenter;
   private double sunZ = 1/Math.sqrt (3) , sunY = sunZ, sunX = -sunZ,
      inprodMin = 1e30, inprodMax = -1e30, inprodRange;
   private Vector w = new Vector();        // World coordinates
   private Point3D[] e;                     // Eye coordinates
   private Point2D[] vScr;                  // Screen coordinates
   private Vector polyList = new Vector();  // Polygon3D objects
```

```java
    private String fName = " ";                    // File name

    boolean read(String fName)
    {  Input inp = new Input(fName);
       if (inp.fails())return failing();
       this.fName = fName;
       xMin = yMin = zMin = +1e30F;
       xMax = yMax = zMax = -1e30F;
       return readObject(inp); // Read from inp into obj
    }

    Vector getPolyList(){return polyList;}
    String getFName(){return fName;}
    Point3D[] getE(){return e;}
    Point2D[] getVScr(){return vScr;}
    Point2D getImgCenter(){return imgCenter;}
    float getRho(){return rho;}
    float getD(){return d;}

    private boolean failing()
    {  Toolkit.getDefaultToolkit().beep();
       return false;
    }

    private boolean readObject(Input inp)
    {  for (;;)
       {  int i = inp.readInt();
          if (inp.fails()){inp.clear(); break;}
          if (i < 0)
          {  System.out.println(
                "Negative vertex number in first part of input file");
             return failing();
          }
          w.ensureCapacity(i + 1);
          float x = inp.readFloat(), y = inp.readFloat(),
                z = inp.readFloat();
          addVertex(i, x, y, z);
       }
       shiftToOrigin(); // Origin in center of object.
       char ch;
       int count = 0;
       do   // Skip the line "Faces:"
       {  ch = inp.readChar(); count++;
```

```
  } while (!inp.eof() && ch != '\n');
  if (count < 6 || count > 8)
  { System.out.println("Invalid input file"); return failing();
  }
  // Build polygon list:
  for (;;)
  { Vector vnrs = new Vector();
    for (;;)
    { int i = inp.readInt();
      if (inp.fails()){inp.clear(); break;}
      int absi = Math.abs(i);
      if (i == 0 || absi >= w.size() ||
        w.elementAt(absi) == null)
      { System.out.println("Invalid vertex number: " + absi +
        " must be defined, nonzero and less than " + w.size());
        return failing();
      }
      vnrs.addElement(new Integer(i));
    }
    ch = inp.readChar();
    if (ch != '.' && ch != '#') break;
    // Ignore input lines with only one vertex number:
    if (vnrs.size() >= 2)
      polyList.addElement(new Polygon3D(vnrs));
  }
  inp.close();
  return true;
}

private void addVertex(int i, float x, float y, float z)
{ if (x < xMin) xMin = x; if (x > xMax) xMax = x;
  if (y < yMin) yMin = y; if (y > yMax) yMax = y;
  if (z < zMin) zMin = z; if (z > zMax) zMax = z;
  if (i >= w.size()) w.setSize(i + 1);
  w.setElementAt(new Point3D(x, y, z), i);
}

private void shiftToOrigin()
{ float xwC = 0.5F * (xMin + xMax),
        ywC = 0.5F * (yMin + yMax),
        zwC = 0.5F * (zMin + zMax);
  int n = w.size();
  for (int i=1; i<n; i++)
```

```java
        if (w.elementAt(i) != null)
        { ((Point3D)w.elementAt(i)).x -= xwC;
          ((Point3D)w.elementAt(i)).y -= ywC;
          ((Point3D)w.elementAt(i)).z -= zwC;
        }
     float dx = xMax - xMin, dy = yMax - yMin, dz = zMax - zMin;
     rhoMin = 0.6F * (float) Math.sqrt(dx * dx + dy * dy + dz * dz);
     rhoMax = 1000 * rhoMin;
     rho = 3 * rhoMin;
  }


  private void initPersp()
  { float costh = (float)Math.cos(theta),
          sinth = (float)Math.sin(theta),
          cosph = (float)Math.cos(phi),
          sinph = (float)Math.sin(phi);
    v11 = -sinth;    v12 = -cosph * costh;    v13 = sinph * costh;
    v21 = costh;     v22 = -cosph * sinth;    v23 = sinph * sinth;
                     v32 = sinph;             v33 = cosph;
                                              v43 = -rho;

  }


  float eyeAndScreen(Dimension dim)
     // Called in paint method of Canvas class
  { initPersp();
    int n = w.size();
    e = new Point3D[n];
    vScr = new Point2D[n];
    float xScrMin=1e30F, xScrMax=-1e30F,
        yScrMin=1e30F, yScrMax=-1e30F;
    for (int i=1; i<n; i++)
    { Point3D P = (Point3D)(w.elementAt(i));
      if (P == null)
      { e[i] = null; vScr[i] = null;
      }
      else
      { float x = v11 * P.x + v21 * P.y;
        float y = v12 * P.x + v22 * P.y + v32 * P.z;
        float z = v13 * P.x + v23 * P.y + v33 * P.z + v43;
        Point3D Pe = e[i] = new Point3D(x, y, z);
        float xScr = -Pe.x/Pe.z, yScr = -Pe.y/Pe.z;
        vScr[i] = new Point2D(xScr, yScr);
        if (xScr < xScrMin) xScrMin = xScr;
```

```
            if (xScr > xScrMax) xScrMax = xScr;
            if (yScr < yScrMin) yScrMin = yScr;
            if (yScr > yScrMax) yScrMax = yScr;
        }
    }
    float rangeX = xScrMax - xScrMin, rangeY = yScrMax - yScrMin;
    d = 0.95F * Math.min(dim.width/rangeX, dim.height/rangeY);
    imgCenter = new Point2D(d * (xScrMin + xScrMax)/2,
                            d * (yScrMin + yScrMax)/2);
    for (int i=1; i<n; i++)
    {   if (vScr[i] != null){vScr[i].x *= d; vScr[i].y *= d;}
    }
    return d * Math.max(rangeX, rangeY);
    // Maximum screen-coordinate range used in CvHLines for HP-GL
}


void planeCoeff()
{   int nFaces = polyList.size();

    for (int j=0; j<nFaces; j++)
    {   Polygon3D pol = (Polygon3D)(polyList.elementAt(j));
        int[] nrs = pol.getNrs();
        if (nrs.length < 3) continue;
        int iA = Math.abs(nrs[0]), // Possibly negative
            iB = Math.abs(nrs[1]), // for HLines.
            iC = Math.abs(nrs[2]);
        Point3D A = e[iA], B = e[iB], C = e[iC];
        double
            u1 = B.x - A.x, u2 = B.y - A.y, u3 = B.z - A.z,
            v1 = C.x - A.x, v2 = C.y - A.y, v3 = C.z - A.z,
            a = u2 * v3 - u3 * v2,
            b = u3 * v1 - u1 * v3,
            c = u1 * v2 - u2 * v1,
            len = Math.sqrt(a * a + b * b + c * c), h;
            a /= len; b /= len; c /= len;
            h = a * A.x + b * A.y + c * A.z;
        pol.setAbch(a, b, c, h);
        Point2D A1 = vScr[iA], B1 = vScr[iB], C1 = vScr[iC];
        u1 = B1.x - A1.x; u2 = B1.y - A1.y;
        v1 = C1.x - A1.x; v2 = C1.y - A1.y;
        if (u1 * v2 - u2 * v1 <= 0) continue; // backface
        double inprod = a * sunX + b * sunY + c * sunZ;
        if (inprod < inprodMin) inprodMin = inprod;
```

```
          if (inprod > inprodMax) inprodMax = inprod;
      }
      inprodRange = inprodMax - inprodMin;
   }

   boolean vp(Canvas cv, float dTheta, float dPhi, float fRho)
   {  theta += dTheta;
      phi += dPhi;
      float rhoNew = fRho * rho;
      if (rhoNew >= rhoMin && rhoNew <= rhoMax)
         rho = rhoNew;
      else
         return false;
      cv.repaint();
      return true;
   }

   int colorCode(double a, double b, double c)
   {  double inprod = a * sunX + b * sunY + c * sunZ;
      return (int)Math.round(
         ((inprod - inprodMin)/inprodRange) * 255);
   }
}
```

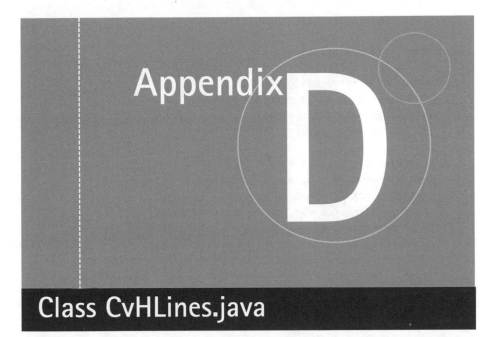

Appendix D

Class CvHLines.java

The following class is used in program *HLines.java*, listed in Section 6.8:

```java
// CvHLines.java: Used in the file HLines.java.
import java.awt.*;
import java.util.*;

class CvHLines extends Canvas3D
{   private int maxX, maxY, centerX, centerY, nTria, nVertices;
    private Obj3D obj;
    private Point2D imgCenter;
    private Tria[] tr;
    private HPGL hpgl;
    private int[] refPol;
    private int[][] connect;
    private int[] nConnect;
    private int chunkSize = 4;
    private double hLimit;
    private Vector polyList;
    private float maxScreenRange;

    Obj3D getObj(){return obj;}
    void setObj(Obj3D obj){this.obj = obj;}
```

```
      void setHPGL(HPGL hpgl){this.hpgl = hpgl;}

      public void paint(Graphics g)
      {  if (obj == null) return;
         Vector polyList = obj.getPolyList();
         if (polyList == null) return;
         int nFaces = polyList.size();
         if (nFaces == 0) return;
         float xe, ye, ze;
         Dimension dim = getSize();
         maxX = dim.width - 1; maxY = dim.height - 1;
         centerX = maxX/2; centerY = maxY/2;
         // ze-axis towards eye, so ze-coordinates of
         // object points are all negative. Since screen
         // coordinates x and y are used to interpolate for
         // the z-direction, we have to deal with 1/z instead
         // of z. With negative z, a small value of 1/z means
         // a small value of |z| for a nearby point.

         // obj is a java object that contains all data,
         // with w, e and vScr parallel (with vertex numbers
         // as index values):
         // - Vector w (with Point3D elements)
         // - Array e (with Point3D elements)
         // - Array vScr (with Point2D elements)
         // - Vector polyList (with Polygon3D elements)

         // Every Polygon3D value contains:
         // - Array 'nrs' for vertex numbers (n elements)
         // - Values a, b, c, h for the plane ax+by+cz=h.
         // - Array t (with n-2 elements of type Tria)

         // Every Tria value consists of the three vertex
         // numbers A, B and C.
         maxScreenRange = obj.eyeAndScreen(dim);
         imgCenter = obj.getImgCenter();
         obj.planeCoeff();        // Compute a, b, c and h.

         hLimit = -1e-6 * obj.getRho();
         buildLineSet();

         // Construct an array of triangles in
         // each polygon and count the total number
```

```
    // of triangles.
    nTria = 0;
    for (int j=0; j<nFaces; j++)
    {  Polygon3D pol = (Polygon3D)(polyList.elementAt(j));
       if (pol.getNrs().length > 2 && pol.getH() <= hLimit)
       {  pol.triangulate(obj);
          nTria += pol.getT().length;
       }
    }
    tr = new Tria[nTria];    // Triangles of all polygons
    refPol = new int[nTria]; // tr[i] belongs to refPol[i]
    int iTria = 0;

    for (int j=0; j<nFaces; j++)
    {  Polygon3D pol = (Polygon3D)(polyList.elementAt(j));
       Tria[] t = pol.getT(); // Triangles of one polygon
       if (pol.getNrs().length > 2 && pol.getH() <= hLimit)
       {  for (int i=0; i<t.length; i++)
          {  Tria tri = t[i];
             tr[iTria] = tri;
             refPol[iTria++] = j;
          }
       }
    }
    Point3D[] e = obj.getE();
    Point2D[] vScr = obj.getVScr();
    for (int i=0; i<nVertices; i++)
    {  for (int j=0; j<nConnect[i]; j++)
       {  int jj = connect[i][j];
          lineSegment(g, e[i], e[jj], vScr[i], vScr[jj],
             i, jj, 0);
       }
    }
    hpgl = null;
}

private void buildLineSet()
{  // Build the array
   // 'connect' of int arrays, where
   // connect[i] is the array of all
   // vertex numbers j, such that connect[i][j] is
   // an edge of the 3D object.
   polyList = obj.getPolyList();
```

```
        nVertices = obj.getVScr().length;
        connect = new int[nVertices][];
        nConnect = new int[nVertices];
        for (int i=0; i<nVertices; i++)
        nConnect[i] = 0;
        int nFaces = polyList.size();

        for (int j=0; j<nFaces; j++)
        {  Polygon3D pol = (Polygon3D)(polyList.elementAt(j));
           int[] nrs = pol.getNrs();
           int n = nrs.length;
           if (n > 2 && pol.getH() > 0) continue;
           int ii = Math.abs(nrs[n-1]);
           for (int k=0; k<n; k++)
           {  int jj = nrs[k];
              if (jj < 0)
                 jj = -jj; // abs
              else
              {  int i1 = Math.min(ii, jj), j1 = Math.max(ii, jj),
                    nCon = nConnect[i1];
                 // Look if j1 is already present:
                 int l;
                 for (l=0; l<nCon; l++) if (connect[i1][l] == j1) break;
                 if (l == nCon)  // Not found:
                 {  if (nCon % chunkSize == 0)
                    {  int[] temp = new int[nCon + chunkSize];
                       for (l=0; l<nCon; l++) temp[l] = connect[i1][l];
                       connect[i1] = temp;
                    }
                    connect[i1][nConnect[i1]++] = j1;
                 }
              }
              ii = jj;
           }
        }
    }

    int iX(float x){return Math.round(centerX + x - imgCenter.x);}
    int iY(float y){return Math.round(centerY - y + imgCenter.y);}

    private String toString(float t)
    // From screen device units (pixels) to HP-GL units  (0-10000) :
    {  int i = Math.round(5000 + t * 9000/maxScreenRange);
```

```
   String s = "";
   int n = 1000;
   for (int j=3; j>=0; j--)
   {  s += i/n;
      i %= n;
      n /= 10;
   }
   return s;
}

private String hpx(float x){return toString(x - imgCenter.x);}
private String hpy(float y){return toString(y - imgCenter.y);}

private void drawLine(Graphics g, float x1, float y1,
   float x2, float y2)
{  if (x1 != x2 || y1 != y2)
   {  g.drawLine(iX(x1), iY(y1), iX(x2), iY(y2));
      if (hpgl != null)
      {  hpgl.write("PU;PA" + hpx(x1) + "," + hpy(y1));
         hpgl.write("PD;PA" + hpx(x2) + "," + hpy(y2) + "\n");
      }
   }
}

private void lineSegment(Graphics g, Point3D p, Point3D q,
   Point2D pScr, Point2D qScr, int iP, int iQ, int iStart)
{  double u1 = qScr.x - pScr.x, u2 = qScr.y - pScr.y;
   double minPQx = Math.min(pScr.x, qScr.x);
   double maxPQx = Math.max(pScr.x, qScr.x);
   double minPQy = Math.min(pScr.y, qScr.y);
   double maxPQy = Math.max(pScr.y, qScr.y);
   double zP = p.z, zQ = q.z;    // p and q give eye-coordinates
   double minPQz = Math.min(zP, zQ);
   Point3D[] e = obj.getE();
   Point2D[] vScr = obj.getVScr();
   for (int i=iStart; i<nTria; i++)
   {  Tria t = tr[i];
      int iA = t.iA, iB = t.iB, iC = t.iC;
      Point2D aScr = vScr[iA], bScr = vScr[iB], cScr = vScr[iC];

      // 1. Minimax test for x and y screen coordinates:
      if (maxPQx <= aScr.x && maxPQx <= bScr.x && maxPQx <= cScr.x
       || minPQx >= aScr.x && minPQx >= bScr.x && minPQx >= cScr.x
```

```
      || maxPQy <= aScr.y && maxPQy <= bScr.y && maxPQy <= cScr.y
      || minPQy >= aScr.y && minPQy >= bScr.y && minPQy >= cScr.y)
         continue; // This triangle does not obscure PQ.

      // 2. Test if PQ is an edge of ABC:
      if ((iP == iA || iP == iB || iP == iC) &&
          (iQ == iA || iQ == iB || iQ == iC))
         continue;  // This triangle does not obscure PQ.

      // 3. Test if PQ is clearly nearer than ABC:
      double zA = e[iA].z, zB = e[iB].z, zC = e[iC].z;
      if (minPQz >= zA && minPQz >= zB && minPQz >= zC)
         continue;  // This triangle does not obscure PQ.

      // 4. Do P and Q (in 2D) lie in a half plane defined
      //     by line AB, on the side other than that of C?
      //     Similar for the edges BC and CA.
      double eps = 0.1; // Relative to numbers of pixels
      if (Tools2D.area2(aScr, bScr, pScr) < eps &&
          Tools2D.area2(aScr, bScr, qScr) < eps ||
          Tools2D.area2(bScr, cScr, pScr) < eps &&
          Tools2D.area2(bScr, cScr, qScr) < eps ||
          Tools2D.area2(cScr, aScr, pScr) < eps &&
          Tools2D.area2(cScr, aScr, qScr) < eps)
         continue;  // This triangle does not obscure PQ.

      // 5. Test  (2D)  if A, B and C lie on the same side
      //     of the infinite line through P and Q:
      double pqa = Tools2D.area2(pScr, qScr, aScr);
      double pqb = Tools2D.area2(pScr, qScr, bScr);
      double pqc = Tools2D.area2(pScr, qScr, cScr);

      if (pqa < +eps && pqb < +eps && pqc < +eps ||
          pqa > -eps && pqb > -eps && pqc > -eps)
         continue;  // This triangle does not obscure PQ.

      // 6. Test if neither P nor Q lies behind the
      //     infinite plane through A, B and C:
      int iPol = refPol[i];
      Polygon3D pol = (Polygon3D)polyList.elementAt(iPol);
      double a = pol.getA(), b = pol.getB(), c = pol.getC(),
         h = pol.getH(), eps1 = 1e-5 * Math.abs(h),
         hP = a * p.x + b * p.y + c * p.z,
```

```
      hQ = a * q.x + b * q.y + c * q.z;
   if (hP > h - eps1 && hQ > h - eps1)
      continue;   // This triangle does not obscure PQ.

   // 7. Test if both P and Q behind triangle ABC:
   boolean pInside =
      Tools2D.insideTriangle(aScr, bScr, cScr, pScr);
   boolean qInside =
      Tools2D.insideTriangle(aScr, bScr, cScr, qScr);
   if (pInside && qInside)
      return;   // This triangle obscures PQ.

   // 8. If P nearer than ABC and inside, PQ visible;
   //    the same for Q:
   double h1 = h + eps1;
   if (hP > h1 && pInside || hQ > h1 && qInside)
      continue;   // This triangle does not obscure PQ.

   // 9. Compute the intersections I and J of PQ
   // with ABC in 2D.
   // If, in 3D, such an intersection lies in front of
   // ABC, this triangle does not obscure PQ.
   // Otherwise, the intersections lie behind ABC and
   // this triangle obscures part of PQ:
   double lambdaMin = 1.0, lambdaMax = 0.0;
   for (int ii=0; ii<3; ii++)
   {   double v1 = bScr.x - aScr.x, v2 = bScr.y - aScr.y,
              w1 = aScr.x - pScr.x, w2 = aScr.y - pScr.y,
              denom = u2 * v1 - u1 * v2;
      if (denom != 0)
      {   double mu = (u1 * w2 - u2 * w1)/denom;
         // mu = 0 gives A and mu = 1 gives B.
         if (mu > -0.0001 && mu < 1.0001)
         {   double lambda = (v1 * w2 - v2 * w1)/denom;
            // lambda = PI/PQ
            // (I is point of intersection)
            if (lambda > -0.0001 && lambda < 1.0001)
            {   if (pInside != qInside &&
               lambda > 0.0001 && lambda < 0.9999)
               {   lambdaMin = lambdaMax = lambda;
                  break;
                  // Only one point of intersection
               }
```

```
                        if (lambda < lambdaMin) lambdaMin = lambda;
                        if (lambda > lambdaMax) lambdaMax = lambda;
                    }
                }
            }
            Point2D temp = aScr; aScr = bScr;
            bScr = cScr; cScr = temp;
        }
        float d = obj.getD();
        if (!pInside && lambdaMin > 0.001)
        {   double iScrx = pScr.x + lambdaMin * u1,
                   iScry = pScr.y + lambdaMin * u2;
            // Back from screen to eye coordinates:
            double zI = 1/(lambdaMin/zQ + (1 - lambdaMin)/zP),
                   xI = -zI * iScrx / d, yI = -zI * iScry / d;
            if (a * xI + b * yI + c * zI > h1)
                continue;  // This triangle does not obscure PQ.

            Point2D iScr = new Point2D((float)iScrx, (float)iScry);
            if (Tools2D.distance2(iScr, pScr) >= 1.0)
                lineSegment(g, p, new Point3D(xI, yI, zI), pScr,
                    iScr, iP, -1, i + 1);
        }
        if (!qInside && lambdaMax < 0.999)
        {   double jScrx = pScr.x + lambdaMax * u1,
                   jScry = pScr.y + lambdaMax * u2;
            double zJ =
                1/(lambdaMax/zQ + (1 - lambdaMax)/zP),
                   xJ = -zJ * jScrx / d, yJ = -zJ * jScry / d;
            if (a * xJ + b * yJ + c * zJ > h1)
                continue;  // This triangle does not obscure PQ.
            Point2D jScr = new Point2D((float)jScrx, (float)jScry);
            if (Tools2D.distance2(jScr, qScr) >= 1.0)
                lineSegment(g, q, new Point3D(xJ, yJ, zJ),
                    qScr, jScr, iQ, -1, i + 1);
        }
        return;
            // if no continue-statement has been executed
    }
    drawLine(g, pScr.x, pScr.y, qScr.x, qScr.y);
        // No triangle obscures PQ.
  }
}
```

Appendix E

Some Applications

This appendix demonstrates how to generate data files for other interesting 3D objects by special programs, in a similar fashion to the cylinder example in Section 6.6. The generated files are accepted by the programs *HLines.java* (see Chapter 6), *Painter.java* and *ZBuf.java* (see Chapter 7).

E.1 PLATONIC SOLIDS

We will first discuss the generation of 3D files for five well-known objects. Let us begin with two definitions.

If all edges of a polygon have the same length and any two edges meeting at a vertex include the same angle, the polygon is said to be *regular*. If all bounding faces of a polyhedron are regular polygons, which are congruent (that is, which have exactly the same shape), that polyhedron is referred to as a *regular polyhedron* or *platonic solid*. There are only five essentially different platonic solids; their names and their numbers of faces, edges and vertices are listed below:

Platonic solid	Faces	Edges	Vertices
Tetrahedron	4	6	4
Cube (= hexahedron)	6	12	8
Octahedron	8	12	6
Dodecahedron	12	30	20
Icosahedron	20	30	12

Note that what we call a *tetrahedron*, a *hexahedron*, and so on, should actually be referred to as *regular tetrahedron*, *regular hexahedron*, etc., but since in this section we are only dealing with regular polyhedra, we omit the word *regular* here.

The above numbers of faces, edges and vertices satisfy Euler's theorem, which also applies to non-regular polyhedra:

$$Faces + Vertices = Edges + 2 \qquad \text{(E.1)}$$

E.1.1 Tetrahedron

An elegant way of constructing a tetrahedron is by using the diagonals of the six faces of a cube as the edges of the tetrahedron, as Figure E.1(a) shows.

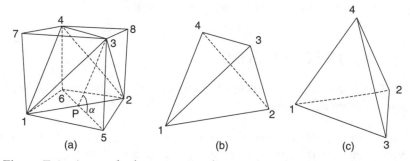

○ **Figure E.1: A tetrahedron: (a) inside a cube; (b) cube omitted; (c) after rotation**

Using a cube with edges of length 2 and with its center as the origin of the coordinate system, we can easily write down the contents of the data file, say, *tetra.dat*, for the tetrahedron proper (without the surrounding cube):

```
1    1  -1  -1
2   -1   1  -1
```

```
3    1   1   1
4   -1  -1   1
Faces:
1 2 3.
2 4 3.
1 4 2.
1 3 4.
```

Supplying this file to program *HLines.java* results in a poor representation of a tetrahedron, identical to what we obtain if we omit the dashed line (and the vertex numbers) in Figure E.1(b). Most people would fail to recognize the result as a 3D object, unless Figure E.1(a) was also given. The surrounding cube in the latter figure can be obtained by adding vertices 5, 6, 7 and 8 to the first part of the above input file and twelve lines of vertex-pair numbers, for the cube edges, to the second part.

A much better representation is Figure E.1(c), in which the tetrahedron has been rotated about the edge 1–2, in such a way that the face 1-2-3 becomes horizontal. The angle of this rotation is equal to

$$\alpha = \arctan \sqrt{2}$$

As Figure E.1(a) shows, α is the angle included by the edges P-5 and P-3 in the right-angled triangle P-5-3, where P is the point of intersection of the lines 1–2 and 5–6. Since the cube edge 3–5 has length 2 and the line segment P-5, being half the diagonal 6-5 of the bottom plane, has the length $\sqrt{2}$, we have tan $\alpha = 2/\sqrt{2} = \sqrt{2}$, which explains the above value of α.

Fortunately, we have already developed a general and useful class, *Rota3D*, for 3D rotations. We used it in Section 3.9 in the program *Rota3DTest.java* to rotate a cube about a given axis AB through an angle of 180°. This time, vertices 1 and 2 will act as points A and B, while rotation will take place through the angle α we have just discussed. We will use the file *tetra.dat*, listed above, as input, to derive the file *tetra1.dat*, describing the rotated tetrahedron, from it. Note that the classes *Point3D* and *Rota3D*, both defined in Section 3.9, and the class *Input* of Section 5.5 must be available (in the form of *.class* files) in the current directory.

```
// Rota3DTetra.java: Rotating a tetrahedron that
//   has horizontal top and bottom edges, in such
//   a way that it obtains a horizontal bottom face.
//   Uses: Point3D, Rota3D (Section 3.9), Input (Section 5.5).
import java.io.*;
```

```
public class Rota3DTetra
{  public static void main(String[] args)
       throws IOException
   {  // Specify AB as directed axis of rotation
      // and alpha as the rotation angle:
      Point3D A = new Point3D(1, -1, -1),
              B = new Point3D(-1, 1, -1);
      double alpha = Math.atan(Math.sqrt (2);
      Rota3D.initRotate(A, B, alpha);
      Point3D P = new Point3D (0, 0, 0);
      Input inp = new Input("tetra.dat");
      if (inp.fails())
      {  System.out.println("Supply file tetra.dat, see Section E.1");
         System.exit(0);
      }
      FileWriter fw = new FileWriter("tetra1.dat");
      for (;;)
      {  int i = inp.readInt();
         if (inp.fails()) break;
         P.x = inp.readFloat();
         P.y = inp.readFloat();
         P.z = inp.readFloat();
         Point3D P1 = Rota3D.rotate(P);
         fw.write(i + " " + P1.x + " " +
            P1.y + " " + P1.z + "\r\n");
      }
      inp.clear();
      // Copy the rest of file tetra.dat to tetra1.dat:
      for (;;)
      {  char ch = inp.readChar();
         if (inp.fails()) break;
         fw.write(ch);
      }
      fw.close();
   }
}
```

This program changes only the coordinates of the four vertices. With the above input file, *tetra.dat*, the resulting output file, *tetra1.dat*, is listed below:

```
1 1.0 -1.0 -1.0
2 -1.0 1.0 -1.0
3 1.7320508 1.7320508 -1.0
```

```
4 0.57735026 0.57735026 1.309401
Faces:
1 2 3.
2 4 3.
1 4 2.
1 3 4.
```

Since we now have $z = -1.0$ for vertices 1, 2 and 3, we see that triangle 1-2-3 is now horizontal. This is illustrated by Figure E.1(c), which, except for the text and the dashed edge, is the result of applying the program *HLines.java* to the above file *tetra*1. *dat*.

E.1.2 Cube or hexahedron

The cube, also known as a hexahedron, is perhaps the most common 3D object because of its simplicity. With the rather unusual vertex numbering of Figure E.1(a), this cube (with edges of length 2 and with the origin as its center) is described by the following file:

```
1     1  -1  -1
2    -1   1  -1
3     1   1   1
4    -1  -1   1
5     1   1  -1
6    -1  -1  -1
7     1  -1   1
8    -1   1   1
Faces:
1 5 3 7.
5 2 8 3.
2 6 4 8.
6 1 7 4.
7 3 8 4.
1 6 2 5.
```

E.1.3 Octahedron

An octahedron has eight faces, which are equilateral triangles. One way of constructing this platonic solid is by starting with a cube and using the principle of *duality* or *reciprocity*. The numbers of faces and vertices shown in the table:

Platonic solid	Faces	Edges	Vertices
Cube (= hexahedron)	6	12	8
Octahedron	8	12	6

suggest that each face of a cube might be related to a vertex of an octahedron and vice versa. This is indeed the case: a cube and an octahedron are said to be *dual* or *reciprocal*, which implies that the centers of the faces of one can be used as the vertices of the other. Starting with a cube, we can simply use the centers of its six faces as the vertices of an octahedron. The following data file for an octahedron is based on such a cube with edges of length 2 and with O as its center:

```
1   1  0  0
2   0  1  0
3  -1  0  0
4   0 -1  0
5   0  0 -1
6   0  0  1
Faces:
1 2 6.
2 3 6.
3 4 6.
4 1 6.
2 1 5.
3 2 5.
4 3 5.
1 4 5.
```

If we use this file as input for program *HLines.java*, we obtain the octahedron shown in Figure E.2 on the right. On the left we see the way the vertices are numbered and the surrounding cube.

E.1.4 Icosahedron and dodecahedron

Let us again take a look at the following numbers of faces and vertices:

Platonic solid	Faces	Edges	Vertices
Dodecahedron	12	30	20
Icosahedron	20	30	12

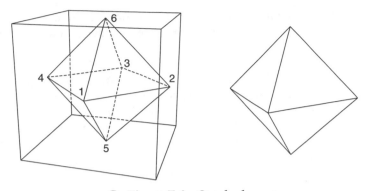

Figure E.2: Octahedron

Since the number of faces of one of the two polyhedra is equal to the number of vertices of the other, a dodecahedron and an icosahedron are reciprocal polyhedra. Figure E.3 illustrates this. For example, vertex 1 of the dodecahedron has been constructed as the center of the face 1-2-3 of the icosahedron, vertex 2 of the dodecahedron as that of face 1-3-4 of the icosahedron, and so on. Since showing this dodecahedron in Figure E.3 in its original position would have been confusing, the dodecahedron has been shifted to the right after its construction.

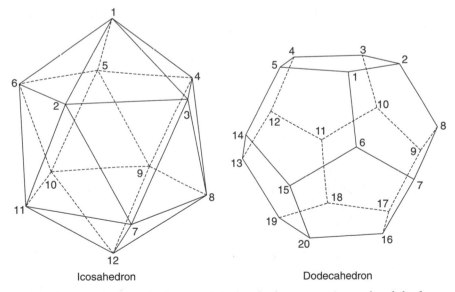

Icosahedron   Dodecahedron

Figure E.3: Icosahedron and dodecahedron as reciprocal polyhedra

It follows that constructing an icosahedron is the only remaining problem: once the coordinates of its vertices are known, we can derive the dodecahedron from it.

Both polyhedra are based on regular pentagons, as you can see in Figure E.3. In the icosahedron shown here, there are two horizontal pentagons: 2-3-4-5-6 and 7-8-9-10-11. They have both been constructed with their vertices on (horizontal) circles with radius 1. Curiously enough, these two horizontal pentagons lie a distance 1 apart, while the 'north pole' 1 and the 'south pole' 12 lie a distance $\sqrt{5}$ apart. A proof of these facts is omitted here, because it would be rather lengthy and only very loosely related to computer graphics. Interested readers are referred to books about geometry, such as Coxeter (1961).

With O as the center of the icosahedron, we can now define the coordinates of all twelve vertices of an icosahedron as follows:

i	x_i	y_i	z_i
1	0	0	$\frac{1}{2}\sqrt{5}$
2, 3, 4, 5, 6	$\cos\{(i-2)\times 72°\}$	$\sin\{(i-2)\times 72°\}$	0.5
7, 8, 9, 10, 11	$\cos\{36° + (i-7)\times 72°\}$	$\sin\{36° + (i-7)\times 72°\}$	−0.5
12	0	0	$\frac{1}{2}\sqrt{5}$

We can easily program the above formulas to obtain the numerical values of the vertex coordinate in question, as we will see shortly. These values are listed in the following 3D data file, in which the faces of the icosahedron are displayed on five text lines, instead of on 20 lines as generated by the program. Also, the layout of the first part of the file has been improved for the sake of readability:

```
 1  0.0        0.0          1.118034
 2  1.0        0.0          0.5
 3  0.309017   0.95105654   0.5
 4 -0.809017   0.58778524   0.5
 5 -0.809017  -0.58778524   0.5
 6  0.309017  -0.95105654   0.5
 7  0.809017   0.58778524  -0.5
 8 -0.309017   0.95105654  -0.5
 9 -1.0        0.0         -0.5
10 -0.309017  -0.95105654  -0.5
11  0.809017  -0.58778524  -0.5
12  0.0        0.0         -1.118034
Faces:
```

```
 1  2  3.     1  3  4.     1  4  5.     1  5  6.
 1  6  2.     2  7  3.     3  7  8.     3  8  4.
 4  8  9.     4  9  5.     5  9 10.     5 10  6.
 6 10 11.     6 11  2.     2 11  7.    12  8  7.
12  9  8.    12 10  9.    12 11 10.    12  7 11.
```

E.1.5 Dodecahedron

As mentioned above, we use the center of the first face, 1-2-3, of the icosahedron as vertex 1 of the dodecahedron. For example, we have

$$x_1 \text{(of the dodecahedron)} = \frac{x_1 + x_2 + x_3 \text{ (all three of the icosahedron)}}{3}$$

The faces in the above icosahedron file are to be read line by line, so that the center of face 1-3-4 provides vertex 2 of the dodecahedron, that of face 1-4-5 provides vertex 3, and so on. The second part of the dodecahedron file is more difficult. You can check it by comparing both polyhedra of Figure E.3. For example, the vertices of the dodecahedron's face 1-6-7-8-2, in that order, are the centers of face 1 (1-2-3), face 6 (2-7-3), face 7 (3-8-7), face 8 (3-8-4) and face 2 (1-3-4) of the icosahedron. In the data file for the dodecahedron below, you can find this face 1-6-7-8-2 as the second one after the word *Faces*:

```
 1   0.436339     0.31701884    0.7060113
 2  -0.16666667    0.51294726    0.7060113
 3  -0.53934467    0.0           0.7060113
 4  -0.16666667   -0.51294726    0.7060113
 5   0.436339     -0.31701884    0.7060113
 6   0.7060113     0.51294726    0.16666667
 7   0.26967233    0.82996607   -0.16666667
 8  -0.26967233    0.82996607    0.16666667
 9  -0.7060113     0.51294726   -0.16666667
10  -0.872678      0.0           0.16666667
11  -0.7060113    -0.51294726   -0.16666667
12  -0.26967233   -0.82996607    0.16666667
13   0.26967233   -0.82996607   -0.16666667
14   0.7060113    -0.51294726    0.16666667
15   0.872678      0.0          -0.16666667
16   0.16666667    0.51294726   -0.7060113
17  -0.436339      0.31701884   -0.7060113
18  -0.436339     -0.31701884   -0.7060113
19   0.16666667   -0.51294726   -0.7060113
20   0.53934467    0.0          -0.7060113
Faces:
```

```
 1  2  3  4  5.     1  6  7  8  2.     2  8  9 10  3.
 3 10 11 12  4.     4 12 13 14  5.     5 14 15  6  1.
20 19 18 17 16.    20 15 14 13 19.    19 13 12 11 18.
18 11 10  9 17.    17  9  8  7 16.    16  7  6 15 20.
```

Since this book is about programming aspects of graphics, a Java program to generate both above files (in a slightly different format) is listed below:

```java
// IcoDode.java: Generating input files for
//     both an icosahedron and a dodecahedron.
//     Uses: Point3D (Section 3.9), Tria (Section 5.5).

import java.io.*;

public class IcoDode
{  public static void main(String[] args)throws IOException
   {  new Both();
   }
}

class Both
{  Point3D[] icoV;
   Tria[] icoF;

   Both()throws IOException
   {  outIcosahedron();
      outDodecahedron();
   }

   void outIcosahedron()throws IOException
   {  double zTop = 0.5 * Math.sqrt (5);
      // Vertices (icoV[1], ..., icoV[12]):
      icoV = new Point3D[13];
      icoV[1] = new Point3D(0, 0, zTop); // North pole
      double angle36 = Math.PI/5, angle72 = 2 * angle36;
      for (int i=2; i<=6; i++)
      {  double alpha = (i - 2) * angle72;
         icoV[i] = new Point3D(Math.cos(alpha),
            Math.sin(alpha), 0.5);
      }
      for (int i=7; i<=11; i++)
      {  double alpha = angle36 + (i - 7) * angle72;
         icoV[i] = new Point3D(Math.cos(alpha),
```

```
            Math.sin(alpha), -0.5);
   }
   icoV[12] = new Point3D(0, 0, -zTop);
   // Faces (icoF[1], ..., icoF[20]):
   icoF = new Tria[21]; //
   icoF[ 1] = new Tria (1, 2, 3);
   icoF[ 2] = new Tria (1, 3, 4);
   icoF[ 3] = new Tria (1, 4, 5);
   icoF[ 4] = new Tria (1, 5, 6);
   icoF[ 5] = new Tria (1, 6, 2);
   icoF[ 6] = new Tria (2, 7, 3);
   icoF[ 7] = new Tria (3, 7, 8);
   icoF[ 8] = new Tria (3, 8, 4);
   icoF[ 9] = new Tria (4, 8, 9);
   icoF[10] = new Tria (4, 9, 5);
   icoF[11] = new Tria (5, 9, 10);
   icoF[12] = new Tria (5, 10, 6);
   icoF[13] = new Tria (6, 10, 11);
   icoF[14] = new Tria (6, 11, 2);
   icoF[15] = new Tria (2, 11, 7);

   icoF[16] = new Tria (12, 8, 7);
   icoF[17] = new Tria (12, 9, 8);
   icoF[18] = new Tria (12, 10, 9);
   icoF[19] = new Tria (12, 11, 10);
   icoF[20] = new Tria (12, 7, 11);
   FileWriter fwI = new FileWriter("icosa.dat");
   for (int i=1; i<=12; i++)
   { Point3D P = icoV[i];
      fwI.write(i + " " + P.x + " " + P.y + " " + P.z + "\r\n");
   }
   fwI.write("Faces:\r\n");
   for (int j=1; j<=20; j++)
   { Tria t = icoF[j];
      fwI.write(t.iA + " " + t.iB + " " + t.iC + ".\r\n");
   }
   fwI.close();
}

void outDodecahedron()throws IOException
{ FileWriter fwD = new FileWriter("dodeca.dat");
   for (int j=1; j<=20; j++) writeVertexInCenter(fwD, j);
   fwD.write("Faces:\r\n");
```

```
      // Horizontal, at the top:
      writeFace(fwD, 1, 2, 3, 4, 5);
      // Slightly facing upward:
      writeFace(fwD, 1, 6, 7, 8, 2);
      writeFace(fwD, 2, 8, 9, 10, 3);
      writeFace(fwD, 3, 10, 11, 12, 4);
      writeFace(fwD, 4, 12, 13, 14, 5);
      writeFace(fwD, 5, 14, 15, 6, 1);
      // Horizontal, at the bottom:
      writeFace(fwD, 20, 19, 18, 17, 16);
      // Slightly facing downward:
      writeFace(fwD, 20, 15, 14, 13, 19);
      writeFace(fwD, 19, 13, 12, 11, 18);
      writeFace(fwD, 18, 11, 10, 9, 17);
      writeFace(fwD, 17, 9, 8, 7, 16);
      writeFace(fwD, 16, 7, 6, 15, 20);
      fwD.close();
   }

   void writeVertexInCenter(FileWriter fwD, int j)throws IOException
   {  Tria t = icoF[j];
      Point3D A = icoV[t.iA], B = icoV[t.iB], C = icoV[t.iC];
      float x = (float)((A.x + B.x + C.x)/3),
            y = (float)((A.y + B.y + C.y)/3),
            z = (float)((A.z + B.z + C.z)/3);
      fwD.write(j + " " + x + " " + y + " " + z + "\r\n");
   }

   void writeFace(FileWriter fwD, int a, int b, int c, int d, int e)
      throws IOException
   {  fwD.write(a + " " + b + " " + c + " " + d + " " + e + ".\r\n");
   }
}
```

An icosahedron, as generated by this program, will be useful to generate (better) approximations of spheres, as we will see in the next section.

E.2 SPHERE REPRESENTATIONS

There are several ways of approximating a sphere by a polyhedron. A very popular one is the globe model with north and south poles at the top and the bottom, horizontal circles called *lines of latitude*, and circles called *lines of longitude* in vertical planes through the poles, as shown in Figure E.4. A program to generate such a globe should preferably be based on a single integer n, indicating both the number of horizontal slices and half the number of lines of longitude. In other words, angles of $180°/n$ play an essential role, both in horizontal and vertical planes. In Figures E.4(a) and (b) we have $n = 6$ and $n = 30$, respectively. Programming this is left as an exercise (see Exercise 6.6).

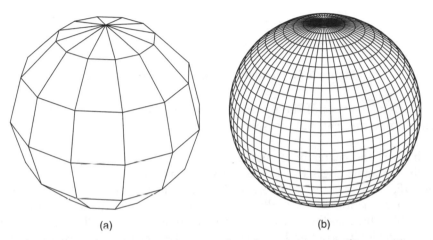

(a)   (b)

○ **Figure E.4: Approximations of a sphere:** (a) $n = 6$; (b) $n = 30$

The above way of approximating a sphere has two drawbacks:

1. The faces are unequal in size and have different shapes: except for the triangles at the poles, each face is a trapezium, whose size depends on its distance from its nearest pole.

2. These spheres have an 'anisotropic' appearance: which may be undesirable. For example, a view from above looks much different from a view from the front. We may prefer all faces to look alike, so that the image should not significantly change if we turn the sphere a little.

We will therefore discuss different models of a sphere, in such a way that we cannot easily tell the poles and the other vertices apart.

E.2.1 Spheres based on an icosahedron

As Figure E.3 illustrates, an icosahedron and a dodecahedron are very poor approximations of a sphere. However, we can use the former as a basis to generate a much better one. The idea is to divide each triangular face of an icosahedron into four triangles, as shown in Figure E.5, and to use the sphere

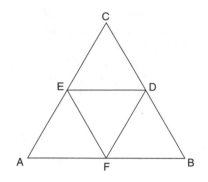

○ **Figure E.5: Dividing a triangle into four smaller ones**

to which all vertices of the icosahedron belong. For the icosahedron we have constructed, the center of this sphere is O and its radius is $\frac{1}{2}\sqrt{5}$.

With O as the center of the icosahedron and D, E and F as the midpoints of three triangle edges BC, CA and AB, we have to extend the lines OD, OE and OF, such that the new vertices D, E and F (like A, B and C) lie on the sphere just mentioned. Actually, we may as well change the lengths of all six lines OA, OB, ..., OF, such that the new points A, B, ..., F lie on a sphere with center O and radius 1. Doing this for all 20 faces of an icosahedron, we obtain a polyhedron that has $20 \times 4 = 80$ triangles. Since each of the 30 original edges gives a new vertex (its midpoint), and there were already 12 vertices, this new polyhedron has $12 + 30 = 42$ vertices. It follows from Equation E.1 that it has $80 + 42 - 2 = 120$ edges. Note that the four triangles of Figure E.5 are equilateral (that is, they have three edges of the same length), but this is the case only as long as the six points A, B, ..., F lie in the same plane. Consequently, the 80 faces of our new polyhedron are *not* equilateral triangles.

Instead of writing a program just to generate this polyhedron, we will make the program much more general. It will accept the names of an input file and an output file. The input file can be any file (in our 3D format) for a convex polyhedron that has only triangular faces and whose center is the origin O of the coordinate system (provided the vertex numbers 1, 2, 3, ... are used and appear in that order in the first part of the file). In the output file we obtain a polyhedron that has four times as many (triangular) faces as the given one, and whose vertices lie on a sphere with center O and radius 1. This will enable us to use the program several times, starting with the file *icosa.dat*, generated by program *IcoDode.java*, and each following time to use the previous output file as input. Using names of the form *sphx. dat*, where *x* is the number of faces, we can proceed as follows:

icosa.dat $\Rightarrow$ *sph80.dat* $\Rightarrow$ *sph320.dat* $\Rightarrow$ *sph1280.dat* $\Rightarrow$ . . .

Figure E.6 shows the results of applying program *HLines.java* to these four files, of which the last three have been generated by the program we are discussing.

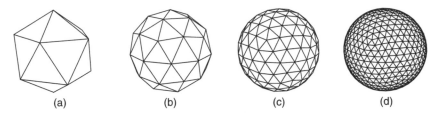

(a) (b) (c) (d)

Figure E.6: Icosahedron and three other polyhedra derived from it by program *SphTria.java*: (a) 20 faces (see Section E.1); (b) 80 faces; (c) 320 faces; (d) 1280 faces

Program *SphTria.java* takes the names of its input and output files as program arguments. After generating the file *icosa.dat* by using program *IcoDode.java* of Section E.1, we obtain the files for the other three sphere approximations above as follows:

```
java SphTria icosa.dat sph80.dat
java SphTria sph80.dat sph320.dat
java SphTria sph320.dat sph1280.dat
```

Like some other programs in this book, *SphTria.java*, listed below, uses the classes *Point3D*, *Tria* and *Input*, discussed in Sections 3.9 and 5.5:

```
// SphTria.java: Generating a 3D object file for a sphere
//     approximation consisting of triangles. In the output file there
//     are four times as many triangles as in the input file. Suitable
//     input files are icosa.dat, produced by program IcoDode.java, and
//     the output files produced by this program (SphTria.java) itself!
//     To run this program, enter, for example,
//         java SphTria icosa.dat sph80.dat.
//     Uses: Tria, Input (Section 5.5), Point3D (Section 3.9).

import java.io.*;
import java.util.*;
public class SphTria
{ public static void main(String[] args)throws IOException
   { if (args.length < 2)
      { System.out.println("Command:\n"
        + "java SphTria InputFile OutputFile");
```

```
         }
         else
            new SphTriaObj(args[0], args[1]);
      }
   }

   class SphTriaObj
   {  Vector v = new Vector(); // Vertices
      Vector t = new Vector(); // Triangular faces
      int nV, codeRadix;
      Hashtable ht = new Hashtable();
      String inputFile, outputFile;

      SphTriaObj(String inputFile, String outputFile)throws IOException
      {  this.inputFile = inputFile;
         this.outputFile = outputFile;
         readFile();
         computeMidpoints();
         toUnitCircle();
         writeFile();
      }

      void readFile()throws IOException
      {  Input inp = new Input(inputFile);
         if (inp.fails()) error();
         v.addElement(new Integer (0) ); // Start at position 1
         for (;;)
         {  int nr = inp.readInt();
            if (inp.fails()) break;
            nV = nr;
            float x = inp.readFloat(), y = inp.readFloat(),
                  z = inp.readFloat();
            v.addElement(new Point3D(x, y, z));
         }
         inp.clear();
         codeRadix = nV + 1;
         inp.clear();
         while (inp.readChar() != '\n' && !inp.fails());
         // Rest of line 'Faces:' has now been skipped.
         for (;;)
         {  int a = inp.readInt(), b = inp.readInt(), c = inp.readInt();
            if (inp.fails()) break;
            t.addElement(new Tria(a, b, c));
```

```
        inp.readChar(); // Skip '.'
    }
    inp.clear();
}

void error()
{   System.out.println("Problem with file input file " + inputFile);
    System.exit(1);
}
void computeMidpoints()
{   for (int j=0; j<t.size(); j++)
    {   Tria tr = (Tria)t.elementAt(j);
        int a = tr.iA, b = tr.iB, c = tr.iC;
        addMidpoint(a, b); addMidpoint(b, c); addMidpoint(c, a);
    }
}

void addMidpoint(int p, int q)
{   if (p < q)
    {   ht.put(new Integer(codeRadix * p + q), new Integer(++nV));
        Point3D P = (Point3D)v.elementAt(p),
                Q = (Point3D)v.elementAt(q);
        v.addElement(new Point3D(  // at position nV
        (P.x + Q.x)/2, (P.y + Q.y)/2, (P.z + Q.z)/2));
    }
}

int getMidpoint(int p, int q)
{   int key = p < q ? (codeRadix * p + q) : (codeRadix * q + p);
    Integer iObj = (Integer)ht.get(new Integer(key));
    return iObj.intValue();
}

void toUnitCircle()
{   for (int i=1; i<=nV; i++)   // nV = v.size() - 1
    {   Point3D P = (Point3D)v.elementAt(i);
        float r = (float)Math.sqrt(
           P.x * P.x + P.y * P.y + P.z * P.z);
        P.x /= r; P.y /= r; P.z /= r;
    }
}

void writeFile()throws IOException
```

```
   {  FileWriter fw = new FileWriter(outputFile);
      for (int i=1; i<v.size(); i++)
      {  Point3D P = (Point3D)v.elementAt(i);
         fw.write(i + " " + P.x + " " +
            P.y + " " + P.z + "\r\n");
      }
      fw.write("Faces\r\n");
      for (int j=0; j<t.size(); j++)
      {  Tria tr = (Tria)t.elementAt(j);
         int a = tr.iA, b = tr.iB, c = tr.iC;
         int mab = getMidpoint(a, b),
            mbc = getMidpoint(b, c),
            mca = getMidpoint(c, a);
         fw.write(a + " " + mab + " " + mca + ".\r\n");
         fw.write(b + " " + mbc + " " + mab + ".\r\n");
         fw.write(c + " " + mca + " " + mbc + ".\r\n");
         fw.write(mab + " " + mbc + " " + mca + ".\r\n");
      }
      fw.close();
   }
}
```

Each edge of a triangle of the given polyhedron is also an edge of a neighboring triangle. Since for each triangle its vertices are specified in counter-clockwise order, the ordered vertex number pair p, q representing an edge of one of these two triangles will appear as q, p for the other triangle. To avoid adding the midpoint of this edge twice, we accept the pair p, q only if p is less than q, as the test at the beginning of the method *addMidpoint* shows. Note that we process all given triangles twice, first, in *computeMidpoints*, to add the midpoint of every edge (exactly once) to the list of vertices v, and later, in *writeFaces*, to construct the new, smaller triangles. In the first of these two actions, we associate a new midpoint, say, vertex number m, with a certain edge p, q. This must be stored in such a way that later, in *writeFaces*, when we encounter this edge p, q again, we can use this pair to find this same vertex number m. We can do this efficiently and conveniently by using a *hash table*, writing

```
Hashtable ht = new Hashtable();
```

The pair p, q, or rather, a large integer *codeRadix* $* p + q$, where *codeRadix* is a large constant and $p < q$, is used as a key. By storing the pair (key, m) in the hash table *ht*, we can later retrieve the midpoint vertex number m using the same key. This explains both the statement

```
ht.put(new Integer(codeRadix * p + q), new Integer(++nV));
```

in *addMidpoint* (called in *computeMidpoints*) and

```
Integer iObj = (Integer)ht.get(new Integer(key));
```

in *getMidpoint* (called in *writeFile*).

The sphere that program *SphTria.java* produces obviously depends upon its input file. The file *tetra.dat* of Section E.1, like *iscosa.dat*, describes a polyhedron consisting of equilateral triangles and has O as its center. Note that the latter is not the case with the file *tetra*1. *dat*, obtained by the program *Rota3DTetra.java* because this program rotates the tetrahedron about the edge 1–2. Another polyhedron satisfying the conditions just mentioned is the octahedron, also discussed in Section E.1. This gives a better, though rather peculiar, result. If we start with the file *octa.dat*, describing the octahedron shown in Figure E.7(a), we obtain

$$octa.dat \Rightarrow sph32.dat \Rightarrow sph128.dat \Rightarrow sph512.dat$$

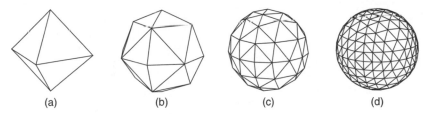

Figure E.7: Octahedron and three other polyhedra derived from it by program *SphTria.java*: (a) 8 faces (see Section E.1); (b) 32 faces; (c) 128 faces; (d) 512 faces

E.3 A TORUS

We will now discuss a program to construct a *torus*, as shown in Figure E.8. The input data of this program will consist of three program arguments:

- *n*, the number of small vertical circles; on each of these, *n* points are used as vertices to approximate the torus;
- *R*, the radius of a large horizontal circle containing the centers of the *n* smaller circles;
- the name of the output file.

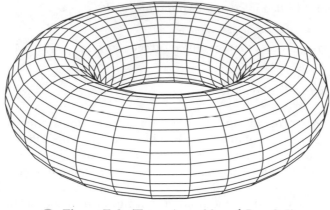

Figure E.8: Torus ($n = 30$ and $R = 2.5$)

All small circles will have the same radius, $r = 1$. You can see the large horizontal circle (with radius R) and one of the small vertical ones in Figure E.9. Since the smaller circles must not intersect each other, we require that

$$R \geq r(= 1)$$

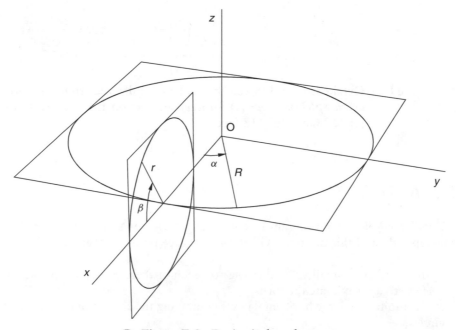

Figure E.9: Basic circles of a torus

A parametric representation of the large circle is

$$x = R \cos \alpha \quad y = R \sin \alpha \quad z = 0$$

If we take $\alpha = 0$ in these equations, we obtain the center of the small vertical circle shown in Figure E.9, which has the following parametric representation (where $r = 1$):

$$x = R + r \cos \beta \quad y = 0 \quad z = r \sin \beta$$

This small circle belongs to $i = 0$. By rotating it about the z-axis through angles $\alpha = i\delta$, where $i = 1, \ldots, n - 1$ and $\delta = 2\pi/n$, we obtain the remaining $n - 1$ small circles. As for the vertex numbers of the torus, we select n points on the first small circle (corresponding to $i = 0$) and assign the integers $1, 2, \ldots, n$ to them: the point obtained by using parameter $\beta = j\delta$ is assigned vertex number $j + 1$ $(j = 0, 1, \ldots, n - 1)$. The next n vertices, numbered $n + 1, n + 2, \ldots, 2n$, lie on the neighboring circle, corresponding to $i = 1$, and so on. In general, we use the n^2 vertex numbers $i \cdot n + j + 1 (i = 0, 1, \ldots, n - 1; j = 0, 1, \ldots, n - 1)$.

We will now rotate the small vertical circle drawn in Figure E.9 about the z-axis through the angle $\alpha = i\delta$. As follows from Section 3.2, this rotation can be written

$$\begin{bmatrix} x' & y' \end{bmatrix} = \begin{bmatrix} x & y \end{bmatrix} \begin{bmatrix} \cos \alpha & \sin \alpha \\ -\sin \alpha & \cos \alpha \end{bmatrix}$$

In our case the basic small circle lies in the xz-plane, so that $y = 0$, which reduces this matrix product to

$$x' = x \cos \alpha$$
$$y' = x \sin \alpha$$

(which we could also have derived directly from Figure E.9, without using the above matrix multiplication).

As you can see in the following program, we use most of the above formulas in the inner loop, in which the variable x denotes the x-coordinate of a point of the small circle in the xz-plane (see Figure E.9), while $x1$ denotes the x-coordinate of that point after rotation through α about the z-axis:

```
// Torus.java: Generating a data file for a torus. R is the radius of
//    a large horizontal circle, on which n equidistant points will be
//    the centers of small vertical circles with radius 1. The values
//    of n and R as well as the output file name are to be supplied as
//    program arguments.

import java.io.*;
```

```java
public class Torus
{  public static void main(String[] args)throws IOException
   {  if (args.length != 3)
      {  System.out.println("Supply n (> 2), R (>= 1) "
            + "and a filename as program arguments.\n");
         System.exit(1);
      }
      int n = 0;
      double R = 0;
      try
      {  n = Integer.valueOf(args[0]).intValue();
         R = Double.valueOf(args[1]).doubleValue();
         if (n <= 2 || R < 1)
            throw new NumberFormatException();
      }
      catch (NumberFormatException e)
      {  System.out.println("n must be an integer > 2");
         System.out.println("R must be a real number >= 1");
         System.exit(1);
      }
      new TorusObj(n, R, args[2]);
   }
}

class TorusObj
{  TorusObj(int n, double R, String fileName)throws IOException
   {  FileWriter fw = new FileWriter(fileName);
      double delta = 2 * Math.PI / n;
      for (int i=0; i<n; i++)
      {  double alpha = i * delta,
            cosa = Math.cos(alpha), sina = Math.sin(alpha);
         for (int j=0; j<n; j++)
         {  double beta = j * delta, x = R + Math.cos(beta);
            float x1 = (float)(cosa * x),
                  y1 = (float)(sina * x),
                  z1 = (float)Math.sin(beta);
            fw.write((i * n + j + 1) + " " +
               x1 + " " + y1 + " " + z1 + "\r\n");
         }
      }
      fw.write("Faces:\r\n");
      for (int i=0; i<n; i++)
```

```
    { for (int j=0; j<n; j++)
      { int i1 = (i + 1) % n, j1 = (j + 1) % n,
            a = i  * n + j  + 1,
            b = i1 * n + j  + 1,
            c = i1 * n + j1 + 1,
            d = i  * n + j1 + 1;
        fw.write(a + " " + b + " " + c + " " + d + ".\r\n");
      }
    }
    fw.close();
  }
}
```

E.4 BEAMS IN A SPIRAL

Our next example is a spiral built from horizontal beams with length $2a$ ($a \geq 0.5$), width 1 and height 1. The bottom of the lowest beam lies in the xy-plane; this beam is parallel to the y-axis and its maximum x-coordinate is equal to a (see Figure E.10). Each next beam can be obtained by lifting the previous one a distance 1, and by rotating it about the z-axis though a given angle α. There are n beams. The integer n, the two real numbers a and α (the latter in degrees) and the output file name, in that order, are supplied as program arguments.

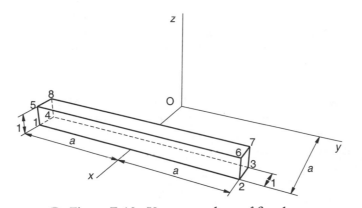

○ **Figure E.10: Vertex numbers of first beam**

The beams in Figures E.11(a), (b) and (c) have lengths ($2a =$) 2, 8 and 1, respectively, which implies that the beams are actually cubes in Figure E.11(c).

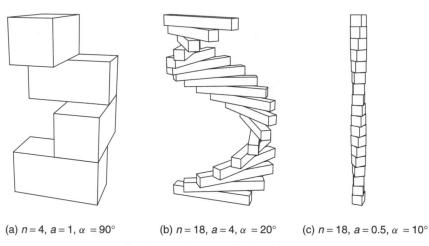

(a) $n = 4$, $a = 1$, $\alpha = 90°$ (b) $n = 18$, $a = 4$, $\alpha = 20°$ (c) $n = 18$, $a = 0.5$, $\alpha = 10°$

◯ **Figure E.11: Spirals of beams**

The data files for program *HLines.java* to produce the three spiral images of Figure E.11 were generated by running program *Beams.java* three times as follows:

```
java Beams 4 1 90 FigE11a.dat
java Beams 18 4 20 FigE11b.dat
java Beams 18 0.5 10 FigE11c.dat
```

Although we could have used the class *Rota3D*, discussed in Section 3.9, the rotation about the z-axis is as simple as a 2D rotation about O (see Section 3.2), so that we may as well program it directly, as is done in the nested for-loop in program *Beams.java*, listed below:

```java
// Beams.java: Generating input files for a spiral of beams. The
//    values of n, a and alpha (in degrees) as well as the output
//    file name are to be supplied as program arguments.
//    Uses: Point3D (Section 3.9).
import java.io.*;

public class Beams
{  public static void main(String[] args)throws IOException
   {  if (args.length != 4)
      {  System.out.println(
           "Supply n (> 0), a (>= 0.5), alpha (in degrees)\n" +
           "and a filename as program arguments.\n");
```

```
        System.exit(1);
     }
     int n = 0;
     double a = 0, alphaDeg = 0;
     try
     {  n = Integer.valueOf(args[0]).intValue();
        a = Double.valueOf(args[1]).doubleValue();
        alphaDeg = Double.valueOf(args[2]).doubleValue();
        if (n <= 0 || a < 0.5)throw new NumberFormatException();
     }
     catch (NumberFormatException e)
     {  System.out.println("n must be an integer > 0");
        System.out.println("a must be a real number >= 0.5");
        System.out.println("alpha must be a real number");
        System.exit(1);
     }
     new BeamsObj(n, a, alphaDeg * Math.PI / 180, args[3]);
   }
}

class BeamsObj
{  FileWriter fw;

   BeamsObj(int n, double a, double alpha, String fileName)
      throws IOException
   {  fw = new FileWriter(fileName);
      Point3D[] P = new Point3D[9];
      double b = a - 1;
      P[1] = new Point3D(a, -a, 0);
      P[2] = new Point3D(a,  a, 0);
      P[3] = new Point3D(b,  a, 0);
      P[4] = new Point3D(b, -a, 0);
      P[5] = new Point3D(a, -a, 1);
      P[6] = new Point3D(a,  a, 1);
      P[7] = new Point3D(b,  a, 1);
      P[8] = new Point3D(b, -a, 1);
      for (int k=0; k<n; k++)
      {  // Beam k:
         double phi = k * alpha,
            cosPhi = Math.cos(phi), sinPhi = Math.sin(phi);
         int m = 8 * k;
         for (int i=1; i<=8; i++)
         {  double x = P[i].x, y = P[i].y;
```

```
            float x1 = (float)(x * cosPhi - y * sinPhi),
                  y1 = (float)(x * sinPhi + y * cosPhi),
                  z1 = (float)(P[i].z + k);
            fw.write((m + i) + " " + x1 + " " + y1 + " " + z1 +
              "\r\n");
       }
    }
    fw.write("Faces:\r\n");
    for (int k=0; k<n; k++)
    {  // Beam k again:
       int m = 8 * k;
       face(m, 1, 2, 6, 5);
       face(m, 4, 8, 7, 3);
       face(m, 5, 6, 7, 8);
       face(m, 1, 4, 3, 2);
       face(m, 2, 3, 7, 6);
       face(m, 1, 5, 8, 4);
    }
    fw.close();
  }

  void face(int m, int a, int b, int c, int d)throws IOException
  {  a += m; b += m; c += m; d += m;
     fw.write(a + " " + b + " " + c + " " + d + ".\r\n");
  }
}
```

E.5 FUNCTIONS OF TWO VARIABLES

Although the programs *Painter.java*, *ZBuf.java* and *HLines.java* were primarily intended to represent solid objects, they can also be used for other purposes, such as displaying surfaces that correspond to functions of the form

$$z = f(x, y)$$

For example, Figure E.12 shows such a surface for the function

$$z = f(x, y) = \frac{10 \cos \sqrt{x^2 + y^2}}{2 + \sqrt{x^2 + y^2}} \tag{E.2}$$

As usual, the x-axis points towards us, the y-axis points to the right and the z-axis points upwards. Note that each of the three coordinate axes is partly visible and partly hidden. The lines on the surface connect points (x, y, z), where

$$-6 \le x \le 6 \text{ and } -6 \le y \le 6, \text{ with step sizes } \Delta x = \Delta y = 0.25 \tag{E.3}$$

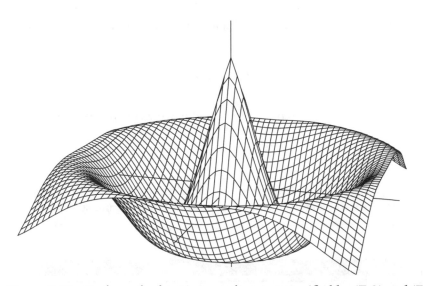

Figure E.12: Surface of a function $z = f(x, y)$ as specified by (E.2) and (E.3)

Instead of dealing only with this particular function, we will discuss a very general program, based on an *expression evaluator*. Using a graphical user interface (as we also did in Section 6.6), we will enable the user to enter both an expression for the function in question and the intervals and step sizes for x and y. Such expressions are similar to what we write in our programs, although the set of available operators and standard functions is very limited:

1. An *expression* consist of one or more terms, separated by + and −.
2. A *term* consists of one or more factors, separated by * and /.
3. A *factor* can be
   (a) a real number (such as 12.3, 4 or −25; number representations such as 1e7 are not allowed),
   (b) a variable x or a variable y (and no other variables),
   (c) an expression, as defined in point 1, written between parentheses, such as the one occurring in 3 * $(x + y)$,
   (d) a function call of one of the following three forms (and no others):
       sin(*expression*)
       cos(*expression*)
       pow(*expression*, *expression*).

The last three standard functions are the same as those in the *Math* class of Java. For example, we write *pow*(x, 0.5) for $x^{0.5}$. There is no special *sqrt* function. As usual, blank spaces are allowed in expressions.

For example, the function given by Equation E.2 can be written as the following expression:

```
10 * cos(pow(x*x + y*y, 0.5))/(2 + pow(x*x + y*y, 0.5))
```

As for the intervals and step sizes for x and y, we write, for example,

```
-6  (0.25)  6
```

indicating that the variable in question ranges from -6 to 6, with step size 0.25. The dialog box to be used to enter expressions, intervals and step sizes is shown in Figure E.13.

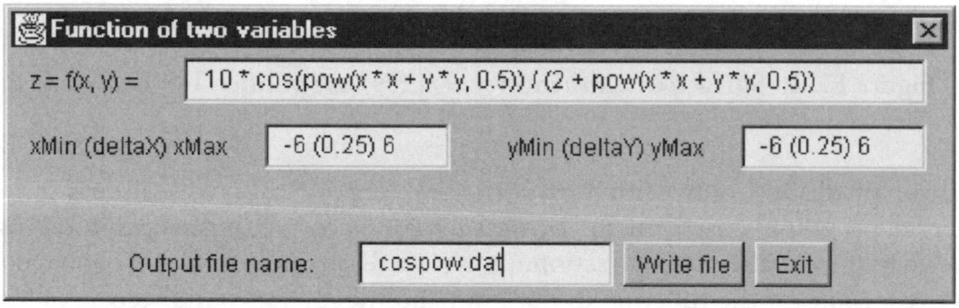

Figure E.13: Dialog box for program Func.java

There is also a text field in which the user has to enter the name of the output file. After filling in all text fields, the user can click the button *Write file* to generate the desired file. Since this does not terminate the program, there is also an *Exit* button. Although the program *Func.java* produces only a file, such as *cospow.dat* in this example, we can quickly see the 3D surface in question by executing the two programs *Func.java* and *HLines.java* at the same time. After pressing the button *Write file*, in the former program, we use *File |Open* in the latter to see the result. If we want to change any data, such as shown in Figure E.13, we go back to *Func.java*, which is still running; after doing this, we click the *Write file* button and switch to *HLines.java* again, and so on.

If the expression entered for $z = f(x, y)$ cannot be interpreted because it is syntactically incorrect, the computer gives an audible signal. Such a beep also occurs if an interval or a step size is incorrect; this happens, for example, if *xMin* is greater than *xMax – deltaX*. It follows from this that error handling is not the strongest point of the program we will discuss, and neither is its speed. However, although the given expression is not converted into more efficient intermediate code (such as postfix), it is much faster than the hidden-line program that follows; improvements with regard to error handling and efficiency were deliberately omitted because many readers will find the program already complex enough in its current form. After having a look at the program listed below, we will discuss some of its internal aspects.

```java
// Func.java: A function of two variables x and y.
import java.awt.*;
import java.awt.event.*;
import java.io.*;

public class Func extends Frame
{  public static void main(String[] args){new Func();}
   Func(){new FuncDialog(this);}
}

class FuncDialog extends Dialog
{  TextField tfFun = new TextField (50),
   tfX = new TextField (10), tfY = new TextField (10),
   tfFileName = new TextField (15);
   Button buttonWriteFile = new Button("Write file"),
          buttonExit = new Button(" Exit ");

   FuncDialog(Frame fr)
   {  super(fr, "Function of two variables", true);

      addWindowListener(new WindowAdapter()
      {  public void windowClosing(WindowEvent e)
         {  dispose();
            System.exit(0);
         }
      });

      Panel p1 = new Panel(), p2 = new Panel(), p3 = new Panel();
      p1.add(new Label("z = f(x, y) = "));
      p1.add(tfFun);
      p2.add(new Label("xMin (deltaX) xMax"));
      p2.add(tfX);
      p2.add(new Label("      yMin (deltaY) yMax"));
      p2.add(tfY);
      p3.add(new Label("Output file name: "));
      p3.add(tfFileName);
      p3.add(buttonWriteFile);
```

```
p3.add(buttonExit);
setLayout(new BorderLayout());
add("North", p1);
add("Center", p2);
add("South", p3);

buttonWriteFile.addActionListener(new ActionListener()
{  public void actionPerformed(ActionEvent ae)
    {  float xa=0, dx=0, xb=0,
            ya=0, dy=0, yb=0;
        String sX = tfX.getText();

        xa = (new xyExpression(sX)).factor();
        sX = sX.substring(sX.indexOf('(')+1);
        dx = (new xyExpression(sX)).factor();
        sX = sX.substring(sX.indexOf(')')+1);
        xb = (new xyExpression(sX)).factor();

        String sY = tfY.getText();
        ya = (new xyExpression(sY)).factor();
        sY = sY.substring(sY.indexOf('(')+1);
        dy = (new xyExpression(sY)).factor();
        sY = sY.substring(sY.indexOf(')')+1);
        yb = (new xyExpression(sY)).factor();

        if (xa + dx > xb || dx <= 0 ||
            ya + dy > yb || dy <= 0)
        {  Toolkit.getDefaultToolkit().beep();
            return;
        }
        String s = tfFun.getText(),
            fileName = tfFileName.getText();

        xyExpression xyE = new xyExpression(s);
        try
        {  xyE.generate(xa, dx, xb, ya, dy, yb, fileName);
        }
        catch (IOException ioe){}
    }
});
buttonExit.addActionListener(new ActionListener()
{  public void actionPerformed(ActionEvent ae)
    {  dispose();System.exit(0);
```

```
            }
        });

        Dimension dim = getToolkit().getScreenSize();
        setSize(6 * dim.width/10, dim.height/4);
        setLocation(dim.width/5, dim.height/2);
        show();
    }
}
class xyExpression
{   String buf;
    float x, y, lastNum;
    char lastChar;
    int pos;
    boolean OK;

    xyExpression(String s){buf = s; OK = true;}

    void generate(float xa, float dx, float xb,
        float ya, float dy, float yb, String fileName)
        throws IOException
    {   FileWriter fw = new FileWriter(fileName);
        int nx = Math.round((xb - xa)/dx),
            ny = Math.round((yb - ya)/dy), nr = 0;
        float za = 1e30F, zb = -1e30F;
    outer:
        for (int j=0; j<=ny; j++)
        {   float y = ya + j * dy;
            for (int i=0; i<=nx; i++)
            {   float x = xa + i * dx;
                nr = j * (nx + 1) + i + 1;
                float z = eval(x, y);
                if (!OK)
                {   Toolkit.getDefaultToolkit().beep();
                    break outer;
                }
                if (z < za) za = z;
                if (z > zb) zb = z;
                fw.write(nr + " " + x + " " + y + " " + z + "\r\n");
            }
        }
        // x, y and z axes:
        float dz = (zb - za)/10,
```

```
    xa1 = Math.min(xa - 2 * dx, 0), xb1 = Math.max(xb + 2 * dx, 0),
    ya1 = Math.min(ya - 2 * dy, 0), yb1 = Math.max(yb + 2 * dy, 0),
    za1 = Math.min(za - 2 * dz, 0), zb1 = Math.max(zb + 2 * dz, 0);
    fw.write(++nr + " " + xa1 + " 0 0\r\n");
    fw.write(++nr + " " + xb1 + " 0 0\r\n");
    fw.write(++nr + " 0 " + ya1 + " 0\r\n");
    fw.write(++nr + " 0 " + yb1 + " 0\r\n");
    fw.write(++nr + " 0 0 " + za1 + "\r\n");
    fw.write(++nr + " 0 0 " + zb1 + "\r\n");
    fw.write("Faces:\r\n");
    for (int i=0; i<nx; i++)
    {  for (int j=0; j<ny; j++)
       {  int k = j * (nx + 1) + i + 1,
              m = k + nx + 1, k1 = k + 1, m1 = m + 1;
          fw.write(k + " " + -m1 + " " + k1 + ".\r\n");
          fw.write(k1 + " " + m1 + " " + -k + ".\r\n");
          fw.write(k + " " + -m1 + " " + m + ".\r\n");
          fw.write(m + " " + m1 + " " + -k + ".\r\n");
       }
    }
    int k = (nx + 1) * (ny + 1);
    fw.write(++k + " " + ++k + ".\r\n"); // x-axis
    fw.write(++k + " " + ++k + ".\r\n"); // y-axis
    fw.write(++k + " " + ++k + ".\r\n"); // z-axis
    fw.close();
    System.out.println("Ready!");
}

boolean readChar()
{  char ch;
   do
   {  if (pos == buf.length())return false;
      ch = buf.charAt(pos++);
   }  while (ch == ' ');
   lastChar = ch;
   return true;
}

boolean nextIs(char ch)
{  char ch0 = lastChar;
   if (readChar())
   {  if (ch == lastChar) return true;
      pos--;
```

```
   }
   lastChar = ch0;
   return false;
}

float eval(float x, float y)
{  this.x = x; this.y = y;
   pos = 0;
   OK = true;
   return expression();
}

float expression()
{  float x = term();
   for (;;)
   {  if (nextIs('+')) x += term(); else
      if (nextIs('-')) x -= term(); else break;
   }
   return x;
}

float term()
{  float x = factor();
   for (;;)
   {  if (nextIs('*')) x *= factor(); else
      if (nextIs('/')) x /= factor(); else break;
   }
   return x;
}

float factor()
{  float v = 0;
   if (!readChar()) return 0;
   if (lastChar == 'x') return x;
   if (lastChar == 'y') return y;
   if (lastChar == '(')
   {  v = expression();
      if (!nextIs(')')){OK = false; return 0;}
      return v;
   }
   char ch = lastChar;
   if (ch == 'c'      // cos(expression)
      || ch == 's'    // sin(expression)
```

```
           || ch == 'p')   // pow(expression, expression)
    {   while ((OK = readChar()) && lastChar != '(');
        if (!OK) return 0;
        float arg = expression();
        if (ch == 'p')
        {   if (!nextIs(',')){OK = false; return 0;}
            double exponent = expression();
            v = (float)Math.pow(arg, exponent);
        }
        else
            v = (float)(ch == 'c' ? Math.cos(arg) : Math.sin(arg));
        if (!nextIs(')')){OK = false; return 0;}
        return v;
    }
    pos--;
    if (number()) return lastNum;
    OK = false;
    return 0;
}

boolean number()
{   float x=0;
    int nDec = -1;
    boolean neg = false;
    do
    {   if (!readChar()) return false;
        if (lastChar == '-')
        {   neg = true;
            if (!readChar()) return false;
            break;
        }
    }   while (Character.isWhitespace(lastChar));
    if (lastChar == '.')
    {   if (!readChar()) return false;
        nDec = 0;
    }
    if (!Character.isDigit(lastChar)){OK = false; return false;}
    for (;;)
    {   if (lastChar == '.' "" nDec < 0) nDec = 0; else
        if (Character.isDigit(lastChar))
        {   x = 10 * x + (lastChar - '0');
            if (nDec >= 0) nDec++;
        }   else
```

```
        {   pos--;
            break;
        }
        if (!readChar()) break;
    }
    while (nDec > 0){x *= 0.1; nDec--;}
    lastNum = (neg ? -x : x);
    return true;
  }
}
```

The given expression is evaluated when the first part of the output file is generated. In the class *xyExpression* we find the method *generate*, in which, five lines after the label *outer*, the following call to *eval* occurs:

```
float z = eval(x, y);
```

This method *eval* calls the method *expression*, whose task is to scan an expression, stored in the array *buf*, and to return its value. According to our above definition of *expression*, defining an expression as a sequence of terms separated by + and − operators, the method *expression* calls the method *term*, which scans a term and returns its value, and so on. This way of *parsing*, that is, analyzing expressions that satisfy a given *grammar*, is referred to as *recursive descent*. This adjective *recursive* will be clear if we note that our above syntactic definition of *expression* and the corresponding method are recursive. An *expression* can contain a *factor* that again contains an *expression*. Accordingly, in the program, *expression* calls *term*, which calls *factor*, which may again call *expression*. We immediately evaluate the syntactic entities we are dealing with, or, as we normally say, we *interpret* the source code. Instead, we might have generated intermediate code. More information about recursive descent parsing can be found in Ammeraal (1996).

In the program, parsing is done by using two simple methods, *readChar* and *nextIs*, as well as the variable *lastChar*, all belonging to the class *xyExpression*:

```
boolean readChar()
```

This method scans the next character, if possible, places this in the variable *lastChar* and returns *true*. If this is not possible because the end of the expression is encountered, it returns *false*. This methods skips any blank spaces.

```
boolean nextIs(char ch)
```

This method tests if the next character to be scanned is equal to the argument *ch*. If so, it scans this character and returns *true*; if not, it leaves the scan position unaltered and returns *false*.

After this discussion of parsing (which is unusual in a book on computer graphics) let us now turn to the graphics aspects of this program. It goes without saying that the vertices of a polygon, as specified in our 3D data files after the word *Faces*, should lie in the same plane. This is obviously the case for rectangles (or squares) such as 7-8-12-11 in Figure E.14(a) if we regard these as lying in the plane $z = 0$.

However, the corresponding four points on the surface may or may not lie in the same plane. We therefore prefer triangles to rectangles in this case. Remember, the three points of a triangle always lie in the same plane. Instead of the rectangle 7-8-12-11, we can specify the two triangles 7-8-12 and 7-12-11. However, we must pay attention to these two aspects:

1. Diagonals, such as 7–12, must not be drawn; we solve this problem by using minus signs, as discussed in Section 6.4.
2. Each triangle has two sides; since we do not know in advance which will be visible, we have to specify both. Recall that we have discussed this subject of 'individual faces' in Section 6.5.

According to this second point, the vertices of each triangle in Figure E.14(b) will occur twice in the data file: clockwise and counter-clockwise. Using minus

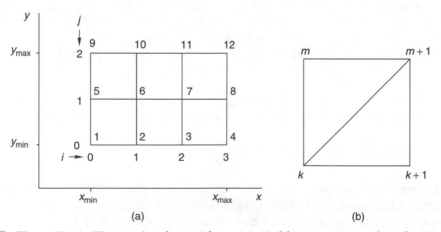

(a)   (b)

⭕ **Figure E.14: Two triangles with an invisible common edge forming a rectangle** signs, as discussed in the first point, we use four lines in the data file for the 'rectangle' $k, k + 1, m + 1, m$ of Figure E.14(b), as shown below:

k	$-(m + 1)$	$k + 1.$	(lower-right, clockwise)
$k + 1$	$m + 1$	$-k.$	(lower-right, counter-clockwise)
k	$-(m + 1)$	$m.$	(upper-left, counter-clockwise)
m	$m + 1$	$-k.$	(upper-left, clockwise)

You can find the code that writes these four triangles to a file in the method *generate*.

Appendix F

Hints and Solutions to Exercises

1.1 Numbers of pixels:

```
g.drawLine (10, 20, 100, 50); // 100 - 10 + 1 = 91 pixels
g.drawRect (10, 10, 8, 5);    // 2 * 8 + 2 * 5 = 26 pixels
g.fillRect (10, 10, 8, 5);    // 8 * 5 = 40 pixels
```

1.2 Program to draw many squares:

```
// ManySq.java: This program draws n x n sets, each
//    consisting of k squares, arranged as on a chessboard.
//    Each edge is divided into two parts with ratio
//    (1 - q)  : q. The values of n, k and q are program
//              arguments.

import java.awt.*;
import java.awt.event.*;

public class ManySq extends Frame
{  public static void main(String[] args)
   {  if (args.length != 3)
      {  System.out.println("Supply n, k and q as arguments");
         System.exit(1);
```

```
      }
      int n = Integer.valueOf(args[0]).intValue(),
          k = Integer.valueOf(args[1]).intValue();
      float q = Float.valueOf(args[2]).floatValue();
      new ManySq(n, k, q);
   }
   ManySq(int n, int k, float q)
   { super("ManySq: Many squares");
     addWindowListener(new WindowAdapter()
      {public void windowClosing(
             WindowEvent e){System.exit(0);}});
     add("Center", new CvManySq(n, k, q));
     setSize (600, 400);
     show();
   }
}

class CvManySq extends Canvas
{ int centerX, centerY, n, k;
  float p0, q0;

  CvManySq(int nn, int kk, float qq){n=nn; k=kk; q0=qq; p0 =
             1-q0;}

  int iX(float x){return Math.round(centerX + x);}
  int iY(float y){return Math.round(centerY - y);}

  public void paint(Graphics g)
  { Dimension d = getSize();
    int maxX = d.width - 1, maxY = d.height - 1,
       minMaxXY = Math.min(maxX, maxY);
    centerX = maxX/2; centerY = maxY/2;

    float r = 0.45F * minMaxXY / n;
    for (int x=0; x<n; x++)
    for (int y=0; y<n; y++)
    { float xCnew = (2 * x - n + 1) * r,
           yCnew = (2 * y - n + 1) * r,
        xA, yA, xB, yB, xC, yC, xD, yD,
        xA1, yA1, xB1, yB1, xC1, yC1, xD1, yD1, p=p0, q=q0;
      if (x % 2 + y % 2 == 1){p = q0; q = p0;}
      xA = xD = xCnew - r; xB = xC = xCnew + r;
      yA = yB = yCnew - r; yC = yD = yCnew + r;
```

```
        for (int i=0; i<k; i++)
        {  g.drawLine(iX(xA), iY(yA), iX(xB), iY(yB));
           g.drawLine(iX(xB), iY(yB), iX(xC), iY(yC));
           g.drawLine(iX(xC), iY(yC), iX(xD), iY(yD));
           g.drawLine(iX(xD), iY(yD), iX(xA), iY(yA));
           xA1 = p * xA+q * xB; yA1 = p * yA+q * yB;
           xB1 = p * xB+q * xC; yB1 = p * yB+q * yC;
           xC1 = p * xC+q * xD; yC1 = p * yC+q * yD;
           xD1 = p * xD+q * xA; yD1 = p * yD+q * yA;
           xA = xA1; xB = xB1; xC = xC1; xD = xD1;
           yA = yA1; yB = yB1; yC = yC1; yD = yD1;
        }
      }
    }
  }
```

1.3 To draw all edges as exactly straight lines and to make the vertices of inner squares lie exactly on the edges of their surrounding squares, use device coordinates, starting with a pair of very small squares ($\diamond$ and $\square$), and making the squares of each next pair exactly twice as large as those of the preceding pair.

1.4 The radius r of the circumscribed circles for the hexagons is supplied by the user. Based on this radius r, the following fragment (in which the variable names are self-explanatory) may be helpful:

```
int iX(float x){return Math.round(centerX + x/pixelSize);}
int iY(float y){return Math.round(centerY - y/pixelSize);}

void drawLine(Graphics g, float xA, float yA, float xB, float yB)
{  g.drawLine(iX(xA), iY(yA), iX(xB), iY(yB));
}
...

float halfr = r/2, horpitch = 1.5F * r,
  w = r * (float)Math.sqrt (3), h = w/2, marginleft,
                marginbottom;
int nhor = (int)Math.floor((rWidth - 2 * r) / horpitch) + 1,
    nvert = (int)Math.floor(rHeight/w);
marginleft = -rWidth/2 + 0.5F * (rWidth - halfr - nhor *
                horpitch);
marginbottom = -rHeight/2 + 0.5F * (rHeight - nvert * w);
for (int i=0; i<nhor; i++)
```

```
{  float x = marginleft + r + i * horpitch,
      y0 = marginbottom + (1 + i % 2) * h; // center of lowest
               hexagon
   int m = nvert - i % 2;
// There will be nvert hexagons in each column for i = 0, 2, 4,
            ...
// while there will be nvert - 1 in each column for i = 1, 3, 5,
            ...
// Special case: if nvert = 1 and nhor > 1, then x is increased
               by
// horpitch/2 because otherwise there will be an empty column on
               the
// right.
   if (nvert == 1 && nhor > 1)
      x += horpitch/2;
   for (int j=0; j<m; j++)
   {  float y = y0 + j * w;
      drawLine(g, x + halfr, y + h, x - halfr, y + h);
      drawLine(g, x - halfr, y + h, x - r, y);
      drawLine(g, x - r, y, x - halfr, y - h);
      ...
```

1.5 We begin by computing the length

$$L = \sqrt{u_1^2 + u_2^2}$$

where

$$u_1 = x_B - x_A$$
$$u_2 = y_B - y_A$$

Since there should be a dash, not a gap, at each endpoint, and we use gap widths that are about equal to *dashLength*, we use the equality

$$L = (2n - 1) \times dashLength$$

to compute n, the number of dashes. Writing $h_1 = u_1/(2n-1)$ and $h_2 = u_2/(2n-1)$, and denoting the dashes by $i = 0, 1, \ldots, n-1$, we draw dash i as a straight line with endpoints $(x_A + 2ih_1, y_A + 2ih_2)$ and $((x_A + (2i + 1)h_1, y_A + (2i + 1)h_2)$.

2.1 After rotating the vector $\mathbf{v} = (v_1, v_2)$ through $90°$ counter-clockwise, we obtain the vector $(-v_2, v_1)$. Setting $\mathbf{v} = (v_1, v_2) = (x_B - x_A, y_B - y_A)$, we can therefore find the points D and C by adding $(-v_2, v_1)$ to the coordinates of A and B, respectively.

2.2 To determine the position of P relative to the triangle ABC, we first test whether P lies on one of the three sides of the triangle, using the method *onSegment*, discussed in Section 2.10. If this is not the case, we test whether P lies inside ABC, using the method *insideTriangle* of Section 2.8. To do this properly, we need to know the orientation of A, B and C, for which we can use the method *ccw* of Section 2.6. If this orientation is clockwise, we use C, B and A, in that order, as the first three arguments of *insideTriangle*, so that the orientation of these arguments is counterclockwise, as required. If P lies neither on a triangle side nor inside the triangle, it lies outside it.

2.3 Section 2.11 shows how to compute the distance between a point and a line. We perform this computation three times to determine which of the three triangle sides AB, BC and CA (or rather the infinite lines through these sides) lies closest to point P. We then use the method *projection* of Section 2.12 to compute the projection P′ of P on the triangle side in question (or on an extension of it). We draw both the triangle and the line segment PP′. If the projection point P′ lies on an extension of a side, we also connect this point to the side (AB, BC or CA), to indicate clearly which of the three lines has been used. For example, if P′ lies on an extension of BC (not between B and C), we can draw P′B.

2.4 Using the vector $\mathbf{AB} = \mathbf{u} = (u_1, u_2) = (x_B - x_A, y_B - y_A)$ and the parameter λ, we can represent the line through A and B by the following vector form:

$$\mathbf{A} + \lambda\mathbf{u}$$

Similarly, with $\mathbf{CD} = \mathbf{v} = (v_1, v_2) = (x_D - x_C, y_D - y_C)$ and parameter μ, the line through C and D is represented by

$$\mathbf{C} + \lambda\mathbf{v}$$

We find the intersection point S by solving

$$\mathbf{A} + \lambda\mathbf{u} = \mathbf{C} + \lambda\mathbf{v}$$

for λ (rewriting this vector equation as a system of two linear equations, using the x- and y- coordinates of A and C as well as u_1, u_2, v_1 and v_2). We then use the value of λ computed in this way to find

$$\mathbf{S} = \mathbf{A} + \lambda\mathbf{u}$$

When deriving the desired value of λ, we will have to perform a division by the expression $u_2v_1 - u_1v_2$ (which is a determinant). If this determinant is zero, the lines AB and CD do not have a unique intersection point because these lines are parallel or coincide. Since the points A, B, C and D are

obtained by clicking and there are (very small) rounding-off errors, we
had better replace the condition

$$determinant = 0$$

with this one:

$$|determinant| \leq epsilon$$

where *epsilon* is some very small positive value. To make this independent
of the units of length and in view of the way the determinant is computed,
a reasonable value is

$$epsilon = 10^{-3}(u_1^2 + u_2^2 + v_1^2 + v_2^2)$$

2.5 To construct the bisector of angle B, we can compute the two vectors
$\mathbf{u} = \mathbf{BA}/|\mathbf{BA}|$ and $\mathbf{v} = \mathbf{BC}/|\mathbf{BC}|$. We can view these vectors as arrows
starting at B and pointing to A and C, respectively. Since both $\mathbf{u}$ and $\mathbf{v}$
have length 1, the sum vector

$$\mathbf{w} = \mathbf{u} + \mathbf{v}$$

can then be regarded as another arrow starting at B but lying on the
desired bisector, so that, with parameter α, the vector form

$$\mathbf{B} + \alpha\mathbf{w}$$

denotes the bisector of angle B. The intersection point D of this bisector and triangle side AC can then be found in the same way as in
Exercise 2.4.

2.6 Using $\mathbf{AB} = \mathbf{u} = (u_1, u_2) = (x_B - x_A, y_B - y_A)$ and $\mathbf{v} = (v_1, v_2) = (-u_2, u_1)$,
we can write the following vector form for the perpendicular bisector
of AB:

$$\mathbf{A} + 0.5\mathbf{u} + \lambda\mathbf{v} \qquad \text{(F.1)}$$

To find the circumcenter D of triangle ABC, write a similar vector
form, say,

$$\mathbf{B} + 0.5\mathbf{w} + \mu\mathbf{t} \qquad \text{(F.2)}$$

for the perpendicular bisector of BC. You can then find the intersection of
these two lines by solving the vector equation

$$\mathbf{A} + 0.5\mathbf{u} + \lambda\mathbf{v} = \mathbf{B} + 0.5\mathbf{w} + \mu\mathbf{t}$$

for λ (or μ). Then the circumcenter D is found as the point of intersection by using this value λ in Equation (F.1). After computing the radius
$r = |\mathbf{AD}|$, and using the methods iX and iY to convert real logical coordinates into integer device coordinates, you can draw the circle through A,
B and C by writing:

```
int xLeft = iX(xD - r), xRight = iX(xD + r),
    yTop = iY(yD + r), yBottom = iY(yD - r);
g.drawOval(xLeft, yTop, xRight - xLeft, yBottom - yTop);
```

2.7 Compute the center C and the radius *r* of the circle through P, Q and R (see Exercise 2.6). Although there is a method *drawArc* in Java, this is not suitable for our present purpose because it requires angles to be specified (in degrees) as integers; especially if *r* is large, this may cause too large rounding-off errors with regard to both endpoints of the arc. We therefore simply use a great many straight line segments. We can do this by using *Point2D* objects for C, P, Q and R (see Section 1.5). Taking the orientation of P, Q and R into account by means of the method *area2* of class *Tools2D* (see Section 2.13), we can write:

```
double alpha = Math.atan2(P.y - C.y, P.x - C.x),
       beta  = Math.atan2(R.y - C.y, R.x - C.x);
if (Tools2D.area2(P, Q, R) > 0)
   arcCcw(g, C, r, alpha, beta);
else
   arcCcw(g, C, r, beta, alpha);
```

The method *arcCcw*, used here, is listed below. Working counterclockwise, it draws the arc with start and end angles *alpha* and *beta* and belonging to the circle with center C and radius *r*:

```
void arcCcw(Graphics g, Point2D C, double r,
   double alpha, double beta)
{  double pi2 = 2 * Math.PI, delta = beta - alpha;
   // Reduce delta to the interval [0, 2pi):
   delta = (delta + pi2) % pi2;
   int X0=0, Y0=0,                        // Arc length = r * delta
      n = (int)Math.ceil(r * delta / 0.02); // 0.02 = rWidth/500
   double theta = delta / n;
   for (int i=0; i<=n; i++)
   {  double phi = alpha + i * theta,
         x = C.x + r * Math.cos(phi),
         y = C.y + r * Math.sin(phi);
      int X = iX((float)x), Y = iY((float)y);
      if (i > 0) g.drawLine(X0, Y0, X, Y);
      X0 = X; Y0 = Y;
   }
}
```

2.8 We can use the first of the two methods *projection* of Section 2.12 to find the projection D' of D on AB. Since the center M of the circular arc lies on the bisector of the angle ABC, we compute the unit vectors $\mathbf{u} = \mathbf{BA}/|\mathbf{BA}|$ and $\mathbf{v} = \mathbf{BC}/|\mathbf{BC}|$ and $\mathbf{w} = (\mathbf{u} + \mathbf{v})/|\mathbf{u} + \mathbf{v}|$, which start at B and point to A, C and M, respectively. We now have to find a scale factor λ, so that $\mathbf{BM} = \lambda w$. Since the cosine of the angle D'BM is equal to $\mathbf{w} \cdot \mathbf{v}$ and using $\mu = |\mathbf{BD'}|$, we can compute $\lambda = \mu/(\mathbf{w} \cdot \mathbf{v})$. We then find the endpoint E of the arc on BC and the center M as follows: $\mathbf{E} = \mathbf{B} + \mu\mathbf{v}$, $\mathbf{M} = \mathbf{B} + \lambda\mathbf{w}$. Obviously, the radius of the arc is $r = |\mathbf{MD'}|$. We can now compute the start and end angles α and β and draw the arc by choosing between two calls to the method *arcCcw*, depending on the orientation of the points A, B and C (see Exercise 2.7).

2.9 Refer to Exercise 2.8 for bisectors of angles and to Exercise 2.1 for the intersection of two lines. This will provide you with the centers of the four circles. You can use the radius of each circle as the distance of its center to one of its tangents. Recall that we have discussed the distance of points to lines in Section 2.11.

2.10 Use vector $\mathbf{AB} = (u_1, u_2)$ to find the points $\mathbf{D} = \mathbf{A} + (-u_2, u_1)$, $\mathbf{C} = \mathbf{D} + (u_1, u_2)$ and $\mathbf{E} = \mathbf{D} + 0.5\{(u_1, u_2) + (-u_2, u_1)\}$.

3.1 $M = \begin{bmatrix} s_x & 0 & 0 \\ 0 & s_y & 0 \\ x_C(1 - s_x) & y_C(1 - s_y) & 1 \end{bmatrix}$

3.2 Similar to Exercise 3.1.

3.3 For shearing a set of points with reference to point C, we replace the shearing equations at the end of Section 3.2 with the similar ones

$$x' - x_C = (x - x_C) + a(y - y_C)$$
$$y' - y_C = (y - y_C)$$

which reduces to $x' = x + a(y - y_C)$, $y' = y$.
The sharing operation will transform the circle into an ellipse with a non-horizontal axis, so that we cannot use the Java method *drawOval*. Therefore, for some large value of n, we approximate a circle with center $C(x_C, y_C)$ and radius r by computing the following n points (x_i, y_i) of this circle:

$$x_i = x_C + r \cos i\theta$$
$$y_i = y_C + r \sin i\theta$$

where $\theta = 2\pi/n$ and $i = 0, 1, \ldots, n - 1$. Instead of immediately connecting these points by straight lines, which would produce the circle, we first subject each x_i to the above shearing formula.

3.4 Just compute the product AA^{-1} to obtain the identity matrix I. For example, the upper-left element of this product is equal to the inner product of the first row of A and the first column of A^{-1}, which is $a_{11}(a_{22}/D) + a_{12}(-a_{21}/D) = D/D = 1$.

3.5 If there are many points for which we have to check whether they lie within a single triangle (or on an edge of it), the method *insideTriangle* of the following class is more efficient than the one discussed in Section 2.8, since most of the work is done here by the constructor, which need be called only once for that triangle:

```
class TriaTest
{  private Point2D C;
   private double a1, a2, b1, b2, c1, c2, d1, d2, det;

   TriaTest(Point2D A, Point2D B, Point2D C)
   {  this.C = C;
      a1 = A.x - C.x;  a2 = A.y - C.y;
      b1 = B.x - C.x;  b2 = B.y - C.y;
      det = a1 * b2 - b1 * a2;
      if (det != 0)
      {  c1 = b2/det;  c2 = -a2/det;
         d1 = -b1/det; d2 = a1/det;
      }
   }

   double area2(){return det;}

   boolean insideTriangle(Point2D P)
   {  double p1 = P.x - C.x, p2 = P.y - C.y,
         lambda, mu;
      return (lambda = p1 * c1 + p2 * d1) >= 0 &&
         (mu = p1 * c2 + p2 * d2) >= 0 &&
         lambda + mu <= 1;
   }
}
```

4.1 Adapt the Java program for Bresenham's algorithm by drawing pixels from both of the endpoints towards the middle of the line. Either calculate where the middle point is beforehand or check on-the-fly (that is, within the loop) when the two pixels merge in the middle. There may be one or two middle points depending on whether the line consists of an odd or even number of pixels. If there is only one, it is a good idea to draw this pixel after exiting the loop. Check if your solution also works correctly for very short lines, consisting of one or two pixels. You solution should be very general in that it works for any two endpoints P and Q.

4.2 You should add a second for-loop in which the roles of x and y are interchanged. For example, the calls to *putPixel* should have $++y$ as their third argument instead of $++x$ as their second. If $|y_Q - y_P| \leq |x_Q - x_P|$, the first loop should be executed; otherwise the second.

4.3 The following program produces only Figure 4.19. You should extend it, enabling the user to specify the two endpoints of a line segment and both the center and the radius of a circle.

```java
// Bresenham.java: Bresenham algorithms for lines and circles
//                 demonstrated by using superpixels.
import java.awt.*;
import java.awt.event.*;
import java.util.*;

public class Bresenham extends Frame
{  public static void main(String[] args){new Bresenham();}

   Bresenham()
   {  super("Bresenham");
      addWindowListener(new WindowAdapter()
       {public void windowClosing(WindowEvent e)
               {System.exit(0);}});
      setSize (340, 230);
      add("Center", new CvBresenham());
      show();
   }
}
class CvBresenham extends Canvas
{  float rWidth = 10.0F, rHeight = 7.5F, pixelSize;
   int centerX, centerY, dGrid = 10, maxX, maxY;

   void initgr()
   {  Dimension d;
      d = getSize();
      maxX = d.width - 1;
      maxY = d.height - 1;
      pixelSize = Math.max(rWidth/maxX, rHeight/maxY);
      centerX = maxX/2; centerY = maxY/2;
   }
```

```
int iX(float x){return Math.round(centerX + x/pixelSize);}
int iY(float y){return Math.round(centerY - y/pixelSize);}

void putPixel(Graphics g, int x, int y)
{  int x1 = x * dGrid, y1 = y * dGrid, h = dGrid/2;
   g.drawOval(x1 - h, y1 - h, dGrid, dGrid);
}

void drawLine(Graphics g, int xP, int yP, int xQ, int yQ)
{  int x = xP, y = yP, D = 0, HX = xQ - xP, HY = yQ - yP,
      c, M, xInc = 1, yInc = 1;
   if (HX < 0){xInc = -1; HX = -HX;}
   if (HY < 0){yInc = -1; HY = -HY;}
   if (HY <= HX)
   {  c = 2 * HX; M = 2 * HY;
      for (;;)
      {  putPixel(g, x, y);
         if (x == xQ) break;
         x += xInc;
         D += M;
         if (D > HX){y += yInc; D -= c;}
      }
   }
   else
   {  c = 2 * HY; M = 2 * HX;
      for (;;)
      {  putPixel(g, x, y);
         if (y == yQ) break;
         y += yInc;
         D += M;
         if (D > HY){x += xInc; D -= c;}
      }
   }
}

void drawCircle(Graphics g, int xC, int yC, int r)
{  int x = 0, y = r, u = 1, v = 2 * r - 1, E = 0;
   while (x < y)
   {  putPixel(g, xC + x, yC + y); // NNE
      putPixel(g, xC + y, yC - x); // ESE
      putPixel(g, xC - x, yC - y); // SSW
      putPixel(g, xC - y, yC + x); // WNW
```

```
        x++;  E += u;  u += 2;
        if (v < 2 * E){y--;  E -= v;  v -= 2;}
        if (x > y) break;
        putPixel(g, xC + y, yC + x);  // ENE
        putPixel(g, xC + x, yC - y);  // SSE
        putPixel(g, xC - y, yC - x);  // WSW
        putPixel(g, xC - x, yC + y);  // NNW
      }
  }

  void showGrid(Graphics g)
  {  for (int x=dGrid; x<=maxX; x+=dGrid)
        for (int y=dGrid; y<=maxY; y+=dGrid)
          g.drawLine(x, y, x, y);
  }

  public void paint(Graphics g)
  {  initgr();
     showGrid(g);
     drawLine(g, 1, 1, 12, 5);
     drawCircle(g, 23, 10, 8);
  }
}
```

4.4 Since an unknown number of curve segments are to be dealt with, we can
use the Java concept of *Vector*, as we have also done in Section 1.5 and
elsewhere to store *Point2D* objects representing the vertices of a polygon.
In this case it makes sense to define a class *CurveSegment* and to use a
Vector of *CurveSegment* objects, as this fragment shows:

```
class CurveSegment
{  Point2D[] P;
   CurveSegment(Point2D[] P){this.P = P;}
   ...
}
```

Writing

```
Vector curves = new Vector();
```

and using the array *P*, declared as

```
Point2D[] P = new Point2D[4];
```

containing the most recent four points, as we did in program *Bezier.java* in Section 4.6, we can add a new curve segment to *curves* by writing

```
curves.addElement(new CurveSegment(P));
```

The object *curves* can store several curves, each consisting of some consecutive elements.

4.5 In program *Bspline.java* of Section 4.7, pressing a key is interpreted as a signal to terminate the process of extending the curve. Insert the line

```
char ch = evt.getKeyChar();
```

in the method *keyTyped* so that you can use the character *ch* to differentiate between different characters entered by the user and to use them as commands.
Use a *Vector* element for each array representing a curve. Recall that we have used the statement

```
V.copyInto(P);
```

in the *paint* method of program *Bspline.java*, to copy the *Vector* object *V* into the array *P*. Using a different *Vector* object, say, *curves*, we can now add the array *P* to *curves*. The deletion of the last curve, as required by the *d* command, is then implemented as

```
curves.setSize(curves.size()-1);
```

4.6 Represent the grid on the screen by drawing ten equidistant horizontal lines that intersect ten equidistant vertical lines. If the user clicks on (or near) a point of intersection of these lines, transform the device coordinates to gridpoint coordinates, ranging from 0 through 9, and use these gridpoint coordinates to select P and Q. Draw the line PQ after Q has been defined. On the right of all these horizontal and vertical lines, display the strings

$$algorithm[0], algorithm[1], \ldots, algorithm[7]$$

below each other, where the array *algorithm* is defined and initialized as follows:

```
String[] algorithm = {
    "int x=xP,y=yP,d=0,dx=xQ-xP,c=2*dx,",  // 0
    "    m=2*(yQ-yP);",                      // 1
    "for (;;)",                              // 2
    "{  putPixel(g, x, y);",                 // 3
```

```
"   if (x == xQ) break;",            // 4
"   x++; d += m;",                   // 5
"   if (d > dx){y++; d -= c;}",      // 6
"}"};                                // 7
```

As soon as the user has defined point Q, the line stored as *algorithm*[3] should be highlighted, indicating that the call to *putPixel* is about to be executed. You can realize this by using a variable, say *i*, indicating which of the above eight program lines (if any) should be displayed in red (or equal to, say, −1 if all program lines are to appear in black). All lines *algorithm*[*j*] with *j* ≠ *i* are displayed in black. You can use a switch statement to test the value of *i* in a method *stepPressed*. For example, you can write a fragment of the following form in the constructor of your canvas class:

```
addMouseListener(new MouseAdapter()
{  public void mousePressed(MouseEvent evt)
    {  // When the mouse is clicked, determine where
       // it is on the screen and do the appropriate
       //   action, if any.
       int xClick = 0, yClick = 0;
       // Get the coordinates
       xClick = evt.getX();
       yClick = evt.getY();
       // Check to see if STEP button was pressed
       if (xClick, yClick lies within the rectangle representing
                                              the Step button)
          stepPressed();
       else
       if (xClick, yClick) lies within grid area
       {  ...
       }
       repaint();
    }
});
```

In the switch statement just mentioned, you should execute actions defined in the program line (stored in the *algorithm* array) that was previously highlighted and update the variable *i* mentioned above. Your method *paint* will use this variable *i* to display the correct program line in red and the others in black.

5.1 As Figure 5.11 shows, nine cube edges are visible and three are invisible. In the *paint* method of program *CubePers.java*, replace the calls to the method *line* with this fragment:

```
// Visible edges:
line(g, 0, 1); line(g, 1, 5); line(g, 5, 4); line(g, 4, 0);
line(g, 1, 2); line(g, 2, 6); line(g, 6, 7); line(g, 7, 4);
line(g, 5, 6);

// Invisible edges:
g.setColor(Color.blue);
line(g, 0, 3); line(g, 3, 2); line(g, 3, 7);
```

If you did Exercise 1.5 and have a class *Lines*, containing the method *dashedLine*, available, you may be able to replace the last two of the above lines with

```
dash(g, 0, 3); dash(g, 3, 2); dash(g, 3, 7);
```

while adding the following method to the class *CvCubePers*:

```
void dash(Graphics g, int i, int j)
{  Point2D P = obj.vScr[i], Q = obj.vScr[j];
   Lines.dashedLine(g, iX(P.x), iY(P.y), iX(Q.x), iY(Q.y), 8);
}
```

Figure F.1 shows the result of this solution with dashed lines.

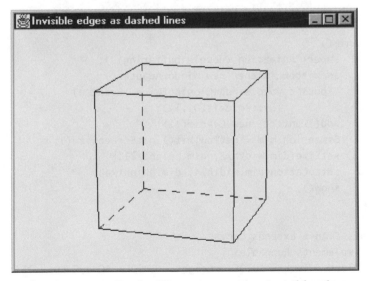

○ **Figure F.1: Dashed lines representing invisible edges**

5.2 There are two *fillPolygon* methods: one taking a *Polygon* object as an argument and the other taking two arrays x and y instead. In either case, do not forget to convert logical to device coordinates, using the methods *iX* and *iY*. Use *setColor*, with different colors before each of the three calls to *fillPolygon*.

5.3 To replace Figure 5.11, begin by sketching two cubes, say, one on either side of the xz-plane, and by assigning the numbers 0–7 to the vertices of the first and 8–15 to those of second cube. With this sketch, and using arrays w and $vScr$ with length 16 instead of 8, you can easily update the program as requested. Remember to increase the value of *objSize*, which is used to compute both the object distance ρ and the screen distance d.

5.4 The following program demonstrates the principle of animation (with double buffering) for a simple case: a line segment is rotated about one of its endpoints, which is the center of the canvas. Every 20 ms, the angle α is increased by 0.01 radians and the line from the origin O (in the center of the canvas) to point $(r\cos\alpha, r\sin\alpha)$ is drawn. The effect is that of a running clock with only one hand:

```
// Anim.java: Animation with double buffering.
import java.awt.*;
import java.awt.event.*;
public class Anim extends Frame
{  public static void main(String[] args){new Anim();}

   Anim()
   {  super("Animation (double buffering)");
      addWindowListener(new WindowAdapter()
        {public void windowClosing(WindowEvent e)
              {System.exit(0);}});
      add("Center", new CvAnim());
      Dimension dim = getToolkit().getScreenSize();
      setSize(dim.width/2, dim.height/2);
      setLocation(dim.width/4, dim.height/4);
      show();
   }
}
class CvAnim extends Canvas
   implements Runnable
{  float rWidth = 10.0F, rHeight = 10.0F, xC, yC, pixelSize;
   int centerX, centerY, w, h;
   Dimension d;
   Image image;
```

```
Graphics gImage;

float alpha = 0;
Thread thr = new Thread(this);

public void run()
{  try
   {  for (;;)
      {  alpha += 0.01;
         repaint();
         Thread.sleep (20);
      }
   }
   catch (InterruptedException e){}
}


CvAnim(){thr.start();}

void initgr()
{  d = getSize();
   int maxX = d.width - 1, maxY = d.height - 1;
   pixelSize = Math.max(rWidth/maxX, rHeight/maxY);
   centerX = maxX/2; centerY = maxY/2;
   xC = rWidth/2; yC = rHeight/2;
}

int iX(float x){return Math.round(centerX + x/pixelSize);}
int iY(float y){return Math.round(centerY - y/pixelSize);}
public void update(Graphics g){paint(g);}
public void paint(Graphics g)
{  initgr();
   if (w != d.width || h != d.height)
   {  w = d.width; h = d.height;
      image = createImage(w, h);
      gImage = image.getGraphics();
   }
   float r = 0.8F * Math.min(xC, yC),
      x = r * (float)Math.cos(alpha),
      y = r * (float)Math.sin(alpha);
   gImage.clearRect (0, 0, w, h);
   // Every 20 ms, the following line is drawn.
   // Each time, its endpoint (x, y) is a
   // different point on a circle:
```

```
            gImage.drawLine(iX(0), iY(0), iX(x), iY(y));
            g.drawImage(image, 0, 0, null);
      }
   }
```

5.5 The following program produces two rotating cubes, illustrated by Figure 5.15. Remember, this program works only if the class file *Rota*3D. *class* (see Section 3.9) is available in the current directory:

```java
// CubRot2.java: Two rotating cubes with double buffering.
//   Uses: Point2D (Section 1.5),
//         Point3D, Rota3D (Section 3.9)
import java.awt.*;
import java.awt.event.*;

public class CubRot2 extends Frame
{   public static void main(String[] args){new CubRot2();}

   CubRot2()
   {   super("Rotating cubes (double buffering)");
       addWindowListener(new WindowAdapter()
         {public void windowClosing(WindowEvent e)
                 {System.exit(0);}});
       add("Center", new CvCubRot2());
       Dimension dim = getToolkit().getScreenSize();
       setSize(3 * dim.width/4, dim.height/2);
       setLocation(dim.width/8, dim.height/4);
       show();
   }
}

class CvCubRot2 extends Canvas
   implements Runnable
{   int centerX, centerY, w, h;
   Obj2 obj = new Obj2();
   Image image;
   Graphics gImage;

   double alpha = 0;
   Thread thr = new Thread(this);

   public void run()
```

```
{  try
   {  for (;;)
      {  alpha += 0.01;
         repaint();
         Thread.sleep (20);
      }
   }
   catch (InterruptedException e){}
}

CvCubRot2(){thr.start();}
public void update(Graphics g){paint(g);}

int iX(float x){return Math.round(centerX + x);}
int iY(float y){return Math.round(centerY - y);}

void line(int i, int j)
{  Point2D P = obj.vScr[i], Q = obj.vScr[j];
   gImage.drawLine(iX(P.x), iY(P.y), iX(Q.x), iY(Q.y));
}
public void paint(Graphics g)
{  Dimension dim = getSize();
   int maxX = dim.width - 1, maxY = dim.height - 1;
   centerX = maxX/2; centerY = maxY/2;
   int minMaxXY = Math.min(maxX, maxY);
   obj.d = obj.rho * minMaxXY / obj.objSize;
   obj.rotateCube(alpha);
   obj.eyeAndScreen();
   if (w != dim.width || h != dim.height)
   {  w = dim.width; h = dim.height;
      image = createImage(w, h);
      gImage = image.getGraphics();
   }
   gImage.clearRect (0, 0, w, h);
   // Horizontal edges at the bottom:
   line (0, 1); line (1, 2); line (2, 3); line (3, 0);
   // Horizontal edges at the top:
   line (4, 5); line (5, 6); line (6, 7); line (7, 4);
   // Vertical edges:
   line (0, 4); line (1, 5); line (2, 6); line (3, 7);
   // Same for second cube:
   line (8, 9); line (9, 10); line (10, 11); line (11, 8);
   // Horizontal edges at the top:
```

```
      line (12, 13); line (13, 14); line (14, 15); line (15, 12);
      // Vertical edges:
      line (8, 12); line (9, 13); line (10, 14); line (11, 15);
      g.drawImage(image, 0, 0, null);
    }
  }

class Obj2 // Contains 3D object data for two cubes
{   float rho, theta=0F, phi=1.3F, d;
    Point3D[] s, w; // World coordinates
    Point2D[] vScr; // Screen coordinates
    float v11, v12, v13, v21, v22, v23,
      v32, v33, v43, // Elements of viewing matrix V.
      xe, ye, ze, objSize = 8;

    Obj2()
    {  s = new Point3D[16]; // Start situation
       w = new Point3D[16]; // After rotation
       vScr = new Point2D[16];
       // Bottom surface:
       s[0] = new Point3D( 1, -3, -1);
       s[1] = new Point3D( 1, -1, -1);
       s[2] = new Point3D(-1, -1, -1);
       s[3] = new Point3D(-1, -3, -1);
       // Top surface:
       s[4] = new Point3D( 1, -3,  1);
       s[5] = new Point3D( 1, -1,  1);
       s[6] = new Point3D(-1, -1,  1);
       s[7] = new Point3D(-1, -3,  1);
       // Bottom surface:
       s[8]  = new Point3D( 1,  1, -1);
       s[9]  = new Point3D( 1,  3, -1);
       s[10] = new Point3D(-1,  3, -1);
       s[11] = new Point3D(-1,  1, -1);
       // Top surface:
       s[12] = new Point3D( 1,  1,  1);
       s[13] = new Point3D( 1,  3,  1);
       s[14] = new Point3D(-1,  3,  1);
       s[15] = new Point3D(-1,  1,  1);
       rho = 15; // For reasonable perspective effect
    }

    void rotateCube(double alpha)
```

```
{  Rota3D.initRotate(s[0], s[4], alpha);
   for (int i=0; i<8; i++)
      w[i] = Rota3D.rotate(s[i]);
   Rota3D.initRotate(s[13], s[9], 2 * alpha);
   for (int i=8; i<16; i++)
      w[i] = Rota3D.rotate(s[i]);
}

void initPersp()
{  float costh = (float)Math.cos(theta),
         sinth = (float)Math.sin(theta),
         cosph = (float)Math.cos(phi),
         sinph = (float)Math.sin(phi);
   v11 = -sinth;
   v12 = -cosph * costh;
   v13 = sinph * costh;
   v21 = costh;
   v22 = -cosph * sinth;
   v23 = sinph * sinth;
   v32 = sinph;
   v33 = cosph;
   v43 = -rho;
}

void eyeAndScreen()
{  initPersp();
   for (int i=0; i<16; i++)
   {  Point3D P = w[i];
      float x = v11 * P.x + v21 * P.y;
      float y = v12 * P.x + v22 * P.y + v32 * P.z;
      float z = v13 * P.x + v23 * P.y + v33 * P.z + v43;
      Point3D Pe = new Point3D(x, y, z);
      vScr[i] = new
         Point2D(-d * Pe.x/Pe.z, -d * Pe.y/Pe.z);
   }
}
}
```

6.1 The desired input file is listed below:

```
1  1 -1 0
2  1  1 0
3 -1  1 0
```

```
4  -1 -1  0
5   0  0 -2
6   0  0  2
Faces:
1 2 3 4.
4 3 2 1.
5 6.
```

6.2 Use the vertices 1, 2 and 3 as triangle vertices in the plane $z = 0$, such that the origin O lies inside the triangle. Let vertex 4 be the origin and vertices 5 and 6 the same line endpoints as in the above solution to Exercise 6.1. Then, when specifying the triangle, use the invisible lines 1–4, 2–4 and 3–4 in the same way as the line 7–10 in Figure 6.14. In other words, define each of the two sides of the triangle as a rather complex polygon, specified as a sequence of ten numbers by visiting, for example, the vertices 1, 2, 4, 2, 3, 4, and so on, in that order, using minus signs for invisible lines.

6.3 See Section 6.4 for holes in polygons. Figure 6.27 was obtained by using a data file of the same structure as the above one (see Exercise 6.1), but with 16 vertices and four faces. Based on Figure F.2, the first of these faces was specified as follows:

1 2 3 -7 6 5 8 7 -3 4.

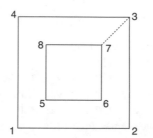

Figure F.2: One of the four faces for the square rings of Figure 6.27

6.4 A simple solution to this problem is obtained by adding some code to draw *all* polygon edges (visible as well as invisible) as dashed lines. In addition to this, the visible edges are drawn as solid lines without any modification to the hidden-line algorithm. In other words, every visible edge is drawn as coinciding solid and dashed lines, which gives the effect of a solid line. Although HP-GL provides the command *LT* (Line Type) to draw dashed lines, we obtain better results if we draw our own, computed dashes, which are required for screen output anyway. Note that every dashed line in Figure 6.28 begins and ends with a dash of the same length as the other ones. To implement all this, modify the program file *HLines.java* (see Appendix D) as follows:

a. Disable back-face culling by deleting the following program line in the method *buildLineSet*.

```
if (n > 2 && pol.h > 0) continue;
```

b. Insert the following method in the class *CvHLines* (see also Exercise 1.5):

```
void dashedLine(Graphics g, float xA, float yA,
      float xB, float yB, float dashLength)
{   float u1 = xB - xA, u2 = yB - yA,
      L = (float)Math.sqrt(u1 * u1 + u2 * u2);
   int n = Math.round((L/dashLength + 1)/2);
   float h1 = u1/(2 * n - 1), h2 = u2/(2 * n - 1);
   for (int i=0; i<n; i++)
   {   float x1 = xA + 2 * i * h1, y1 = yA + 2 * i * h2,
            x2 = x1 + h1, y2 = y1 + h2;
      drawLine(g, x1, y1, x2, y2);
   }
}
```

c. Just before the call to *lineSegment* in the *paint* method, almost at the end of the program file, insert the following line:

```
dashedLine(g, P.x, P.y, Q.x, Q.y, 8);
```

6.5 A program to generate an open book is shown below. It was executed twice (with $n = 4$ and $n = 150$) to produce the two open books of Figure 6.29. Refer to the analysis of Exercise 6.6 below for the way we design this type of program.

```
// BookView.java: Generating a data file for an open book.
import java.io.*;

public class BookView
{  public static void main(String[] args)
       throws IOException
   {   if (args.length != 4)
       {   System.out.println(
           "Supply nr of sheets, width, height and file name\n"+
```

```
            "as program arguments.");
            System.exit(1);
      }
      int n;
      float w, h;
      FileWriter fw;
      n = Integer.valueOf(args[0]).intValue();
      w = Float.valueOf(args[1]).floatValue();
      h = Float.valueOf(args[2]).floatValue();
      fw = new FileWriter(args[3]);
      int spineTop = 1, spineBottom = 2, outerTop, outerBottom;
      float theta = (float)Math.PI/(n - 1);
      float xTop = 0, xBottom = h;
      fw.write(spineTop + " " + xTop + " 0 0\r\n");
      fw.write(spineBottom + " " + xBottom + " 0 0\r\n");
      for (int i=0; i<n; i++)
      {  float phi = i * theta,
            y = w * (float)Math.cos(phi),
            z = w * (float)Math.sin(phi);
         outerTop = 2 * i + 3; outerBottom = outerTop + 1;
         fw.write(outerTop + " " + xTop + " " +
            y + " " + z + "\r\n");
         fw.write(outerBottom + " " + xBottom + " " +
            y + " " + z + "\r\n");
      }
      fw.write("Faces:\r\n");
      for (int i=0; i<n; i++)
      {  outerTop = 2 * i + 3; outerBottom = outerTop + 1;
         fw.write(spineTop + " " + spineBottom + " "
            + outerBottom + " " + outerTop + ".\r\n");
         fw.write(spineTop + " " + outerTop + " "
            + outerBottom + " " + spineBottom + ".\r\n");
      }
      fw.close();
   }
}
```

6.6 Before writing the program code we have to assign numbers to vertices and find mathematical expressions for the x-, y- and z-coordinates of these vertices. We will now discuss how this can be done for a sphere, but the same approach applies to any program that generates 3D data files.

The model of a sphere in question has two poles; let us assign vertex number 1 to the north pole. Since it is given that there are n horizontal slices, there will be $n-1$ horizontal planes between them, each corresponding with a horizontal circle, or line of latitude, on the sphere. There will also be $2n$ vertical circles, or lines of longitude. Every vertex (other than the two poles) of our sphere model is a point of intersection of such a horizontal and a vertical circle. As for the faces, $2 \times 2n$ of them are triangles at the two poles. There are $n-2$ remaining horizontal slices, so that the number of remaining faces is equal to $(n-2) \cdot (2n) = 2n(n-2)$. Each of these is a parallelogram with two horizontal edges. Altogether, there are $4n + 2n(n-2) = 2n^2$ faces, and, as we will see below, $2(n^2 - n + 1)$ vertices. We will use two angles, θ and φ, as shown in Figure 5.3. Using a sphere radius 1, we can express the level of the $n-1$ horizontal circles by their z-coordinate

$$z = \cos \varphi$$

Writing $\delta = \pi/n$, we will only use horizontal circles corresponding to the following angles:

$$\varphi = i \cdot \delta \ (i = 1, 2, \ldots, n-1)$$

On each of these circles we have to use $2n$ vertices, which correspond to the angles

$$\theta = j \cdot \delta \ (j = 0, 1, \ldots, 2n-1)$$

Thus, each pair (i, j) is associated with a vertex, so that we can devise a means of associating a vertex number with it. Since 1 has been used for the north pole, we start with vertex number 2 on circle $i = 1$. With $2n$ vertices on each horizontal circle, the first vertex number available for circle $i = 2$ will be $2n+2$, and for circle $i = 3$ it will be $4n+2$, and so on. In general, on circle i, we begin with number $(i-1) \cdot 2n + 2$. Since on each circle there are $2n$ vertices, identified as $j = 0, \ldots, 2n-1$, we have

$$\text{number for vertex } (i, j) = (i-1) \cdot 2n + 2 + j$$

As we have seen in Section 5.2, the x-, y- and z-coordinates for this vertex (i, j) is computed as $x = \sin \varphi \cos \theta$, $y = \sin\varphi \sin\theta$ and $z = \cos \varphi$, where θ and φ depend upon i and j as shown above.
Finally, we have to assign a vertex number to the south pole. As we already have used $1 + (n-1) \cdot 2n$ vertex numbers, the one for the south pole will be

$$1 + (n-1) \cdot 2n + 1 = 2(n^2 - n + 1)$$

which is also the total number of vertices.

6.7 Analyze this problem in the same way as was done for Exercise 6.6. Here each triangle (at the south pole) and each parallelogram is to be specified both counter-clockwise and clockwise, since either side of the curved surface can in principle be visible. Unlike Exercise 6.6, we had better use the variable n for the number of slices of *half* the sphere in this problem, so that there are $4n$ instead of $2n$ vertices on every horizontal circle that we use, giving altogether $n \cdot 4n + 1 = 4n^2 + 1$ vertices.

6.8 Use program arguments for the numbers of squares in each of the three directions x, y and z. Remember, the word *Faces* can occur only once in the file, so we have to specify the vertices of *all* cubes before we start specifying the faces.

6.9 Let us start with a torus such as the one in Section E.3, that is, a horizontal one with O as its center, and let the second torus be a vertical one, with its center on the positive x-axis. We will make the sizes of the tori and their numbers of vertices identical; only their positions are different. As in Section E.3, the size of a torus (and its shape) is completely determined by the radii R and r, where $r = 1$. Since the hole in each torus must be wide enough for the other to pass through, it is required that $R \geq 2r$, that is, $R \geq 2$.

For each vertex of the first torus, there is a corresponding one on the second. As we have seen in Section E.3 there are n^2 vertices for each torus, so we can use the numbers i and $i + n^2$ for each pair of corresponding vertices. To obtain the second torus, we have to shift the first one a distance R towards the positive x-axis, after which we turn it through the x-axis though 90°. (Because of this special angle, no complicated computations are required for this rotation, so it is not worthwhile to use the class *Rota3D* of Section 3.9 in this case.) Writing (x, y, z) for vertex i and (x', y', z') for the corresponding vertex $i + n^2$, we now have $x' = x + R$, $y' = -z$, $z' = y$.

Although, in the first part of 3D data files, we usually supply the vertices in ascending order of the vertex numbers, this is not required. It is therefore possible to write pairs of lines of the following form in the first part of the data file:

$$
\begin{array}{cccc}
i & x & y & z \\
i + n^2 & x' & y' & z'
\end{array}
$$

Similarly, in the second part of the file, we can write faces in pairs, with vertex numbers in the second face of each pair n^2 higher than those of the first of that pair. In this way, the desired program for two tori can be obtained from *Torus.java* by adding only a few statements.

6.10 If necessary, you might refer to the method *genCylinder* in program *Cylinder.java* of Section 6.6 for the cylindrical pole in the middle of the staircase. If you do, bear in mind that the situation here is simpler because this cylinder is solid (as is the case in program *Cylinder.java* with $rInner = 0$).

You can use program *Beams.java* of Section E.4 to see how the steps can be constructed, or you can use the class *Rota3D* (see also Exercise 5.5), provided that you also perform a translation, adding a constant to the z-coordinates of each new step. As for the railing, recall that the data file, after the word *Faces*, can contain line segments specified as two vertex numbers followed by a period, as discussed in Section 6.5.

7.1 In Figure F.3, the two outer faces on the left and right are parallel, but the corresponding inner faces are not, as the distances 18 and 19 indicate. The latter faces, which are visible here, become invisible if we view the object from very far away, as Figure F.4 shows.

Recall that, with eye coordinates, the x-axis points to the right, the y-axis upwards and the z-axis towards us. Let us focus on the inner face that is visible in Figure F.3 on the right but invisible in Figure F.4. Estimating the normal vector $\mathbf{n} = (a, b, c)$ and the value h, as specified in the exercise and discussed in Section 5.5, for this face, we find:

a is almost equal to -1, because $\mathbf{n}$ almost points toward the negative x-axis;

b is almost zero, but positive because we view the object slightly from above;

c is almost zero, but negative because $\mathbf{n}$ points a little to the back.

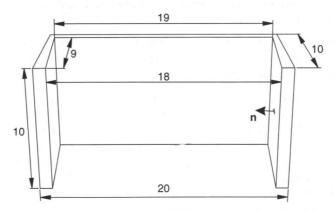

○ **Figure F.3: Object nearby: two inner faces visible**

These values, and in particular c, are independent of the viewing distance. By contrast, the inner product $h = \mathbf{n} \cdot \mathbf{x}$, where $\mathbf{x}$ is a vector from the viewpoint E to any point of the face in question, depends on the viewing distance. You should verify this by drawing a sketch similar to Figure 7.12 but applied to this example. As a result, you will find that h is negative in Figure F.3 but positive in Figure F.4. This example demonstrates that, to

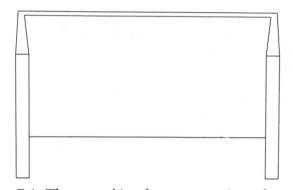

○ **Figure F.4: The same object far away: two inner faces invisible**

determine if a face is a back face, we should use the sign of h, not that of c. The correct practice of using h for this purpose is equivalent to back-face culling based on the orientation of three points: if this orientation on the screen is the same as when the object is viewed from outside, the face is visible. Using c instead of h would be equivalent to using the eye coordinates x and y instead of the screen coordinates in determining the orientation of image points. This would work correctly for most situations, but it may result in wrongly deciding that faces are invisible, especially if the object is viewed from nearby, as Figure F.3 illustrates. Recall that we also briefly discussed this in Section 7.1.

7.2 We can use back-face culling to decide which faces of the cube are visible. Refer to the solutions to Exercises 5.4 and 5.5 for the implementation of animation and rotation, respectively.

7.3 In the previous exercise we could have realized the effect of a rotation about a vertical axis by changing the angle θ and leaving the cube unchanged. This is no longer the case here because we now want to use two rotations. Figure 7.13 was obtained by rotating each cube about one of its vertical edges, with different rotation speeds, the latter simply meaning that we use different angles in each step. As in the solution to Exercise 5.5, you need to supply only one method *run*, in which only one infinite loop occurs.

7.4 Change the class *CvPaint* (in the program file *Painter.java*) as follows:
a. At the beginning of the class *CvPaint*, before {, add the line

```
implements Runnable
```

b. After {, add the following lines:

```
Image image;
```

```
Graphics gImage;
double sunTheta = 0;
Thread thr = new Thread(this);
```

c. Insert the method *run*, similar to the one given above for Exercise 5.4, but containing statements to update the spherical coordinate *sunTheta* (see Section 5.2) and the variables *obj.sunX* and *obj.sunY*; you can use a constant value for *sunPhi*, which makes *obj.sunZ* also a constant. By using spherical coordinates, with radius $\rho = 1$, the light vector will have length 1.

d. Insert the program lines

```
int w, h;
CvPainter(){thr.start();}
public void update(Graphics g){paint(g);}
```

e. Modify the *paint* method, using the variables *image* and *gImage* as well as *g*, in about the same way as was done in program *Anim.java*, listed above as help for Exercise 5.4.

7.5 For the format of the desired file see the file for Exercise 6.1. As for the program to generate 3D data files, refer to Section 6.6 and Appendix E, if necessary.

8.1 In the program *FractalGrammars.java*, there is the following fragment, which draws a line from the current point (*xLast*, *yLast*) to the new point (*xLast* + *dx*, *yLast* + *dy*), which, after the call to *drawTo*, will automatically be the current point (*xLast*, *yLast*).

```
case 'F': // Step forward and draw
   // Start: (xLast, yLast), direction: dir, steplength: len
   if (depth == 0)
   {  double rad = Math.PI/180 * dir, // Degrees -> radians
      dx = len * Math.cos(rad), dy = len * Math.sin(rad);
      drawTo(g, xLast + dx, yLast + dy);
   }
```

Besides *xLast* and *yLast*, introduce the variables *xCorner* and *yCorner*, indicating the cornerpoints that we will not really visit because of the rounded corners. Each time, instead of drawing a line as discussed above, draw two lines. The first is one from the current point (*xLast*, *yLast*) to (*xCorner* + *dx*/4, *yCorner* + *dy*/4) to approximate the rounded corner. After this, the point just mentioned is now automatically stored as the new point (*xLast*, *yLast*) to enable you to used *drawTo* again. Then update the variables *xCorner* and *yCorner* by increasing them by *dx* and *dy*, respectively, so they indicate the next cornerpoint. Then you draw the second line, from the current point (*xLast*, *yLast*) to (*xCorner* − *dx*/4, *yCorner* − *dy*/4). Note that this last line is half as long as the full line drawn in the above fragment, since a quarter of it at the beginning and a quarter of it at the end are now replaced with the approximated rounded corners.

8.2 In the *paint* method of the program *Koch.java* in Section 8.2, there is only one call to *drawKoch* preceded by setting *dir* = 0. All you have to do is add two other such calls, each preceded by assigning an appropriate value to *dir* so that the turtle starts in the right direction.

8.3 You can generate a random number between 0 and 1 by calling *Math. random*(), and derive the thickness of a branch from the height of that branch in the tree. A line of any thickness can be realized by using the method *fillPolygon*.

8.4 This hint is based on the program *FractalGrammars.java* and the string grammar *Tree2* of Section 8.3. In this example, we have

$$strX = "F[+X]F[−X]+X"$$

Each time the second *F* in this string is encountered a branch is drawn that should have a leaf at its end. So in the switch statement you should add a fragment to draw a leaf in the *case F* part after the call to *drawTo*, provided that the position counter *i* for *strX* is equal to 5. One way of drawing a closed figure that approximates the shape of a leaf is to draw a sequence of filled circles (by means of *drawOval*) whose centers lie on a line that has the same direction (*dx*, *dy*) as the branch in question.

8.5 Use methods *iX* and *iY* to convert logical to device coordinates and methods *fx* and *fy* for the inverse conversions. Restricting this discussion to *x*-coordinates, we can use

```
int iX(float x)
{  return (int)(xDevCenter + (x - xLogCenter)/pixelSize);
}

float fx(int x)
{  return xLogCenter + (x - xDevCenter) * pixelSize;
}
```

As usual, we use *d* defined as

```
Dimension d = getSize();
```

Let us denote the current boundaries of the logical *x*-coordinates by *xLeft* and *xRight*. For example, we can initially set these boundaries equal to those of the device coordinates, that is, to 0 and *d.width*(), respectively. In the method *mouseReleased*, we obtain the device coordinates *xs* and *xe* for the left and right boundaries of the cropping rectangle. We then apply the method *fx* to these to obtain the corresponding logical coordinates, writing, for example,

```
xLeftNew = fx(xs);
xRightNew = fx(xe);
```

Then these new values are assigned to *xLeft* and *xRight*, and used to compute

```
pixelSize = Math.max((xRight - xLeft)/d.width,
                        (yTop - yBottom)/d.height);
xLogCenter = (xLeft + xRight)/2;
```

Let us now discuss the plausibility of these statements (rather than proving them rigorously). Normally, *mouseRelease* provides us with a range (*xs*, *xe*) that is smaller than the width of the drawing rectangle. Then after applying *fx* and *fy*, the new logical *x*-range (*xLeft*, *xRight*) will also decrease, and the same applies to *pixelSize*. As a result of the latter, the value added to *xDevCenter* in the above method *iX* will be larger than it was before, so that the figure will appear on a larger scale. As for panning, let us assume that the new *x*-range selected by the user is on the left half of the screen. Then the new center *xLogCenter* of the logical *x*-range will be smaller than it was before, which will increase the value computed by the method *iX*. This should indeed be the case, since the part of the image displayed in the selected *x*-range on the left half of the screen should be displayed in the center of the drawing rectangle, or, in other words, it should shift to the right.

8.6 Modify the *MandelbrotZoom.java* program and the *paint* method for Julia sets. Combine the two programs so that the latter will draw Julia sets in a side window.

Bibliography

Ammeraal, L. (1996) *Algorithms and Data Structures in* C++, Chichester: John Wiley.

Ammeraal, L. (1998) *Computer Graphics for Java Programmers*, Chichester: John Wiley.

Arnold, K., and J. Gosling (1996) *The Java Programming Language*, Reading, MA: Addison-Wesley.

Burger, P., and D. Gillies (1989) *Interactive Computer Graphics*, Wokingham: Addison-Wesley.

Coxeter, H. S. M. (1961) *Introduction to Geometry*, New York, NY: John Wiley.

Flanagan, D. (1997) *Java in a Nutshell*, 2nd Edition, Cambridge, MA: O'Reilly.

Foley, J. D., A. van Dam, S. K. Feiner, J. F. Hughes, and R. L. Phillips (1990) *Computer Graphics – Principles and Practice*, 2nd Edition, Reading, MA: Addison-Wesley.

Foley, J. D., A. van Dam, S. K. Feiner, and J. F. Hughes (1994) *Introduction to Computer Graphics*, Reading, MA: Addison-Wesley.

Glassner, A. S. (1990) *Graphics Gems*, Boston, MA: Academic Press.

Gosling, J., and F. Yellin (1996) *The Java Application Programming Interface*, Reading, MA: Addison-Wesley.

Hearn, D., and M. P. Baker (1986) *Computer Graphics*, Englewood Cliffs, NJ: Prentice-Hall.

Hill, F. S., Jr (2001) *Computer Graphics Using Open GL*, 2nd Edition, Prentice-Hall.

Horstmann, C. S., and G. Cornell (1997) *Core Java*, Mountain View, CA: Sun Microsystems.

Kreyszig, E. (1962) *Advanced Engineering Mathematics*, New York, NY: John Wiley.

Newman, M. N., and R. F. Sproull (1979) *Principles of Interactive Computer Graphics*, New York, NY: McGraw-Hill.

O'Rourke, J. (1993) *Computational Geometry in* C, Cambridge: Cambridge University Press.

Rokne, J. G., B. Wyvill, and X. Wu (1990) Fast Line Scan-Conversion, *ACM Transactions on Graphics*, Vol. 9, No. 4, 376–388.

Salmon, R., and M. Slater (1987) *Computer Graphics – Systems & Concepts*, Wokingham: Addison-Wesley.

Watt, A. (1989) *Fundamentals of Three-Dimensional Computer Graphics*, Wokingham: Addison-Wesley.

Wu, X. and J. G. Rokne (1987) Double-Step Incremental Generation of Lines and Circles, *Computer Vision, Graphics, and Image Processing*, Vol. 37, 331–344.

Index